ALSO BY CHRISTOPHER BENSON

Special Interest: A Novel

DEATH OF INNOCENCE

RANDOM HOUSE
NEW YORK

DEATH OF INNOCENCE

THE STORY OF THE HATE CRIME
THAT CHANGED AMERICA

Mamie Till-Mobley

and Christopher Benson

RANDOM HOUSE and colophon are registered trademarks of
Random House, Inc.

Library of Congress Cataloging-in-Publication Data
Till-Mobley, Mamie, d. 2003.
Death of innocence: the story of the hate crime that changed
America / by Mamie Till-Mobley and Christopher Benson.
p.   cm.
ISBN 1-4000-6117-2
1. Till, Emmett, 1941–1955—Death and burial.   2. Lynching—
Mississippi.   3. Hate crimes—Mississippi.   4. African American
youth—Crimes against—Mississippi.   5. Racism—Mississippi.
6. Trials (Murder)—Mississippi.   7. Mississippi—Race relations.
I. Benson, Chris, 1953–   II. Title.
HV6465.M7T55 2003   364.1'34—dc21   2003046928

Random House website address: www.atrandom.com
Printed in the United States of America on acid-free paper
1   2   3   4   5   6   7   8   9   10
First Edition

Book design by Victoria Wong

DEDICATED TO
EMMETT LOUIS TILL

We cannot afford the luxury of self-pity. Our top priority now is to get on with the building process. My personal peace has come through helping boys and girls reach beyond the ordinary and strive for the extraordinary. We must teach our children to weather the hurricanes of life, pick up the pieces, and rebuild. We must impress upon our children that even when troubles rise to seven-point-one on life's Richter scale, they must be anchored so deeply that, though they sway, they will not topple.

MAMIE TILL-MOBLEY
November 5, 1989
Dedication of the Civil Rights Memorial,
Southern Poverty Law Center Headquarters,
Montgomery, Alabama

God's magnificent women.

God chooses ordinary people to do extraordinary things when they honor His will and His way. Dr. Martin Luther King, Jr., contended all cannot be famous because all cannot be well known, but all can be great because all can serve.

The struggle for our emancipation is a history of strong women who by their courage, commitment, and craftiness made America honor her creed of ". . . life, liberty, and pursuit of happiness . . ." for all. Magnificent women: Harriet Tubman, Sojourner Truth, Ida B. Wells, Constance Baker Motley, Madam C. J. Walker, Fannie Lou Hamer, Rosa Parks, Gertrude Johnson Williams, mother of John H. Johnson. In that tradition of a high league of service has stood Mamie Till-Mobley. She was an emancipation heroine.

Magnificent women.

Strong women don't merely birth children. They cultivate them to render service. One example is that of the mother of the Biblical Moses.

When the government's decree was issued to kill the firstborn babies, she didn't just cry and pray and hope. She acted. She crafted a plan, made a basket, hid him in the water, floated him toward Pharaoh's daughter, who, in turn, would become emotionally connected to the baby and adopt Moses. Later, Moses' mother volunteered to "babysit" her own baby.

Magnificent women who made a difference.

Mother Mary traveled by donkey to Bethlehem, and gave birth outdoors in a stable. When King Herod was frustrated that he couldn't find Baby Jesus, he ordered all firstborn babies killed. The impression is that most mothers wept and wailed. Mary was so committed to Jesus she traveled to Africa to hide Him. Likewise, Gertrude Johnson Williams said to her son John, the dreamer, "I will give you all I have; my prayers, my love, my five hundred dollars, and put my furniture in hock." Women of faith are courageous, committed, and crafty.

All these women went beyond giving birth, all the way to magnificent action. Mamie lost her only son so that we might have salvation. She planned to be a mother, yet she became a freedom fighter. In 1954, *Brown v. Board of Education* broke the legal back of segregation. But the murder of Emmett Till broke the emotional back of segregation. Emmett's death—and Mamie's life—gave us the backbone to resist racism.

The 1954 legal victory changed the assumptions of our lives, but hardly our emotional mind-set. I remember in 1954 my grandparents trying to describe what integration meant, because the law had changed, but nothing around us had changed.

On August 28, 1955, when Emmett Till was killed, unlike with *Brown* there was no need for definition. It shook the consciousness of a nation. It touched our bone marrow, the DNA of our dignity.

People tend to want to cover up a lynching. But Mamie put the struggle for emancipation and her outrage above personal privacy and pride. She allowed the distorted, water-marked body from the Tallahatchie River to be displayed in an open casket, at that time the largest single civil rights demonstration. More than 100,000 demonstrated their disgust at that casket. Each one of those people who saw how her son was defaced left telling their own story. They were never the same again. Mamie's courage unsettled people of conscience into action.

Mamie empowered the media to nationalize the lynching. *Jet* magazine exploded, and the tragedy became the *Chicago Defender*'s finest hour. It was an earthquake and Mamie used the aftershocks of that earthquake to awaken, to transform a people, and to redirect our course. Montgomery, Alabama, in 1955; Little Rock, Arkansas, in 1957; Greensboro, North Carolina, in 1960 are aftershocks of the murder of Emmett Till and the genius of his mother.

We often think of the modern civil rights movement as beginning in Montgomery in 1955 because of the dramatic arrest of Rosa Parks and the emergence of Dr. King. But that is not so. There is a scientific theory that the earth was born through the big bang. One could make the case that Emmett Till was "the big bang," the Tallahatchie River was "the big bang" of the civil rights movement.

When Ms. Parks was asked "Why did you not go to the back of the bus after such threats?" she said she thought of Emmett Till and said she couldn't go to the back.

Usually death stops everything. That is the calculation of the enemy. But here, death started everything. The murderers of Emmett Till miscalculated the power of people who have faith in God. People of faith are convinced and are able to say, "Though you slay me yet will I trust you, God." The enemy puts faith in death. They feel death can protect their tyranny. If Pontius Pilate and the Roman government had known the power of the resurrection beyond the crucifixion they would have gone another way. If they had known when they lifted Him up on the cross that He would draw men unto Him, they would not have chosen state-sponsored murder, resulting in a religious movement known as Christianity.

If the men who killed Emmett Till had known his body would free a people, they would have let him live.

God had the last answer. Even death cannot stop our God. Mamie turned a crucifixion into a resurrection. Well done, Mamie, well done. You turned death into living. Well done. You awakened the world. Well done. You gave your son so a nation might be saved. Well done.

A magnificent woman.

REVEREND JESSE L. JACKSON, SR.
Chicago
January 11, 2003

ACKNOWLEDGMENTS

W e have been truly blessed with loving support from so many dedicated people who wanted this book to be published, and who helped in countless ways to make it a reality.

For that, we are indebted, and so very grateful to:

Melody Guy, our editor, for your perfect vision, your steady hand, your unwavering enthusiasm for this project, and for being so good at what you do. To Melody's assistant, Danielle Durkin, for handling all those critical production details and absorbing so much of the pressure. And to the entire Random House family for its support.

Manie Barron, our agent and collaborator, a true believer, for knowing just what this book would need, and knowing how to get it; for your hands-on involvement, and for never letting go.

Attorney Lester L. Barclay, for being a great advocate, for your determination to have this story told, and for going to such lengths to safeguard the legacy.

Reverend Wheeler Parker, Jr., and Simeon Wright for the important roles you played in this story, the vital roles you played in the telling, and for never forgetting Emmett.

Crosby Smith, Jr., Bertha Thomas, and Abe Thomas for rising to the occasion, always answering the call with advice and materials, and doing so much to make sure that everything was handled to keep this project moving forward.

Reverend Wealthy and Euphemia Mobley, Lillian Gene Jackson, and Thelma Wright Edwards for your constant availability, your high level of support, and your eagerness to share so much of yourselves.

Ollie and Airicka Gordon, Anna Laura Williams, Priscilla Sterling, and

Deborah Watts for everything you've done to keep the family story alive and well.

Earlene Greer and Shep Gordon for unceasing devotion and loving care.

The many loving family members and friends who are such a cherished part of this story.

Rosa Parks, a woman of courage, conviction, and compassion, for the loving embrace of friendship, and for pointing the way.

Reverend Jesse L. Jackson, Sr., for committed friendship and never failing to find the perfect words for the perfect sentiment.

Ollie M. Williams, a true friend for life, for always being there at just the right time.

Dr. Ann Brickel, a dear and faithful friend, for constant inspiration and guidance.

Elaine Eason Steele, keeper of the flame, for uncommon devotion and support.

Willie Reed, for your courage and your determination to reveal the truth in the face of such great odds.

Maria Johnson, for the bond only two mothers can share, for showing such strength and dedication in overcoming so much to continue moving forward.

David Barr for the many things you did to get this project started. It wouldn't have happened without you.

Odel Sterling III for daring to dream and showing so many others how to make dreams come true.

Alice Elzy and Clifton Anthony Goins, for your indispensable help and spiritual support.

The wonderful members of Evangelistic Crusader Church of God in Christ for the many years of loving support, and for sharing the blessings.

Doris Saunders, for so much advice, insight, positive energy, and for being a tremendous resource.

Robert Miller, Michael Flug, and Tammy Hampton of the Vivian Harsh Collection at the Carter G. Woodson Regional Library in Chicago, for outstanding research assistance, and the high level of devotion to this project that made all the difference.

John H. Johnson for sharing the Emmett Till story with the nation and keeping it alive over the years. And to Linda Johnson Rice, for making it possible for Chris Benson to work on this project.

Simeon Booker for being the reporter other reporters want to be and for sharing so much insight on this and other important stories over the years. And to the other dedicated people who courageously covered the

1955 murder trial and who were so willing to relive the experience: Clotye Murdock Larsson, Moses Newson, Franklin McMahon, and Ernest
Withers.

William Parker, Milton Parker, Tillman Mallory, Tyrone Modiest, Sam
Lynch, Donny Lee Taylor, and Lindsey Hill for the laughter and the mem-
ories in the back of the Esquire Barbershop in Argo, and to Roosevelt
Crawford for all that you added to the story.

Stephanie Parker-Weaver, for taking care of business in Mississippi and
keeping track of all the important details.

Vernon Jarrett, for the compelling historical perspective and the encouragement to tell important stories.

Dr. Bennie Goodwin, Jr., for the most special blessing.

Annyce Campbell and Audley Mackel, Jr., for the significant recollections of Dr. T.R.M. Howard and Mound Bayou.

Col. Eugene Scott, *Chicago Defender,* for your generous support and
willingness to help.

Lois Walker, *Chicago Defender,* Deborah Douglas, *Chicago Sun-Times,* and
Sandra Spikes, *Chicago Tribune* for recognizing the importance of this story,
and for providing invaluable assistance leaving no stone unturned in digging up such significant photographs.

Geoff Brown, Brenda Butler, Raymond Thomas, and Charles
Whitaker for early and enduring support, and for the faith, confidence,
and encouragement that meant so much.

Keith Beauchamp and Alvin Sykes for your dedication to fighting the
good fight.

Renny Cushing, for unceasing advocacy, keen insight, and valued assistance.

Gary Flowers, John Mitchell, and Marnie Trotter, Rainbow/PUSH
Coalition, for your relentless efforts on our behalf.

Charles and Alice Tisdale, *Jackson Advocate,* for the vital Mississippi information.

Penny Weaver, Southern Poverty Law Center, for your eager support
and never-ending assistance.

Karen L. Blackwell, for uncommon generosity.

Wini R. Benson for all those colorful "Bronzeville" memories, and to
Pauline M. Clark for that important Atlanta connection.

Kaye C. Benson for the feedback, the candid critique and advice, and all
the love you put into those perfect transcripts.

Additional appreciation to Trish Phipps, University of Virginia Press;
Barbara Lanphier, Strahorn Library, Illinois Railway Museum; Joan
Harms, Denver Public Library; Peggy Price, McCain Library and

Archives, University of Southern Mississippi; Writer's House, New York; Harpo, Inc., Chicago; Optimus, Chicago; and Lab One, Chicago.

The following sources were very helpful in providing insight and context, and refreshing the memory:

Books

Baldwin, James, *Blues for Mister Charlie.* New York: Vintage Books, 1964.

Bullard, Sara, ed., *Free at Last: A History of the Civil Rights Movement and Those Who Died in the Struggle.* Montgomery, Alabama: Teaching Tolerance/Southern Poverty Law Center, 1989.

Carson, Clayborne, David J. Garrow, Gerald Gill, Vincent Harding, Darlene Clark Hine, eds., *The Eyes on the Prize Civil Rights Reader: Documents, Speeches and Firsthand Accounts from the Black Freedom Struggle.* New York: Penguin Books, 1991.

Evers, Myrlie, *For Us, the Living.* Garden City, New York: Doubleday & Co., 1967.

Halberstam, David, *The Fifties.* New York: Villard Books, 1993.

Hudson-Weems, Clenora, *Emmett Till: The Sacrificial Lamb of the Civil Rights Movement.* Troy, Michigan: Bedford Publishers, Inc., 1994.

Metress, Christopher, ed., *The Lynching of Emmett Till: A Documentary Narrative.* Charlottesville and London: The University of Virginia Press, 2002.

Whitfield, Stephen J., *A Death in the Delta: The Story of Emmett Till.* Baltimore: The Johns Hopkins University Press, 1988.

Williams, Juan, *Eyes on the Prize: America's Civil Rights Years 1954–1955.* New York: Viking Penguin, 1987.

Articles

Booker, Simeon, "A Negro Reporter at the Till Trial," *Nieman Reports,* January 1956.

Faulkner, William, "Can We Survive?" *New South,* September 1955.

Hicks, James L., "New Till Evidence Disclosed in Letter," *Philadelphia Afro-American,* November 26, 1955.

Hicks, James L., "Why Reporter Went Back to Mississippi," *Baltimore Afro-American,* November 26, 1955.

Porteus, Clark, "New Till Evidence: Reporter Finds It," *Memphis Press Scimitar,* September 21, 1955.

Wilson, L. Alex, " 'Too Tight' Talks: Defender Tracks Down Mystery Till 'Witnesses,' " *Chicago Defender,* October 8, 1955.

Unpublished

Beito, David T., and Linda Royster Beito, "T.R.M. Howard: Pragmatism Over Strict Integrationist Ideology in the Mississippi Delta, 1942–1954."

Whitaker, Hugh Stephen, "A Case Study in Southern Justice: The Emmett Till Case." Master's Thesis, Florida State University, Tallahassee, 1963.

Documentaries/Television

Eyes on the Prize: Awakenings 1954–1956. Blackside, Inc. Henry Hampton, executive producer; Judith Vecchione, producer. 1987.

"The Murder and the Movement." NBC, *Channel 5 News,* Chicago. Anna Vasser, producer; Bob Webb, director; Rich Samuels, reporter and writer. 1985.

The Murder of Emmett Till. Firelight Media. Stanley Nelson, producer and director; Marcia A. Smith, writer. 2003.

"The Untold Story of Emmett Louis Till." *Till Freedom Come.* Keith Beauchamp, writer, producer, and director; Ceola J. Beauchamp, Edgar Beauchamp, Ali Bey, Steven Laitmon, executive producers; Yolande Geralds, producer. 2002.

"Unsolved Hate Crimes, Part 10: Witnesses of Murders During the Civil Rights Era." The *Oprah Winfrey Show.* Debra DiMaio, executive producer. October 13, 1992.

Newspapers/Periodicals

Amsterdam News
Atlanta Journal-Constitution
Baltimore Afro-American
Chicago American
Chicago Defender
Chicago Sun-Times
Chicago Tribune
Jackson Advocate
Jackson Clarion-Ledger
New York Post
Pittsburgh Courier
The Crisis
The New York Times
The Washington Post

Hardly a moment goes by when I don't think about Emmett. There are constant reminders. I see his face everywhere. It is on my datebook, on the calendar on my wall, on a special T-shirt I wear. Everywhere. Pictures and mementos fill my house, his presence fills my life. At times I will think about something he said or did—something funny, something so many years ago—and it will still make me laugh, each time just like the first time. When I am out and about, people recognize me and they want to talk about him, what his death meant to them, what I mean to them still. They just can't help it. On the news, there are human interest stories about mothers and sons and grandsons, and I find myself thinking about what life might have been like if I still had a son to look after me in my old age, or grandsons whom I might look after, and spoil rotten. Then there are the tragic reports of child abductions and hate crimes. I know about these things. I know about them the only way you really can know about them. And I quietly pray for the grieving mothers of other missing or murdered children, hoping they will find the peace and the meaning that took me so long to find. We are connected, these other mothers and I. We share a bond, the knowledge of an exclusive few: that there can be no greater suffering than the pain of a mother who must bury her child, and be left alone to wonder if there might have been even one small thing she could have done to make a difference.

Hardly a moment goes by when I don't think about Emmett and the promise of a lifetime. There are constant reminders. But, then, a mother really doesn't need reminders. Just as you always remember the agony of childbirth, you can never forget the anguish of losing a child. You don't need to be reminded of the horror you have seen—even for a brief moment—in your boy's battered body. That vision plays back forever like a perpetual nightmare. Emmett Louis Till, my only son, my only child, was kidnapped, tortured, and murdered at the hands of white racists on August 28, 1955. That was so many years ago, yet it seems like only yesterday to a mother who needs no reminders. After all, every shattered piece of my heart has its own special memory of Emmett.

They say there are lessons to be learned from every experience in life. It has taken practically all my life to sort out the lessons here. I couldn't see how there might possibly be any good to come of something so evil. What could the lesson have been? How could anyone deserve this? Then there was the mistreatment, the indifference of those who I thought really cared, the betrayal by those I trusted, the injustice at the hands of the justice system.

It has taken all these years of quiet reflection to recognize the true meaning of my experience, and Emmett's. It took quite a while for me to accept how his murder connected to so many things that make us what we are today. I didn't see right away, but there was an important mission for me, to shape so many other young minds as a teacher, a messenger, an active church member. God told me, "I took away one child, but I will give you thousands." He has. And I have been grateful for that blessing.

That is why, for forty-seven years, I wasn't quite ready to write this book. It took a long time for me to reach this kind of deep understanding. I have been approached, oh, so many times by people who wanted to tell my story or put words in my mouth to tell their version of my story. But I just couldn't do that. I owe Emmett more than that. I owe him the absolute understanding I finally have come to appreciate; the deep understanding of why he lived and died and why I was destined to live so long after his death. You see, my story is more than the story of a lynching. It is more than the story of how, with God's guidance, I made a commitment to rip the covers off Mississippi, USA—revealing to the world the horrible face of race hatred. It is more than the story of how I took the privacy of my own grief and turned it into a public issue, a political issue, one which set in motion the dynamic force that led ultimately to a generation of social and legal progress for this country. My story is more than all of that. It is the story of how I was able to pull myself back from the brink of desolation, and turn my life around by digging deep within my soul to pull hope from despair, joy from anguish, forgiveness from anger, love from hate. I want people to know about all of that and how they might gain some useful understanding for their own lives from my experience. But I also want people to know my Emmett, the way they might have known him had they met him so many years ago—as the driven, industrious, clever boy that he was at age fourteen. Forever fourteen.

Thankfully, Emmett has helped to steer me in my lifelong odyssey. He does still. I often hear his voice guiding or chiding, the voice of a boy much older than his years. In fact, as I began discussions for this book, I sat down at my kitchen table, my workspace. As I sometimes do, I asked that a trifold picture frame of images of Emmett and me be taken down from atop the china hutch in my living room and placed on the table in front of me. I focused on my son while I considered this book. I scanned the pictures that portrayed a life from infancy through boyhood into adolescence. I prayed and asked for help in making this important decision. The result is in your hands. Now, only now, I can share the wisdom of my age. I am experienced, but not cynical. I've been disappointed by so many of the people I've trusted over the years, but still I am hopeful that we all can be better than we are. I've been brokenhearted, but I still maintain an oversized capacity for love.

It is not that I dwell on the past. But the past shapes the way we are in the present and the way we will become what we are destined to become. It is only because I have finally understood the past, accepted it, embraced it, that I can fully live in the moment. And hardly a moment goes by when I don't think about Emmett, and the lessons a son can teach a mother.

DEATH OF
INNOCENCE

I will always remember the day Emmett was born. It was July 25, 1941. A Friday. But I'm getting a little ahead of my story, because this is not where it really begins. You see, my mother had brought me to the hospital on Wednesday. And the fact that it was my mother and not my husband who took me to the hospital to have a baby probably tells you just about everything you need to know about Louis Till. He was at work that day, I think. He worked at the Corn Products Refining Company in Argo, Illinois, where we lived, just outside Chicago. I guess you might call Argo a suburb, but it didn't have anything at all in common with the big city, except for being close to it. It was a sleepy little town where whites called blacks by their first names and where blacks would never dare do the same thing. It was a place where most little black girls dropped out of school by age sixteen to get married and where I was considered an old maid because I had waited until I finished high school to marry Louis at age eighteen. That was just the year before. Argo was also a place where it seemed the greatest ambition of most black men, like my father and my husband, was to work for Corn Products, and the greatest ambition of their wives was to take care of things at home for their husbands. So it was with my mother, who did what my mother always seemed to be there to do. She took care of me, and on that Wednesday when she drove me to Cook County Hospital in Chicago, I really needed care. I was going into labor and I didn't understand much about that except for this: those pains were *talking* to me. They were saying: "Any minute now, Mamie Till. Any minute, girl."

Now, Cook County was a public hospital and it was one place you were sure black folks could get treated. That's not to say that we were treated well. The nurses decided right away that this was not an emergency. But, then, of course, they were feeling no pain. They put me into a room with another lady and it seems that I was the only one who noticed that this woman was screaming and hollering and cursing and she was going through every four-letter word she could think of, teaching me a few in the process. That was about the time *my* pain stopped. I felt so sorry for her that I forgot my own troubles. I got up out of my bed after everyone left and started trying to comfort her, help ease her pain. I didn't understand a lot of things back then. I mean, I was so naive it wasn't safe for me to walk the streets alone. And listening to the screams of that poor woman really frightened me because I didn't understand any of it. My God, was this what was in store for me? No one had prepared me for any of this. Why hadn't my mother talked to me about these things? And why on earth did this woman want to kill her husband? I guess it was her husband. "That man," I think is what she kept saying. Anyway, she told me that I would soon find out why.

Over the next couple of days, I was in and out of pain—terrible pain—and my mother was in and out of the room checking on things, taking care of me. That room always seemed dark, like a government office, not cheerful the way I thought it should look for such a blessed event. But that was Cook County Hospital. Louis never came to see about me. I would have thought that he would be excited about the baby, but he didn't seem to care. On Friday during one of my mother's visits, I told her what I had been telling the nurses: that I needed to go, that if the pain was a sign, then it was definitely time. I didn't think I could take another minute of it. But they weren't paying me any attention. Mama asked if my water had broken. I told her I thought it had and that I had asked somebody to come and change my bed. But when they didn't, I just pulled the blanket up and got back on top of the bed. Well, Alma Gaines was having none of that. My mother called the nurse, who checked my situation and quickly got me into the labor room. And that's where things really got serious. The doctor there began to examine me. He said something that I didn't get, but I could hear the urgency in his voice. What I understood was that they had to get busy. They had to take my baby. The baby was coming butt first. It was a breech birth. I had no idea how serious that could be, but even *I* understood the anxiety I heard in the doctor's voice, and the tense way things were moving in that room.

"What have you been doing?" he asked, like he was accusing me of murder.

Now I knew; it was my fault. Whatever was happening to my baby was all my fault. The only thing I could recall was that Louis and I had moved into a new place not that long before all of this. As the medical team rushed to prep me, I thought about that move from my mother's house to a little apartment down the street. I was so proud of that little place, our first apartment. I had bought curtains. Everything had to be perfect. I mean, I was such a perfectionist. And now, of course, I know better, but I didn't know anything then. I was hanging curtains and I was cleaning cobwebs high up on the windows. And somebody came by and saw me and told me I shouldn't reach overhead like that. So, it was my fault that all this was happening, all because I wanted a nice, clean place for the baby to live and play. Now, in the delivery room, I was being punished for it, but I didn't want my baby to have to suffer for my mistake. The agony was so severe, I finally understood why that woman back in the room wanted to kill "that man." Somehow, though, I didn't think that would help. At that moment, I thought there could be no greater pain than giving birth to a child. I couldn't imagine then how much more pain a mother might have to endure. Someone placed a cone over my mouth and told me to count backward from one hundred. The last thing I remember was ". . . ninety-nine . . ."

When I finally awakened, it seemed as if I had been dreaming. I was back in the room, but there was no baby there. In fact, I had never even seen my baby. I wanted to know where they had taken the baby. All they told me was that I was very sick, and they really didn't want to bring him to me and they had taken him to do whatever it is they do to babies. "Him." A boy. I kept insisting on seeing my baby boy and, finally, they gave in and brought him to me, probably just to keep me quiet, knowing how mothers are. But I didn't care. I was so happy to see my baby, all six and three-quarters pounds of him.

Happy, that is, until I looked down at him in my arms.

I reacted right away with a frown. "Oooh, no . . ." I said, before thinking much about it.

His skin color was very, very light and he had blond hair and blue eyes. I looked up at the nurse, but I was assured that they had handed me the right baby. There was more. It had been such a difficult birth that they had used forceps and clinched him at the temples. He was scarred on his forehead and on the nose, and his little face looked distorted. My reaction must have startled him. His eyes grew wide, and he began to cry.

I pulled him closer to my bosom and rocked him gently. "Oh, honey. Mama loves you."

That was our first connection, mother and son. I was so contrite after that and I would remember all of my life how my son looked when he came into the world, and how I reacted to it.

The attending nurse needed a name to complete the birth certificate form. I had been ready for some time. Now, this was long before you could tell what sex a baby was going to be ahead of time, the way people do these days. But I just knew I would have a boy. After all, I had decided, a boy first, then a girl, then another boy and then another girl. So, weeks before I went to the hospital, I asked my husband what he wanted to name our son. He just shrugged and sort of brushed me off. Then I thought about my favorite uncle, who didn't seem much concerned, either, when I asked him. That's when I decided myself on the name Emmett Louis, after my favorite uncle and my husband, because they didn't care and I did.

We didn't have long together during that first visit. Emmett was taken from me again right away. I was running a temperature and at a certain point, I think I became delirious. It's all a blur. They had given me eighteen stitches inside and I don't know how many outside. But I began scratching at the stitches and, in my state of mind, I guess I was causing problems, making things worse. Infection set in and I had to be looked after. Emmett was in even worse shape. His neck, right knee, and left wrist had been constricted by the umbilical cord. He could have choked to death. Thank God, he didn't. His wrist was swollen and his knee was swollen even more. It was as big as an apple. The circulation had been cut off. Apparently, that was what kept him from being delivered normally, what caused the breech birth and what forced the doctors to use the forceps to help him into the world. And it was why that doctor seemed to be accusing me of being a bad mother even before I *became* a mother; all because I hadn't been taught how to prepare for such an important part of my life.

There are certain things that a parent owes a child. One is to prepare him for the world outside. I know this, not only because I became a mother, but because I learned so much from what my mother hadn't taught me. My mother was good at a lot of things. She was a good teacher and once kept me up until three in the morning drilling me on my multiplication tables, then got me up to make the 8 A.M. school bell that same morning. She was a good nurturer, making sure that I and just about everybody else in our neighborhood was well fed. She was a firm disciplinarian, with strong Mississippi-bred church values. But she wasn't so good at opening up to me and telling me some things I really needed to know. At age sixteen, I finally heard my mother's version of the facts of life.

"If you run around here kissin' these little boys, you'll come up in a family way."

That was it. I didn't even know what "pregnant" was. I'd never seen that word. That same year, my mother let me go to the birthday party of a friend. The parents—church members and friends of my mother—weren't home. A boy there leaned over and kissed me on the mouth. Oh, God. If Mama knew I was up there kissing . . . I would get beheaded. I slapped that boy. Slapped him silly. But I knew it was too late. I *knew* I was pregnant. I left the party right away and ran home. When Mama came in, I was in the bathroom gagging. I had a toothbrush almost down to my tonsils.

She just stood there. "Gal, what's wrong with you?"

"I'm gonna have a baby," I declared.

"Oh, my," she said. "*What* have you been doing?"

That's when I told her about the boy kissing me. And instead of her telling me everything was all right, instead of telling me that I couldn't possibly get in a family way that way, she simply dismissed it, turned, and walked off. And I was left there, all alone with my biggest fear and a toothbrush down my throat. I waited, and waited, and waited for that baby to arrive.

One day, I just couldn't take it anymore. I worked up the nerve to ask Mama when the baby would be coming. We hadn't talked about it, so what did I know?

Finally, she said something. "Gal, you're not pregnant." And that was it. Until I really did become pregnant with Emmett. Eventually, I discovered where babies came from. I learned at the hospital, during labor. In the delivery room, I told the doctors and nurses to get the bedpan because I thought I was having a different kind of problem. And the doctor told me that was the baby. I asked where the baby was coming out and the doctor told me that the baby was coming out the same way he went in. Ooohhh, I was embarrassed to pieces. I should have known that the doctor knew how the baby got there, but I just couldn't face the doctor knowing that I had slept with a man. Even though the man was my husband. Well, I was pretty educated by the time I got out of the hospital. I surely knew a lot more than I knew when I went in.

Still, I struggled with it all. There had been so many things my mother didn't tell me; things that might have helped me avoid so many difficulties along the way. I just don't know what her problem was, but it left me feeling vulnerable. My mother and father were divorced and my stepfather was a very nice man. But it was my mother who always was the source of strength for me. A stately, sturdy woman, who seemed so much taller than five-foot-three, she had the look of someone who could handle anything that came her way. And she always seemed to be guided by traditional values—the kind of things you learned in Sunday school more than everyday school. She taught me these things, how to be a good person, but still something was missing.

There were several incidents that occurred during my early years, events that I wish I had been better prepared to take on. Because I was used to her taking care of me, I thought I could rely on her to handle them, or at least show me she understood. There was this neighbor of ours, one of our church deacons. I was about seven, an only child, and I always loved playing with his children, three girls and a boy. One day he sent all the kids out of his house, but he told me to stay behind with him. He was cooking a turtle and asked me if I wanted to look at it. Of course I did. He picked me up and I looked over in the boiling pot and I could see the turtle's heart beating. He told me that the turtle's heart was like a timer, that it would not stop beating until the turtle was done. I was fascinated, but I knew right away that I did not want any turtle soup, or whatever it was he was making. That might have been the only thing I would ever remember about that man, if it hadn't been for the other thing. He kept holding me up in his arms even though I was getting uncomfortable and told him I wanted to get down, to go out. The other kids had already left and I wanted to be with them, not him.

"No, you're gonna stay in here with me," he said. Although I was a very naive child, I knew *something* was wrong. And I was right. He finally set me down, but he didn't let me leave. He began to pull my pants down. Why was he doing this to me? He was a deacon in our church, a man I was taught to respect, but this was not what a good man was supposed to do. This was bad, and I wasn't quite sure what I should do about it.

Well, he gave me the answer, by asking the question. "Who you gonna tell?"

"I'm gonna tell my mama," I blurted out without any hesitation. I was afraid and I didn't know what else to say. I figured my mother could fix anything. She always did.

"Oh, no, you can't do that," he said, as if he was really surprised by my threat. What did he think I would do?

Then he asked me again, and I repeated that I would tell my mother. I held to it because I meant it. This didn't seem like something he should be doing, and I was going to tell her. If I could get to her. Finally, I guess he decided it wasn't worth the risk. He let me go, sent me out to play with the other kids. But I couldn't wait to tell Mama. What happened next was as surprising to me as what had happened in the first place. When I told Mama everything that had gone on, she didn't have any reaction. I wanted to know what she was going to do. But she just shooed me off somewhere. She never acted like she thought it was anything of consequence. But she did make me stay around our house from then on. I don't know to this day whether Mama spoke to that man or not. I can't help but wonder about it, though.

There was another incident. I was about fourteen by this time, and I wanted to go to a dance with my dearest friend, Ollie Colbert. I could *never* go to dances. They were just off-limits. But I begged Mama so, and Ollie's mother told Mama that I would have adequate supervision. Mama reluctantly let me go, but I had to be home by nine o'clock. The dance didn't start until eight, so I had one hour. As it turned out, I wouldn't even have that long. I had just gotten there, had one dance, and the music was sounding so good. Oh, it was just glorious. I had never experienced such excitement. I felt like a cat in a fish market. Then, all of a sudden, somebody tapped me on the shoulder. I turned around and saw that it was the son of one of our church officers. He was very handsome and charming, but he wasn't asking me for a dance. Mama had sent this young man to pick me up. Oh, I was so upset. But I had to do what she told me to. Now, we were only about five blocks from my house when he and I got in the car and he began driving. But then he started going the wrong way, taking the long way up and down streets in the white neighborhoods. Oh, my goodness, where was he going, what was he doing? Just as I was asking myself these questions, the answer came. He made a proposition. He suggested things I had never even *thought* about, sexual things. How strange, that the one person my mother had trusted to make sure I got home safely was the very person she would have wanted me to avoid that night.

"No. Absolutely not," I said, wondering if I could just get out of the car and run home. Then I told him what I had told that demon deacon so many years before. I threatened to tell Mama.

Unlike the man in that earlier incident, this young man seemed so calm about it all. "She won't believe you," he said.

Well, that scared me more than anything. He seemed so sure about it, I began to really worry. He was such an upstanding, outstanding young man in the neighborhood that he figured he could get away with this. After all, his family was involved in our church and everyone saw him drive his mother and sister to and from church every Sunday. The whole community knew him and respected him.

Somehow, we wound up right in front of my house and then he really came on strong. He tried to touch me. And I threatened to scream. Finally, he jerked back, and at that moment, I opened that car door and left it swinging as I ran up the steps of my house.

For some reason, Mama was not there, looking out the door like she always did when she waited for me to come home. In fact, she was nowhere to be seen. I finally found her way in the back of the house just as calm as could be, I guess because she trusted this young man so much. I rushed to tell her this story about the fine, young trustworthy church boy and asked her what she planned to do.

She looked at me for a long moment. "I'm going to pray on it."

I'm not sure how her prayers were answered. That was the last time it ever came up.

There was a lesson in these experiences. I realized that, sometimes, you can suffer the greatest harm at the hands of the people you trust the most. Unfortunately, that would be a lesson I would come back to later in life. But I shouldn't have had to learn it in this way. I was caught off guard because of my mother's failure to open my eyes to so many possibilities in life. She taught me to always see the best in people, and never seemed to think it was important that I should also be prepared for the worst. Just in case. My mother was good at a lot of things. She was the best there was. I can't help but wonder, though, how much different my life would have been had I known all the things children need to know as they grow to become adults, all the things a mother should share to make sure a child can make it in a world where there may be no mother around to take care of things. I decided that I could not let Emmett face that world unprepared. It was my obligation as a mother, as his mother, to make sure he would have the survival skills that I had lacked. But there was something else, something very compelling about my start with Emmett and all the problems we had to overcome in those early days—problems that seemed to be all my fault.

Something happens when a child faces a life-and-death situation, as Emmett did. It leaves an indelible mark on the mother. Somewhere deep inside I knew that everything I did had consequences in the life of my child. And I had to make sure that I always did the right thing, the best thing, for him. I knew that each moment was a blessing and that each moment was to be nurtured and protected, as was my son. It would become such a stressful balancing act, to do enough without doing too much. To protect my child without stifling him, snuffing out his independence and his sense of adventure, the very things that would make him such a special little boy.

CHAPTER 2

There had been so many complications during those first few weeks. The doctors had told me Emmett would probably be disabled for life, and that he should be institutionalized. I was not about to accept that. Even so, Emmett and I wound up going back and forth, in and out of the hospital so much that it was a month after his birth before we finally settled in at home together. And I was so happy then. He was the most precious thing I had ever had in my life. Better than all the little dolls my mother had given me with their painted-on hair. Now I had a *living* doll. His skin and hair color were finally reaching their natural brown and his eyes had gone from blue to hazel brown. That was a good thing, since his appearance had been causing quite a stir in our close-knit little community in Argo. Oh, my, the neighborhood gossip. And just because Emmett looked so, well, different at first. Most people had bet on the milkman, a white man, just because he had always been so nice to me—nice enough to give me a bottle of chocolate milk every now and then. The iceman also got his share of votes from nosy neighbors, because he would treat me to a little chunk of ice he'd break off when it was hot outside. Why, I even had to convince my own mother at one point that Louis Till was the only man I had ever slept with. She should have known. When Louis and I decided to get married, Mama took me to a doctor. I thought she just had to get me checked out for the marriage license. But that wasn't it at all. Not until many years later did I finally come to understand what that doctor meant when he put me up on the table, examined me in a very strange way, and then made his announcement to Mama.

"Well, Alma," he said, "you've got a good girl here."

Anyway, I was glad to see little Emmett finally starting to look like Louis and me, and I was so relieved that he seemed to be okay after all the trouble we had gone through. And, my goodness, did I make up for lost time with Bobo. That was the playful name a young family friend had given to my baby while I was still carrying him. She would bring me things all the time, announcing that they were for "the little Bobo." It stuck. I pampered Bo, and bathed him constantly. I used Castile soap. I remember it left his cheeks so rosy. I had no idea why. Mama complained that the soap was too strong for him and that I was washing his skin off. She wound up insisting that I bring him to her when it was time to bathe him.

It was so nice learning about him and how to respond to him. I mean, he was just marvelous. When he wanted something, he would give you a warning. He would simply say, "Uh-uh." I learned that meant "come and see about me." Actually, I learned it the hard way, by not coming quickly enough. When I came right away, that's all I would get, that one little "uh-uh." But if I didn't come right away, he would give me another call. And, by the time he gave me a third call, well, everybody in the neighborhood heard it. I mean, he just let go. Mama helped with the translation.

"He *told* you to come and see about him," she said. "What do you want this baby to do, send you a letter?"

Emmett truly was a miracle baby. It was a miracle that he'd even gotten here, and that he didn't have to be institutionalized after all. I hadn't had the proper prenatal care. Of course, I knew some things, because people in the neighborhood knew things they would pass on. But I never even went to a clinic to get treated. In fact, the first time I set foot in the hospital during my pregnancy was when I checked in with labor pains. Well, I just didn't understand why my mother hadn't taken me to get checkups before that.

It was only after we had been home together for a short while that I learned that Emmett was having a new problem. An acquaintance, a woman from the neighborhood, wanted to come by and bring her baby to visit my baby. Her baby was about six weeks old, just like Emmett at this point. She was a striking woman, with a look that could make everybody else in the room feel like they needed to go touch up a little. She was a bit older than I was, much more glamorous, and appeared so confident. Unlike me, she didn't seem at all like a woman who had a newborn, yet she seemed to know all about having one. To look at her, you could tell she was used to finer things, and she had a way of letting you know that. I remember she looked down at little Emmett lying in the dresser drawer where he slept, and she wondered why we didn't have a bassinet for him. It was the best we could do. I wasn't working and Louis, well, that's a different story, but we just didn't have the money yet for such luxuries as a

crib or bassinet. Soon after she got there, Emmett began to cry. I had noticed that whenever I finished feeding my baby, he seemed to start crying.

"Mamie, your baby is hungry," this woman told me.

But I had just fed him.

"Do you mind if I feed him?" she asked.

I sure did. I mean, I really did. But I looked at her calmly and simply
said, "Just a minute." I ran to get a wash pan, added soap and water,
grabbed a towel, and brought everything back to her. I wanted her to wash
her breasts first. She looked at me and sort of shook her head. But then she
shrugged and she did it. I was amazed. She nursed Emmett and he went to
sleep. That had to be about eight or nine o'clock in the evening. He stayed
asleep during her whole visit and did not wake up until ten o'clock the
next morning. For the first time, he slept the clock around. Later that next
day, I saw the woman walking up the street. Actually, it was more of a strut
than a walk. That was her way. Anyway, I ran to the porch when I saw her
coming. I just couldn't wait to tell her.

"Emmett slept all night," I said with such glee. "You were right. He was
just hungry."

She gave me a sly smile as if she already knew what I was going to tell
her before I told her, as if she knew a lot of things I had yet to learn.
"Mamie, take your baby to the health center and they'll give you a formula
to feed him," she said. "Your milk is just not doing the trick."

I took her advice and the people at the health center put Emmett on
formula, yellow cornmeal, and Carnation milk with Karo syrup. Now,
Emmett was just a baby. I didn't think he even should have been eating
solid food yet. But he ate a whole bowl. That woman had been like an
angel to me and Emmett. I don't know what would have happened if she
hadn't come by that day. Later, I would learn that she had quite a reputation around Argo. Not for helping new mothers, but for helping their
husbands. Not only had she suckled my baby, but I found out she also had
serviced my man.

If only that had been the worst of it with Louis Till. Things were to get
worse still. Much worse.

Trouble had a way of finding Louis Till. He was a big, strapping man,
an amateur boxer who just couldn't get enough of the sweet sport. Even
though we were the same age, Louis was a lot more sophisticated than I
was. Of course, that didn't take much back then, but he had been out on
his own for so long, and was quite accustomed to taking care of himself.
He had a presence when he stood that made you feel secure to be with
him and very uneasy if you were against him. He had a no-nonsense look
that was all business, even when he was at play. His favorite game was dice.

Or maybe it was poker. I'm not really sure, but I do know he was a gambler. He never did it at home, but he did it all the time on the way home. Which is why he often got home late, and, just as often, with no money in his pocket. One such night, he came home ready to blame me for his bad luck. I could tell. It didn't even take *me* long to get the pattern. My friend Ollie was there that evening. My mother was keeping Emmett and she had sent over some greens. I also had made a pot of chili. Louis resented my close relationship with my mother—probably because he had grown up an orphan and never experienced a loving household—and, of course, anything connected to her. On this particular night, it was the greens. He walked in just as I was about to put a forkful in my mouth. I knew he had been drinking and gambling again. And I figured he wouldn't have the money for the rent again. But I thought at least I could enjoy my greens and figure the rest out later.

"Don't put that in your mouth," he said.

Ollie excused herself from the table and left the apartment. But I knew what this was all about, so I paid him no attention. Besides, Mama's greens were too good to waste. I brushed him off and ate. The next thing I knew, he had pounced on me. I didn't know what to do at that moment, but knew I was no match for Louis Till. I found myself on the floor with Louis choking me, squeezing my neck as I coughed up the greens, squeezing harder and harder until I just blacked out.

When I came to, there was no one around. I don't know how long I had been out, but it probably was just a short while. At first I couldn't tell whether I was dead or alive, but surely God would have delivered me to a better place than that tiny old apartment. I could feel the soreness at my neck where Louis had squeezed. That's when I knew I was still alive and better act quickly. Louis would probably be coming back and I had to be ready. Either he was coming in peacefully, or he was going out peacefully. Feet first.

I took a poker and placed it on the embers of a wood-burning stove we had. I wanted it to get good and hot. Then I filled a pot with water and placed it on top of the stove to boil. I turned out the lights again. And waited. And thought about how I had gotten in that position, lying in wait for the man I had married only one year before. How I had been so charmed by Louis, yet so terribly wrong about the man.

It was such a thrill to me when Mama finally let me walk to Berg's Drugstore with Louis. She would never let me go to the show, and even though he had come over a few times, our version of a date up to that point had been just sitting on the front porch. Louis was a dashing, good-looking guy who was very popular. He had only recently come to Argo from New Madrid, Missouri, to work in the Corn Products plant. I felt lucky that he was paying attention to me and even luckier to have been given a break by Mama. As we approached Berg's, Louis asked me if I wanted a banana split. Well, I was insulted. I had no idea what a banana split was, but I thought I was good enough to have a *whole* banana to myself. Why should I have to split one with him? He just shook his head at this little country bumpkin and took me inside the drugstore, where he ordered a couple of banana splits. I couldn't believe my eyes as I watched the clerk prepare them. First, the banana, then the three scoops of ice cream—which I just loved—then the syrup, the pineapples, the whipped cream, nuts, everything. I was just imagining how good this was all going to taste as the clerk began packaging everything and Louis stopped him.

"No," he said, "we'll eat them here."

What was he thinking? I realized he was new in town, but he was about to get us into some real trouble. Louis very casually pointed me in the direction of the booth by the window and we sat there and began eating our banana splits. I could hardly enjoy mine, I was so nervous. Just as I was about to taste a spoonful, Mr. Berg himself rushed out to our booth. He was so upset.

"Mamie," he shouted, "you know better than this. I'm going to tell Alma."

Before I could say anything, Louis stood, and he did it so slowly that he seemed to unfold right there, all five feet eleven inches of him, in a way that told Mr. Berg to back off. Louis never spoke a single word, but Mr. Berg left just as quickly as he had come out. Louis calmly sat again at our booth and asked if I liked the banana split. I must have nodded or something, but all I could think about was how much trouble he was getting me into. And to think, this was just our first date. How in the world would I be able to explain all this to Mama? That's when I noticed something else. Other black people on the street were passing by and doubling back to take a second look at us sitting in a window booth at Berg's. I'm sure they were as shocked as Mr. Berg had been. But then they started doing something I never would have expected. They began coming in, ordering something or other, and sitting at other booths to eat. Before long, it turned into a mob scene as word spread all over Argo that Louis and Mamie had integrated Berg's Drugstore. Everyone came in to be part of it, I guess. I really didn't want to have anything to do with it and kept looking through that window expecting to see Mama storming down that street to pull me out of that booth. But it never happened. Even after I finally made it back home, Mama never said anything. It was as if it was all a matter of pride that Louis had stood up to Mr. Berg and opened the doors for everyone in our neighborhood. From that day on, I really admired Louis Till, looked up to him. I had always been taken care of and it seemed that he could take good care of me. I felt safe when I was with him, like I had nothing to fear.

The longer I sat there in the darkened room of my apartment waiting for Louis to come back, the less afraid I became. The hot poker and the boiling water were both within reach. No matter how much bigger Louis was, he would be no match for me now. Sure enough, he came back, and started calling out to me.

"Mamie. Mamie." He sounded so sweet, so pitiful, so sincere. But I wasn't falling for any of that. As I heard him moving in my direction, I grabbed the boiling pot and threw it at him. All I heard was this bloodcurdling scream as he ran from the apartment, and I grabbed the hot poker. Just in case he doubled back.

The next thing I knew, there was a call from my mother. He had run down the street to her house, probably to get his version of the story in first. Mama told me she had to peel his shirt off his back, pulling pieces of skin off in the process. I told her she should pour iodine on his wounds, and explained what had happened. Mama came through for me this time. She called the police, but they didn't arrest him. They figured he had already been punished enough.

Eventually, I got a protective order to keep Louis away from me. Without Louis, though, I didn't have enough money to keep the little apartment. The landlord was sympathetic. I guess that's what he was trying to be. He suggested that there were two ways to pay the rent. There was money, and then, well, that's when I knew I had to leave. I mean, I was not that kind of girl. Besides, he was ugly.

I moved back to Mama's. But things were different. I was different. Something had shifted in me. You reach a point in life where you simply must take a stand. I realized that when Louis had stood up to Mr. Berg. That took courage. And it took courage for me to do what I had to do—leave Louis in a town where women were defined by their relationships. I was a wife and a mother, but I only became a woman on that day—the day I stood up to my man.

As it turns out, Louis just couldn't help himself. He kept violating that court order, confronting me in the street, arguing with me about getting back together again. Finally, we had to go back to court, where the judge was considerate enough to give Louis a choice: jail or the army. It seemed to take no time at all for Louis to get into basic training. And it was months before I heard from him again. It was around Thanksgiving and he just showed up on our doorstep. I have to say he really looked good standing there in the uniform. We spent time together and he finally seemed to bond with Emmett. He told me he had made arrangements for me to receive a portion of his military pay. We talked about reconciling, but I wasn't sure. Before he could weaken my resolve, there was a knock at the door. It was the military police. Louis had gone AWOL. I don't know what all they might have charged him with, but I know they threw him in the stockade before shipping him out.

Over the next few years, the money came quite regularly from Louis. Not only did we receive his military spousal allotment, but we also got money he was making from boxing and gambling. It really helped to supplement the little money I was making at the time. We were getting about four hundred dollars a month from Louis, and Mama started a bank account for me with the money. She showed me at one point where we had put away more than five thousand dollars. Oh, my, that seemed like all the money in the world to me back then.

In 1945, however, the money stopped coming. It was on July 13 of that year—just two weeks before Emmett's fourth birthday—when I received the telegram. Louis Till was dead, killed in Italy. There wasn't much of an explanation. In fact, the telegram raised more questions than it answered. Like the words "willful misconduct." It was all too much. I collapsed when I read the news. Later, I considered the whole thing further and thought about the Louis Till I had known. "Willful misconduct." What a fitting epitaph, it seemed. And that's probably about all that would ever be said about Louis Till again, except that he left a very special gift, a remembrance. The army would return a few of his personal belongings to me. Among them was a plain silver ring. I learned that Louis bought the ring in Casablanca and had it engraved with his initials, LT, and the date MAY 25 1943. I would have to find just the right moment to share it with Emmett.

Over time, I would think about the sum total of Louis's life as I'd gaze at the son we created, the beautiful life, the active little boy, stretching his arms and his legs, getting stronger all the time as he began to rush forward to explore his world. I realized that Emmett was the one thing that gave meaning to Louis's life. He hadn't been a good husband, hadn't been a good father, and seemed to do his best to show the world that he wasn't a good person. But Emmett was his singular achievement, his one accomplishment, and in the end, perhaps, his only reason for being.

For Bo and me, life with Mama was as close to perfect as you could get, and as perfectly close as you would ever want. That's not to say that it was quiet. My goodness, there were times when Mama's house seemed like the intersection of State and Madison in downtown Chicago—one of the busiest, bustling blocks in the whole city. I read somewhere that more than two hundred thousand black people moved to Chicago between the 1920s and the 1950s. Mostly, they came from the South, and at least half of these Southerners came from one state, Mississippi. As I was growing up, it really seemed like almost everybody from Mississippi was coming through our house—the Ellis Island of Chicago. Actually, it was more like a terminal on the Underground Railroad. And Mama, well, Mama was kind of like Harriet Tubman. She took in relatives and friends of relatives and some people even our *relatives* didn't know. But she also helped all these people settle into a new life, a life with a whole lot more promise than the one they had left behind. She took people around, either to Corn Products or to the homes she had cleaned, the homes of white people. Mama helped so many folks find jobs; she helped them readjust, gave them every reason to look forward, never back.

As a result, we came to call Argo "Little Mississippi," but that description really only told half the story. For us, it meant the joy of the familiar, of family and friends, and, of course, runaway ambition. But there was that other half—the part that was more understood than talked about, and talked about mostly between the lines of other talk around our dinner table. It was the part that was dominated by what people knew they had fled. And, even though they thought they had put that part behind them, it always seemed to be lurking there in those quiet spaces between the words, as a reminder, and as a warning.

No one knew that better than my mother, Alma Carthan. We had come to Argo from just outside Webb, Mississippi, where I was born, near Sumner. My daddy, Wiley Nash Carthan, had come up a couple of months ahead of us and found work at Corn Products. Mama and I joined him in January 1924, when I was just a little over two years old. As far as Mama was concerned, we didn't come a moment too soon. All kinds of stories came out of Mississippi with the black people who were running for their lives. There had been talk of a lynching in Greenwood, Mississippi. It was the sort of horrible thing you only heard about in the areas nearby. But it seemed like that was the whole point: to send a signal, to make sure that black people in the area were kept under control. Maybe it was that Mama just knew she could never be controlled, or maybe she just knew that there had to be a better life for us somewhere else. And just about any place else would have been better than Mississippi in the 1920s.

There were other stories. I don't really know when I first heard this one. Maybe it was around the table, in one of the many dinner conversations we would have with family and friends at our house. Maybe it's just one of those stories that grows and is cultivated, like cotton in the Mississippi sun. It seems as if it was always there in my awareness. But there was a black woman who brought her little girl to work with her when she cleaned, cooked, and did laundry for a white family in the South. The little girl became a playmate of the daughter of this white family. One day something happened that upset the little white girl and she ran to her daddy as he came down the drive after work. The man listened to his daughter, then confronted the little black girl, and became so angry with her that he pushed her hard against a tree. Just slammed her. Now, that girl's mother had to finish her day's work before she could even look after her daughter, who was left there writhing in pain the rest of the day. Eventually, the little girl died from her injuries. That story left a mark on me, because I could see myself in that kind of situation. For black people, every generation has a cautionary tale like this. A story based on events, on shared experiences that teaches us something important. Was this a true story? I don't know. But I do know this: Somewhere between the fact we know and the anxiety we feel is the reality we live.

Despite the stories and the warnings, I was to get a small taste of what my family wanted to spare me. It was when I returned to Mississippi as a confident little twelve-year-old to spend time with relatives. I was so excited to see my grandparents. Now, the town of Webb was really not much of a town at all. To tell the truth, it was more like a commercial strip in search of a town. There was a white side of the main street—the *only* street, really—and there was a black side, just about a block and a half long. If you walked down the street, turned the corner, walked another half block, well, that was pretty much it. You were at the edge of town. I remember that at the end of that walk, there was a diner with a jukebox that really caught my attention. There was no way to ignore it. That was the *loudest* jukebox I had ever heard in my life and I really believe you could have heard it all over that little town. That probably would have been about the only point of interest in Webb for a curious youngster like me, but it wasn't music that I was looking for on this particular trip into town with my grandfather. What I was looking for was in the drugstore, the only one in town, the one on the *other* side of the street.

Now, my grandfather had let me wander a bit while he took care of something or other, and I had the bright idea to be helpful, to do what I thought might be a good deed with the little bit of money I had. When I had seen how my grandparents were using the pages out of the Sears, Roebuck catalog, well, I thought they had just run out of toilet paper. No one could possibly *choose* to use that slick, uncomfortable catalog paper that way. I mean, you really had to work with it. So I figured they must have run out and just didn't have time to run down to the store to get some more. I was always trying to help with one thing or another, so I headed across to that drugstore on the other side. I was going to buy some toilet paper. That, and an ice cream cone, because, after all, every good deed deserves a reward.

When I walked into the store, I got a whole lot of attention. Now, I was used to getting a lot of attention, but this, this was different. Very different. A mean-looking white man came up to me right away, but not in the right way, more like an aggressive kind of way.

He looked down on me. "What do *you* want?"

Even with that sharp, nasty tone, I really thought he was asking me what I wanted, not "How did you have the nerve to walk across the street and come into my store?" Which I think is what he really meant. But, I proceeded to answer the question I thought he was asking me. Politely, because that's the way I was taught to speak to everyone.

"I want two rolls of toilet paper," I said, "and an ice cream cone."

He kind of narrowed his eyes as if he were playing my voice back in his head, evaluating, the way a wild animal might size you up just before he pounces. "Where y'all from?"

I know my chest must have swelled. "I'm from *Chicago*," I said. That always seemed to impress people when my grandparents would take me around and introduce me. And I was very proud that I was from Chicago.

But apparently pride wasn't a good thing for a little black girl to have in the Mississippi Delta of the 1930s.

Well, he just looked like he was about to spit as he collected himself. "You know what? I'm gonna give you that ice cream cone," he said. "But I'm *not* going to sell you no toilet paper." He turned his back on me, but he kept talking. "You go on home, use corncobs like everybody else."

What? Now, really. Those glossy catalog pages were bad enough, but *corncobs*? I drew my breath, preparing to say something I *know* I would have regretted, some smart remark, because, I mean, what did I know? I must have thought I was still in Chicago or something. But at that moment, I was made aware of just where I stood. My grandfather walked through the door.

John Carthan, my daddy's daddy, was a well-respected man. He actually had his own land, with sharecroppers working for *him*. And there was a "plantation" store he owned, where people could come and get whatever they needed, from cloth to grits to candy. Everything, of course, except toilet paper. So, when Papa Carr came in, the white man recognized him.

"Does she belong to you?" the man asked.

My grandfather smiled, gently placed his arm on my shoulder. "Yes, sir, that's my baby."

I did get my ice cream cone, as well as a tongue-lashing from my grandfather once he got me on the other side of the street. He warned me never again to cross over by myself, and how I should never lose sight of him, and how I should always let him know when I moved away from him. He told me about the great danger that I had just faced, how I simply could have disappeared. And then what? He made me think about what Mama and Daddy would have thought, what they would have felt. Oh, that really shook me up. I mean, he just pounded the fear of every black person in the state of Mississippi into me. I would never forget that incident, and, my goodness, that talk with Papa Carr. The lessons of that moment would always stay with me. In Mississippi, there were certain things that black people were denied by white people. The freedom of movement. The luxury of choice. And a roll of toilet paper.

So Mama must have felt she had every reason in the world to help people get out of that place. I do believe that she must have single-handedly contributed to the growth of Argo, Illinois, in the process. Our whole neighborhood was like an extended family. Aunt Marie and Uncle Kid and June Bug lived west of us. Uncle Crosby and his family lived to the east of us. In back of us were Aunt Babe and Uncle Emmett, and in front of us was Bo's great-uncle Lee Green. It was a place of open arms and open doors. In fact, whenever we had to go away for a while, my mother would lock the door behind us, but she would put the key under the front door-mat. That was so people could let themselves in while we were away. You see, we were among the few people in the neighborhood who had a telephone back then and we shared everything with everyone. Some people didn't, but Mama always wanted to be there for everyone, even when she wasn't there. So she would leave the key and a little container next to the phone. She asked only that people remember to leave the key under the mat behind them and, well, to leave a nickel in the container for the phone call. It was an honor system. We never bothered to question people. And sometimes we would find nickels underneath the phone weeks later. There were people who must have believed that was the safer thing to do.

Mama was constantly doing something for somebody. Like cooking. People came over for dinner all the time, but especially on Sundays, which I have to admit didn't always make me happy as a child. There were just so many people. Our house was the meetinghouse, the gathering place, the center of the community. It was the place where Mama had helped to found the Argo Temple Church of God in Christ, and where she recruited new church members with practically each new Mississippi migrant. So, I guess it shouldn't have been much of a surprise when each Sunday Mama would host dinner for at least four ministers. The funny thing about it was that all these preachers lived outside Argo. And they were Baptists and Methodists. We were neither. I couldn't understand that one at first. I mean, those Baptist women were very good cooks. Maybe we could have switched up a bit. But every Sunday, it was dinner at Alma's. At least one of those four ministers was someone my mother and father knew from Mississippi. His name was C. J. Rogers, but they called him "One-Eyed" Rogers. That was because, well, because he had one eye. But, oh, that man could preach. And he would punctuate his sermons with a little hop and a squeak that would get everybody moving and filled with the holy spirit. Goodness gracious, the women would just throw their pocketbooks and everything. I never thought of One-Eyed Rogers as disabled. He kind of made me realize that there are people in this world who are able in a different way. That when God takes something away from you, He gives you so much in return. Anyway, that's the way it was on Sundays. Four ministers, Mama, Daddy, family, friends, strangers, and little Mamie Elizabeth Carthan, who almost couldn't make a way to the table.

Besides all that, I was the one who had to do the shopping much of the time. I don't know how my mother could afford all those chickens. They were more than a dollar apiece. And she would make me walk forever to save three cents on a stick of butter, seven blocks out of the way to buy butter at seven cents a stick, and to get three pounds of neck bones for a dime. Of course, this was Argo, and since just about everybody worked at the Corn Products plant, that meant just about everybody stocked the products they made at Corn Products. I once heard they made more than a hundred items from a grain of corn at that place. Sugar, starch for your clothes, Mazola corn oil, Karo syrup, and, oh, I just loved the lemon meringue pies Mama made with that Argo cornstarch.

It was a special time back then. And even though, from time to time, I might have gotten impatient with all the activity in our home as a child, that feeling didn't last very long. I loved listening to the conversation of people who were set on moving forward. It was a time filled with love and support and I felt it all very strongly. And then there was Mama, who had a way of calming me down. It wasn't so much something she said as just the way she was. A deeply religious woman, and a committed one, who believed in family as well as God. She was a very strong woman, the matriarch, and she took her strength from her faith, but also from her folks. She seemed to pull on a deep awareness of one fundamental truth: Above all else, you must always keep your family close. Without really knowing why, I came to understand that. But I wouldn't fully appreciate it for a long time, nearly a lifetime.

Not only did it seem that the world was beating a path to our door, but it also seemed that the whole world was within a short distance of our door. Argo was like that. It was a small town in a large metropolitan area, living in the shadow of everything around it. The total population was only thirteen thousand. Archer Avenue was our main street of small storefront shops, and there were tidy little residential streets of mostly single-family homes with big-family values. There was an elementary school, a high school, and a number of community churches. That was basically it. That, and the huge thirty-acre Argo Corn Products Refining Company squatting on the southwest edge of town. Like a fat man on a seesaw, the plant supported everything else on the other end. Our end. And you could pretty much see it all from our end, on the sidewalk in front of my home. The elementary school right across the street, the church not too far down the street, and to the right, filling up the distant horizon, was the Corn Products plant. Our whole world.

As important to me as anything else in that world was the fact that, to the left of our place, only several doors down, was the home of my dearest friend, Ollie Colbert. You know you are truly blessed when you find your life filled with special people who will do anything for you, without thinking about it, without being asked, without batting an eye. Certainly your family, but also friends who are so much like family you almost can't tell the difference. That is the kind of relationship I have had with Ollie for as far back as I can remember.

My household was so strict that it seemed like my one social activity was spending time with Ollie. Even though we were a year apart in school, I feel like we were inseparable. There were so many mornings when Ollie would come by my house for breakfast, listen for the school bell, and then run with me to make it to class on time. As we grew older, our bond became closer. And the list of things we wouldn't do for each other grew shorter. When I was about fifteen, Mama began teaching me to drive. One day Ollie stopped by after school and we talked about errands she had to run. She wasn't sure how she was going to get everything done and carry everything back. We looked at each other and knew right away, the way close friends know things without saying them. I looked for Mama's keys, slipped the car out of the garage, and we made it back without ever being missed.

Ollie took the plunge for me too. Literally. At Argo Community High School, I was an A student, and the first black to make the honor roll. I liked school. I liked it a lot, and I wanted so much to do well. Since things were so strict at home, mostly all I ever did was study, anyway. And, obviously, it was paying off in tough subjects like Latin and science. I even had a flair for poetry and found myself writing on my own when I didn't have poetry assignments. I wanted to make National Honor Society, but there were two things standing in my way. One was geometry, and the other was swimming. Actually, they were one-and-the-same problem, because I had the same instructor for both.

First, geometry. Now, I would bring my books home every night. I would memorize theorems and get Mama's help, calling out numbers that I could just close my eyes and visualize. I felt that I knew it all cold. But then something happened. I always recopied my notebook for the week before handing it in, as we were required to do. One week, my book was taken, probably by some boys I knew who wanted to get my notes. That meant I didn't have anything to turn in. I got a failing grade that week from a teacher who didn't seem to like me very much anyway. Well, I wasn't going to take that. I had gotten nothing but A's each week. I went to the principal's office and dazzled him by showing that I knew what I was doing, proving to him that my notebook really had been taken. He was convinced and made the teacher change my grade. Oh, she did not like that. And that brings us to the swimming problem.

Even though I was getting perfect grades, the National Honor Society wanted its candidates to be well rounded. So, I took swimming. There were three problems with this choice. First, the geometry teacher also was the swimming instructor. Second, that same teacher also was on the board for the National Honor Society. And the third problem was, well, I couldn't swim, but it was the only gym class left. Now, I loved to dive, I just didn't know what to do once I made it into the water. And we were all standing at the deep end. The teacher, the one who had given me the failing grade in geometry, the one who was ordered by the principal to restore my A, well she was really critical of the students who were just standing there, afraid to jump in. Students like me. As she kept walking back and forth, I felt something behind me. It was a nudge and the next thing I knew, I was in deep, flailing about, going down. Ollie saw all this. Now, even though Ollie could swim, she hadn't yet received her junior lifesaving pin. That didn't stop her. The next thing I knew, she was pulling me out of the water.

Ollie had risked her life for me, I had risked Mama's wrath for her, and to tell you the truth, I don't know who was taking the biggest chance. We laughed about both incidents for years, the many years that we have been close friends, and sometimes competitors, the way friends drive other friends to do their very best. After high school, when I found out Ollie was making twenty-five dollars a week working for the federal government, while I was making only fifteen dollars at the Coffey School of Aeronautics, I applied right away for the federal job, because, well, I just could not be outdone. And although I went on in 1940 to become only the fourth black to graduate from Argo Community and the first to graduate first in her class, one thing bugged me for a while: Ollie made National Honor Society. I didn't.

Over the years, Emmett would call her Aunt Ollie. And when Ollie had children, they called me Aunt Mamie. Fitting, really, for two best friends who thought of themselves as sisters.

So, this was the world I had brought Emmett into. It was the world that would shape him, define him. A world of strong values where you kept your family close and you kept your friends for life. It would become his world too, surrounded on all sides by people who loved him dearly. If it's true what they say, that it takes a village to raise a child, then Argo was that village, Emmett was that child. That's why for Bo and me, life with Mama and the community she helped to create was as close to perfect as you could get. This would be the place he'd know best. This would be the life he'd know best how to live. And he'd always know who he was in this place. Argo's favorite son. And he'd always know where he stood. At the center of our universe. After all, to even the most casual outside observer, it would seem like we had realigned the planets just to revolve around him.

Emmett took his first little baby steps when he was about eleven months old. Within a few months of that, there would be yet another step forward. A big one.

At the time, I was still working as a clerk-typist at the Coffey School of Aeronautics. It was a good job and it paid well enough, even though I always turned everything over to Mama: my paycheck, as well as the money I was getting while Louis was still alive. Mama, in turn, had complete control over Bo. Then again, Mama had complete control over everything in her household, and practically every other household within shouting distance, for that matter. Anyway, when I got home this one night, Mama was telling me what she had prepared for dinner and then she glanced at Bo, measuring the distance between them as he made his busy little way around the kitchen. She turned back to finish spelling it all out to me.

"And I made some *J-E-L-L-O*," she said in a hushed voice, as if spelling it wouldn't have been safe enough.

Suddenly, from behind her came this proud little-bitty voice. "Jell-O."

Mama turned around in shock. "He can talk."

I was even more amazed. "He can *spell*."

Now, I don't know; when you sound out the letters *J-E-L-L-O*, it does kind of sound like the actual word "Jell-O" to me. And Bo loved it enough to have been paying special attention to each syllable. But still, just to be there to hear him speak his first word, and to know that he had translated it from the letters, well, it sent an unbelievable charge through my whole body and through that entire kitchen. Mama must have felt it, too, because she moved into action. Right away, as if on command, she got a bowl and went into the icebox. The Jell-O wasn't even firm yet, but that didn't seem to matter. Bo loved it. I mean, he would scream for Jell-O. And, from this point on, he would know how to say it as he screamed for it. For the time being, we were content to savor the special moment, as Mama served the Jell-O, and Bo slipped into baby bliss, and she and I continued to spoon-feed new words to him. Now, I would have preferred his first word to have been "Mama," but maybe this was the next best thing. Our relationship would—well, I guess you could say it would *gel* through just this kind of care and nurturing and fun.

Now that he could walk and talk, there was no stopping our little Emmett. "Mama" wasn't far behind "Jell-O" in his ever-growing vocabulary. I made sure of that. Then came "Ma-moo." That's what he called his grandmother. I was Mama, she was Ma-moo. I'm sure that was his way of helping us figure out who he was calling on. Probably made no difference whatsoever to him. You see, as far as he was concerned, he had two Mamas. And, as far as my mother was concerned, she had two babies. Yes, now it was two children for Mama. I was the big kid, Emmett was the little kid. And this was the beginning of the special relationship we always would have. We were so much like brother and sister, like friends back then, and it added a unique dimension to the mother-son bond we would forge over the years ahead.

"Jell-O" might have been dessert for Bo, but it was just an opening for Mama. Once she saw Emmett was ready to learn, she didn't waste any time at all teaching him. Everything, starting with his ABC's. She took this on with the same kind of intensity she had when she'd kept me up all night teaching me my multiplication tables or drilling me on geometry theorems until I could simply close my eyes and dream the solutions to all my problems. She wanted to make sure that Bo could count and spell long before he started school. She became his personal "Big Bird."

Of course, Mama just loved being the caregiver. I mean, she *really* loved it. There seemed to be nothing that pleased her more back then than attending to every possible need her *babies* might have. And Mama would give Emmett everything. Her love, her attention, her devotion. Everything. Over the years, Emmett would have all that he wanted and probably more than he needed. We lavished him. And we made sure he looked good, too. Bo would always be a clotheshorse, although, early on, I guess he was just a clothes pony. I went out of my way to buy him the best outfits. The earliest ones had sort of a theme. Armed services. First, there was the cutest little sailor suit and then we turned to the army. After all, it was the 1940s. Military was in style.

Later my mother gave him a suit that, I'm sorry, I just did not like at all. It had plaid sleeves on a solid-colored body and—well, I had spent so much money on his clothes and that one, I don't know, it just looked bargain basement to me. But then he put it on and told his grandmother he looked better than he'd ever looked in his life. And, my goodness, that was such a slap in the face for me. Even back then, it seems, he had a sense of what was important and how to make the important people around him happy. I might have been making the money, but Mama was making the Jell-O. I have to say that Bo was becoming quite the little diplomat.

It's no wonder, then, that Mama couldn't even think about leaving him behind when she planned to make a trip to Mississippi. Emmett was not quite two at the time, and it would be a tense trip for her, but I knew I didn't have to worry about anything as long as he was in my mother's care. One of Mama's sisters, Elizabeth Wright, was expecting another child. Mama felt she simply had to travel down to Money, she had to look after Aunt Lizzy, who was the most fragile of Mama's fourteen brothers and sisters. She had lost three of her ten kids through difficult childbirths. Mother wanted to go down there to insist that Aunt Lizzy's husband, Moses Wright, would take her sister to a doctor. Now, Papa Mose was a preacher and a sharecropper and just as tough as Mama. If she was considered the matriarch of our very large family, then Papa Mose was considered the patriarch. He didn't budge on his decision to use the midwife. But Mother was there to supervise, to monitor, and, of course, to holler out if things didn't go well. They did go well. They went very well. And when the baby came, Mama was the one who came up with the name: Simeon Brown Wright.

Mama and I weren't the only ones who treated Emmett in a very special way. Part of that was due to my mother's dominance in the family. She just commanded attention for herself and her offspring. I was the oldest grandchild on my mother's side and on my father's side, and had always done so well in school that most of my relatives tended to dote on me, thinking Mamie Lizzie was the be-all and end-all. But beyond all that, everyone in our family simply adored Emmett. How could they not? He was irresistible. With his sandy hair and twinkling hazel brown eyes, he was the cutest little boy. And, by the time he was two, he had gotten way beyond all of the problems we suffered during his birth. The facial scarring had disappeared, and his legs had gotten stronger, so much so that it was hard to keep him down. He got a kick out of pulling a little mischief every once in a while, then running to hide under the bed, waiting for people to come after him, playfully. Within a few seconds, he must have felt the coast was clear and he would peek-a-boo his way out from under the bedspread, and there I'd be, just waiting for that little rascal. But then we both would have such a wonderful laugh that he'd wind up getting a hug instead of a spanking. For Emmett, pranks and hugs were inseparable, wrapped up together in one big loving bundle.

Not that anybody needed a reason to hug him. With so many relatives around, we almost had to develop a time-share plan for Emmett. My young cousin Thelma Wright was living there at the time. She was one of the daughters of Papa Mose and Aunt Lizzy and had come to stay with us in 1939, when she was in the third grade. Her parents thought she had promise and wanted to give her a chance to take advantage of everything the world outside Mississippi had to offer. She was about ten when Emmett was born and she was always there to pitch in, helping Mama with everything that needed to be done. It took a few tries for young Thelma to get the hang of changing Bo's diapers, though; they kept falling off at first. Over the years, they were so close, talking and playing together, that Bo would come to think of "Thel-moo" as his sister, and she would think of him as a brother.

There were others. Plenty of them. We had a very big family and a lot of friends. They all were practically standing in line. Every so often one of my uncles might come by and take Bo uptown, which was only about two or three blocks away. They would walk him up there just to spend a little time and, of course, buy him some ice cream or some other treat.

Several of Emmett's older cousins made it their business to take him out every Saturday. There was a Cadillac that seemed to get passed around them. And there was a rush to see who could get up the earliest on Saturday morning, take the keys to this Cadillac, and head to Argo. It became such an intense competition that they were getting up as early as five in the morning. On a Saturday morning. Bo was the prize, although riding around in that fancy car must have made him feel like the winner. He was just a toddler and he was already going first-class. Whoever got to our place first on Saturdays always seemed overjoyed to get to spend time with my baby. The others, the latecomers, would try to wait it out. It was like they were on the "Emmett shift," talking to me, eating, but mostly hoping to get a turn when Bo got back. Oh, and when he got back, he would be so full of junk that he would have an upset stomach. They were feeding him all kinds of stuff at places like Riverview Amusement Park in Chicago. Caramel corn, popcorn, cotton candy, hot dogs, and anything else they could stuff in the poor kid. I know they thought they were doing a good thing, entertaining him, showing him a fun time, but they were making more work for the rest of us who had to take care of Bo after they dropped him off, bathing him, calming him down, putting him to bed.

Even with the upset tummy, though, Emmett was having a great time. He loved the amusement park. Later he would take on the roller coasters, but at this point, the wildest thing he could handle was the horse on the merry-go-round. And it had to be a horse, too. His cousins would try to get him onto one of the benches so they could sit with him, but he insisted on sitting on top of a horse. And he wanted to sit there by himself, although someone would always be right there next to him. Already at two, Emmett was showing signs of that independent spirit that would only get stronger in time.

There also were his little friends in the neighborhood. Mama was much more lenient with Bo than she had been with me. He was actually able to go outside and play with the other kids all the time, not just sometimes. When I was coming up, there was so much I couldn't do. No movies, no hopscotch, no hide-and-seek, and definitely no dancing. Even after I got married. In the first six months of my marriage to Louis Till, we lived with Mama and actually asked permission to go to the show. I'm not kidding. Mama's hold on me had been so strong that I didn't realize that I was fully grown until I was nineteen years old and had been married for six months.

When Emmett was about three, he was either out right in front of our house or in our yard. We had an enclosed yard, and it seemed to be a meeting place for the whole neighborhood. The *whole* neighborhood. My mother once told me that if you put one child out in the yard, by the time you came back, you'd find a flock of children. She was right. Bo was like a kiddie magnet. They were drawn to him. I never imagined that children could find so many activities in a front yard and on a front porch. Oh, yes, and on the sidewalk. There would be so many kids on the sidewalk in front of our house that people had to step off just to get by. There was always food, plenty of games, and water. A steady stream of kids to the water fountain. At first all these children had to go all the way through our house—the front room, dining room, past a bedroom and bathroom, and finally into the kitchen. And I think we had the thirstiest children in all of Argo. Every time you turned around there was some little person asking for water. Finally we decided to tap into a pipe to install a faucet outside for all the kids. And that became a real attraction. Of course, you add a water spout to kids outside in a yard and you wind up with mud. We had mud puddles for days, but the children had good times they would remember for a whole lot longer.

It didn't hurt that Emmett had so many toys to play with. In fact, throughout his childhood, Emmett would have everything any child might want. From the time he lay in his crib playing with the rattle I had suspended there, kicking it with his little feet, laughing, there was always something around to occupy him. Wooden blocks, toy animals, bikes, wagons. When he was about five, I bought him a Lionel train set, one with all the bells and whistles. Not to mention smoke pellets that made it look so real as it would come chugging along to the special little depot I bought, the stop where the train would pick up little passengers and cargo. It was a very nice train, the deluxe model. I don't remember exactly what it cost, but I know it wasn't cheap. And Emmett really liked it. At least, he seemed to like it, as he sat on the side watching all the adults play with it. I guess it was kind of hard for the poor little fellow. Whenever he would try to operate something, some cousin or uncle would yell, "No," or "Wait," or "Don't touch that." Now that I think about it, we were all much more excited about the train than he was. All my friends would come by to play with it. Eventually, Emmett lost interest. Even early on, he clearly wanted to be a player, not a spectator. He wanted to be in the game, not on the sidelines.

Besides, he was strictly an outdoor man. Mama loved to take him to Brookfield Zoo. Even when he was a toddler, we would strap him in his stroller and push him right along. It was one of my mother's favorite activities, especially when we had visitors from the South. Mama had to take them to the zoo. It was new in those days and our relatives from the South had never seen a zoo before. Bo loved the polar bears, who would dive and box and thrill him so. But Mama's favorite spot in the whole place was the monkey house. There always was a show with those monkeys. I'll never forget the time Aunt Georgia came to visit us from Mississippi. I was pushing Bo and he kept trying to get out and walk. But I knew if I let him out in the monkey house, he'd wind up being one of the monkeys. I couldn't take that chance. So, I kept him strapped in. Those monkeys were doing their monkeyshines that day. I mean, they were really showing their—well, what monkeys show when they're showing out. Aunt Georgia had never seen anything like it and she began to laugh like I had never heard anybody laugh before, with a very loud voice, slapping her thighs and making this high-pitched sound to the point where Bo kept looking back and forth. At the monkeys, then at Aunt Georgia. He studied her so intently that he must have been trying to figure out whether Aunt Georgia and the monkeys were communicating somehow. We caught the attention of others, too, as more and more people stopped looking at the monkeys and started watching Aunt Georgia. I'll never forget that day, when we went to the monkey house at Brookfield Zoo, and Aunt Georgia became the entertainment.

Mama thought my twenty-fifth birthday should be a memorable event. It would be. But not for a reason we ever would have imagined. The date—

November 23, 1946—was approaching and Mama made sure everything was worked out. She and I planned it together, but, as always, she was in charge. She took care of everything, even all the cooking. She prepared a twin-turkey dinner. Unbelievable. Two whole turkeys. I don't know how she did it, but she wanted to make sure everything was done right. That was a good thing, too, because it seemed like everybody in Argo wound up at our house on my special day. And it *was* special, too. When I was coming up, there was no music or dancing in our house. But now the whole town was dancing the night away. I don't know how it all started. It seemed to have been a spontaneous kind of thing. I mean, it was a party, and that's how parties can be. But I was nervous when all the dancing started. Once it did, it was hard to hold people back. I knew Mama, and I didn't know when she was going to just lose it. As it turns out, Mama didn't complain, she took it all in stride. But I believe she was just holding her peace. Until it seemed the house just couldn't take it anymore. People were dancing so hard, the floor looked like it was starting to sag. I guess, after all those quiet years, that old house just couldn't stand all this activity. Even without the dancing, though, the party went on.

At some point, somebody convinced me to try a little rum in my Coke. Just a little. Enough to smell the rum more than anything else. But why not? After all, you only have one twenty-fifth birthday. Now, I wasn't a drinker, but it was my party and I didn't see anything wrong with it, even though I wasn't too sure what Mama would think. She knew about it. She knew about everything going on in her house, and then some. But she didn't say anything about it. Believe me, that was startling. Now, since I wasn't a drinker, I would take a little sip and then put my glass down, walk around mixing with my guests, and then come back, only to find my glass was missing. I'd get another drink and the same thing would happen again. In fact, it happened a few times before I really started wondering about it. Why did my glass keep disappearing like that? No sooner had I asked myself the question than I thought of the answer: Mama. I started looking around, but she was nowhere near me. Then I looked down. Oh my God. Emmett had been trailing me around the party picking up my "Coke" glass, drinking after his mama. By the time I noticed, he was in a pretty good mood. He seemed to think everything was funny. Well, I took him up in my arms and up to bed. He was so limber, not stiff at all, just very relaxed, passive. I saw that he was all right, and I relaxed, too. There hadn't been much rum in those glasses to begin with. Even so, he wound up sleeping like, well, like a baby. Through the noise, the music, all the way through the night.

There was no more rum and Coke for me that night, or any night, for that matter. Even before Mama talked to me about the whole thing. Of course, she noticed. And she had a way of coming back at you when you'd least expect it. She really didn't have to drive the point home. Seeing Bo with my glass was a sobering experience. He was only five years old. Very impressionable. And I knew that the impressions I made would be lasting. I decided that he would never see me with a drink in my hand again.

I have learned over the years that there are many ways that children learn. But one of the most important is by watching adults, especially their parents. There was a valuable lesson in this experience, a valuable lesson for *me*. I learned from Bo that he was learning from me and that I had better pay attention to what I was teaching him. Everything I did as a mother would have an effect on my son. And I decided at that moment that I had to set the right example for him. I would always remember that lesson. But if I ever forgot, even for a moment, I'm sure Mama would have been there to remind me.

Chicago was more than five hundred miles and at least a hundred years away from Mississippi. Even though there were no visible signs of discrimination outside the buildings in the North, there were subtle reminders just behind the facades.

It was 1947. I was twenty-five years old and working for the federal government in downtown Chicago before I finally began to show a little independence. I remember when I first started working, at age eighteen, my mother would travel with me to and from work each day. Even when she didn't have a car, she would ride public transportation. But she would always be there for me, until the day she couldn't and I had to work my way through it, find my way home. I feel like I grew a lot as a result. So, by the time I was twenty-five, I thought I knew my way around, at least between home in Argo and my job in downtown Chicago. The Loop was an exciting place to walk around. I loved to look in the department store windows and dream about the things I might buy myself, or Mama, or Emmett. One day I decided to stop dreaming, and I had a rude awakening. I walked into Marshall Field's like I *was* Marshall Field. Like I knew my way around, at the very least.

So, I was surprised when the security guard stopped me. "Are you looking for something?"

I didn't think I looked like I needed directions. And I really wouldn't know what I was looking for until I found it. "Well, I was just going to do a little shopping," I said.

He gave me a stern look. "Then you'll have to go to the basement."

Oh, no. Not here. Marshall Field's had a reputation as a fine department store. I figured the only discriminating you'd find there was in taste.

There were no signs, so how could I have known that I was not welcome? The store motto was "Give the lady what she wants." I guess if the lady was black, though, they would have to give it to her in the basement. I just turned on my heels and took my business down the street, to Carson Pirie Scott and Wieboldt's, and down to the South Side to the black shopping mecca at Sixty-third and Halsted streets. That was the last time I would shop at Field's for nearly twenty years. And when I finally went back, I didn't go to the basement.

The way I looked at it, discrimination was somebody else's problem: It was the problem of the person who was doing the discriminating. In this case, Field's didn't get my business, and I always loved to shop. But I had choices and I would make sure my son had choices. In the community where we lived, the kind of problem I ran into when I walked into Marshall Field's just would not occur. Not since Louis and I integrated Berg's. People there wanted our business, and our friendship. And that's all Bo would know. In time, he would also know whites, children in school, even adults he would do business with. We made sure he would never be self-conscious around them. He would not see the signs, or the attitudes behind the facades. For him, they would not exist. There would come a time, though, when that strength would make him vulnerable.

During this same period, Mama took Emmett on his second trip to Mississippi to escort Aunt Lizzy back to Money after an extended visit in Argo. While they were down there at the home of Aunt Lizzy and Uncle Mose, Bo borrowed a hammer from the white plantation boss. He wanted to work on something. Little Bo was always working on something. After some time, the man came back to ask for his hammer.

Bo looked up at him. "Just a minute," he said. "I'm not finished yet."

Mama rushed in to handle the situation. The man got his hammer. Mama got Bo out of there.

People in Argo valued our family for so many reasons. But most of the reasons were Mama, and the way she could step in and handle situations. In addition to running her one-woman settlement house, my mother was the people's choice for all kinds of advice. If she had been a man, she might have been considered the "Godfather" of Argo. When people had problems, they brought them to Alma Gaines. She had remarried by this time, Tom Gaines, after she and my father divorced. And she could draw on that experience to counsel neighbors on family problems. She was a walking resource, who pointed people to social services when there was a need, and she always led them in the direction of her church. It was no surprise, then, that she was able to get so much help when it came time to sell fish sandwiches door-to-door or anything else that might be needed to raise funds for the church. Fifteen cents a sandwich. The bricks came from the streetcar tracks removed by the town. The Argo Temple Church of God in Christ was Mama's heart and soul. It had been organized right there in our home. Mama was into community building.

By 1947, my cousins Hallie and Wheeler Parker decided they were ready to leave Mississippi and bring their three children north. Hallie wrote to Mama and asked her whether she could help them with the move. Wheeler Senior had already come up to scout around. Of course Mama would help. In fact, there was a place right next door to us that had been available for some time. It was the house where my uncle Crosby Smith had lived with his family. For some reason we never really understood, Uncle Crosby had decided to move back to Mississippi a couple of years earlier. Everybody else was coming the other way about that time, but he wanted to go back. Anyway, an elderly couple had occupied the place for a while, but it had been vacant since they died. It was empty so long, in fact, that people had time to start inventing stories about the place. They declared they could see the elderly couple walking around at night, and nobody wanted to run into those ghosts. So the place stayed vacant for a while. But my mother brushed all that off, and the Parkers didn't know about it, so they moved in.

They never saw a single ghost. But, with three boys, Wheeler Junior, William, and Milton, the Parkers began to see as many kids hanging out at their house as we did next door. Bo became friends with all the Parker boys, but he and Wheeler developed a special relationship. Wheeler was seven at the time, two years older than Emmett, but they had the greatest time playing together. Even though I didn't always approve of their games. Their relationship started out as a sort of back porch kind of thing. It was one porch to the other. Ours was high with a railing and Wheeler's porch was much lower. I couldn't believe it when I saw those boys standing up on my railing and jumping down and across the way to Wheeler's porch. I guess they figured it was a shortcut, but that was so frightening to me. They could have fallen and broken something. An arm, a leg, anything.

When I called out to them to stop, Emmett tried to make me feel more comfortable. I guess that's what he thought he was doing. "Aw, Mama, nothing to it," he said. "Look."

Then, to my amazement, he did it again. Finally, I got tired of looking. I got tired of talking. I got me a switch and tanned his little legs. That broke up the jumping for both of them, since Wheeler also learned a lot from Bo's lesson.

There was another time I had to get after Bo for taking chances. I had told him not to play around an abandoned garage in our neighborhood.

But boys always have a sense of adventure about such things. They seem to be drawn to them. Word got back to me that he was playing around that place again. Word got to him that I was on my way, to give him a spanking. He rushed and made it home down the back way while I was headed for that garage the front way, down our street. By the time I realized what had happened and made it back home, he was already there, acting like he had been there all along. Except that he was breathing hard from running all the way home.

Bo loved to fish with Mama. Wheeler would go along with them sometimes to a spot along the Des Plaines River nearby. The boys would set up their poles at a bend where Mama could keep an eye on them. But, while she could still see their poles set up there, lines in the water, the boys were slipping just out of sight around that bend, where they could splash at the water's edge. Scaring away all the fish. One time, though, Emmett managed to catch one. Mama had shown him how to reel it in and yank it out of the water. But he hadn't quite worked the whole thing out yet. He was beside himself with excitement, and maybe his coordination was a little off to begin with. He managed to yank the fish out of the water, all right, just as he had been taught. But he couldn't hold on to it. The fish fell to the ground and got dirty. Well, Bo could not stand dirt on anything. So, he picked up his prize catch with his chest all puffed up, so proud of what he had done. He walked right up to the edge of the river and dipped the fish to wash it off. Well, in the river is exactly where a fish wants to be. That little thing just wriggled out of Bo's hands and swam away. Bo fell back on the riverbank and he and Wheeler were left there with so much laughter. That, and a fish tale.

Sometime during the summer Emmett turned six, I noticed something very odd. He always played hard and he played all the time. At least, he wanted to play all the time. First thing I saw when I got home from work was Emmett, ripping and running. Well, I thought when I got home it was time for him to come in. I figured he had been out most of the day. Naturally, he didn't agree, and he would pitch a fit. By the time we settled him down inside, he would just completely deflate. That's what was so odd to me, because Emmett always seemed to have unlimited energy. Mama blamed me for upsetting him by bringing him in. As far as she was concerned, this was just a childish reaction to me making Emmett do something he didn't want to do. Within a couple of days, we started to realize there was a more serious problem. He would be active all day and then fall into this slump at night when I'd force him inside. But there was more. His temperature was beginning to soar at night.

Strange. He seemed just fine during the day, then at night, he would fall into a slump; he would be so lethargic. And now, a high temperature. We couldn't figure it out. I searched high and low to find fault, to find a place to lay blame. I mean, someone had to be blamed. Someone had to be responsible for this, whatever "this" was. My mother was the most responsible person I knew. So I blamed Mama. I thought she wasn't paying enough attention. Bo would get up in the morning and want to get out right away, every day. She would just let him. He was only a baby, not even six years old. How could he really know what he wanted to do? Mama *told* me what to do. I had no choices. But she was so light on him, so lenient. As far as she was concerned, he could do no wrong. But something *was* wrong with this situation. Something was very wrong.

We started using home remedies, rubbing him down with goose grease and serving him hoof tea. We set a lot of stock by this stuff. These remedies were supposed to cure a lot of things. I never knew why or how. I didn't even know what kind of hoof came in that little box of hoof tea. All I knew was that we would wash it, then boil it, strain it, and the poor fellow would have to drink it. No sugar. Horrible taste. The goose grease was rubbed all over his body. I didn't know what this was supposed to do, either. I just knew that all our folks from Mississippi used it. It might have been uncomfortable, but Emmett put up with the goose grease. At least he didn't have to drink it.

He wasn't showing any improvement with our home remedies. In fact, he seemed to be getting worse. We finally decided we better call the doctor. This was when doctors would still make house calls. After examining Emmett, the doctor gave us the diagnosis that broke my heart: polio. I felt ill. Mama nearly collapsed. Polio was the worst thing that could happen to you back then. It didn't kill you, but it could take your life away from you just the same. It was sneaky and it was controlling and it scared people nearly to death. But we didn't have time to think about that right then. The doctor urged us to rush Emmett to the hospital immediately. We didn't have a car at the time and couldn't get anyone to drive us. We were desperate. A private ambulance even turned us down. Finally we were able to get Bo to the hospital in a police squad car.

This was pure agony for me. We had no way of knowing what to expect. All we had was a vision of what might be in store. In those days, you would see the casualties everywhere. Children, mostly, in iron lungs because their own muscles had failed them. Wheelchair-bound children whose legs had shriveled, or with different forms of paralysis. And then there was my son. What was to become of little Emmett? I had defied the doctors who told me he would be crippled for life following the complications at birth. We got through that. Now there was this.

The doctors at the contagious disease center weren't able to tell us anything reassuring at first. In fact, what they were telling us was anything but reassuring. What we heard from the medical specialists was talk about permanent limb damage, and the possibility that Emmett might be disabled for the rest of his life, and, oh, my God, there was just so much to absorb.

We turned to prayer. We prayed hard. I had heard this kind of talk from doctors before. I didn't accept it then, and I couldn't bring myself to accept it now. We tried to figure it out. Where had this come from? It was often hard to tell with polio. As far as we knew, no one in Argo had been diagnosed. Our best guess was that Emmett must have been exposed to it in a pool. But we never really knew. So, we kept praying.

Emmett had to be quarantined at home. We could go out, but he had to stay in, and no one else could come over. We kept praying. There were good signs. Emmett's little legs and arms were still moving and our baby didn't seem to have any brain damage. We were overjoyed. I mean, we were so grateful. He was recovering, he really was. His only problem was keeping still. Mama had to sit with Emmett all the time, practically holding him in the bed. And he just couldn't stand that. But that was a good sign. I called constantly from work to check, and I looked after him when I got home at night. Then, on one of his regular visits to our home, the doctor finally discharged Emmett. It had been thirty days, and Emmett had recovered. He had beaten it. He was up and running again and practically tore a hole in the screen to get out.

After Emmett's recovery, I remember we went to church one night. Mama testified how God had brought her baby through. And the whole church just started shouting. It was such a wonderful, "glory hallelujah" time. I heard Mama's testimony, saw the church just going up in thanks, and, as the congregation rose, all I could do was sit there and cry. Tears of joy.

Although it was a great relief to learn that Emmett hadn't lost any of his motor skills, it wasn't long before we noticed a related problem. It was devastating to us. Emmett's bout with polio had caused some muscle damage after all. He was left with a speech defect. He stuttered. It was especially bad when he got excited or nervous. It could just take over at times in those early days. Nobody could understand him. Nobody but Mama and me. We knew what this could mean and we refused to accept it. We were very proud people, and we didn't want anything to stand in the way of Em-

mett's success. We didn't want him held back because of people's prejudices, because they might hear him speak and think he had limitations.

Good speaking skills had always been important to Mama. She was a
very proper and dignified lady. She had an aunt named Rose Taliafero. Actually, I think it was Tolliver and she changed it to Taliafero. But, anyway,
she worked in the political arena with the black Chicago congressman,
Oscar DePriest. And Mama fell completely under the spell of Rose Taliafero, who was a lady's lady, and who placed a heavy emphasis on appearance and speech. The kind of person who said "to-mah-to." That was
"Ant." And every time somebody would say something incorrectly, Ant
was right there to stop him in his tracks, back him up, and make him repeat the phrase correctly. Ant was a lady of grace, charm, and, above all
else, first impressions. Mama knew what she had learned from Ant, that
people judge you by the way you present yourself, and that those judg-
ments can be very important for your success in life.

We couldn't bear the thought that Emmett might somehow be misjudged for something that was not his fault. So we worked on that problem very hard. We started taking him to doctors, to clinics. I would have to
take him on Saturdays, and we had to travel quite a way by streetcar. Oh,
that was rough. But it was for Bo, and we kept at it. In the end, the doctors
couldn't find a remedy, although speech therapy helped. They said he
would outgrow it. It seemed we had little choice but to wait. Even so, we
would never stop trying to help. In the meantime, we would do everything we could to keep Emmett's outlook strong and positive. That wasn't
hard at all. It was becoming clear to us that there was no problem Emmett
wouldn't try to solve, no difficulty he wouldn't try to overcome. And,
somehow, he would always maintain his sense of balance, and his sense of
humor.

From the very beginning with Emmett there was laughter. He could
find a way to enjoy himself in most situations. He was always trying to en-
tertain me with jokes he picked up, early on from his uncle Emmett, who
lived across the alley. Uncle Emmett would tell him a joke, then he would
run back home to tell me. Oh, gee, I heard about more chickens crossing
more roads, and knock-knock this and knock-knock that. All those tired,
old jokes that were still so new to him. Sometimes, he would tell riddles
that he seemed to have been making up, because they didn't make sense.
Or maybe you just had to be six years old to get them. He had the right
style of joke telling. He would raise his voice just at the right time and
punch the ending like he must have heard Uncle Emmett doing, and then
it just didn't make sense. But you would laugh just as he must have been
laughing at jokes that weren't making sense to him yet. After all, it was the

laughter that was important. For Emmett, life was laughter and laughter was life-giving. There was so much joy in his carefree world that he just wanted to share with everyone around him. He did it the only way a young boy knows how to do it. He made people laugh.

Emmett couldn't wait to start school, and we were encouraged by that. As it turns out, he wanted to be with his friends who were going. Wheeler was ahead of him by a couple of years, and Bo just had to be with Wheeler. After all, Wheeler was his idol. Almost every day, Emmett wanted to know why he couldn't go to school. It wasn't enough to explain to him that he wasn't old enough, that he would be going in September. What sense does that make to a little boy? But when school was ready for him, he was ready for school. Mama had been tutoring him all along. My mother had been a teacher in the South. She didn't have a college degree. She came up in a simpler time. Among black people back then, if one person was ahead of the group, that person became the teacher. Mama was that person. And although she hadn't been trained, she had strong values and she recognized the value of good education. And that's the way it worked.

When Bo was about to start, we talked to him. We always stressed discipline. And we told him what an important thing it was to start school. We let him know that he was getting to be a big boy now. He had to take it all seriously; he was not going to school to play. We told him he was going to school to learn all he could learn so that, when he became a man, he would have something to depend on. This was the kind of encouragement we kept giving him. And we figured that it would sink in over time. But, at that moment, just before his first day of school, an excited boy as young and playful and sociable as Bo had to be thinking that school was the place where he could see all his friends most of the day. And that was all that mattered to him.

Mama and I had really enjoyed shopping for Bo's clothes for the start of school. Mama talked me into getting some blue jeans, and we bought him shirts and shoes. I got him everything he needed. Of course. And then, when winter came, we had to fight. The boots and the heavier coats and sweaters, they were all fine. But the long underwear? No way. Oh, he complained, he protested. He didn't want to wear those things. "Nobody else is wearing them," he said. But he was no match for Mama. She ruled the roost. I remember how she made me wear long, white stockings in the winter. And I hated those stockings. She also made me wear long underwear, and then pull my stockings up over them. When I'd get to school, I would go straight to the washroom and I would pull the legs of those drawers up as high as they would go and then I would pull my stockings back up over my bare legs. Then I'd have to go to the washroom again at just about three o'clock every day.

One day the teacher couldn't resist any longer. "Why is it that you have to go to the bathroom every day at three o'clock?"

She had gotten wise to me. Or somebody had told on me. It didn't matter how she knew, she wasn't letting me go. And that meant that I had to go home without readjusting myself, and face Mama. Bo wouldn't stand a chance. Thanks to me and a teacher who wouldn't let me go to the washroom, Mama knew all the tricks.

Emmett was always looking for something to do to make some extra money or get a treat. It started with the milk truck. Emmett would help the deliveryman carry bottles of milk from the truck to the front doors of all the customers on our block. Bo would wind up getting a bottle of chocolate milk for his troubles. The next thing I knew he was picking up bottles in alleys and collecting the deposits. He even ran down the hill to the train yard where the railcars were delivering coal to fire up the furnaces of the Corn Products plant. Coal would always fall off the coal cars. Bo had a scuttle. He'd pick up spilled coal, carry it back to our block, and walk up and down yelling, "Coal. Coal man. Coal." He could sell a scuttleful for ten to twenty-five cents. Then he'd run back to the train yard to collect more spilled coal to sell. But his favorite "job" was ice delivery. He'd run ahead of the man on the ice truck, knock on doors, and take orders from the houses. Then he would tell the iceman how much each customer would buy. Twenty-five pounds here, fifty pounds there. Bo actually even tried to carry a twenty-five-pound block of ice once. Just once. The iceman appreciated the help. He liked Bo and gave him a chunk of ice wrapped in a little rag for him to enjoy on the hot days. But that wasn't all. He also paid Bo a quarter.

A strong sense of responsibility was an important quality to have back in Argo, when Emmett was coming up. In a way, our section of town was a community of immigrants. That's what we were, really, all those black folks from the South. People coming to a strange, new land—the land of milk and honey—in search of the kind of grand opportunities they would never have back home. There is always something special about people like that. They don't look back. They don't let anything stand in their way. Every day, the people in our little Argo community could see the Corn Products plant spread out there on the horizon, dominating our landscape. It stood there as a constant reminder that the gateway to a better life was hard work. So, even those folks who had no jobs worked in whatever way they could to make a way for themselves. Bo saw them, he watched them, he learned from them. Now, a six-year-old boy really doesn't need a job. And, with everything we gave Bo, he certainly didn't need money. What he did need, though, was a sense of his place in his world. A sense of belonging. And to belong, you had to make a contribution. Making a contribution had its value, but it also had its rewards. At the time, for little Emmett, that reward was only twenty-five cents. But it was a good start.

CHAPTER 6

E ven though I've always believed that we're strengthened by our values, sometimes I think we can be limited by our customs. As a child in Argo, I learned somehow that the most important thing for a little girl was to grow up to become some man's wife. I wasn't the only one. So many of the little black girls in our community had quit high school by age sixteen to marry that there were only four blacks in my entire 1940 graduating class. In fact, I felt like I was at risk. Even at the top of my class, it seemed that I was still falling short of success. I really was beginning to think that I was on the brink of becoming an old maid when I waited until I was eighteen—almost nineteen—to marry Louis Till. As I got closer to thirty, I began thinking all over again about all the things I had been taught to think about marriage and family and what it meant for a woman to have a significant life. My mother had married for the third time. Papa Tom Gaines died in 1945 and she married Henry Spearman in 1947. Mama moved to Chicago. Bo and I stayed behind in Argo surrounded by other relatives, yet still feeling that something was missing. I was working regularly for the federal government and thinking that I really should start working regularly on getting married again before Emmett got too much older. There should be a father figure, at least, to replace his real father.

Now, apart from that one trip to Berg's Drugstore with Louis, I'd never had any experience with dating, so I didn't even know the first rule of that game. If I could have limited my choices to Argo, I wouldn't have felt so uneasy about it all. I knew Argo. I knew all the people in Argo, so many people with familiar backgrounds that would make it seem less like a stab in the dark. But, as we started closing in on a new decade, what I knew most of all was that there were no real prospects in Argo. People I knew were married already. That's how people were in that place. That was the custom of that place.

As it turns out, there was a fellow I thought I would like from Maywood, another nearby community. He came to take me out once and we wound up at a popular spot, the Rum Boogie. This was one of the elite clubs on Chicago's South Side. There were two shows a night with big bands, chorus girls, singers, and comedians. There was dancing, and so many tables on the main floor and the mezzanine, and bars on both levels, and, oh, so many people, fashionable people who were moving to a different beat. The atmosphere was charged, so very exciting. I was dazzled, and maybe just a little overwhelmed. After all, I was used to sleepy little Argo. But I figured this guy knew his way around. He certainly knew his way to this spot. I figured he could take care of anything that might come up. So I tried to relax with it all, sit back and enjoy myself. The conversation started. He was a good talker and, as he started talking, I listened to the words and looked at the man behind the words to see if there was somebody there I might want to spend more time with. Someone I might want to spend more time with Emmett. So he talked about his job and his life and his wife and his children and . . . Wait a minute. *Wife? Children?* How did this happen? How did I wind up there in a nightclub on a date with a married man? Oh, my goodness. What was I supposed to do? I began to question everything and he simply said that he thought I already knew he was married. Now, really. How could I have known that? I guess you're supposed to ask, but it never occurred to me to ask about his status, because I never dreamed that a married man would ask me out. What did I know about these things? Well, I demanded that he take me home at once. He did, and just vanished into the night. This was not a good start and the road ahead didn't look too promising.

Meanwhile, my cousin Ruby kept writing to me, telling me what a great time she and another cousin, Juanita, were having in Detroit. I felt very close to these cousins; they had spent quite a few of their summer vacations with me. By this time, Ruby was encouraging me to relocate to Detroit, telling me, among other things, that I would be able to meet somebody, a good person, probably with a good job in the automobile industry, somebody who could help me with Emmett. My father also was living in Detroit at the time. He had moved there after he remarried.

It became clear to me that I was going to have to leave Argo. The little town that had been my home for so long, the place that had been so comfortable, the place that had nurtured me and my son was no longer an option if we were going to look to our future. It also was clear to me that I was going to need some help, as I had always gotten in Argo. I needed a support network, people who could look out for me, expose me and protect me all at the same time. People who might be able to help me screen the prospects, and avoid another Rum Boogie. So the choice came down to Chicago or Detroit. Mama was in Chicago. Daddy was in Detroit. I didn't think Mama could help much at all at this point. Besides, her last husband, Papa Tom, had adored Bo and was always there to pitch in with his care. Her newest husband, Henry Spearman, was, well, he was a good man, but children weren't his strong suit. And there was nobody else I could really count on at the time. Without that support, Chicago could be a strange and overpowering place. So, even though Chicago was nearby, it was more distant in a strange kind of way. As I saw it, I did have family in Detroit, and family could make any place closer.

Still, there was a problem I would have to sort out. A major one.

For a number of years, I had lost contact with my dad. One morning in 1932, when I was eleven years old, my father got up, got dressed, gave me a nickel, and drove away. I didn't think anything about it at the time. I was used to my father going away on the weekend, returning on Monday morning, usually in time to make it to work at Corn Products. He would be disheveled when he got back, looking like he'd walked down ten miles of bad road. And that struck me because my father was so handsome and so meticulous about his appearance. Still, I was always happy to see him. But, Mama, oh, would she make a fuss. She was very unhappy about all this. To say the least. But what could she do? She couldn't whip him. And she couldn't make him obey her. So, instead, she did what a duty-bound wife did in Argo. Mama would pour coffee and get the tub ready for him to take a bath. We didn't have a tub in the bathroom, so he had to get in the tin tub behind the heater in the dining room, and I had to go to my room and lock the door until he finished. I couldn't hear everything that was going on. I didn't have a clue.

It was only later that I would find out where my father went on these weekends away from us.

There was some kind of dive over on Forty-third Street in Chicago, sort of a juke joint, where he would play the piano and sing. All night. All weekend. People in the bar would keep a whiskey glass filled on his piano. They paid him in drinks. He wouldn't eat. He would just sing and play the piano, and that whiskey kept him going.

This went on for a while and was causing so much stress in our home. Still, I was always happy to see my dad come home. One day, I thought I would do something to show him that I loved him, something that would make him feel he had a reason to stay at home with us. He had a couple of pairs of knob-toed shoes. One pair was black, the other burgundy. My daddy loved those shoes and used to have them shined so bright that they'd look like "a puppy dog's eyes under the bed." Well, I knew what I was going to do. I decided to shine my daddy's shoes. I pulled both pairs from under the bed and found the shoe polish. All he had was black, but I figured that would work. Polish was polish. And I polished those shoes and polished them, bright like "a puppy dog's eyes." I couldn't wait to show him what I had done. I couldn't wait for him to give me a great big hug to thank me for what I had done.

He came home, and I ran to get the shoes. I was so proud as I handed the two pairs over to him. "Daddy, look what I did for you."

He looked down at the shoes, the black pair with black polish, the burgundy pair with black polish, and his face fell. "Gottuh-mighty-knows!"

I never knew exactly what that meant, but I knew it wasn't good, especially when he pulled off his belt. Daddy gave me a whipping that day for polishing his new shoes. Black polish on burgundy shoes. It was the only whipping I ever got from my daddy. There would be no need to whip me again. That one stung for years.

So, there came a day when my daddy handed me a nickel and drove away. I thought it was just like all the other weekends, until Monday came and my daddy didn't. I was asking Mama, "Where's Daddy?" And Mama would always tell me she didn't know. Her best guess was that he must have come to town and gone on straight to work. But then the morning shift ended, and Daddy still didn't come home. When somebody you love just disappears like that, you find every way to avoid the obvious conclusion, the one that makes sense in your head but not in your heart. You find every way to avoid facing the reality that becomes more and more apparent. Finally, I had to accept the fact that Daddy had driven out of our lives forever. And he hadn't even said good-bye. I guess the nickel was supposed to make up for it. Compensate somehow. That's what he left me. A whole nickel. A buffalo nickel. I wish I had held on to it.

Mama moved on. She remarried, Tom Gaines, but I kept letting it all pull me back. I loved Daddy so much, and, since he could do no wrong, I convinced myself that I was somehow to blame. I'm sure it had something to do with what would happen to me within the next year.

I was twelve at the time, in sixth grade, and suddenly noticed that I was having a problem concentrating on my reading. There was a raw feeling in my chest. And with every heartbeat, I could feel the rawness intensify. I just started crying and asked the teacher if I could go home. After being excused, I walked to my house and knocked on the door. Nobody answered. Mama had to be there. Mama was *always* there. But nobody answered and the door was locked. There was no key under the mat, and the pain in my chest was getting worse, probably because I was getting worried about finding Mama. I *had* to find her. She would know what to do. My stepfather had a daughter, three blocks away. That seemed to be my best bet. But I had already walked from school. Every step seemed like it caused my heart to go faster and faster and, oh, I was in such pain. I knew if I found Mama, she could fix it. Mama could fix anything.

Finally, I did find Mama, two doors down from where I thought she might be. I told her how sick I felt. She must have thought it was something routine because she told me to go and lie down on the couch, and she just kept talking. After waiting there forever, I begged Mama to take me home. She did, but told me to carry one of the three bags she had to take with her. I wasn't able to carry it, but I made it. I wouldn't complain. I just didn't know how to make Mama understand. Every step seemed like it would be the last one. And when I finally got home, I just sat down on the steps. I didn't think I could make it upstairs. Mama urged me on and insisted that I have dinner. Well, I knew what eating dinner would mean. That would mean doing the dishes after dinner. That was not negotiable. That was my job. But I knew I would not be able to do those dishes. Even so, I got up and I struggled up the steps, put the groceries away, and sat down again. It seemed like my heart was going to jump out of my chest. It was just beating terribly fast. And when I ate, it got worse. I told Mama I wanted to go to bed. She told me to wash the dishes first so I wouldn't have to worry about getting up later to do them. I washed those dishes with my tears that night. I felt so sick, worse than I had ever felt in my life. Finally, I told Mama she had to call the doctor. That's when she began to take it all very seriously.

Our family doctor examined me and told Mama that I had an enlarged heart. It seems that I had been exposed to rheumatic fever. A classmate of mine had developed it and died. I had shaken it off without incident, but apparently it had left me with a leaky valve, which would affect me all my life. So, I had an enlarged heart, which sounded like it should have been a good thing to a young girl. But it wasn't a good thing. It wasn't good at all.

The doctor ordered me to bed immediately. No lights. I could not read. No company. The shades had to be drawn. There could be nothing to excite me or stimulate my heart. My mother had to hook up a bell, and we developed a code so that she would know what I needed by the number of times I'd ring for her.

I was confined to bed for more than three months, and at some point during that time I was able to begin reading books again, to catch up on my schoolwork, and finally to return to school, which made me very happy. It was a close call. Mama never really said any more about it, but it stayed with me and helped me to understand that anything out of the ordinary could be a big deal. A raw feeling in my chest wound up being something quite serious, a heart problem. My father had left my mother and me, and that had hurt me very deeply. The doctor had given us a logical explanation, said I suffered from an enlarged heart, a leaky valve, a byproduct of rheumatic fever. But I knew differently. I knew that what I really suffered was a broken heart.

By the time I started thinking about the Detroit move, Daddy and I had already reestablished some limited contact. I talked to my mother and told her what I had been thinking about doing and she encouraged me to call my father. As it turned out, I was happy that she and I talked. She let me know that what had happened between her and Daddy was between her and Daddy. It was not my problem. It was not my fault. And it should not be my burden to carry around for the rest of my life. She reminded me that Wiley Nash Carthan was my father and that I should treat him like my father. Her words meant a lot, but it was the message in between the words that was even more meaningful. For in that space was acceptance and absolution. And if Mama could take that position, then certainly I could. I was thankful for that talk, one that was long overdue. It was a transforming experience, and it would allow me to once again share with my father my life, and now my son.

I made the call. I made the arrangements. I made ready to leave Argo. This was a big deal for me. A very big deal. And I had mixed feelings about the move. On the one hand, I was apprehensive, but then I knew I would have family around to look out for me. On the other hand, I was eager to set out on a new trail, head for a new adventure. I was so eager for a new life that I convinced myself that Bo shared that excitement, never realizing what that kind of eagerness might cost a person.

Daddy had been all too happy to accommodate Bo and me. He would try to help me find a job and a permanent place to stay. Meanwhile, we were welcome to stay with him and his wife, A.D. While Daddy was eager to help, A.D. had a different attitude about the whole thing. They hadn't been married long. She'd once been married to a preacher who passed, and she was a "first lady." I mean she was as proud and snobby as she needed to be. Anyway, I settled into the small room Bo and I would call home for a short while. And that room was so tiny. It had a small bed and a vanity-style dresser with a little stool that went under the dresser. And that was it, that's all that you could get into that room. If I wanted to make the bed, I had to crawl over it and reach and tuck it in on the other side. But I knew this was a temporary arrangement, and I was grateful for the accommodations.

There also was perfume on that vanity, which, of course, I would never touch. But there was so much of it. The whole surface of the vanity was taken up by fragrance bottles, so I didn't have anywhere that I could put a bottle or a jar for myself. I wound up using a little box that I would put under the bed, and all of my toiletries were in that little box. The interesting thing was that one of the fragrances A.D. had was White Shoulders. Somebody had given me some White Shoulders also. One morning, I put on my White Shoulders. I had never smelled it before, but I liked it. She must have recognized it because, while I was out that day, she came and cleared all her fragrances out of the room. Every last bottle.

Soon I got a job at the Ft. Wayne Induction Center. I was working very long days, but the good thing was that I was able to pay Daddy and his wife something for the room. I also had to cook on Sundays, come hell or high water, since A.D. had cooked all week. I would be so tired sometimes and I really wanted to clean my room. I mean, that house was immaculate. It was stressfully clean, no dust anywhere, and I was beginning to feel the pressure. But I never had time to do everything. I was working seven days a week sometimes, twelve, thirteen, fourteen, sixteen hours a day. It was a pressure job and I was kind of in the lead of the group of clerk-typists. That meant that I had a lot of responsibility. I had to work and I had to make sure the other people were working as well.

One Sunday I baked chicken for dinner with dressing and gravy and vegetables and all that stuff. And when I got the kitchen all cleaned up, I went back and I pulled out the vanity and the little stool so that I could scrub the floor. As soon as I pulled that vanity and that stool into the living room, A.D. came out and sat on the couch. She crossed her legs and started swinging her foot. "Well, well, well," she said. "Who would have thought it? Miracles do happen." As if to say, "It's about time you did some work around here."

She sat there bobbing her leg, making comments like that for the next couple of hours as I cleaned my room and the living room. From then on, all of my spare time was filled with chores to give her a break. Since she was the stepmother, I guess I must have been Cinderella.

Daddy and I kind of bridged the gap during this time. He was so good to me. He was glad I was there and he was trying to be a buffer between his wife and me. He also was happy that he had a chance to bond with Bo. Dad worked for a drugstore and he'd bring a quart of ice cream home every night and share it with Bo. Vanilla, strawberry, banana, or, if Bo asked for chocolate, Dad would pack it himself to bring home. Even though A.D. wasn't necessarily looking after Bo during the day, apparently he was getting in her way. He had always been well cared for and was used to that. Not demanding, but not ignored. Bo was a kid. He might come in and want a sandwich. And she would have to fix it. He was nine at the time and he was used to so much more space. It was hard to contain all his energy. He would go out to play and come in sweating. He might plop down on the floor, get dirt on the rugs. The kind of things boys do. The kind of things he never had to worry about back in Argo, where he could do no wrong. Here, it seemed, he could do no right. A.D. just didn't want to be bothered with children. It wasn't long before Dad had to come in and give us the talk. I could see in his eyes that he didn't want to do it. He said Bo was going to have to go back to Argo. When I stalled long enough, Daddy came back for a second talk. He had found another place for Emmett and me to live. I admit that it was a little more crowded there for his wife with Bo and me. I imagine it was something of an intrusion for her. I just wish we hadn't been made to feel that way. Still, I am grateful for the time we were able to spend with my father. He and I had a chance to have many wonderful conversations, and that made me feel that I could call on him again if I ever needed him, the way a daughter might need to call upon her father. While we never talked about what had come between us, I appreciate all that we did have a chance to say, and, of course, the message in between all the words we spoke.

Thanks to my father's help, Emmett and I moved into another house with another family, the Harrises, an older woman, her husband, and another relative. They rolled out the welcome mat, and they gave me the front room for a bedroom, the best room in the house. And they fell in love with my boy. They just went crazy over Emmett. There were no children in the house and Mr. Harris practically adopted my son. He just took him away from me. On Saturdays they always had somewhere to go: the circus, the movies, a ball game, from early in the morning until late in the afternoon. Of course, that meant that Bo couldn't do much for me. Not that there was much that he could do anyway, but he was starting to channel his energy, make a contribution around the house. For one thing, he was learning how to cook and that was a big help to me when I'd come home from a long day, bone tired. But there would be more surprises from this industrious little boy.

One day I came home from work and both women were sitting in the kitchen. It was like they were watching a performance. In a way, they were. I wound up joining them.

Bo was in the pantry working. The first day, when we'd moved in, Bo and I noticed immediately that the Harrises had a roach problem. It was a big problem. Bigger still because Bo just couldn't take roaches. So he'd taken it upon himself to go out and buy some D-Con, the liquid kind you mop with a brush. Now he went into the pantry and, starting at the top shelf, he pulled everything down, washed the shelf, mopped it with the D-Con, and put newspaper on the shelf. That shelf belonged to Mrs. Harris, because she was tall. The next lady was about five-two or -three, so she got the middle shelf. Emmett cleared that one. As he cleared the shelves, he washed and organized everything that he took down. He put everything back on the middle shelf, and then he got to mine. I had the bottom shelf, because he was little and I'm barely five feet tall myself. He went through the same process there. When he finished with the pantry shelves, he got down on his knees and painted the kitchen and pantry baseboards with D-Con.

Then he wanted to clean the refrigerator. I don't know how he knew this, but he had told Mrs. Harris that roaches would live in the back of your refrigerator. She just let him go for it. He cleaned back there, and then he wanted to clean the inside of the refrigerator. I held my breath. He took everything out, but thank God he didn't put any D-Con in there. I exhaled. He just washed it and put everybody's stuff back in it. Finally, he scrubbed the kitchen floor. It was such a big kitchen. But he did the whole thing.

When he finished, I stepped in. "Now you have to take a bath," I told him.

He looked so pretty after he got cleaned up, with his cheeks all rosy from the scrubbing. I just wanted to keep looking at him, this very special child of mine. And I wanted to hold on to that moment, to cherish it.

As busy as I was with work and caring for Emmett, I did find a little time to socialize with my cousins Ruby and Juanita. Juanita was engaged and took me once to visit her fiancé, Alfonso. That's where I met Alfonso's next-door neighbor, Pink Bradley. Since Juanita was going over there all the time, and since I seemed to be hanging out with her whenever I could, I wound up running into Pink quite often. He seemed like the nicest person. A sturdy five-foot-ten, he towered over me. He was very dark and appeared to be a strong man, which is what I needed. And he had a good job. I knew that because Juanita had started whispering in my ear. He worked for Chrysler Corporation, a company that apparently was generous with overtime. I mean, those boys were working, making money like nobody's business. That's what she was telling me, or words to that effect. Meanwhile, Alfonso was whispering in Pink's ear. Basically, he told Pink not to let me get away.

We started seeing each other. He would take me out to dinner, to the movies, and we went to dances and house parties, where I'd walk around all night with the same scotch and soda. No refills for me. I hated the taste, but I liked the sophisticated look. We seemed to fit in together nicely. We went to Joe Louis's Farm once. Pink seemed impressed by it all, but I couldn't even pretend to be. It was smelly. And I didn't like trying to ride the horse. It was sort of an amusement park, a big attraction there in Detroit and I knew he wanted to show me a good time, but it must have been obvious to him that I wasn't having one. Now, they had good food, but because of the smell, I couldn't really enjoy it.

Pink also seemed to get along with Bo and he would do anything I asked him to do for Bo, running errands or taking him where he needed to go. But maybe I should have been paying closer attention. As I said, Pink did anything I asked him to do, but nothing he thought of on his own. He never took initiative with Emmett. Soon Emmett took himself out of the picture.

Despite the pleasant times I thought we were having, things were still unsettled and cramped. Bo just could not contain his restlessness, his boundless energy. He had not adjusted to his new life with me in Detroit. He was unhappy and, as a result, he wasn't doing so well in school. Bo was aching to go back to Argo and he kept on me about letting him go live with Ma-Moo in Chicago. He knew his grandmother's place would be the gateway to Argo. I couldn't stand the thought of being apart from him. This was the first time I had been able to be around him without the whole family taking over. And things seemed to be moving in the right direction with my new job and all. But I didn't think it would be fair to make him stay, especially as long as we still didn't have a place of our own. When I talked to my mother about it, she agreed to have him come. But we had to figure out the rest of it. Her husband, Henry Spearman, would not go for it. Now, he liked Bo. He would stand up and fight for Bo, but he just didn't want kids living in his house. So Mama worked it out with Aunt Marie and Uncle Kid—John Carthan—Daddy's youngest brother. Perfect for Emmett. He'd have familiar relatives who would be responsible for his care and getting him back and forth to school. Best of all, Bo could be with all his friends in Argo and he would live right next door to where we used to live. He was happy to be with Aunt Marie and Uncle Kid, and I was content that he would be all right there until I could find a place for the two of us in Detroit.

Meanwhile, Pink was not letting up. He seemed so interested. I think I was at a stage in my life where I was vulnerable. I felt that I needed somebody I could depend on. It wasn't easy trying to raise a boy and trying to work and trying to have a life. And I have to admit, I was so flattered by all the attention, and that somebody wanted me, that I was not over the hill. That meant a lot to me back then. Besides, I did want very much to be married. I thought I was supposed to have a husband, an anchor. We had only been seeing each other about three or four months when we married on May 5, 1951.

It had been an intense courtship and Pink had always been the nicest fellow. Until we got married.

Mama met Pink when she came to the wedding, and brought Emmett. She gave her blessing, and wasn't critical of Pink. I think she told me one day that "If you love him and he loves you, that's my only concern." Now looking back, I think Mama could see through the marriage from the very beginning. She knew that we were not equally yoked. Bo stayed for a short while, then wanted to go back to Argo. I still believed I could make a place in Detroit that he would enjoy, especially now with two incomes.

Pink and I settled into a lovely new place in a nice area. The woman we were staying with was someone my family knew from Mississippi. So she was a stranger to me, but I wasn't a stranger to her. The way her house was built, we could go up the stairs and into our living quarters and we had everything we needed, *except* the kitchen sink. We had to come downstairs to cook, but our new landlady was nice about the whole thing and I felt quite comfortable.

Then, almost as soon as we settled in, Pink got laid off. I thought he should be out looking for work, but all he did was wait for me to come home, where he'd greet me with "I'm hungry." I wondered why "I'm" didn't cook. I thought he should have had *my* food ready when I got home. We did have a—well, I guess you'd call it a *discussion* about that. He said he didn't want to cook in somebody else's kitchen. And all I ever heard was "I'm hungry."

He was insistent. "If I tell you to get up at three o'clock in the morning and make me some biscuits, you should get that batter going."

Really? I didn't even make biscuits. Didn't know the first thing about making a biscuit. I made yeast rolls. But that was beside the point. The point was that I did not have time for this foolishness and just kept brushing him off.

I had problems of my own. I was having a hard time getting back and forth to the Ft. Wayne Induction Center. I told my mother I needed a car. I had talked to her and she had sent me the down payment. I bought a gray

1947 Plymouth. That was the best car. They had reconditioned it and there was nothing wrong with it. It would go where you wanted it to go. Pink wasn't accustomed to a car, so this was like instant riches for him. He was so excited about owning an automobile he just went berserk. When I told him that I was going to use the car to get back and forth to work, he had the nerve to get upset. He wanted to know what he was supposed to do all day. I couldn't say. But I knew what I was going to do. I was going to drive that car. I was not about to wait on the corner for buses while he piled his friends into my car and drove out to that smelly Joe Louis's Farm. I knew that much.

In one of our quieter times, I agreed to prepare a meal for Pink, some of his friends, my two cousins, and some more people I had met. Ten people altogether. Our landlady said it was okay. She was nice enough to leave the house so that I would feel relaxed about using her kitchen to cook for my guests. She suggested that I use the pressure cooker, which I did for my green beans. She gave me some quick instructions, but I was in such a hurry that I was only half paying attention. How hard could this be, anyway? I found out.

I'd never been exposed to a pressure cooker before in my life. I was getting this big dinner ready all by myself and I was angry because Pink was not there helping me. He was out somewhere wasting time again and expecting me to have everything ready. To tell the truth, I don't even know why I was using a pressure cooker for green beans in the first place. But at one point, I took the little jiggler off the top of the pot. I think that's what my landlady told me to do. Then I tried to lift the top off. But it wouldn't move. That's because it was still sealed by the steam, and since I had not been paying attention, I didn't realize that until I started trying to pry the top off with a knife. I heard this hissing sound like a bomb about to explode. I didn't know if air was going in or coming out, or what, but just at that moment, I remembered that I wasn't supposed to lift the top until the steam went down. Too late. The top shot up and banged the ceiling so hard, it left a big dent. Beans flew all over the place, the ceiling, down my back, all over my arms. Oh, God, they were so hot. The place was a wreck, my dinner party was in ruins, and I was in pain. I just broke down in tears. And I felt so sick. I mean, I was so badly burned that even Pink realized he had to do something when he finally came in and looked at me.

He rushed me to the emergency room. I was in bad shape: bean burns on my back, on my arms, my face. I was "beaned" up. I have bean marks on my back to this day from that incident. At some point during the treatment, I told Pink that I didn't know if I'd be able to make dinner. He would not have that. We were there arguing in the emergency room about whether I should keep my obligation.

"Well, I don't promise somebody something and don't do it," he said.

I just looked at him. What could I say to that? I mean, who did he care about, me or all those people? The hospital came up with the answer: I had to stay overnight. I don't know whether Pink had that dinner or not. I don't know whether people came or not. Maybe my cousin Ruby finished everything. Maybe they were able to pull it all together. The roast beef was done. The cornbread was in the oven. And the green beans, well, they were on the ceiling.

I ran back to Chicago every chance I got. Usually once a month, by train. Emmett never called. He was having a great time, so much fun with Wheeler, Uncle Emmett, Uncle Kid, all his friends. He was happy as a bug in a rug. I was eager to see him, and he seemed happy to see me when we'd visit. But his gang was waiting. He would spend some time, but he was always kind of eager to get out with his buddies. For me, it was such a precious time whenever I'd see him because I hadn't seen him in a while. But it was becoming clear to me that he was drifting away. I had always thought he would rejoin me in Detroit once I got settled in, but it hadn't worked out that way. And it didn't seem to distress him that he was not with me. After all, he had his grandmother, his aunt and uncle, and his friends. All I had was a husband and a deep longing for my son. On top of that, I have to admit I was a little jealous. I talked it over with Mama, who urged me to take responsibility for Bo myself. With her telling me that, and when I saw Bo pulling away, I decided the quicker the better. Mama had sold the house in Argo, and used that money, along with some of my money, as a down payment on a two-flat building at 6427 South St. Lawrence in Chicago. Back in Detroit, I went in to my job and resigned right away. Didn't hesitate. Didn't waste any time. I had to pull up stakes.

I moved back to Chicago in November 1951. Pink came, too. Mama got him a job at Corn Products. We took the second-floor apartment in my mother's building. Oh, I was so glad to see my baby again. I wondered how in the world I had let him be away from me as long as I had. How had I avoided losing my mind? I couldn't hug him hard enough. I couldn't wait to make up for the lost time. Pink was another matter. Bo and Pink got along. They got along fine. But they weren't buddy-buddy. Pink never had time to talk like a father or participate in any of Emmett's games or take him out. That was my job, my reward.

Even though I thought Pink felt at home with Bo and me in Chicago, apparently, that is not the way he felt at all. He kept going to Detroit, his real home. Every weekend he would take *my* car and all *his* money and he would go to Detroit. To see his mother. During the week, he really didn't spend much time with Bo, or even with me, for that matter. He went to work, he came home—"I'm hungry"—he slept, and on the weekends he'd disappear. It was a reminder of what I didn't want to remember. After all, I had just rebuilt my relationship with Daddy, who used to disappear on weekends. So, finally, I decided that maybe I should just go with Pink. To see his mother. When we got to Detroit, Pink's best buddy was waiting for him. They went somewhere. I stayed with his mother. We became very good friends, his mother and I, since we spent so much time together that weekend. Oh, I don't know, that marriage was a miracle. Which is not to say it was a good thing. What I mean is that it just seemed to happen, just appeared out of thin air, and seemed to continue for reasons no human could possibly explain.

I kept letting Pink come in and out of our lives, but that next Christmas season marked the end of the year 1952 and the end of us, really. He came in and got dressed one night. He grabbed a bottle of Johnnie Walker Black Label I kept around for holiday guests. He put the bottle in his inside coat pocket. Then he picked up the telephone and made a call. I could tell he was making plans with somebody to go somewhere, a party or something. It sounded like they were making a date. On my phone? I flew into a rage, grabbed the phone out of his hand, and learned that the person on the other end was "Margaret."

I introduced myself to her. It was the polite thing to do. "I'm Pink's wife."

By the time Pink made it back to our place after he went wherever he was going with Margaret, he found the locks had been changed. And he found his clothes. They were on the front lawn. I had flung them out the second-floor window, every last stitch. As far as I was concerned, he had made his move and might as well just keep on moving. Helping him out was the least I could do.

I had gone to Detroit looking for a new world of possibilities, and wound up finding it just where I had left it. Back home. I have always been strengthened by my values and I place a great value on marriage and family. But now I know that it wasn't necessarily a good thing for me to be married at all costs, just to conform, just to live up to some local community standard, to do what people thought I should do, to be what people thought I should be. I talked with some friends after Pink and I separated.

"Why did you let me do that?" I asked. They told me he seemed like a nice guy and he had a good job. But life is about more than that, and maybe it took a trip to Detroit for me to see it. Living in Argo had been good for me as a child, but leaving Argo was good for me as an adult. It was time for me to burst out of my cocoon, to emerge and strike out on my own, discover the things about myself I might not have known had I stayed in that sheltered environment. I would always value marriage, but not at the expense of my values. Some things should never be sacrificed. Nothing is more important than being true to yourself. Besides, what good is a no-good man?

CHAPTER 7

For the first time, Emmett and I were on our own together. We were closer than we ever had been, looking out for each other, taking care of each other, having fun together. Unfortunately, we still were one emotional step away from ridding ourselves of Pink Bradley.

Not long after I had "evicted" Pink, he stopped by. Now, we were separated, and I can't say what made me do it, but I let him in. Emmett was sick, some flu bug. When Pink found out, he said he wanted to see Bo. I don't know why. He never really had been much of a father figure when he'd had the chance. As it turns out, before he even got to Bo's room, he started talking some stupid talk about what he ought to do to me. I just remember he had a very threatening tone. It's funny, and sad, how women nurture men, only to have them turn on us like that. Even so, I figured I could handle it. I mean, I had handled Pink before. So I told him I wanted him to go, and thought I could make him leave. But no sooner had I said this than I noticed Bo standing there in the doorway. He had gotten out of his sickbed in his long underwear and had come to see what the fuss was all about. That was my first concern, just seeing him standing there, knowing how sick he was. But that wasn't the part that startled me. It seems that Emmett had taken time to stop in the kitchen on his way in. At his side, he was holding a knife, a butcher's knife.

Well, everything just sort of froze right then and there. I didn't know what to do. Apparently, neither did Pink.

Finally, Bo broke the ice, very calmly, very smoothly, very slowly, taking his time to get it all out without faltering. "Pink, Mama wants you to go and I think you should go." And his next words sounded like he had been saving them up for a very long time. In fact, the whole time I had been married to Pink. "And if you put your hands on her," he said, "I *will* cut you."

Pink measured him up and down for a minute. Bo was only eleven, but he was the one holding the knife, a pretty long knife at that. I knew I had to step in, get Pink out. He was kind of stubborn about leaving, and struggled some. I knew he felt challenged, and might do something stupid just to make a point. I had no idea what that might be, and I was caught there in the middle, but it didn't matter. All I knew was that I had to break this up. In a way, I was helping Pink save face. Finally, I got him out the door and locked it. I think that's about when I started breathing again.

My God, that frightened me so. I didn't want my baby to wind up hurt by this man, or in jail over something that had started out as a stupid disagreement. Pink wasn't worth the trouble. Things were still unsettled for a moment after Pink left, and I went over to feel Bo's little heart. It was racing a mile a minute. He was very upset, even though he had seemed so calm. Really, I think I was even more worked up about it. I don't know what I would have done if something had happened to Bo. I hugged him, held him close, held him tight, but it was as much a comfort to me as it was to him. I knew at that precious moment that I would never let Pink into our home again.

Later, Emmett and I talked about it all and I told him that he should never, ever, get between me and somebody else when we were arguing. I warned him that he might get hurt, that just because he was a kid, there was no guarantee that someone wouldn't knock him down. Or worse. I told him that if he ever thought a situation was getting too serious, that he shouldn't try to step in to fight. He should call the police. That's what they're for, to take care of things like this. He insisted that he could defend himself and he could defend me, too. He said he could duck if he had to, and I had to fight back a little chuckle. Emmett was like that. He never seemed to be aware of his limitations. Maybe it was because he had struggled so hard to get beyond so many difficulties so early on. Time would tell whether that was a good thing. But, at that moment, all he could think of was that he wanted to protect me, and from then on, he wasn't ever going to let anybody hurt me. I told him I felt the same way about him, and that's pretty much where we left it. But I thought about it from time to time, that whole thing, how Emmett and I had put each other in danger, and how each of us could think of nothing else but how to protect the other.

For Bo and me, this was a turning point. We formed a new and stronger bond. It was almost like a partnership. He started taking on more responsibility. Like cooking. He loved pork chops and would go shopping some afternoons and bring home two packages, one for him, one for me. He'd cook them in separate skillets. Heaven forbid that *I* might get one of *his* pork chops. And then there was the corn, another one of his favorites. But, oh, my goodness, he would just empty the pepper can into that corn. At least that's the way it seemed to me. I mean, the corn was yellow *and* black. He thought it was delicious. And I would eat it. I *had* to eat it. I was his mother. And I was hungry. Eventually, I had to plead with him, "Honey, please. Let up on the pepper." So that was a typical dinner he made, pork chops and "pepper" corn, and he served it the same way each time. His pork chops went by his plate, mine went by my plate, and the skillet of corn sat in the middle of the table. That was our community dish.

Over time, Emmett got accustomed to doing most of the cooking. He even expanded the menu. I appreciated that. He figured out how to boil potatoes, even though he would add too much salt. And he'd cook green peas, pork and beans, hot dogs, and soup. It was simple, but I was grateful, as a mother would be. Besides, I was too tired to worry about cooking myself when I got home from my Social Security Administration job.

Emmett wanted to take on even more. With Pink out of the picture, it was clear that he wanted to be the man of the house. One evening I came home and I was bone tired. Emmett had been down the street playing and he ran to meet me at the steps of our building. He looked at me and he could tell that I was exhausted. That's when he set out the plan, telling me then that if I had to go to work every day to make the money, then the least he could do would be to take care of the house. And I just handed it over to him. At that moment, I was in no mood to debate. I felt as if a huge load had been lifted off me. By him. It was just beautiful the way he took on that responsibility without being asked. It did take him a while, though, to tell me he would do the washing.

Emmett was very industrious. He could take care of the house. It had started in Detroit, when he was just nine, and felt some great need to clean up the Harrises' place. He always wanted everything to be a certain way. But now he was reaching new levels. He would see that something needed to be done and he would do it. Just like that, no questions asked. If we needed to lay a rug, Bo would tell me, "We can do it." Which usually meant *he* could do it. Sweep, mop, wash walls, paint—"We can do it," he'd say. When I saw he could handle it all, I really loaded him up. He kept a good attitude about it, a sense of humor. Emmett could find humor in anything he was doing. He and I saw a cartoon once where two of the characters had swept some dirt into a little pile under a rug. Now, I thought it was cute, but Emmett just thought it was the funniest thing. And I could see the wheels turning in his mind and I knew him well enough to know where this might lead. I knew I needed to keep that boy in check. I warned him in a playful kind of way that if I ever found out that he was sweeping dirt under my rug, I was the one who would have the last laugh. I think he got the message. He didn't really say anything. He just looked at me, smiling, with that mischievous gleam in his eye.

Soon, he would show me skills I never knew he had. I had bought a piece of linoleum to install in the dining room. As it turns out, we got a big snowfall on the day I was supposed to get help laying the linoleum. Mama was even planning to come over to supervise the whole thing. Of course. But that snow just kept coming and I knew my help was not. Everyone was snowed in. So I sat there, wondering how I was going to get that linoleum laid, wondering *when* it was going to be laid, for that matter. The roll had already been sitting in my apartment for the last twenty-four hours, getting up to room temperature as we were supposed to let it do. Oh, I was so upset. That big roll would have to sit there in the way, blocking everything, for another week while we waited.

Emmett walked up. He looked over the situation for a minute. He started nodding his head. "We can do it ourselves. We can lay that linoleum," he said.

I didn't take him seriously. "Oh, honey," I said, "I can't let you mess up Mama's linoleum trying to learn how to lay it."

He insisted, "Mama, we can do it. I know we can." He wouldn't let it go. "Look," he said, "all we have to do is move all the stuff from the front to the back and when we get back there, we move all the stuff back to the front."

Oh, was *that* all we had to do? He kept working on me, telling me new pieces of his plan, and walking me through it all, and, I don't know, it was still snowing, and what else were we going to do that day? He talked me into it. But that doesn't mean I ever relaxed about it.

Right from the start, we were facing obstacles. We had cleared the first section of the room at the front. But there was a built-in china cabinet that couldn't be moved. We would have to go around that. It had a shape that kind of reflected the bay window along the dining room wall, as if it had been a puzzle piece pulled from that section of the wall. It came out from the corner at an angle, then it ran straight across, then back at an angle to the wall on the other side. That was going to be one tough corner. To make matters worse, right next to the cabinet was a radiator. How on earth were we going to get that linoleum under there?

"Don't worry about it." Bo smiled. He looked so confident, like he had already figured out how to do it. "Just let me handle that," he said. "I'll take care of it."

Well, you can imagine how nervous I was. The piece had to be cut just right to work around the china cabinet and all the way to the wall under the radiator. If it was off even a fraction of an inch, I knew that would be the only fraction of an inch I would ever see in that room from then on: every family dinner, every time I walked to the hutch, every day for the rest of my life. Okay. All right. He said we could do it, and if ever I was going to trust my son, I guess this would have to be the time. Besides, we already had moved everything from one end to the other.

Bo measured out that section of space around the cabinet and the radiator. Then he measured the entire piece of linoleum and decided how far we would have to cut into it. Next, he took off all the molding around the room—*all* of it.

I was in shock. "What are you doing with the molding? You're tearing up my floor." Waiting another week was starting to look better and better to me.

He simply made a calming sign with his hands and explained that he would put it all back once the job was done. He got a tape measure, drew lines, then somehow drew circles for the feet of the radiator and the pipe from the floor. He made all his marks precisely, and took a lot of care to set the linoleum out perfectly, at the proper distance between the radiator and the wall. Then my heart stopped. He was about to cut. His back was to me, but he must have felt me eyeing him like a hawk on a chicken, ready to swoop. Didn't seem to faze him. He was so calm.

I was so worked up that his voice startled me when I finally heard it. "Don't bite your fingernails off," he said, teasing me, disarming me. But just for a heartbeat.

He started cutting out the space for the china cabinet, then he moved to the radiator legs, then along the wall, around the bay window, and the rest. My mouth was open, but I wasn't speaking a word. We took a cutting break to move everything back to the other end. And by the time he got to the front wall, it was all so easy. The door? No problem. He worked it all out to perfection.

He stood up, and looked around the room at our new flooring, then over at me with that little sparkle in his eyes. "How do you like it?"

My eyes must have been as wide around as dinner plates and I know I was beaming. "Perfect," I said. "Just wait until Mama sees this. She is not going to believe it." He knew that was the highest compliment I could pay. After all, we both thrived on Mama's approval, and we knew that she did not expect us to do any of the work unless she was available to engineer, to supervise the job.

Well, when Mama came and saw what her children had done, she had nothing but admiration and accolades. For Bo. We had a great time, celebrating the moment, walking back and forth across our new floor, singing Emmett's praises. When Mama got through talking to him and telling him what a smart guy he was, and how talented he was, and all that, he puffed up like a frog. There was nothing more I could say.

Except to share my next brilliant idea. "So, Mama, tell us, how do you go about tiling a floor?"

After we all finished laughing, Mama actually did explain it. And Bo and I wound up laying tile in every available space—the kitchen, the bathroom, even a section of the hallway. Emmett did a beautiful job on that project, too. And I came to expect that of him. I knew there was nothing I couldn't ask him to do for me. There was no chore too difficult, no problem he couldn't solve. "We can do it" was all he would say. And I was confident that everything I asked of him would be done with the same kind of loving care he used on the linoleum project, when he made my heart skip a beat.

Emmett was meticulous. Always. For one thing, that boy loved his clothes and he wanted to make sure they looked good. In between taking care of more and more things for me, he made sure he took care of his own things. I had taught him how to crease his brown dungarees on the ironing board. But then he showed me the shortcut he had developed. He'd take great care to fold his pants, creasing them with his fingertips, then placing them on the radiator, where they would wind up getting steamed. He would hang shirts on the line, press them with his hands, and when they dried, they would look like they had been professionally laundered.

He never shied away from hard work, even though he teased his cousins about it. Thelma Wright came to live with us again in 1953, joined by her sister Loretha. Thelma was attending Northern Illinois University and Loretha was working. As he was helping them move into the room the girls would share, he made a wink of a remark. "You better act like you're lazy. Otherwise, Mama will work you to death." They all laughed. But I was serious about housework. So much so that eventually, the girls and I had a falling-out about it. I don't know if anybody can recall exactly what it was all about. What I do remember is that one thing led to another, and Thelma and Loretha wound up leaving to stay with other relatives.

Well, that really bugged Emmett. He could never stand that kind of tension. Not anywhere, really, but especially not in the family. And these girls were close to him. After all, he had grown up thinking of Thelma, I mean,

Thel-moo, as his big sister. It hurt him. He could not accept the fact that there was some sort of problem between us.

He was not going to let it go and he kept working on me. "Look at yourself," he'd say to me. "Don't you feel silly about this?"

Oh, he just kept on with it, pushing me to make up with the girls. Finally, I gave in. It was a Saturday night, and Bo and I just showed up where the girls were staying. We made up and everybody was so happy about it. Especially Bo. We wound up staying there very late that night and had so much fun, laughing and talking and playing music, like nothing had ever happened. Mama knew about the tension, but had no idea that Bo had talked me into making up with Thelma and Loretha. She was so relieved, and, of course, she gave Bo all the credit. I agreed, figuring he should have won a Nobel Peace Prize for those negotiations.

Emmett was always so confident about his ability to talk his way through things that you could forget that he still had a problem talking. After he had recovered from polio as quickly as he had done, at such an early age, the doctors figured he could lick this problem, too. And we did everything we were supposed to do. The speech therapy classes helped some, but the stutter was still apparent at eleven and then at twelve, in normal conversation, but especially when he got excited. If he was going to outgrow it, then when was that supposed to happen? He was growing pretty big, pretty fast.

Sometimes I would watch him through the window as he played with friends and talked. He didn't seem to have a problem communicating with them or relating to them. I saw that he held everybody's attention. Even when he was in a new group of children in Chicago, rather than the more familiar group of friends from Argo, people seemed to accept him. There was always a group of boys congregating on my porch talking to Bo.

I knew how cruel kids could be. And early on I had worried about that. But then I saw that I didn't have anything to worry about when it came to my son's acceptance. Everybody liked Bobo, and they never poked fun at him. I don't know of a single fight he ever had. Over anything. He had such good friends, who would just wait patiently until he could get himself together and go and say what he wanted to say. Of course, there were times when he might get impatient with himself, and hold on to a friend's arm, pulling or pushing when he was really getting stuck.

Even though the stutter obviously wasn't holding him back, I agonized over it so much. Still, I hadn't come up with a solution and figured it was just something he and all the rest of us would have to live with. Instead of Bo growing out of it, it was growing on all of us.

Then it happened, quite by accident. One day, I walked in and heard the voice of a television salesman. At least I thought that's what I was hearing. But it was only the familiar tag line of a television salesman. "Lynn Burton, for certain." The speaker was Emmett and he wasn't stuttering.

"Bo," I said, "what are you doing?"

Then the stutter came back as he tried to explain. I had startled him. But I had already seen him in action. He had been racing through that monologue like mad, imitating the commercial. Oh, it was a silly little thing, that commercial, but Emmett seemed to be drawn to silly little things. Twelve-year-old boys can be like that. Still, I was taking this seriously. I realized something after I watched Bo go through the routine without missing a beat, keeping pace with that crazy TV car salesman. When he knew ahead of time where he was going, when he knew what he was going to say, Bo could get through it. That was such a revelation to me. He could improve his speech by practicing, by memorizing and reciting. That would be my solution.

So that's when the pileup began. Poor kid, I had him memorizing everything from the preamble to the Constitution to Lincoln's Gettysburg Address to poetry, everything I knew he was going to encounter. That way, when he'd come across all of this material again, he would already be ahead of everybody else. I felt so sorry for him, because my list of stuff never ran out. I mean, by the time he had half learned one, I was on him with another one. And I had him doing all the gestures, all the expressions. He was good, too.

I was working him so hard, he had to take a time-out. "Mama, you're gonna have to let me come up and breathe," he would say.

He was very pleased with himself, though. And it seemed to help. It proved to him that, once he was certain of something, he could go ahead and execute. But there was something else. I noticed that in pacing himself for the recitation, he would have to control his breathing. That's when it occurred to me to give him a bit of advice.

"If you find yourself stuck on a word," I said, "take in a breath, whistle, and then go ahead and speak." He tried it, and it seemed that when he whistled, it was almost a hypnotic cue that would calm him, steady his breathing, and allow him to finish saying what he had started to say. I guess I was ready to offer anything that might help him through this difficulty.

I only wish he had been as open to my help with his schoolwork. Emmett was always a bright child and he seemed to enjoy school, but mostly for the social aspects of it. He was a student at McCosh Elementary in Chicago. He liked science, but he needed help with math sometimes.

And, even though he was very expressive, he needed help with his writing. Especially the spelling and grammar. Whenever he saw that I felt something was important, then he would take it seriously, especially if avoiding it meant he was not going outside. I let him know that until that homework was done, he was not leaving the house. Still, he would only ask a question when he absolutely had to ask, when he was really stuck on something and couldn't move forward. Even then he didn't want to stick around very long. He caught on pretty fast and would stop me cold: "Okay, okay. I got it. I got it." And then he would just walk off and leave me. He didn't want me to tell him too much, because he wanted to figure out as much as he could on his own. I would never see him work the problem through. But, once he said "Okay, I got it," I knew that's what he meant. And I knew he wanted to do it himself, by himself. He was very independent. Sometimes he was impatient with all the questions I would ask about his homework, what he was doing, how he was doing. "I could be through while you're asking me all these questions," he would say playfully.

I had always taken help myself. As a youngster, I would come home from school ready to interrupt my mother or whoever was there to listen. I would show them everything we did in school that day. Mama would talk to me until she got the job done, and I would sit there still listening. But I came to understand my son and the fact that we wanted different things. I wanted to be there watching every letter he put down, checking every number he subtracted, helping him improve. I wanted to help him solve his problems. He wanted to be left alone to work it out on his own. It was difficult for me to accept, but I did accept it. There would be times when I'd feel that I was not as involved as I should have been with Emmett's schoolwork. But I could see that he was able to handle it. And I thought I was giving him what he needed most. Space. I was giving him the freedom to find his own way. And I had great confidence in his ability to make a way for himself.

Even so, I had to lay down the law from time to time. One day, Bo told me he wasn't feeling well and asked if he could stay home from school. Of course, I told him, if he wasn't feeling well, he should stay home and get some rest. When I got home that evening, I found he had been up, messing around in the kitchen and had made a cake, a Lazy Dazy pound cake. He was so proud, and he was waiting for my reaction.

"Oh, that's great," I said, as I watched his eyes light up. "Guess that means you're well enough to go to school tomorrow."

It was moments like those that probably confused him a little. Way back at Mama's house in Argo, we had established our unique relationship. It sometimes felt more like we were brother and sister. Except, of course, that we got along better than a lot of brothers and sisters, and we were very open with each other. Emmett loved music. I was so excited that he could dance. He tried to teach me the Bunny Hop once. I loved to dance, but had never quite got the swing of it. After all, I'd never danced at home. I was on my knees praying. Finally, Emmett looked at my pitiful coordination and just shook his head. "Give it up," he said. "You will never dance." Then he thought for a moment. "And you'll never ride a bike, either."

We talked a lot and sometimes we even argued. I thought it was important for him to have the freedom to express himself in all situations. So, what better place to start than with me? Oh, he would certainly let me know when there was something he didn't like. I have to admit that he could be very persuasive, as he had been in the situation with Thelma and Loretha. It was hard not to consider the points he made, and even follow his advice. So, I guess it might have caught him off guard at those times when I acted more like his mother than his sister. He wasn't always sure just how to react. Once he got so frustrated with me that he threatened to run away. "Okay," I said, "well then, as soon as you get outside, you go left. Then at the corner, you turn right, and about seven blocks down . . ." After I gave him those directions to the train station, it never came up again. Other times, though, he would tell on me. He'd just pick up the phone and call his grandmother. Sometimes, I'd jump on the phone to tell on him, you know, the way brothers and sisters might do with each other. Whatever it was, she could settle it down. Unlike me, Mama never got confused about what role she played. She was always "Mama."

Things seemed to work out with us, one way or another. I learned from Emmett, a boy setting out to become a man. I learned from this well-nurtured, self-assured son of mine that every problem has a solution. He and I might have had different ways of handling things, but our goal was the same. I was proud of his independence, I was proud of his positive attitude and the way he took on his most difficult challenges with confidence. And I settled into the assurance of a parent who knew her son would look at life the same way he had once looked at that linoleum on a dining room floor: "We can do it."

CHAPTER 8

Something happens when a child is afflicted so early, as Emmett had been with the complications at birth, and then later with polio. Something happens to a child like that under circumstances like those. He develops a new sense. It is a sense of urgency about life. Emmett had such a sense. No doubt about that. It was clear in the way he lived his life. He might not have known why, and we never talked about it. Maybe it was planted in him somehow. In that deep-down place where you know things about life even when you don't know why you know what you know. Maybe it was that he could feel my anxiety, the way I always felt about him, how protective I was. How protective we all were. How fragile we all knew a young life could be after seeing how fragile his had been. Maybe he could feel all that. But, whatever the reason, Emmett definitely had such a sense of urgency. He was two hundred percent boy. It was as if he was trying to squeeze twice as much life into only a fraction of the time. It was as if he somehow felt he had to live that way.

Emmett was always into something. Among so many other things, he still was committed to helping me, and Lord knows I needed help back then. I can only imagine where he got all that energy. I was worn out at the end of my day, but he seemed only to be getting started on his.

I was facing new challenges. I had changed jobs. At the Social Security Administration, I couldn't get a promotion. When I had come to the agency a couple of years earlier, it was integrated, all right, but no blacks were being promoted. So, you could get in, but you couldn't move up. On top of that, I was selected for a very special assignment. I was the one who trained new managers. We were recording everything on cylinders, using something called an "Ediphone." I have to tell you I was dangerous on that

Ediphone. I mean, that thing was talking to me and my foot was dancing all over that control, starting, stopping, and starting the tape all over again. I had a nice rhythm going and never missed a beat. Not only was I fast, but I was efficient. They wound up calling me Mamie "Never-Make-a-Mistake" Bradley. That might have been flattering, but it wasn't necessarily a good thing. The people from the Determination Section would send all their cylinders to me, flagged with my name. That meant that I was working when other people were sitting down doing nothing. Now, that would have been bad enough. But every time somebody new came in, somebody the top people wanted to make into a top person, a manager or a boss, well, every time that happened, I had to train him. Yet I couldn't get a promotion. Well, then, what about a raise? Wages were frozen, I was told. That was it. I couldn't get a promotion, couldn't get a raise, but there was one thing I could get, something I could take for myself: a half-day leave.

Don't tell me wages are frozen, and then expect me to just sit around, hibernating, waiting for a spring thaw. I came back at the end of my half-day leave and I handed in my resignation. I was moving up, two or three floors up, actually, to the offices of the U.S. Air Force, where I'd found a new opportunity, or created one, much the same way Emmett might have done with the iceman back in Argo. When word spread about what I had done, a number of the black girls at the Social Security Administration wound up following me out of that agency and into others where they could get better rewards for their work.

Anyway, as soon as I started working for the U.S. Air Force, I was put through the paces. I mean, those people really tested my skills. And to their credit, they rewarded me when they found out I could handle the job. Not long after I started, they gave me an important assignment: I would work with the Secret and Confidential files. Oh, I was so pleased with the respect they were showing me there. And I knew that it was all because of the quality of my work. It didn't seem to matter at all that I was black. As a matter of fact, I was the only black girl in this office.

Being in charge of those sensitive documents was a lot of responsibility, and I took it seriously. We weren't supposed to talk about the things we'd see in those files and I never did. Of course, I don't even know what I would have said about it all if I had talked about it. So much of it was coded, anyway.

With all that responsibility, though, there were many nights when I would still be at work while all the other people were headed off to their own private lives. Sometimes the only other people left behind were the officer in charge and the head of my department. Just the three of us in that big building. And my days often went late into the night.

That meant I had to lean on Bo even more. Most of the time, when I got home, I was exhausted. And he just fell right in with the routine. He saw things that needed to be done and he took them on. On his own. There were so many things he did that really impressed me. Not only would he make dinner for us, but he would make sure I was not disturbed when I'd come home tired after work. He was so good about taking messages from people and just letting them know that I'd have to call them back later. He really started looking out for me like that, taking care of me. He was quick to assume responsibility and, of course, I was quick to let him.

It had been so different for me coming up. My mother didn't let me take on any real responsibilities as a child, except a few routine chores like washing the dishes as I grew older. I guess it was because, early on, I tried to do things and would always wind up right there in the way. I remember when I was a toddler, not long before we left Mississippi, and I was walking all over the place, always underfoot. Mama went out to milk the cow. I followed. Of course I wanted to help. But she pushed me back in the front door and closed it. Even then, she must have known what my help would have cost her. Only a moment later, as she made her way to the cow, she saw it lunge in the opposite direction. She'd never really liked that cow, mostly because it would act out just like that. But this time it was worse. She saw something that horrified her. It was me. I had made it out the back door and was headed for the cow. Actually, the cow was headed for me—headfirst. Mama was holding the bucket she was going to use to milk the cow, but she wound up putting it to much better use. She beat that cow over the head. Must have been doing a pretty good job, too, because the cow finally moved away. Just in time. Not that I was in danger. No, once Mama stepped in, I was okay. Whenever Mama was around, I was okay. But that poor cow was about to get killed. I kind of moved into the background after that and Mama handled most things around the house. She was quite comfortable with the arrangement. Handling things was what Mama did best.

That wasn't the case with Bo and me. Now, I'm not saying that he was perfect. I admit there were those times when Emmett would get—well, he would get a little distracted. He might be in a hurry to get outside and shove some things under the couch or under a bed, hoping he could get back in time to put it all away before I'd find out. Like any young person, he loved to play and sometimes he would forget what he was supposed to remember.

There was one night when I asked him to go to the store for a loaf of bread. Now, he made it to the store just fine. It was the trip back that seemed to create a problem for him. He ran into some friends playing a little game of baseball. There was no way Emmett could pass up a baseball game, even when he was supposed to be doing something for me. So, I guess he just put down the bread and got in that game. And that's exactly where I found Bo. Bo and that loaf of bread. Of course, by that time, the bread kind of looked like the kids had been using it for second base. I was not happy. And I let him know that I was not happy. I let him know that all the way home. Oh, I fussed so. He just took it, never said a word as we walked. But when we got to the house he said his piece, trying to turn it all around on me.

He was so excited that he began stuttering. But he did manage to get the words out. "How do you feel making a show of yourself out there on the street?"

He was not trying to fast-talk me. No, at that moment, with his excitement and the stutter and all, well, fast talk was not going to happen. And I can't say my son was a smooth talker, necessarily. But that boy was a talker. Like the time he came home late one Sunday night after one of his weekends in Argo. Before I could even get started on him, he began talking about the bus ride home and how he felt women were taking advantage of him, like they could tell he was the kind of boy who would give up his seat, and how they would stand near him until he did, and that it made no difference whether they were black or white, because he would give up his seat to whichever one had the most packages or a child or something like that and . . . I tell you. He just went on and on and I was drawn into it, because he could make conversation like that into something so interesting. By the time we finished talking about all those things, I forgot that I was annoyed with him. And I guess that was the point of it all.

Emmett was confident, and felt he could talk his way out of anything. Even the thing with the baseball game and the loaf of bread. What he had to say at that moment on that night made me stop and think. Emmett was two hundred percent boy. He was always trying to squeeze in twice as much life, twice as much challenge. Now, going to the store and coming straight home with my bread was not quite enough of a challenge for him. But going to the store, then getting into a baseball game and making it home before I ever noticed, *that* was a challenge.

When I think about that kid and the responsibilities that I let him take on, I have to admit that it wasn't hard to overlook a lapse every now and then. As a matter of fact, I appreciated each part of his personality.

"I really like you," I told him once. I couldn't help myself. As I looked at him and saw the way he approached every aspect of his life, I just had to say that. No holding back.

He gave me a puzzled look. "Shouldn't you have said 'I *love* you'?"

I laughed. "Now look," I said, "I can't help but love you. I'm going to love you whether you're good, bad, or indifferent. But to *like* you, now that really *is* something special."

He nodded with a slight smile, as if to show that he accepted my explanation and, at the same time, recognized that this was just how he might try to talk his way out of a corner. But it wasn't fast talk. I meant it. I really did. I mean it still.

I needed to get my nails done. We were having a club meeting, Les Petite Femmes. They were friends of mine, mostly from Argo. That's where it had started, really, about ten years earlier, in 1943. There were around sixteen of us altogether, including my dearest friend, Ollie Colbert. Les Petite Femmes, "the little women," even though some of us were outgrowing that name by this time. We would rotate the club meetings once a month and have dinner at different homes, talking and playing cards well into the night. We would host baby showers for our members and we even held a huge annual ball, a spectacular event that would attract people from all over town. One of our regular meetings was coming up and I just had to get my nails done. I was a Chicago girl now, had a good job, and I knew I should look the part. Chicago girls had their hair done, their nails, too. So, I went out looking for someone to do my nails. To make me look like a Chicago girl.

Somebody told me about a neighborhood shop. It was up at Sixty-fifth and Cottage Grove, right on the corner. When I went in, though, I found out that the manicurist was off for the day. People in that shop pointed out another one across the street, Polk's Barbershop, where Polk's wife was a manicurist. When I walked in, Mr. and Mrs. Polk were there, and had only one customer. Mr. Polk was taking care of him. So I was able to get a walk-in slot just like that. There was another barber sitting high up on the shoe-shine bench, reading a newspaper. His legs were crossed, one foot on the footrest, killing time, I guess, waiting for a walk-in of his own. He kind of looked over the paper at me as I took off my jacket and took a seat with my back to him. I really wasn't paying too much attention to him, because, you see, I was just happy that I was going to get my nails done.

Mrs. Polk and I were having a good old time chatting away as she worked on me. I liked the way she was shaping up my nails, and polishing them, giving me all that attention. We talked about my job and where I lived—right around the corner—and all sorts of things, general chitchat, the way ladies do when they're getting done.

Then, at one point, she slowed down a little and leaned in. "You know that man over there . . . no, don't look," she said, "that other barber over there. You know, he's only pretending to read that paper."

Really? Now why would somebody do something like that?

"He's really looking around that paper," she went on to say. "He's watching you."

O-h-h, my goodness, that just gave me the creepy crawlies all up and down my back. That didn't feel good at all. Not one bit. But I tried to ignore it, just put it out of my head, and I chatted some more with Mrs. Polk until she finished. When she did, I thought my nails looked beautiful. But I needed her to help me with my jacket. I was not about to mess up all that work, especially after working so hard to find somebody to do the work.

Even before I could ask her to help, she spoke up. "Um, Mr. Mobley, can you help this lady with her jacket?"

Oh, my, that boy nearly fell off that bench climbing down. Looking back on it, I'm sure that Mrs. Polk was just messing with him. Messing with me, too, for that matter. But he made his way over to help me out and, as he did, I guess he figured this was going to be his big opportunity.

"I like what I see," he said.

Well, I'm sure I blushed a little. I thought he was being fresh, and I wasn't sure exactly how to respond. But he kept going. He told me his name. Gene. Gennie Mobley. Then he wanted to know my name, my address, my telephone number, and . . . Wait a minute, now. I was not impressed with all this. He wasn't my type. For one thing, I just did not like that conk.

Finally, I had to make it clear to him. "Well, maybe there'll be a time for all that," I said, "but this is not that time."

I didn't see why we should be getting all that familiar. I didn't know anything about this man, except that he was a barber waiting for a customer and giving me the creepy crawlies watching me. I wasn't sure, right then and there, that I wanted to know any more about him than that. But I loved the way the woman in that shop had done my nails. So I went back another time to have her do them again.

Gene was there again. Looking at me again. "You need a line," he said, after I was finished. "Why don't you let me edge your hair?"

I wasn't wearing my hair short then. But a new look kind of got my attention. I touched at my hair. "How much will that cost?" I asked.

"Nothing," he said.

Well, what can I say? The price was right. I wasn't going to walk away from a deal like that. And he wound up doing a good job. He really did. I was impressed, but I knew what he was up to and I decided that was as far as I was going to let this relationship go. I mean, he could cut my hair, but I wasn't ready to let him arch my eyebrows.

Then, at home, I started thinking. Bo needed a haircut. On his regular trips out to Argo, he had been letting one of the neighbors there cut his hair. The man had sort of a barbershop business on his front porch. It seemed like a lot of trouble to go way out there. So I told Emmett that I had met a young man who was a barber, and I thought we should try him out. I guess I was also figuring that Gene might even give me a break on the price. Well, Emmett tried him out and he was just crazy about his haircut. After that first time in Gene's chair, he never went out to Argo for a haircut again.

I kept going back to Polk's, too. On one trip, Gene was about to go out to eat. He asked if I wanted to go with him. I was very hungry that day. So, I accepted the invitation and he waited until Mrs. Polk had finished with me. Gene and I walked about a block and a half to a very special place. I ordered steak. Gene ordered the same thing. When the food came I began to eat. And I ate *everything* on my plate. Like I said, I was very hungry. But Gene hadn't even started. He was sitting there, watching me eat.

I looked over for a moment, and I thought about it. "Are you going to eat your steak?"

He shook his head. "No."

I don't know if he was nervous or what. Maybe he saw this as a date. But I saw it as dinner. So, I just pulled his plate over and ate both steaks. His and mine. He had come with a hankering, I had come with a hunger. And, obviously, I was *not* trying to make an impression. Somewhere with all this eating going on, I finally let my guard down and we were able to talk. I talked about my job, what little bit I could talk about, and the challenges of being a single mother. Gene talked about himself and I found out we had more in common than I had ever imagined. Our paths had been crossing for years, even though we had never met. He was from Mississippi, not far from where I was born. He had been in and out of Argo. He was separated and so was I. And now there was this new connection. The barbershop, nail-salon connection.

Gene worked at the Ford Motor Company. He unloaded heavy parts, half-sides of cars, and got them going through the factory. He would get off from his Ford job about three o'clock in the afternoon, go home, shower, and put on his starched white barber coat and pants, then head to Polk's shop. My goodness, that coat and those pants were crisp and creased. And he looked very nice in that outfit. I had to admit that. Well, I found myself taking a closer look. He was tall, dark as molasses, and had a kind of sweetness about him. Rough around the edges, but smooth at his core, his heart. Not pretty, but fine in other ways that counted. And he had a walk. Oh, he had a walk. It was a confident way he moved that showed you he was in charge. Whatever the situation was.

After we finished our meal, or, I should say, after *I* finished our meal, we walked together back to the barbershop where I had parked my car. On the way we passed some guy Gene must have known and, all of a sudden, Gene put his arm around my shoulder. I guess he was trying to make some point or other, but I was not a point to be made. I took his hand and I flung it off my shoulder.

"You don't know me *that* well," I said, not caring whether the other guy heard me or not. We might have had some things in common, and he was nice and all, but I still didn't think Gene was my type.

Gene did not give up easily. Not at all. I would come home sometimes and find a note from Bo on the dresser, or get a message from Aunt Magnolia or Uncle Mack, who lived downstairs from us in our two-flat building. Bo would have gone to the barbershop and he wanted me to know that he would be home after Gene cut his hair. So that was becoming a routine, and I figured Gene was encouraging it. Then I came home one day to find something else. Hats. Men's hats. On my bed.

"What's this?" I asked Bo.

"Oh," he said, "those are GeGe's hats."

GeGe? "Well," I asked, "what are they doing here?"

He explained that he was running errands, like picking up hats and clothes from the cleaners for "GeGe," and getting tips.

Now, this was right up Bo's alley. He had never lost that drive to get out and hustle, hadn't let up much at all from the time he was six years old and hawking ice and coal back in Argo. More recently, he had been going up to the Jewel food store and helping people carry grocery bags to their cars in the parking lot, or around the corner to their homes. It seemed like everybody lived on the second floor, too. But he would carry those bags all the way up to wherever they lived, and then would even help them put the groceries away before running back to the store for more business. This had all started when he was about ten and had gone up to the store for a couple on our block. Of course, he took forever to get back. And when he finally did, he told us he had stopped to help some people at the store, just stopped to help them carry their groceries to their car, and they had given him a few nickels. So he decided to keep helping people at the store and wound up coming home with a pocket full of change.

It wasn't long before he asked me to buy him a Radio Flyer. His little business was growing. He told me people had gotten accustomed to seeing him and they kind of gravitated to him. They knew they could trust him to get their stuff home and even put it away for them. But his two little arms weren't quite enough. He figured he could make more trips and carry more bags and get more nickels if he had that wagon. Now, a Radio Flyer wasn't cheap, but he promised that he would pay me back. And I guess he did, one way or another. That's how it always was with Bo. If he wanted something, he would go out and work. And he would come back to me with his money in his little hand.

Now, with Gene, Bo was getting more than a few nickels. Gene was giving him a few dollars to run errands for him. My goodness, that was a heap of money back then. First it was the hats from the cleaner's. Then other cleaning, and after that, he wanted Bo to take his shoes out to be shined. Now, they had a shoe-shine stand right there in the barbershop, but he would let Bo take his shoes somewhere to get them shined.

Obviously, Gene saw that whenever Bo was happy, Mamie was happy. So he set out to make Bo happy. And that's when Gene and I started seeing each other. Even so, I do believe Bo was seeing more of him: whenever he needed a haircut, or whenever he needed to earn some money. Gene would take him to baseball games, too, sometimes with his closest brother, Wealthy Mobley. And, of course, there was the shopping.

I came home one night and found a note on my dresser. It was from Bo. "GeGe and I have gone to Sixty-third and Halsted."

By the time they came home, they were loaded down. Bo had a baseball bat, a ball, a glove, some shoes with cleats on the bottom. He was all dressed up.

I was a little upset as I turned to Gene. "Why did you spend that kind of money on him?"

Gene smiled. "He's a good boy," he said. "He deserves it."

They just seemed to really hit it off, building a very strong relationship. And, as a result, my relationship with Gene grew stronger, too. We hadn't been seeing each other long, but Gene was already becoming a father figure to Bo, as if it was supposed to be that way. Funny how at first I didn't think Gene was my type. I guess I just hadn't given him much of a chance to show me what my type really was. Some things happen the way they happen because that's just the way they're supposed to be. I didn't go into Polk's Barbershop that day looking for a man. I went in looking to get my nails done. To look like a Chicago girl. To think I had stopped looking for that perfect man in my life and almost missed him when he finally looked me in the eye. In the end, Gene showed me something very important, something it can take so many years to discover on your own: Sometimes the best way to find what you're looking for is simply to stop looking.

CHAPTER 9

I f you look at Emmett's century, you see that the men who lived important lives, significant lives, were truly gifted. They were blessed with good mothers, mothers who gave them exactly what they needed—unconditional love. That, and the freedom to express themselves, to fulfill their promise. In that way, these mothers helped their sons come to believe that there was nothing they couldn't achieve. This was a gift I gave my own son—a boy of great potential.

Early on, I had a feeling about what Emmett might make of his life. I wanted him to go to college, a dream my mother always had for me. I had a great-uncle, Wade Gordon. Mama had talked once of having me stay with him because he was a minister and a professor at Fisk. When Emmett was still an infant, I wanted this for him, to go to Nashville, to attend Fisk University, maybe even to become a minister.

We had a lot of ministers on my father's side of the family, and two or three on my mother's side. I always thought Emmett would make a wonderful preacher. I thought he might at least become a deacon or a trustee in somebody's church. He liked going to church and he was under the influence of his grandmother, a deeply religious woman. He talked about helping her build a church one day. He attended the one she had helped to build, the Argo Temple Church of God in Christ.

So a minister, maybe, or a deacon, at least, or a trustee. There are so many possibilities when you look at a child's skills, his abilities, his natural tendencies. Emmett was a problem solver. If other people saw problems as locked doors, Emmett always seemed to hold a ring of keys, and an eagerness to see what was on the other side. He looked forward to a life of opened doors. That was Emmett. A solution locked in every problem.

A promise in every solution. Even his stutter. Just as One-Eyed Rogers, the minister and dinner guest from my childhood, never let his life's vision be limited by the loss of an eye, Emmett's stutter was something he always tried to talk, or whistle, his way through. He made us believe that he *would* get through it, too. To know Emmett was to believe in him. That was his way: "We can do it."

He made his analytical and persuasive abilities work for him. He loved working things out with people, to negotiate, to resolve things, as he had done with Thelma, Loretha, and me, and as he did all the time with all his friends. If a problem arose and two guys were ready to go at it, Bo would be the one who stepped right between them and said no. That would be the end of it. No one can recall Emmett ever getting into a fight. And he had an uncanny ability to keep others out of fights. I mean, nobody would buck him. Nobody would talk back to him. That was something that we marveled at. These things helped to make Bo a natural leader among his friends. They loved him. He had so much self-esteem and pride, especially in his appearance. He definitely got that at home. He was a secure boy, very confident in the way he carried himself. He might have stuttered at times, but he knew how to get his point across.

With his natural interest in working things out, he might have made a good lawyer or a politician. Aunt Rose Taliafero, the family "to-mah-to," would have loved that, with her commitment to public service. Who knows? Emmett did have a deep sense of justice. He actually told me once that he wanted to be a motorcycle cop. We thought an awful lot of policemen back then. We saw them as good people doing good works. And we'd hear about the exploits, the dramatic stories. When I was coming up, there was a man everybody talked about named Two-Gun Pete, and by the time Bo came along, the tales of Pete had become legend in our community.

Two-Gun Pete was a man who didn't play. His name made him sound like an outlaw, and he was every bit as tough as one. But Pete was a cop, a local black hero, who worked the trendy Bronzeville section of Chicago's black South Side, mostly in the areas where the nightclubs were located. When he told you to put those hands up, oh, boy, he meant it. He took no stuff, and often took no prisoners. He was known for sometimes shooting first and asking questions later. And, yes, he did carry two guns. He was a two-fisted crime stopper. Street hustlers would clear out just on the rumor that he was headed in. Even if people didn't love him, they sure respected him.

So Emmett wanted to be a motorcycle cop. He liked the work that he saw cops doing. He enjoyed being the peacemaker. And he just loved the uniform. Boys like to look up to heroes. They like to look at themselves as heroes in the making. Emmett was young and probably would have dreamed many things before settling on what he was to become. I was patient, content to let him take his time to make the right choice—whatever that would mean to him. And, with all the uncertainties in life, all the ways that young lives can turn, well, a motorcycle cop would have been just fine with me.

Gene once said that Emmett told him he wanted to be a professional baseball player. That was probably Bo's heart talking. It wasn't his head. It couldn't have been the rest of his body. He might have loved the game; he might have had all the best equipment, thanks to Gene; he might have been able to go to many White Sox games, thanks again to Gene; but Bo was no ballplayer. I know, because so many times I was the umpire when he played with his Chicago friends in Washington Park. Bo tried pitching and catching and he was not very good at either. Now, I really can't talk. As an umpire, I didn't know the strike zone from the ozone, but, like Bo, I was out there trying. What I *did* know was how to get the kids in our neighborhood organized and piled into my car with the soft drinks and other refreshments to head off to their games. Of course, Bo loved that part, since it placed him right at the center of attention. And the center of attention was the place where he felt most comfortable.

Things were no better for him on the baseball field on his weekend trips out to Argo. There was a game one Saturday, the school championship game. Bo had gone out to the park, but he no longer was a student in Argo. He lived in Chicago, so he was going to have to sit and watch all his Argo buddies play. Well, Emmett was never content to sit on any sidelines. He had much too much energy running through him for that. So, he convinced the PE teacher to let him in the game, even though there was no way he could have qualified. The game came down to one out left for Emmett's team, and Emmett came up to bat. He wound up catching a good piece of that ball and he sent it way into right field. Now, by this time Emmett was in seventh grade, and he was getting bigger. Because of his size, he was a slow runner, but he had put enough on that ball to get him all the way to third base. He should have stayed right there, just held up. He didn't. He came around third base, and he got tagged. It wasn't even close. Bo wasn't used to losing. If the game had been marbles, he would have walked away with his pockets full. But this wasn't marbles. This was a championship game. His team lost. His friends lost. But they took it pretty much the way they took most things back then: They grumbled for a moment, then they shrugged it off. They still had half the weekend left. And this would be just another funny story they'd tell over and over again.

Emmett loved those weekends he spent in Argo. The trip might take a good hour on the streetcar from our place in Chicago. But that never seemed to matter, from the time he started making the journey when he was about ten years old. And I never worried about him when he was there. I knew he was in good hands. I knew the entire community was looking out for him. It had always been that way. Kids in Argo couldn't walk to the corner without speaking to every adult they saw, by name. They'd have to do the same thing on the way back. Argo was a good fit for Emmett. Which is why he was drawn back there, again and again. He would hang out with his friends all day on Saturdays and spend a good part of Sundays in church, where, of course, he'd find his friends again. He lived for the fellowship. He lived for the fun. That most of all.

Bo had quite a group of friends out there in Argo, his band of merry young men. There were his cousins Wheeler, William, and Milton Parker; his other cousins Crosby "Sonny" Smith, Sam Lynch, and Tyrone Modiest; along with friends like Donny Lee Taylor and later Lindsey Hill. And when those boys got together, I mean it was nonstop laughter. Many of his Argo friends didn't have televisions yet, so Bo would be all too happy to provide the entertainment, sharing skits and sketches he had seen on his set. Comedy, of course. His favorite was George Gobel. But he also loved Abbott and Costello, and Jerry Lewis and Dean Martin. This was such a novelty to his friends. They hadn't even seen these performers. But they would sure hear about them, getting whole routines from Bo. He had learned a lot about memorizing.

Bo would let his friends get in the act, though. In fact, he would insist on it. He was so hungry for laughter, he would pay for jokes just as he might pay for snacks at Miss Haynes's store in Argo. He would come to town loaded from all those errands he ran for Gene, so he could afford to stand around paying quarters and half dollars and even dollars for jokes. His favorite jokester was Donny Lee, who had a Mississippi knack for storytelling, and had some long rhyming tales Bo would hang around for hours listening to him weave.

"Tell me another one," Bo would say to Donny Lee, or "T. Jones," as he called his friend, referring to a character in one of his stories.

Those two would even stand out for long spells in the cold swapping dollars for jokes and jokes for dollars. It was quite a thing, too, for Donny Lee to tell such long funny stories, since, like Bo, he stuttered. In fact, some of the funniest moments they had together came when they laughed at each other's stuttering. Once it happened while they both got stuck placing orders in Miss Haynes's store around the corner. She asked what the boys wanted to buy.

"I want a p-p-p-pop," Donny Lee said.

"And I want a M-M-M-Moon Pie," Bo added.

They just laughed and laughed over that one. I mean, it was "p-p-p-pop" and "M-M-M-Moon Pie" for the rest of the day. On purpose. That was the way Emmett wanted it. Nonstop laughter. And pranks. On the way back from a beach outing in nearby Michigan, the boys decided to wear their swim trunks and carry everything else home. Donny Lee made the mistake of falling asleep in the car with Bo. He woke up to find that he was wearing his underwear after all. On his head. Another time, when Wheeler and Sonny visited Bo in Chicago, the three boys crossed paths with some tough-looking kids up on busy Sixty-third Street. As they walked by, Bo turned to his cousins and spoke, loud enough for the other boys to hear, "You say you could beat their *what?*"

They all had a good laugh over that one, too. After making a run for it.

In Argo, there was always an adventure, something that touched deep inside a kid who had energy to burn. Oh, goodness, there was so much space there, room to expand, places to explore. It was just that kind of adventurous spirit that carried these boys forward through some of their best times. Naturally, over the years they had their bikes and their wagons and their balls and bats, but they seemed to have just as much fun with the stuff they found or threw together. For boys who knew how to improvise, invention was the game and Argo was one big playground. Their favorite swimming hole was more of a mud hole, a deep pit dug for an expressway bridge and then left to fill up with rainwater. Just enough to entice a group of young explorers. The same spirit of adventure carried them to the top of a nearby hill where they would slide down in oversized cartons, refrigerator boxes that had been thrown out by a local furniture store. It was the kind of daring that could move Bo out on a limb. *Somebody* had to go for it. A terrified cat had been chased up a tree by Miss Haynes's dog. Bo and his cousin Milton worked it all out: Bo would do the climbing and the coaxing, while Milton would wait down below to do the catching. As it turned out, Bo had the easier job. He had seen the lessons in school, the demonstrations showing how cats always land on their feet, lightly. So he wasn't too concerned about the cat's safety once he got it in his arms. But somewhere between the drop from the tree and the landing, well, that little cat got nervous all over again. Very nervous. Poor Milton caught the cat, and he caught the worst of it: the cat's claws.

Those boys would squeeze every last drop out of a day. As hard as they might have wanted to hold on to those moments, though, their days would always end much too soon. Many times they would wind up out in front of the house where Bo had spent so much of his childhood, the house where his cousin Ty now lived, and where Ty's stepfather, Tillman

Mallory, might be coming out to call his boy in as it got dark. Or they might be in front of the house next door to Ty's, where Bo's cousins Wheeler, William, and Milton still lived. So often, the boys would all stand under a lamppost "doo-wopping." Everybody wanted to sing. Everybody wanted to sing lead. Nobody could get it just right. It was the only time they were not in harmony. But this was the fifties, and music was in the air. It was everywhere. For this group of boys standing under a curbside spotlight, the music was off-key, it was out of sync, it was perfect. The grace note of their young lives. And around 8:59 at night, the group would have to take their last bow. The rule of every single black household on that block was that kids had to be on the front porch by nine o'clock sharp. That's what life was like for a bunch of happy-go-lucky boys who knew how to improvise. A championship game that nobody took too seriously, all-day jokes, an adventure in a mud hole or on a hilltop or up a tree, a song under a streetlight where nobody could carry a tune. And nobody seemed to care. For them, it was just right. All of it.

Emmett might have been doing most of the housework—the sweeping, the mopping, the waxing, a lot of the cooking and the laundry—but we took on the big jobs together. Ever since he laid that linoleum so perfectly in the dining room, I kept thinking of more and more redecorating projects we could do. We had already done the tiling and Bo had handled some paint jobs for me. At the time, people were painting their walls navy blue, dark red, dark green. I mean, they were coming up with the craziest colors. And I was following the trend. We had used all those colors in the front room and dining room and in the bedrooms. Bo and I had a great time, moving furniture, covering the floors, taping up the woodwork. As we got closer to Christmas 1954, though, I decided I wanted a new look for the little room across from my bedroom. Bo spent a lot of time there and, even though he had his own bedroom farther back, he liked to sleep up there from time to time. Near me. So I decided on something special. We were going to paper that room. And, oh, the paper I chose, something I picked out on the way home one night. It was red. When I say "red," I mean *red, red, red.* And it had a Japanese theme. There was a lady, a fan, a bridge, all kinds of cultural symbols that repeated in patterns.

Since Emmett had pretty much handled the linoleum single-handedly, I was going to take the credit for this one. I'd never had any lessons in hanging wallpaper, but I figured everything out, and showed Emmett as I was going through it. Well, actually, we figured it out together as we went along. He was so excited about this project. We had to be careful to make sure everything matched up perfectly. I knew Mama would notice if it didn't, anywhere on that wall. There was a little mark on every piece of paper to help you line up each strip with the last, and you had to cut with care to make sure it all came out right. We did a great job, and this time I was the one puffing out my chest when Mama came by for the inspection.

"My Lord," Mama said while she looked over our handiwork, stressing each word she spoke. "What a room."

Now, of course, I thought she was saying how beautiful it was. What she was saying was "Of all the loud, busy patterns . . ." She warned me that I would be sorry about the choice once I came to my senses and decided to choose all over again. "Baby, you can't even cover this stuff up," she said.

I didn't care. Bo and I were very happy with the job we had done. A perfect job, really. And I liked the idea of having something new and trendy, no matter how obnoxious it might have been.

The redecorating was just the beginning. I was determined that this would be a Christmas to remember. The best ever. I had no idea why I would make that decision at that time. I certainly didn't need to be going too deeply into debt. But something just came over me. Call it the Christmas spirit. The first thing I did was to make sure we had a beautiful spruce Christmas tree. We had always bought the cheaper ones and I wanted a nice, fluffy spruce tree. Gennie and Bo took care of that part. It was pretty tall, too, taller than Gene: six, maybe seven feet tall. And I bought everything I could think of to fill up that great big tree. The prettiest decorations.

Since I wanted Bo to get as much enjoyment out of this as I was having, I gave him a hundred dollars. "This is part of my Christmas present to you," I told him. "And you can use it any way you choose."

He chose to spend it on gifts for everybody else. I can't remember a single thing he bought for himself. Now, a hundred dollars could have easily been our entire Christmas. But this year was going to be different. I was feeling good about my job. In fact, it had never been this good for me before. And I wanted to share that good feeling with the people I loved. And I was very generous. I was buying a lot of gifts for Mama and my stepfather, Aunt Magnolia and Uncle Mack, Emmett and Gene, and others. I had accounts at several stores and wound up charging my way into about five hundred dollars of debt. That was a lot of money back then. I just threw caution to the wind.

Gene helped me with Emmett's gifts. We coordinated. He was always helping to dress Bo. Gene was sharp. He always was a very good dresser and Bo always wanted to be one. I can't recall how many times I heard Bo compliment Gene on something he was wearing and then I would find it in Bo's closet. For this Christmas, I bought Bo a black suit, white shirt, and some dress shoes. Gene bought him a wide-brim hat, a beautiful tie, and a gray coat. They picked out that coat together at Carson Pirie Scott. And I hated that coat. I wanted a coat that would conform more to his body, but this was just a big, old loose coat. No belt, no nothing. It made him look big to me. But Emmett assured me that he'd gotten the coat he wanted. It was pretty expensive. I think it cost over a hundred dollars.

Emmett bought Gene some socks and handkerchiefs. He bought just about each woman on his list a box of candy. A Whitman's Sampler. On every occasion, Mother's Day, Valentine's Day, every special day, I could always count on him buying me a box of these chocolates, and I always thought it was the sweetest thing. Every now and then, he would try something different. I remember once he bought me a bottle of Evening in Paris, a drugstore fragrance. I let him know how much I appreciated the thought, and how he didn't have to spend all his money on me. Really. The box of candy would be just fine. But this Christmas, he didn't think that would be enough. Oh, I got my Whitman's Sampler, all right, but Emmett also gave me a beautiful scarf he had shopped several stores to find.

When we got the tree all decorated and the presents spread out around it, I stood back and I looked at it all and thought about how blessed we were, how far we had come. I called Mama and shared the moment with her. I told her we had never seen a Christmas like that one. It was then I realized my Christmas that year was revolving around Emmett. It really was. At that blessed moment, he was the center of everything for me, and I wanted him to feel that way.

As people came in on Christmas Day, most rushed to the tree and grabbed whatever gifts they saw with their name tags. Mama and Papa Spearman spent a long time moving around that tree. It really was something to behold.

"You've been very foolish," Mama finally said to me, all the while looking for her gift. And checking out the other ones along the way. "You'll be paying for this the rest of your life."

Maybe. But at that moment, my whole life was right there in my home with my family. It was all that mattered and I was going to enjoy it, no matter what.

Christmas dinner was a feast at my place that year, truly fit for the kind of day I had hoped it would be. Mama prepared part of the dinner at my apartment, and Aunt Magnolia cooked some of it downstairs at her place. Mama made the turkey, the dressing, the gravy, and the yeast rolls. Aunt

Mag made the greens—because *nobody* could make greens like Aunt Magnolia—and she had potatoes and chits and sweet potato pies. Aunt Mamie made a white potato pie. Now, I had never had one of those before, but it was good. I baked a cake. But that turkey Mama made was a masterpiece, and the centerpiece, so pretty and brown. Oh, my mother could cook.

She could bless a table, too. I mean, she *blessed* that table that night. My mother was the prayer warrior. And she was moved by the spirit of Christmas. Everybody was hungry, but they were just going to have to wait. Mama did not let us forget what was most important. She *talked* to the Lord that night, thanking Him for His bountiful blessings, for bringing us all together, for the love that went from heart to heart and breast to breast. Oh, she went on and on like that until I felt Gene nudging me. I tried not to react. I mean, I wanted to respect this solemn moment. I really did. But I knew what he was trying to tell me, and I didn't want it to distract me. It was what I had told him once, the story about my grandfather, who had gone out to dinner way out in the country at Sister So-and-So's house. The preacher at Sister So-and-So's house was called on to bless the table. Well, that preacher prayed, and he prayed, and he prayed, and he prayed! When the preacher finally said "Amen," Grandpa said, "I was wiping my mouth."

Mama was in the "looking ahead" part of her prayer, seeking the Lord's blessings for all our endeavors in the coming year, keeping our family and our friends close and in the light of God's love and grace. We listened and we listened and we listened to Mama's prayer.

When she said "Amen," Gene was the first to respond. "I was just about ready to start wiping my mouth!"

Everybody laughed, even Mama. That set the tone for the rest of the dinner. We were all happy for the blessings we had enjoyed and just for being together. And it seemed like everybody was there. So many people, they were eating at the dining table, at a card table, and in the kitchen. Oh, it was nonstop "Pass me this" and "Pass me that" and "Pass me something else."

Finally, Uncle Mack had his fill. "Every time I go to put some food in my mouth, somebody's saying 'pass me something,'" he said. "If you want it, you better get up and get it." We all laughed, and promptly got up to serve ourselves, practically turning the dining table into a buffet. It was the best Christmas ever.

It was followed by a great New Year's celebration. Aunt Mag cooked again for everybody who had to have Aunt Mag's greens and black-eyed peas. Greens for money. Black-eyed peas for good fortune. Even so, we weren't about to leave anything to chance. Mama led us all in asking God's blessing.

If Norman Rockwell had ever wanted to do a black family Christmas portrait, he could have turned to us that holiday season, picture perfect and ready to be framed on the cover of the *Saturday Evening Post. If* Rockwell had ever had a mind to do such a thing. *If* the editors of the *Saturday Evening Post* had ever had a mind to feature such a thing. It occurred to me that maybe I could arrange for my own Rockwell moment, or something like it. I could arrange to have photographs made. Since I had gone all out that season, I figured I should at least have some kind of remembrance.

I happened to tell a coworker about our wonderful Christmas and how I wanted to have pictures made to remember it. That's when I found out that he took pictures. He said that he would be happy to take some for me. He never told me how much this was going to cost me, but I figured, with all the money I had already spent, this couldn't be that bad. So we had the pictures taken of all the gifts and the tree and of Bo in all the clothes we had bought him, the coat, the hat, the shirt and tie, leaning on his Philco television, lying across the little bed in the room we had redecorated, and, of course, posed next to me. Our mother-and-son portrait. Eventually, I came around to asking what all this was going to cost me and the man told me I owed him nothing. Nothing? Oh, my goodness. Yet another blessing of that special season. And for that, I was grateful.

I adored the pictures he produced, the giddy moments captured on film, full of the excitement of our holiday. They captured something more than just a moment in time. They caught that perfect light that you see sometimes just before darkness falls. Oh, my, there was a sweetness about them, the sweetness of innocence. There was so much love. That most special gift, which really is Christmas. I held the pictures. I held that moment. I wanted to hold it much longer than I knew I ever could. It was a time of such joy. It was a time that I would one day come to think of only with longing.

CHAPTER 10

Our year began the way every year should. We were happy about our holiday celebrations, we were hopeful about what was in store during the year ahead, and we were very well fed. It wasn't long after the start of the year that I had even worked out how I was going to pay off all the Christmas bills, and I was feeling good about the plan. The only problem was working out the payments. I mean, actually making them, delivering them. I didn't have a checking account, which meant I would have to pay cash each month to all those stores, which meant I would have to make the payments in person, which meant I had a problem. I was working so many hours by this time. Sometimes I didn't get off until eight, nine, ten o'clock at night. Even when I got off in time to make it to the stores before they closed, I would be so tired that walking around from one store to the next paying a bunch of bills—well, that was just the last thing I wanted to do. But I also wanted those bills paid, and I didn't want them paid one day beyond the due date. I was sorting it all out and talking to Emmett one day, half thinking out loud, half looking for his advice. After all, he was the answer man, the problem solver.

He listened to me set out the problem and, without even taking time to think about it, he saw how to handle it. "I can pay those bills for you."

What? Trust him with my money? Well, he might not have had to think about it, but I did. I *really* did. He was only thirteen years old. Sure, he had been taking on a lot of responsibility around the house, and doing a great job. But this was different. This was very, very important. I mean, this was my money. I couldn't take a chance on him running into a baseball game down the street or something with my money in his pocket. Besides, even though he had been riding the streetcar out to Argo for some time, I had never let him go downtown alone. Sure, he had gone with me, but I had to be certain he knew how to handle this on his own. So I asked him and, once again, he spoke without hesitating.

"I would just go up to Sixty-third," he explained, "catch the El, get off at Adams, walk over to the Fair Store. When I get to the Fair Store, Sears is right across the street. I'll come out of Sears, turn right, and keep on up to Wieboldt's. After Wieboldt's, then I work my way up to Carson's."

I had to look at him for a minute. I mean, just like that, he had laid it out for me. The look in his eye showed there was no question in his mind, no anxiety in his heart. "We can do it" was written all over his face. He believed in himself. There was nothing he couldn't do. It was time for me to show, to prove, that I believed in him, too. All I could do was take a deep breath and say, "Okay." I gave him a hundred dollars, gave him the bills for each store, and then I thought for a moment. I pulled out the light bill and gave him that to pay, too.

All the next day at work I was jumpy about what my son would be dealing with. A hundred dollars of my money, a walk through the hustle and bustle, but mostly hustle, of Sixty-third Street, a train ride downtown, and then five stops to make in the Loop. I wondered, at different points in the afternoon, Where is that child with my hundred dollars? What if he loses that money? What if somebody sticks him up? What was I thinking? I had all kinds of nightmares. I might as well have just taken the afternoon off and paid the bills myself. It was a very long ride home for me that night. When I got home, Bo wasn't there. Well, that didn't make me feel any better. I walked into my bedroom and there, on my dresser, was a note. It was sitting on top of the stack of bills. I looked at the bills first. Each one was stamped "Paid." Next to the stack was the change from my hundred dollars. I knew right then and there that Bo and I had reached a very important point in our relationship. It was that critical point where a mother begins to see a boy taking shape as a man. It was the point of no return. I knew then that I could trust my son with everything. I knew he would do what he set out to do. And I knew he'd be paying those bills every month from then on. Then there was the note. Bo wrote that he had taken care of everything and indicated what I had already confirmed, that the bills were paid and he had left the change. And one more thing. Aunt Mag downstairs had given him permission to visit a friend in the neighborhood. *I'll be home before dark,* he wrote. *Don't worry.*

Gene and I were seeing quite a bit of each other by this time. We would go out to clubs like the Blue Note and Joe's at Sixty-third and South Parkway. We saw all kinds of entertainment, including Redd Foxx and Moms Mabley. Oh, we were having a great time going out. But Gene also enjoyed spending time at my place. I knew he was trying to get his foot in my door, but he had a good reason to do it. Lots of them, really. For one, his aunt had talked to him.

"Now, boy," she said, "that's a pretty girl. Don't you let her get away."

All of his friends were pushing for me, too. So he had everybody's approval. For a man, that makes a difference. When a man sees how much other people appreciate a woman, it makes him appreciate her even more. But there was so much more than that. Gene and Bo adored each other and seemed to really enjoy the time they spent together. My mother loved Gene, too. And, oh, he was just crazy about Mama. That boy *loved* my mother, and treated her like she was a mother to him. For a woman, for me, all of that was important. And, well, what can I say? We were falling in love.

Someone once said something that someone once told them, so by now it's officially an adage or something that just makes a whole lot of sense. What they said was that men and women look at their relationships in different ways at the beginning. Men look at their women hoping they'll never change and women size up their men hoping they will. I got to work on Gene right away. The first order of business was that conk. But I have to say that almost as soon as he took it out, I was sorry I had asked him to do it. He looked like such a little boy without that look of his. Then there was that walk. I had to think about that one. I mean, I just couldn't have other women looking at Gene the way I was looking at him. But there are some things, some down-to-the-bone things about a man that make him what he is. Things you can't change. Things you probably shouldn't even try to change. It would be easier just to find another man.

As it turns out, Bo and I weren't the only attraction Gene had when he'd want to come over. He was also drawn to Aunt Mag's cooking. He would say all the time, "Aunt Mag can burn." Now, Aunt Mag was the greatest greens cooker of all time. She cooked greens like nobody's business. In addition to her meat, she put in garlic, onion, green pepper, and celery. Oh-h-h, those greens had such a distinctive flavor. And then she filled them with hot peppers, which I could not tolerate. I would be eating and drinking and crying and drinking. But those greens were too good to pass up. If Aunt Mag was cooking greens, Gene was coming by. He'd want to know if he could have some.

She was only too happy to oblige: "Yeah, come on here, boy."

So, that's what started me cooking them. I mean, I was not going to let Aunt Mag outdo me. First thing, of course, was to get her recipe. Once I got it, I would come home on Fridays with the makings for greens and fish. And I was one happy cook in that kitchen. I would just sing and cook and cook and sing. I think I did a pretty good job of imitating what Aunt Mag was doing with those greens. Gene and Bo were eating them up, that's all I knew. I never could make Aunt Mag's hot-water cornbread, though. I just couldn't make that bread. But I could make regular cornbread, and I would fry that fish. Now Gene Mobley would swallow some fish. Oh, he would eat white buffalo like he was eating a pork chop. But I'd always have to try to get a bone out of his throat. Eventually I stopped making white buffalo and switched to catfish. It wasn't as hard to swallow.

On one of these visits, Gene was complimenting me on the meal and we were playing around and he said he was going to marry me. Just like that. I wasn't sure whether it was his stomach or his heart talking at the time. But then he turned to Bo and told him the same thing, that he wanted to marry me.

Bo shook his head and smiled. "No," he said. "We're not ready."

Well, I thought, I was starting to feel ready *myself*, but we just left it there. Until it came up again, and then again. Mostly, Gene would bring it up in a joking way. He would come over to eat. At some point in the evening he would tell me, "I'm gonna marry you."

Bo would clear his throat, as if to say, "Now, children."

We never talked about it, but I was beginning to believe that Bo was building up his defenses. He thought the world of Gene. But to think of sharing the house and his mother with Gene—well, that was something else. He was the man of the house and wanted it to stay that way. At least, that's what I thought.

Gene was no quitter, though. He brought it up yet again.

Bo said the same thing. "We're not ready yet."

Finally Gene had to know. He asked Bo why he seemed to disapprove of the two of us getting married.

Bo spoke up right away. He didn't have a problem explaining it at all. He told Gene that he was concerned that he might shout at me or hit me. If he did, then Bo would have to take sides, and you know whose side he was going to take. He just liked Gene too much to want to even consider something like that. Because he liked Gene, he didn't want Gene to marry his mama. "We're not ready yet."

So that was it. Emmett had promised to look out for me, to protect me, and this was how he was doing it. That incident with Pink Bradley had left an ugly mark that Gene would have to wipe away. Gene had the warmest and most generous spirit of any man I ever knew. I had no doubt that he would be able to put Bo's mind at ease.

By February of fifty-five, things seemed to be going so well for us. I mean, I was on a roll. I was doing a good job at work, my bills were being paid, and we seemed to have every reason to look forward. I figured, what better way to be on a roll than in a new car? A brand-new car. Now, I had owned several cars before. There was a forty-six Oldsmobile that was about two or three years old when I bought it. I had also bought a Studebaker. And, of course, while I was in Detroit in 1950, my mother sent me the money for that forty-seven Plymouth. They were all good cars that went the way of all cars.

In addition to wanting a new car, I needed one. This would be the first one I would buy completely on my own. But Emmett was going with me to pick it out. He was very, very excited. So was his mama. After all, this was going to be a new experience for me.

The car was a fifty-five Plymouth. Red, with a white top and white interior. I worked out the deal and set up my payments. And when the salesman made the papers out, I looked them over, looked at Emmett, and turned back to the salesman. I told him that I wanted my son to be included as my cosigner. Well, you could just see Emmett straightening up in his chair, preparing to take on this new responsibility.

The salesman looked a little puzzled. "Well, you don't need a cosigner."

I knew he was going to say Emmett was too young, anyway, but I overrode him before he could go on. "My son and I are buying this car together," I told the man. "And he is going to see to it that I'm always able to make these notes." I looked at Emmett again. "Even if he has to go out and do extra work."

Bo was nodding in agreement. That was all right with him. But I knew what he was really thinking. He was thinking that he was going to be the first thirteen-year-old on the block with his own car. Like I was just going to turn the car keys over to him. That was the farthest thing from my mind. But we set everything up just that way, in my name and his. We were traveling down a new road together now. And we'd be traveling it in a brand-new car. Our car.

On one of his streetcar rides home from Argo one Sunday, Emmett saw his cousin Thelma standing outside, waiting for her own streetcar, and they waved at each other as they often did on these weekend trips. Thelma and her sister Loretha still traveled out to Argo for service at the Argo Temple Church of God in Christ. They both sang in the choir. But Thelma recalled this particular encounter, because of what she would learn later. Riding that same streetcar with Emmett was Bennie Goodwin,

Jr., the son of the pastor of Argo Temple who had baptized me. Bennie, Junior, was a student at the Moody Bible Institute in Chicago and the choir director at Argo Temple. He also ministered to boys in the neighborhood through a church-sponsored boys' club. So he knew Thelma and he had seen Emmett around the church, which he attended every Sunday when he was in Argo. Bennie didn't know at the time that Thelma and Bo were related. But he saw them waving. Some time later, he told Thelma about his encounter with Bo on that streetcar. Bennie was reading, studying for upcoming exams, but something kept pulling at him. It was pulling his attention in Emmett's direction, because he recognized him from church. At least he thought that was the reason. Finally, when he realized he was not going to be able to concentrate on his studies, he struck up a conversation with Emmett. At a certain point, he asked if Emmett wanted to pray with him. Emmett said he would and they prayed together on the streetcar. Bennie says that when Emmett raised his head, he looked transformed. It was that moment, Bennie told Thelma, when Emmett accepted Jesus Christ. Bennie would remember that experience for years to come, because he realized that the reason he had not been able to concentrate on his studies was because he was being interrupted by something much more important. It was, as he recalls, the voice of God.

One day, I was standing on my porch talking to Aunt Magnolia and Uncle Mack when I saw my car coming down the street. I knew Gene and Emmett had been out running some errands, so the car coming down the street wasn't a big surprise to me. But what I saw as it came closer was not what I ever expected to see. Gene was on the passenger's side. Bo was on the driver's side. I was beside myself. Apparently, Gene had been teaching Bo how to drive *our* Plymouth. And there was Gene's star pupil, driving with his right hand on the wheel, resting his left hand outside, holding the top of the car, and waving with whichever hand he had left. I had lost count, couldn't tell anymore, because by this time, my God, I was just scared half to death.

They kept going, right on past us, leaving Aunt Mag and Uncle Mack cackling, me in shock, before cruising around the corner to come up the back way to the garage.

Mama had contracted to have that two-car garage built. I had parked the car on the street when I first brought it home. I was so proud to wake up in the morning and look out at it, sitting there on the street—the first car I ever owned with tubeless tires—and I'd smile. Until one morning, I looked out the window and saw that my trunk was slightly open. I went flying downstairs and found that some joker had taken my spare tire. Oh,

I was so unhappy. It was such a traumatic experience. Emmett took it worse than I did. He was angry. After all, the car was his, too. If he could have caught that fellow who broke into his car—oh, my, he just talked and talked about what he would do with him. He calmed down, and I called my mother. Mama came over and, as always, she took care of everything. And after she did, that car stayed in the garage.

By the time Gene and Bo pulled around to the garage through the alley in back, I was standing there, watching with my arms crossed. I couldn't get too upset, though. Not as long as I could remember back when I was a teenager, finding my mother's keys and slipping her car out to run errands with Ollie.

Fortunately, Gene and Bo got out and Gene took charge of the parking. Bo's chest was all puffed up. He looked so pleased with himself. It wasn't just that he had driven the car, it was that I had seen that he had driven the car.

Gene took it all in. My expression. Bo's pride. Then he spoke, looking at Bo, so I didn't realize he was really aiming at me. "Next time, I'm gonna teach you how to back into the garage."

"Oh, don't you dare," I said before I saw that big smile on Gene's face.

Even though I watched Emmett grow through the years, it would always surprise me when I'd look up and notice that he had reached another level. And at each stage, he would see the world differently, react to it differently. It happened when I first saw him running around our old neighborhood in Argo, helping the iceman. I realized then that I didn't have a little baby anymore. I had a little boy. And when I saw him driving our car, I realized that he wasn't a little boy any longer. He was a teenager. In another heartbeat, he would be a man. My God, how had he grown so fast? As much as I had promised myself that I would not make the same mistake my mother had made with me, I realized that there were things I had not told Emmett, things he would need to know to become a man. Maybe that was because he always seemed to know so much already. Maybe that's why I let it slip by. But what about girls? What did he really know about girls?

Emmett never really had a girlfriend. At least none that he mentioned to me. He had one date. It was when he was still eleven years old. It was around Easter, and the little girl lived in Argo. I didn't know Bo had been looking at the girl, really, until he told me he wanted to take her to the show. Well, that's when I got very interested. He told me he was going to have to go out to Argo to get her. Then they would ride the streetcar together back to Chicago to see the movie. Then he was going to ride back to Argo with her, and finally come back to Chicago. That was a whole lot of streetcar riding. After he explained his master plan to me, he asked me for the money. Now, really, who was going on this date, anyway? He promised to pay me back out of his grocery earnings. And that was just fine. I gave him five dollars and he went on his way. They would go to the South Town Theater near Halsted, one of the most beautiful theaters I had ever seen.

Emmett told me about the date when he got home. At the ticket window, he had put two quarters down and the person in the booth looked him over. Now, you had to start paying full price at age twelve. Emmett was still about four months away from his twelfth birthday at this point, but he was big for his age. The ticket person in the booth told him he was not getting in for less than the full price. He tried to explain his age, but it was no use. One dollar for him, and one dollar for his date. Well, Emmett knew he wouldn't have enough money to get home at that rate, but he was the problem solver. He asked the little girl to pay her own way.

Oh, I was so embarrassed when he told me. "You can't do that."

"Why not?" Emmett asked. "That was too much money. I had to take her home. I had to buy her popcorn and pop. So I let her pay her own way in."

They saw the movie and he took her back to Argo. He couldn't stay long because it was getting late, and he had a curfew. Going to Argo took an hour. Coming back took an hour. He had already spent three hours on the road, plus the movie time. So when he took the little lady home, he just said "Bye," turned around, and came back to Chicago.

Then there was his birthday party. The kids were playing games while the adults were in another part of the house. Somehow they turned to spin the bottle. When one of the little girls would spin, Bo would jump from one spot to the next, trying to let the bottle stop on him. But his friends weren't sure it was as much about the girls as it was about Bo. Bo was the life of every party, especially his own. He wanted to be funny. He wanted to win. These were the driving forces of his life.

To tell the truth, for the longest time I never really thought much about having a talk with Emmett. I wasn't trying to encourage him with girls. For one thing, I wanted to keep him to myself. And, of course, I wanted him to focus on his schoolwork. There were a couple of times we sort of talked about the day when he might bring home the girl he wanted to marry, and I acted jealous. He promised he would buy a big house so that he could have his wife and his mother together under one roof. I have to admit, I thought about the grandchildren I might have one day. But I knew that there were things he would need to know to get there. I told Gene what I was thinking, and I asked him if he might want to have a little talk with Emmett. Gene was not in a big hurry to sit down and have any "father and son" chats. Like that, anyway. I don't know if they ever had a talk or not.

Someone would have to speak to Bo at some point. I knew that. I wanted Bo to know how to treat a woman well. I knew how important that would be, for him, for the woman. I knew that from my own experience, such that it was.

Mama arranged my first wedding. She had to. What did I know about anything like that? She took me downtown to get the license. Took me to get the blood test, too, even though that wound up being a full-blown physical. Years later she would explain that she just wanted to make sure I was a good girl. Fortunately, the doctor confirmed that. But, of course, I didn't know how to be anything else. In fact, I knew nothing up to the very moment when I should have known everything.

I married Louis Till in the front room of my mother's house. It was a special little affair with family and friends. Mama was very considerate. After the ceremony, after everyone left, she let us take the back bedroom. No one was in the middle room. She would sleep in front.

When it came time to go to bed, I looked at the few things I had that I could wear. Someone had given me a pink negligee, and, oh, my God, it embarrassed me to pieces. It was just too revealing. I said no to that. I walked up to Mama's room and asked if she had a nightgown I could wear and she said yes. It was October and the weather was not cold. Even so, I went in the drawer and picked out a white flannel gown with images of flowers, mostly roses, I guess. I undressed in the front room and kept my girdle on. Then I put on the gown, which had long sleeves and dragged the floor. After I had stalled for quite a while, I still didn't know how to go in that back room where Louis was. I was nervous. No, I was terrified. I mean, I hadn't been down that path before and had no idea what to expect. I didn't know how much he knew and I didn't know how much you *had* to know. All I knew was what I didn't know, which was everything a person is expected to know. My mother had just not prepared me to become a wife. She'd been too busy keeping me a virgin. I'd talked with other women, who had only told me they liked being with their husbands. But all I could think was, My God, I wish he would just go to sleep before I go to bed. Finally, Louis called me and I walked to the back, to the room.

After that first night, I decided I would stay up late, hoping I could stay awake longer than Louis. But, as it turns out, I didn't have to. I was not well the rest of that week and all we could do was cuddle. I did like that part, even though there was never enough of it. You didn't have to go any farther than that for me back then. The rest of it, my Lord. I didn't know what all the fuss had been about with those other women I had talked to. I figured maybe that's why they called it "the birds and the bees" because, I mean, really, that was for the birds.

There was one good thing about that early experience: In no time, I learned that I was pregnant. Since we really didn't do more than cuddle for a while after that first night, that would mean that my first time ever was the time Emmett was conceived.

Oh, there was so much I wanted for Emmett as he was beginning to take shape as an adult. I wanted him to see his wife's needs and attend to them. I wanted him to be a partner to her and not be one of these guys who only looks out for himself. I wanted him to become a man about the house when it came to repairs or cleaning or anything that needed to be done. I knew where the mistakes had been made by the men I had married, and I wanted Emmett to avoid making those mistakes with the women he would know. I alluded to those things I didn't like, and, of course, he had seen some things himself in my relationship with Pink, how Pink just didn't measure up.

I had to look at Emmett and realize he was already becoming everything I had hoped he might. There were things I had taught him, there were things he just seemed to know. I thought about the way he had treated me, taken care of me, protected me. I thought about the way he had taken to Wheeler Parker's new sister, Alma, after she was born in 1948. Emmett always wanted to be the one to push her stroller, look out for her. He was two hundred percent boy, but that didn't mean he was all play and mischief. It also meant he was a protector, a provider. He had his tender spot, all right, and it showed in the way he always took such care to find just the right cards to express just the right sentiments on just the right occasions, like Mother's Day. I weighed everything as I watched a boy becoming a man and considered the kind of man I was determined he'd become.

As I did, I realized that I had been teaching Emmett all along, teaching him to be the kind of man any woman would want. The kind of man I had wanted in my own life. The kind of man I didn't have in my marriages to Louis and Pink. Although I didn't talk about sexual relationships, I talked to Emmett about the things that mattered most, the essential things that could make a relationship. I knew how important it was for mothers to shape boys, who someday would become men who would marry the women who would mother sons. These were the important things to share with my son. And I figured we would have time to take up the rest of it later.

CHAPTER 11

By summer, I was ready for a vacation, or as close to one as I was going to get. The car was still practically brand-new and I thought it would be so nice to take it out on the road before Emmett had to get back to school. This would have been my first formal vacation since I started working for the federal government twelve years earlier, and I wanted to drive with Gene and Emmett to Detroit and then to Omaha. I planned to take a month off and I was so excited about the trip that I even agreed that Emmett could take the wheel after we got out on the highway. He had only turned fourteen in July, but with Gene and me in the car, well, I figured we could steer him right.

It wasn't long, though, before Emmett started moving in a different direction. My uncle Moses Wright came up to Chicago from Money, Mississippi, in August for the funeral of Robert Jones, the father-in-law of his oldest daughter, Willie Mae Jones. While he was in town staying with Willie Mae, he saw so many of the great sights a big city like Chicago has to offer, and he was impressed. How could he not be? But he preferred the simple pleasures of wide-open spaces and fishing and long summer nights in the Mississippi Delta, and he talked about all that in ways that made you want to be there, to see it for yourself. Emmett got caught up in these images that Papa Mose created. For a free-spirited boy who lived to be outdoors, there was so much possibility, so much adventure in the Mississippi his great-uncle described. But there was something else. Emmett found out that his cousin Wheeler Parker was going to travel to Mississippi with Papa Mose for a visit, and that another cousin, Curtis Jones, Willie Mae's son, was planning to join them later. The boys were looking forward to their visit, and that's all Emmett needed to hear. Wheeler was like his other half. He was determined to go.

The answer was no. Absolutely not. I was against it, my mother was against it. No matter how much people were talking about Mississippi this and Mississippi that, we did not want Emmett to go unless he could go with one of us, as he had done a couple of times before when he was much younger. But Bo refused to let go of it. He couldn't imagine letting his cousins go south without him, especially Wheeler, his best friend. He kept pushing it, I kept saying no. I tried to convince him that we would have just as much fun on the car trip, and that he would be able to drive the car he loved so dearly. But that just didn't compare. It couldn't. I guess he figured he could drive that car anytime, as he already had shown. All the while I was trying to convince him, he was working on me, too. In the end, he was more persuasive.

In one talk we had, he turned to me and began asking questions, questions that were really more like statements. "Why is it that you can take two of Papa Mose's girls and raise them for years, and you won't even let me go to Mississippi and stay a week?" I thought about Thelma and Loretha and how Papa Mose and Aunt Lizzy had entrusted them to Mama's care up in Argo, and to me later in Chicago. "How do you feel about that, Mama?" Bo asked.

He was very convincing. His questions did make me stop and think. Mama and I talked about it. She had been as firm as I had been at first. He couldn't go. But there were other people, besides Bo, who were also sharing their feelings with Mama and me, telling us there was no need to worry so much, that the boys would be looked after. Mama wanted to pray on it. After a while, I decided I would go to talk with Papa Mose about the whole thing. As I was parking my car in front of Willie Mae's house, I saw another car I knew so well, parking across the street. It was my mother's car. I guess Bo had been working on Mama, too. My mother always had a lot of influence over me, but I didn't realize until that moment just how my thinking had been shaped by her. We were reacting in exactly the same way, at exactly the same time. People inside laughed when they saw Mama and me, these "two hens coming to fuss over this one little chick." They thought it was amusing that we would be coming at the same time with the same thing in mind. The real funny part about it was that I had no idea she was going to be there. She had no idea that I was coming either.

As it turns out, we had such a wonderful time that day at Willie Mae's. It was a great joy to be there. We were able to spend time with Papa Mose, Willie Mae, and the rest of her family. And, oh, Willie Mae always wanted to feed you. If you were at her house, you had to eat. That woman made the best fried chicken. I don't know what she did to her chicken, but you could never get enough of it. I mean, every time you ate a piece, you wanted some more. We just had a beautiful evening together. Family had always been so important to us and I felt so relaxed spending time with my family. I began to give in on the journey Bo wanted to make. But Mama and I still wanted to talk to Papa Mose, to get him to assure us that the boys would not be left on their own, ever. He agreed that those boys would not be going off to town alone. He made us that promise. And that was that. I heard Emmett's pleas. I heard Papa Mose's assurances. I heard myself, finally, agreeing to let Emmett go on the trip.

Every generation has its cautionary tale. Mine was the story of that little girl who was punished by the white man her mother cleaned for, the little girl who died slowly and painfully from her punishment while her mother was forced to finish her day's work. That was the story I had heard, somewhere, somehow, growing up. There had been no tales for Emmett. There had been no reason. For Emmett, there had been no danger, no discrimination, no deprivation. He had lived life the way it was supposed to be lived. Without limitation. Which is why he had never seen a difference between himself and white kids he might have encountered in school out in Argo, or white adults like the milkman or the iceman he had hustled for work. It wasn't only that he was taught that he was just as good as anyone else. It was that he was made to feel that way, in every way. It was that he always had that awareness simply because of the way people treated him, the respect people always showed him. I had never had a reason to feel the kind of anxiety about him, about his safety in Argo and in Chicago, that I felt about this trip to Mississippi. Even though I knew he would be with other people who knew how things worked for black folks in the South, I couldn't leave anything to chance. I knew I had to give him the talk. It was the talk every black parent had with every child sent down South back then. It might have been a time of great black migration to the North, but in the summer, there were quite a few black kids from the cities of the North who went south to visit relatives. For our kids, it was as close to summer camp as they were going to get. So, I had to talk to Bo about strange things in a strange, new place, things that lay in wait for him.

He had to understand that he would not be in Chicago and had to act differently. I wanted him to be aware of this at all times. That was so important. We went through the drill. Chicago and Mississippi were two very different places, and white people down South could be very mean to blacks, even to black kids. Don't start up any conversations with white people. Only talk if you're spoken to. And how do you respond? "Yes, sir," "Yes, ma'am." "No, sir," "No, ma'am." Put a handle on those answers. Don't just say "yes" and "no" or "naw." Don't ever do that. If you're walking down the street and a white woman is walking toward you, step off the sidewalk, lower your head. Don't look her in the eye. Wait until she passes by, then get back on the sidewalk, keep going, don't look back.

I'm not really sure where I got all this. It must have been from all those meetings people had at our house as I was coming up. I believe in listening. To my mother, to all those cousins, everybody. Now I wanted Emmett to listen to me. I was trying to make him see that he had to watch everything he did. And I went further, because I wanted to make it look as bad as I could possibly make it look.

"If you have to humble yourself," I said, "then just do it. Get on your knees, if you have to."

It all seemed so incredible to him. "Oh, Mama," he said, "it can't be that bad."

"Bo, it's worse than that," I said.

In fact, if you were a black man in the South, not only should you never look a white woman in the eye, you should never be seen even looking at a picture of a white woman. Now, I couldn't bear the thought of seeing my son get down on his knees in front of some white man. But I figured that putting that image in his head would make him think about everything he did down there, every encounter. I wanted to make sure he was careful.

Emmett just listened. And I kept stressing the points I was making. He finally spoke up again. "Mama," he said, "I know how to act. You taught me how to act."

Then, he went on to remind me of things I had taught him, things I had told him as a child, things he assured me he always did. If he was talking to an adult out in Argo, there was a proper way to do it. As he walked around out there, he had to speak politely to everybody he saw. And he was taught to answer anyone speaking to him by saying, "Yes, Mrs. So-and-So," or "No, Mrs. So-and-So." Never just "yes" or "no."

So, he thought he understood all that he needed to understand. But there were basic things, things that ran deep in the awareness of people who lived in the South, things he couldn't possibly have understood. Everything Emmett had come to believe all his life had to be unlearned as he prepared for the trip. He had developed a sense of dignity, pride, confidence, self-assuredness. He was used to having certain things in his contented life. He was comfortable with himself and the things he had. So I warned him about the ways of the South. And a funny thing occurred to me as we were going through it all: This was the first time I had ever really spoken to Emmett about race. I was giving him some pretty strong instructions about how to avoid problems but, before this, there had never been any reason for race to come up in any way. So, I wondered whether I had done enough to make up for all I had never had to do before. After all, how do you give a crash course in hatred to a boy who has only known love?

A few days before Bo left, we went shopping. There were things he would need for his trip. Some new dungarees and shoes for the country. He also wanted a new wallet. We went to a flea market near Sixty-third and Halsted, and found a nice selection of wallets that all came with stock photos in the photo holder. Bo had the hardest time picking between his two favorite wallets. It wasn't the wallets so much as the photos inside. One had a studio shot of the actress Hedy Lamarr. The other had a picture of Dorothy Lamour. After going back and forth for what seemed like an eternity, Bo finally made his choice. Hedy Lamarr.

He was consumed by the adventure he was about to experience. He talked about it on his visits to Argo. He showed off the new clothes he was going to wear to his friends. And everywhere, he heard the echoes of my voice, my lecture. He stopped by to visit my friend Ollie shortly before he left and told her how much he was looking forward to going. She told him to be sure to behave and to be careful in the way that he talked and the way he carried himself. She knew how independent he was and how he was accustomed to doing whatever he chose in Chicago. He was free to go where he wanted and do what he pleased.

Bo also ran into his cousin Sam Lynch one day when they were both on their way to Wheeler's house in Argo. "We're going down South," Bo said.

"Nice," Sam said. "That's real nice."

Bo couldn't contain himself. "Why don't you go with us?"

"No," Sam said. "I can't go down there."

Bo never wanted to take no for an answer. He offered to ask Sam's parents for him. After all, nothing could have been harder than convincing Mama and me. But Sam explained that Bo would not have to ask his parents for him. He couldn't go because he couldn't get past all the things he had heard about the South. He didn't *want* to go. Bo spent the better part of the next hour walking around Argo with Sam, trying to change his cousin's mind. But Sam's mind was made up. He would not be moved.

Finally, even Bo had to give up. "Okay," he said. "I'll see you when we get back."

I had never said anything to Emmett about his father's death, not about the specifics, anyway. And he had never really asked. Emmett was nearly four when I got the telegram. Much too young to absorb any of it. For him, all that was left of his father's life was the ring that had been returned to me by the army. The one with the initials LT, and the date MAY 25, 1943. Probably the date the ring was inscribed. Emmett had looked at the ring a few times over the years. He even tried it on, but it wasn't a good fit. Just a couple of days before he was to leave for Mississippi, he pulled it out again. With a little tape, it might fit his ring finger. Or maybe he could just wear it on a different finger. And that was when he asked me about his father.

We had talked about the fact that his father was a soldier in World War II and that he had been killed overseas. The only thing I could tell him at that point was the only thing I was told by the army. The cause of death, I explained to Emmett, was "willful misconduct." I didn't know what that meant, and when I tried to find out, I never got a satisfactory answer from the army. A lawyer and friend, Joseph Tobias, had tried to help in 1948. But he was told by the Department of the Army there would be no benefits for me due to the willful misconduct.

At that moment, though, as Emmett and I talked, the only thing that meant anything to him was that silver ring. He wanted to wear it, to show it off to his friends. I agreed. He put it on the middle finger of his right hand. That seemed to work. I thought about how I might try to have another keepsake made for him. A medallion with a picture of Louis Till, in his dress uniform. I could have that made as a gift for Emmett's next birthday. That would give me plenty of time to make the arrangements.

Emmett was about to get back to preparing his things for the Mississippi trip, when he turned to me. I don't know what made him think about it. Maybe it was the conversation we had just had about his father. Maybe it was the thought of having a complete family. Maybe it was all those playful conversations with Gene. I don't know. But whatever it was, it made him smile. "Now, don't you and GeGe run off and get married before I get back."

On Saturday, August 20, 1955, we were in such a state. Everyone was supposed to meet up at the Central Station at Twelfth Street downtown. I was bringing Bo, and Papa Mose would come with Wheeler. But we were running late. My friend Mary Lee had come up from St. Louis to visit with me and other friends. We got to talking and Bo was making last-minute preparations and we knew we were not going to make it downtown. I could see that far enough ahead to tell Papa Mose that we would meet at the train stop at the Englewood Station at Sixty-third and Woodlawn. The *City of New Orleans* left downtown at seven-fifty in the morning, and it left Woodlawn at 8:01. But this change would make a big difference. We were practically around the corner from the Englewood Station. Barely five minutes away. It might have taken us nearly an hour to make it downtown, even at that time of the morning. So that was our plan, and I busied myself getting the food ready for Bo, while he got himself ready. I had fried some chicken. He liked the dark meat. He was not keen on white meat, which was just fine by me, since it meant I could save a little for myself and Mary Lee. There was also some cake, and some treats he had bought for himself, along with something to drink. He would not be able to use the diner on the train, but he would have everything he needed, plenty of food in a shoe box, the same as I always had when I traveled to the South as a child.

Even with our extra time, we still were running late getting to the train station. The train was already there. It was a diesel-powered coach streamliner, with an observation car that seemed to glow there in the early morning, sitting high up on the elevated platform. I had felt so much tension rushing to get Emmett to the station for a trip I had never wanted him to make in the first place. Oh, we had cut it so close. The time was running so fast, I just wanted to slow everything down a bit, to give myself enough time to say good-bye, to hold on. As we bought Emmett's round-trip ticket, there was a loud blast above us, up on the platform. It was the train's horn sounding off, followed by the conductor announcing, "All aboard."

Emmett started up those steps like nobody's business, carrying his suitcase and his box lunch. I called to him. "Bo," I said. "You didn't kiss me good-bye. How do I know I'll ever see you again?"

He stopped, turned around, and headed back. "Aw, Mama," he said, as if he was thinking I could have come up with something else to say. I felt so silly about it at that time. I mean, why would I say something like that? At least he came back, though, and gave me a kiss. Then he took off his watch and handed it to me. He said he wouldn't need it. So I took off my own watch and put his on my wrist. When I asked him about the ring, he told me he wanted to keep that. He wanted to show it to the boys, and that made me happy that I had given it to him.

With that, he bolted up the steps again. I was not allowed to go with him up those stairs to the platform and the train. So I watched him as long as I could. And I was so happy when he got to the top and turned back to wave at me. I waved at him, and then he disappeared, running down the platform. Papa Mose and Wheeler had just about given up on Emmett, when they heard the commotion at the end of the platform and saw him running, finally, to make the train. And they were all relieved when he did.

As the train left the station, Mary Lee and I made our way out, and I began to feel weak, and stumbled. My heart was racing. So were my thoughts. There are certain things a parent owes a child. One is to prepare a child for his journey to the world outside. As I listened to that train pull out of the station, carrying Emmett on his journey, I reviewed everything, to make sure I hadn't missed anything. I considered every detail of every point I had made. As I wondered whether I had done enough to prepare Emmett for all of this, there was one thing I knew for sure: I had not done enough to prepare myself.

By the time we made the short drive back to my place, I felt like something had been ripped from me. I was missing Emmett already, but Mary Lee was more or less saying "poppycock." She and I were going to join another couple of friends and spend the day doing whatever we wanted to do. It was going to be like a reunion for all of us. That's what was on her mind. But, as I was getting out of the car, I told her that I didn't think I was going to be able to run with her that day. She wasn't just disappointed, she was angry. She said she would have been on her way much earlier had she known that. But then she saw that I wasn't well at all. I got out of the car, made it to the steps of my building, and then I just crumbled. I was nearly crawling up those steps. Well, that certainly got Mary's attention. She took my keys, helped me up to my second-floor apartment. She got me inside, managed to get my shoes off, and then got me into bed with all the rest of my clothes on. Then she left to make the rounds.

I just lay there for the longest time, thinking. I knew the train trip Emmett was making. I knew it from memory. I looked at Emmett's watch on my wrist, listened to it tick. Around two that afternoon, the train would be in Cairo, at the southern tip of Illinois, a state that seems to stretch out at that end, to reach a bit, as if trying to hold on to something just a little while longer. Cairo was the place where everything had to be rearranged before the train crossed into Kentucky. Blacks had to change cars, if they were not already in the Jim Crow car up front. As a child, I remembered all the fumes that would pass through that front car, the Jim Crow car, closest to the engine. I had heard that there were ceiling fans in the other cars, the ones where white folks sat. From Cairo on, Papa Mose, Wheeler, and Emmett would have to stay put. I had told Emmett that he was not supposed to go anywhere on that train. But I knew that Papa Mose would be there to take care of everything.

Within a few hours of Cairo, the train would be in Memphis, and then it would arrive in Winona, Mississippi, at 7:25 that night. That's where Papa Mose and the boys would be met by Maurice Wright, the oldest son of Papa Mose and Aunt Lizzy. He would be there waiting with the family's 1946 Ford for the thirty-mile drive down marked roads and dusty back roads to the Wright home just outside Money.

I just lay there in my bed, overwhelmed, thinking of so many things, and of how quickly so many things had passed. From time to time, I would look at Emmett's watch, knowing it would mark the time for me all the while he was away. Ticking away minutes and moments, counting them, keeping track. I've come to know moments. I've come to cherish them, to live in them, to appreciate them as fully as you possibly can. Moments like snowflakes, unique and precious and fleeting. Moments like heartbeats, full of life and joy and love. I once had a moment with Emmett. It was the moment of a lifetime. It was the moment of decision. And balanced on that moment was the tension of motherhood. Two sides of myself at odds. The part of me that longed to provide everything for my son's happiness, the part of me that desperately needed to protect him even at the cost of his happiness. Strange how, before that, I had thought these two parts of myself were one and the same. What if I had paused at that point for just a moment longer and let the other side of me win, and let Emmett lose? How long would his disappointment have lasted? A moment, maybe? I would have a lifetime to consider all that, one moment at a time.

W hen Emmett crossed over into Mississippi, there surely must have been something familiar to him. Not something he recognized with his eyes, but something he felt deep within his soul. Mississippi had always been a part of his life. It was always present in our little community of Mississippi transplants in Argo. It was in our awareness, always there, even if we were only thinking about why we didn't want to think about it anymore. Even in Argo, even in Chicago, Mississippi was still a place we were desperately trying to escape. Why had my son wanted to go back there so badly? What was this deep longing that he felt? It was like he had been programmed at birth to return to the soil of his ancestors, at this time, in this way, and for a purpose he could not possibly have recognized.

It was a strange time for a black boy from Chicago to go to Mississippi. Especially Emmett. Independent and uncompromising in so many ways, he found himself in a place where these qualities were not tolerated in black boys. Self-assured, confident about a future without limitations, he must have gazed out at the wide-open spaces of the Mississippi Delta in amazement. As he surveyed what seemed like an endless plain, he must have seen the ideal place for a boy with unbounded spirit, completely unaware of the boundaries that had begun to close in on him as soon as he got off that train.

The home of Papa Mose and Aunt Lizzy was one of the largest on the 150-acre plantation. It had four bedrooms. Emmett and Wheeler would double up with Maurice, Robert, and Simeon—Emmett's cousins, Wheeler's uncles. Emmett would share the bed with twelve-year-old Simeon. Wheeler slept in another bedroom with Maurice. Willie Mae's son, Curtis, would share the room with Robert after joining the boys down there a week later. Papa Mose had almost a full acre of land to himself. It was set back about fifty feet from the road, behind the trees—cedar, persimmon, pecan, and cottonwood—and at the edge of the cotton fields. The sounds of the country surrounded you in that place. The killdeer whistling on the wing around the lake across the way, the mockingbird everywhere, singing the song of any other bird it could imitate. And there were the farm animals. Plenty of space on this plot for them. There was a cow. And, even though everybody in the house had chores, no one but Papa Mose could mess with that cow. That was the family's source of milk. On his earlier visit, when he was just a little boy, Emmett was amazed to see the milk come from the cow. After all, he had been friends with the milkman in Argo, who had given him a little bottle of chocolate milk for helping out. He could put away a quart of milk all by himself. All he had ever known was that milk came in a bottle from the milkman, or from the store. There was no way he was going to get chocolate milk from a cow anytime soon. He could never work up a taste for the buttermilk the family served up, even on this trip. It tasted sour to him. Aunt Lizzie told me Bo didn't drink any milk while he was there.

So the cow was only for milk. The meat came from the chickens and hogs. Actually, the family got eggs *and* meat from the chickens. Sunday was the first full day for Bo in Mississippi, and that was the best day for meals at the Wright home. The family would have chicken for breakfast and for supper in the evening. The boys would have to catch the chickens for Aunt Lizzy, who would wring their necks, chop their heads off, soak them in hot water, pluck them, and cook them. Oh, my goodness, Bo had never seen anything like this. He bought our chicken all packaged up. He was just amazed to watch all this activity, but he didn't have any problems at all eating chickens from the yard. That was the best-tasting chicken ever.

The hogs were always slaughtered in November, smoked, and put up to carry the family through the winter. Bo wouldn't get a chance to see that during his summer visit. Mostly, though, except for Sundays, the meals were centered around vegetables. And, oh, the gardens they had. There were two big vegetable gardens. Now, Emmett was used to gardens. Everybody in Argo kept one in the backyard, side yard, back porch; wherever people could drop some seeds into some dirt, they were growing things. But he had not seen anything like these gardens. There was cabbage, turnip greens, mustard greens, carrots, lettuce, string beans, butter beans, sweet potatoes, beets, squash, tomatoes, and bell peppers. There were even two apple trees in one of the gardens. The family had to split half and half with the boss man. Only the apple trees, not the vegetables. The boss, the owner of the land, was a German, Grover Frederick. The family called him Mr. Grover. He once asked Papa Mose to give up one of the vegetable gardens so he could plant more cotton. Papa Mose refused. He had to feed his family.

That wasn't the only time he ever stood his ground with the boss man. In addition to picking cotton and sharing half the apples from his trees, Papa Mose also had to tend Grover Frederick's vegetable garden. He got paid by the hour for this work. He kept a log. Once, only once, Grover Frederick questioned Papa Mose on his time. There is an old story about a cropper who went through his tallies with the plantation boss. The boss always found a way to add and subtract so that everything came out even. What he owed the black man for the cotton he picked somehow was always exactly what the black man owed him for provisions. So the white man didn't pay him a thing after all that hard work. One time, the cropper held back one of his fields and waited for the boss to tell him they were even again before telling him he had some more cotton to add to the total amount. "Why didn't you tell me that in the first place?" the boss said. "Now I gotta go through the whole thing all over again to come out even."

Papa Mose didn't come out even. Papa Mose told Grover Frederick in so many words, these are the hours, this is the time, this is what you owe. Pay up.

Papa Mose was well respected around the area. He had been a minister for years and, even though he had stopped preaching in 1949, everyone, even Aunt Lizzy, still called him "Preacher." But he also earned respect because people knew he was a decent man, an honest man, and he always did what he said he was going to do. When he spoke up, people figured he must have an important reason, and they would listen. So Mr. Grover listened as Papa Mose told him he was keeping his two vegetable gardens. The boss man just let that one be, and Papa Mose kept his gardens. It never came up again. Besides, beyond the gardens, everywhere you looked, there was cotton. Plenty of it for picking and selling. In fact, that first Sunday Bo was down there was a special day of rest, because the next day, Monday, would be the first day of cotton-picking season, and my son was about to find out just how hard life could be on a Mississippi farm toward the end of summer.

It was just useless. I couldn't do anything. I was in and out of bed most of the time. Gene and I were still planning to take the vacation I had worked out. We would go to Detroit, pick up one of my cousins, and take her to Omaha, where all of her family lived. But things were not working out according to plan. Not at all. I wasn't doing anything to get ready. I missed Bo. I wasn't worried so much; I just felt some big part of me had been taken away. I was so used to having Bo around. Ever since I had moved back from Detroit, we had always been together, except for those weekends he'd spent in Argo. But that was different from this, and this was *so* much different from that. It wasn't even easy to call him down in Mississippi. Papa Mose and Aunt Lizzy didn't have a telephone. I'd have to call a neighbor and set it all up for them to be in place for my call. In so many ways, this was the most distance Bo and I had ever had between us. Oh, my, I missed him so. Gene checked on me all the time. He was good about that. Whenever I was ready to go, he'd be ready, too. And Mama had even come over to help me get the apartment in order before the trip, but it was useless. I couldn't feed myself. I couldn't cook, couldn't even walk to the kitchen.

I had asked my aunt Mag downstairs if she would give me at least one meal a day. I figured, if she was able to do that, I'd be able to make it. She laughed when I asked her, and said I just wanted some of her food. Well, that was partly true. She was the best cook and everybody would find excuses to come by for something to eat. I mean, she would have company all the time, because people constantly were coming by to see what they could devour. To look at her, you could tell that nobody enjoyed her cooking, or I should say, eating her cooking, as much as she did. And Aunt Mag's heart was as full and as generous as the rest of her. Every day around noon, she would come up those steps with this wonderful plate of food.

Now, climbing those steps was not an easy thing for Aunt Mag to do. She let me know it, too, through the huffing and puffing. "You're going to have to get out of this bed," she said. "I am too heavy to be climbing these steps every day."

Carrying that huge plate of food didn't make it any easier, either. I explained that I would get up when I could, but that I just couldn't walk. My legs didn't seem to be working. She wanted to know what was hurting me. Well, nothing was hurting me. My legs just didn't seem to function. She couldn't see any reason why I was in bed. And I wasn't doing a very good job of explaining, either. So we would go on like that. She would stay until I got through eating, take my plate, and go home. Sometimes she and Uncle Mack might come up in the evening to check me out, to see if I was getting up yet. Through it all, she was faithful in bringing me that food, and a good helping of that "get up" talk.

First call came first thing in the morning at the Wright house. There was no second call. Papa Mose would walk through the rooms in the morning, and he'd call out "Boys" three times, once for each of his sons. He wasn't coming back through there. Maurice, Robert, and Simeon didn't know what would have happened if they hadn't jumped out of bed right away and gotten ready to hit the field. They never tested it, so they never found out.

Late August in a Mississippi cotton field is very hot and very humid. Mid-nineties hot. Sticky hot. Horseflies like vultures. No shade. No place to hide. Whole families would take to the fields under these conditions. The Wrights had to pick thirty acres, the largest field of any of the families' on Grover Frederick's place. But every family had large areas to pick. Even the youngest children might be pressed into duty, usually toting water out to the workers whenever they'd see someone wave a handkerchief in the air. All of Papa Mose's boys picked with nine-foot sacks. Smaller children might carry only six-foot bags. The normal run of a day was about three sacks of cotton. Bo went out to the field on Monday, the first day of cotton-picking season. The bolls had started to open up like flowers. It was a good year for cotton and there was a large crop. The Wright boys showed Bo how to pull the cotton out of the boll. There's a certain way you have to catch it, get right into the boll and pull it clean out so that you don't get all the debris mixed in with it. Nobody wanted dirty cotton. But you also had to take care that you didn't stick your hand on the ends of the bud. And if you didn't get it just right, it *would* stick you. Your cuticles would get cracked, and then you might get sores and those bolls would hit those sores every time. That was not a good feeling. So the boys showed Bo how to do it, but they didn't take very long with him. They had to get to it.

Now, you'd have to walk a row, carrying that nine-foot sack on your back, bending over to pick about ten bolls in succession—very quickly, but very carefully—before you could pause long enough to put the cotton in your bag. A handful at a time. Each boll was less than one ounce, so it took quite a few handfuls to fill up those bags. There were people who could pick four hundred pounds a day at the rate of two dollars for every hundred pounds. Some boys might earn up to twenty-five dollars in a week, which they mostly had to turn over to their parents. Many families worked it out so that kids got to keep all the pay from their Monday pickings. That wasn't all that generous. After they had hung out until late on Sunday—their only day off—most boys weren't worth much on Mondays. So they basically got to keep what they were worth: not much. Even though you picked a sack at a time and got paid by the pound, success was measured by the bale, roughly twelve hundred pounds or so.

Papa Mose surveyed his field and looked forward to about thirty bales that season. That was a lot of cotton. Bo picked about twenty-five pounds that first day before he decided he had just about had enough. Twenty-five pounds meant an automatic whipping for any of the Wright boys. But this was Bo's vacation and Papa Mose gave him a break. That sun was just too hot for Bo, even with a hat on.

Bo continued to work, he just did it around the house, where Aunt Lizzy was in need of some help. There was a full house and a lot of washing to do. She had a new Maytag wringer washing machine. We had the same type at home, so Bo knew how to operate Aunt Lizzy's machine. Since he wasn't going to go out to the field that much anymore, he would get up in the morning and do the wash before breakfast. Then after breakfast, he'd help clean up before going into the vegetable garden with Aunt Lizzy to pick the vegetables for afternoon dinner and supper later on.

The workdays were shorter at the beginning of the picking season. Usually, the pickers would weigh up around noon, eat dinner, and work again until four in the afternoon, when they'd weigh up again. At this time of the year, though, there wasn't much point in working the whole afternoon. So the boys could have a little fun. The Wright boys had been so excited to hear that their Chicago relatives were coming. And, just as in Chicago, Emmett was the center of attention. They enjoyed hearing Emmett tell his stories. Oh, that boy was a talker. One of his Argo cousins said that if a dog could talk, Emmett would have a conversation with it. Emmett would tell his cousins about all the attractions of Chicago. There was the Lincoln Park Zoo and Bushman, the largest gorilla in captivity until he had died a few years before. There was Riverview Amusement Park with all the great rides and the roller coaster. Oh, Chicago had the biggest this and the best that, to hear Emmett tell it, and he told it in a way that made everyone believe it. His cousins were awestruck.

He pulled all kinds of things out of his little bag of tricks. Of course, there was his father's ring. He even let Simeon wear it a couple of days. But it kept getting in Simmy's way when he had to work in the fields, or when the boys played ball. There were plenty of other things for Emmett to share as well. The music the boys heard most was the country music on the radio coming out of Memphis. Emmett shared a new tune. He tried to sing a little Bo Diddley. But there was no mistaking *my* Bo for the other Bo. Couldn't sing a lick. But everybody got the idea. They had never heard of Frankenstein before Emmett showed them the comic book he had brought along, and talked about the movies he had seen. I can only imagine how those boys felt. The first Frankenstein movie was made when I was a little girl. Of course, I wasn't able to go to the show to see it. But the kids would tell me all about it. And, oh, that just made it come alive to me. When I would go to bed at night, I would see Frankenstein hanging on the nail that was holding the coat on my wall. Every time the house would creak, it would scare me to tears: I thought Frankenstein was coming after me. I really became ill from fear. So, I could imagine what effect that might have on kids who had never heard the stories before. Especially out in the country, on a dark Mississippi night, when you might be able to see every star in the sky, but nothing else around you.

Emmett's cousins were impressed. But his cousins had a few things to show him, too. In the afternoons when they weren't working the fields, the boys could swim in the lake directly across from the house. Or maybe down a little way through the woods, down to the Tallahatchie River. Of course, there were places where the boys wouldn't dare swim without beating the water first, making enough commotion to drive the water moccasins out onto the banks on the other side. Someone had once told the boys that water moccasins don't bite in the water. But they never took chances. That's because somebody else said they once saw a man jump out of the water with a bunch of snakes hanging off him. Frankenstein might have been in the movies, but the snakes were right there in the Delta.

The fishing was everything Papa Mose had boasted about in his Chicago visit. Bass and bream and catfish. The boys had a special way they liked to fish. A very creative way. They didn't have rods and reels and lines. They'd place their bait in a glass jar, leave it in the water. The next day, they'd come back and find the jar bobbing up and down, all around. You see, that fish couldn't back out. Now, the trick was that to catch the fish, the boys would have to catch the jar.

In the early evening, Maurice might take the wheel of Papa Mose's car. He loved that car, loved it so much he stripped the gears starting out in too much of a hurry, and had to take a little while now to pop it into second, to get it going. But they'd all pile into that car Maurice loved so much, maybe bring along the Crawford boys, Roosevelt and John, neighbors within hollering distance, and they'd drive the turning roads, the ones that go through the fields. Or they'd drive three miles uptown, into Money, for refreshments after a light supper. The nearby plantation store closed early and didn't sell all the things the boys liked to buy anyway: bubble gum and ice cream and gingerbread cakes and soda pop. All those things they could find at Bryant's Grocery and Meat Market in Money. All those things and a checker game that seemed to go on forever on the store's lazy front porch.

Most nights, everybody would wind up around the family's Philco radio, listening to the popular shows. Robert was in charge of the dial. That meant everybody had to listen to what Robert liked best. But that was okay. They all liked it, too, *The Lone Ranger, Gangbusters, Mr. and Mrs.*

North, Gunsmoke. There was no television. But, somehow, that didn't seem to matter. Emmett's heart was beating to the rhythm of his adventure, his nose was filled with the earthy excitement of this new world, his eyes glowed with the reflection of a billion nighttime stars that could be seen only from this spot. His thoughts already were on the next summer, when he could come back. In a curious kind of way, a way that only makes sense to a fourteen-year-old boy, a boy away from home, away from the familiar world of a doting mother and grandmother, to that boy, Mississippi represented freedom.

I couldn't take it anymore. I just couldn't take it. I needed to talk to Bo. I needed to talk to Aunt Lizzy. Late in the week, I placed a call to one of the neighbors so that I could get Emmett and Aunt Lizzy on that phone. They both sounded so good to me, and they were surprised to hear from me, since they thought I was away on my vacation. Emmett said he was having a good time; Aunt Lizzy said he was a good boy. A fine boy. She told me about all the chores that he did and what a blessing he was to her, and I thought about all the things he had done for me. She told me I should be proud to have such a son. And, of course, I was. They had written letters and sent them to me, thinking I would get them when I got back from Omaha. Emmett told me he needed more money. More money? He had left home loaded, as far as I was concerned. I'd given him about twenty-five dollars and I knew Gene had slipped him something, knowing Gene. But Emmett said he was broke. What in the world was he doing with his money down there, in the middle of nowhere? He told me he was treating other kids to sweets when they'd go to the store in Money. He also asked me to get his bike fixed while he was down there. But he said he'd explained all that to me in the letter.

I had called because I wanted to know how things were going, but mostly to find out that Emmett missed me as much as I missed him, that he wanted to come home as much as I wanted him to. He said he'd be home in a week. Now I knew. He was having too good a time to even think about returning sooner than that.

The mail from Mississippi came Saturday, August 27. Three-cent stamp. Two letters. One envelope. I think they were trying to save on postage. It had been a whole week since I had put Bo on that train and taken to my bed. I was so delighted to read the letters, sort of a summary of what Aunt Lizzy had told me on the phone. What a nice, obedient young man I had raised. Then there was Bo's letter. He asked me to please have his bike fixed by the time he got home. Oh, he really needed that bike. Get his bike fixed and he would pay me back when he got back the following week. On Sunday, Aunt Lizzy wanted to take Bo to visit Uncle Crosby, who had lived next door to us in Argo years ago, before returning to Mississippi.

Mama came by later that day. She also had gotten letters and was so pleased. But she was not happy with me at all. She scolded me for not getting ready to go on my trip. I hadn't packed. She lost patience with me. She wanted me to get out of that bed, get myself ready to go. Then she began to lay out my suitcase. She wanted me to be all ready to get out of there on Monday. I just looked at her and thought, Gee, she doesn't understand. I hadn't been able to get ready to go or to do anything else, for that matter. In fact, I had a meeting of my club, Les Petite Femmes, at my place that night and didn't have a clue about how I was going to get ready for that. I was doubtful that I was going to take the trip. In a way, I think I was really stalling, thinking Bo might still come home in time to go with Gene and me. I was hoping. But I didn't tell her. Maybe I didn't need to. Maybe she really did understand. Maybe she just wanted to help me work through it.

No one had ever seen Emmett cry before. So they didn't know exactly what to do, except keep their eyes on the dark road ahead. It was Saturday night. They were coming back from Greenwood, about twelve miles away from home. Curtis Jones, Willie Mae's son, had just arrived from Chicago earlier that day, and Maurice, Wheeler, and Emmett decided to take him for a ride. Curtis knew people over in Greenwood. But they had stayed too long and had to hurry to get back before Papa Mose laid into them. Maurice had been doing just fine on one of those dusty roads. He had been making good time. But then something had happened. Something had jumped out in front of the car too fast for Maurice to react. Everyone in the car had felt that bump. It was a dog. They had looked around, but couldn't see anything anymore. The dog must have run off somewhere. Maybe it was okay. Maybe it was dying. Emmett had pleaded with Maurice to stop the car, to check on the dog. But Maurice wouldn't do that. He couldn't, really. Maurice knew things Bo didn't know about life on the back roads of Mississippi in the dead of night. If somebody had run across them out there on that road on that night—four black boys in the dark— well, their lives might not have been worth as much as that dog's. Emmett didn't understand that. There was a lot he didn't understand about this place. He had gone out on a limb to rescue a cat back in Argo. The least they could do now was to stop by the side of a Mississippi road to check on a dog. But they couldn't do that and he began to cry. Nobody knew what to say. There wasn't much they could say, really. Nothing that would have made a difference. So Emmett just sat there crying. And everybody else was quiet.

Somehow, hosting our club meeting helped me to break out of my mood. There were about twelve of my friends there that night, including Ollie. And we talked and played cards and, for a moment, at least, I was able to distract myself. We were up so late, talking and laughing, that around one-thirty or two, I wound up making an early breakfast for everyone. I told them all about the letters I had gotten earlier from Aunt Lizzy and Bo and, oh, I just bragged about that son of mine. I told them that instead of making the trip to Detroit and Omaha, I really wanted to go down to Mississippi and bring my son back home.

Then I said something without really knowing why I said it. "If Bo could get his feet on Chicago soil, he would be one happy kid."

Everything stopped for a heartbeat. Complete silence. Why had I said that? Then, just like that, everything started up again. The talking, the laughing, everything.

After everyone left, I tried to get a little sleep before getting up a little later to go to church. The telephone rang like an alarm. I looked at the clock. It was nine-thirty.

I picked up the receiver. "Hello," I said. But there was nothing. "Hello," I said again. Dead silence.

Finally the voice came through. "This is Willie Mae." Curtis had called his mother. "I don't know how to tell you. Bo."

"Bo, what?" I sat up with a jerk, my mind racing. "Willie Mae, what about Bo?"

"Some men came and got him last night."

CHAPTER 13

That call. Early Sunday morning. August 28, 1955. I can never forget that call. As it turns out, Willie Mae had raised more questions than she answered. And I had so many questions to ask. What men? Why had they come? Where had they taken my boy? What was being done about it? But Willie Mae had been much too distraught. She just started crying and wound up hanging up the phone before she could explain anything more than what she had already said. Emmett was missing. Missing in Mississippi. Oh, my God. Oh, dear Lord, no. Please, no. Don't let this be happening. The thing I had feared most, the thing that had made me take so long to even think about letting Bo make the trip, the thing that had kept me immobilized all week long, the most horrible thing any mother could possibly imagine was becoming a reality. I tried to fight back all the things, all the visions that were playing out in my mind. I tried to deny all the things that I could not allow myself to accept. The only thing I really knew was what Willie Mae had said, and that didn't have to mean anything more than that. Somebody had taken Bo out of the house. Maybe that's all there was to it. But she was crying so. What about her son, Curtis? And Hallie's son, Wheeler? Where were they? Were they all right? And the other boys, Aunt Lizzy's sons. What had happened? Aunt Lizzy, Uncle Moses. What was going on?

The thoughts were making my head spin, and my heart ache, and my breathing erratic. But I knew I needed to keep under control. I had to steady myself. I had to think. I had to call Mama, to tell her what Willie Mae had told me. I knew she'd have the same reaction I had. I knew my mother. I knew she felt like she was Bo's mother. And, as I talked to Mama, I realized I was right. She had always been so strong, the rock for all of us. But I could feel her cracking as she told me, or ordered me, or begged me, to come to her. Right then. I called Gene, told him, and he insisted on taking me to Mama's. He wasn't that far away, so okay, fine, I could wait for him. I probably didn't need to drive anyway, not while I was in that frame of mind. So, yes, I would wait. Sit tight. But I couldn't sit still. I needed to do something. I started making my bed. And finally I stopped, I caught myself. Why on earth was I doing *that*? Of all things. What was I thinking? Was I just trying to keep busy, keep from thinking? Lose myself in work to stop me from losing my mind? I couldn't take it. I couldn't stand it. I couldn't stay there. Not one minute longer. I got ready to leave, picked up Emmett's watch, wound it, put it on.

Gene drove up just as I was backing out of the garage. He parked and slid behind the wheel of my car. We had barely made it a mile when I had to take over. I just had to do it. I knew I was in no condition to drive. But he was barely going the speed limit, stopping for all the lights, all the stop signs, and I didn't care about any of that. I drove through everything as fast as I could go. I needed to get to Mama's place. I needed to get to Mama. And I needed to do it fast. The way I figured it, if I had been stopped by the police that morning, then I just would have had a police escort.

We weren't much good for each other at first, Mama and I. She usually knew exactly what to do at exactly the right time to do it. But she was in such an emotional state. Not hysterical. Just very, very quiet, like she had closed down. It wasn't long before Willie Mae came to Mama's, too. She was crying, I was crying, and she told a little more of the story, as much as she knew at the time. They said Emmett had whistled at a white woman.

We knew we had to do something. We kept trying to contact Papa Mose, but we couldn't get through to him. Somehow, we decided to call the newspapers. A number of reporters came out. I had hoped Mama would know what to say, but she couldn't say anything that would have helped. I stepped forward, I talked to the reporters, I told them the only thing I knew at the time. My son, Emmett Till, had been taken away in the middle of the night by white men who came into my Uncle Moses Wright's home in Money, Mississippi.

I kept hoping that Mama would chime in, but she didn't. She couldn't. I still was holding out hope for a lot of things at that point. I hoped that Emmett was all right. I hoped that whoever had taken him had let him go, or that he had escaped. I hoped that he was only hiding out somewhere, and that was the only reason why we hadn't heard from him. But, as I looked at Mama, I began to realize that she already had given up hope. Mama had lived in Mississippi. Mama knew what it meant when white men came in the middle of the night in Mississippi. She had a look that made me pause. It was the look of someone who could see something she didn't want to see. It was as if she had already accepted something I couldn't possibly accept. The unspeakable. She remained silent, and I had to shake it all off. At that moment, I had nothing left but my hope. To let that go would mean I would have nothing.

At some point, Papa Spearman, Mama's husband, suggested we call on his nephew Rayfield Mooty. That wound up being a good call. Papa Henry Spearman was a security guard at Inland Steel Container Company. Rayfield also worked with Inland Steel, and was a union official, head of the Steelworkers Local. He had good contacts. He knew all the big labor people, the steelworkers, the autoworkers, the sleeping-car porters, everybody. Because of his organizing work, he also knew politicians and civil rights people. But I had not gotten along very well with Rayfield. There was some distance between us. He was strictly business. He never seemed to be a man who showed much feeling and I had always found him to be especially cool toward me. In fact, I had always thought he was rather mean. He had taken sides with his uncle against my mother and he knew I did not appreciate that. So, when he came by that Sunday morning, our first moments together were a little tense. I tried to explain things to him, but I couldn't stop crying, blowing my nose. Everything was starting to come out of me by this time.

He was impatient. "Why don't you stop all this," he said. "Just blow your nose, stop crying, and tell me what's going on here."

"They took Emmett," I managed to say. "Some men, in the middle of the night. They took Emmett away."

"Emmett? What, who's Emmett?"

"My son," I said. "Emmett Till. Mr. Mooty, that's Bobo."

He stiffened and his face lost all expression. He said nothing, nothing at all. He just lowered his head, turned, and walked out of the room. I was puzzled by that. Rayfield Mooty was a man of action, and I couldn't believe this would be his only action. To just leave us there like that. It seemed like he was away for about ten minutes. Then he came back. He looked like he was ready to cry. And it made me start crying again. Everybody knew Bo. Everybody knew him by that name. Everybody loved him. He had even touched Rayfield Mooty, who was now prepared to do everything he could to help.

Mama's house was filling up with people, friends, relatives. Ollie was there. She was always there for me. She brought food and unconditional love. Ollie also worked for Inland Steel Container Company. Her supervisor was the head of industrial relations. The company had offices in the

South, in New Orleans and Memphis, and she would see if there was anything her company might do to help.

We still hadn't reached Papa Mose. So we decided to try Mama's
brother, Uncle Crosby. Thank God, we were able to talk to him. Aunt
Lizzy was there. The other boys were okay and Uncle Crosby was going
to the sheriff with Papa Mose.

At the Argo Temple Church of God in Christ, the church Emmett
loved so much, the church his grandmother helped to found, the entire
congregation stood and prayed. The members prayed for Emmett, they
prayed for Mama and me. They prayed that their prayers had come in
time.

Monday morning, August 29, Rayfield arranged for me to meet with the
Chicago branch of the NAACP, and we were referred immediately to
William Henry Huff. He was the Chicago NAACP counsel, the chairman
of the organization's Legal Redress Committee. He was a dignified man
who spoke with assurance and experience. He had been involved in a
number of Mississippi matters, getting people out of that state and out of
danger. He promised to put his resources to work and immediately
reached out to political contacts. Between Rayfield Mooty and William
Henry Huff, things started happening. The story was appearing in the
Chicago papers and I was getting calls. Lots of calls. The local officials
began pressing Mississippi authorities to find Emmett right away. Before I
knew it, Chicago Mayor Richard J. Daley was involved. And so was Illinois Governor William Stratton, and William Dawson, the powerful
South Side congressman. Ollie's boss at Inland Steel Container Company
had talked to the president of the company, who was sympathetic. He contacted the company's Southern offices to put their planes on the lookout
as they flew over the area in Mississippi where Emmett had been taken.

I wanted to catch the first thing smoking to Mississippi, but Uncle
Crosby convinced me to wait in Chicago while he took care of things
down there. That day, Monday, in Mississippi, Leflore County Sheriff
George Smith announced that he had arrested two white men on kidnapping charges. Roy Bryant, owner of Bryant's Grocery and Meat Market,
and his half-brother, J. W. "Big" Milam, who managed cotton pickers for
local plantations. They admitted they had taken Emmett, but said they let
him go. The sheriff was still looking for Roy Bryant's wife, Carolyn, and
one other person in connection with the abduction.

They said they had let Emmett go. Maybe there was some reason to
hope that my boy was okay and would be taken care of. Wheeler had been
put on an early-morning train at Duck Hill, headed back to Chicago, back

home to safety. In Argo, his brother William imagined Emmett making it through the woods after Bryant and Milam let him go. He imagined how Emmett could make it to the home of some nice colored people who would make sure he got back to his own home. If anybody could, he knew, Emmett could. I tried to imagine the same thing.

Things were so hectic at Mama's with people coming in and out constantly, with so many calls coming in. We had to add a second line. That way we'd have one for making calls, one for taking them. We couldn't let a moment pass without trying to reach out to somebody, anybody, who might help us. And we couldn't take a chance that the most important call we could ever receive would get blocked by a busy signal. I spent so much of my time by the phone, taking down notes, dates, times, details. I had to keep busy. I had to keep my mind off my greatest fear, I had to focus on everything around me, all the bustling, all the energy. And the absolute joy when he walked through the door.

Wheeler was just sixteen, a boy becoming a man. He felt things that a boy cannot always express, and a man might try to suppress. I could see that as he began to approach me as I sat there by the phone. He loved Bo. Bo loved Wheeler. I loved Wheeler, too. But I knew there was someone else in the room with even stronger feelings at that moment. I knew that the way only a mother can know such things. That's why I stopped Wheeler in his tracks and said what I had to say: "Go hug your mother."

Somewhere around seven in the evening on Wednesday, August 20, after supper, while Papa Mose was in church, Maurice, Wheeler, Bo, Simeon, Roosevelt Crawford, and Roosevelt's niece Ruthie Crawford climbed into Papa Mose's car and drove uptown. Although there were a couple of hundred people who lived around Money, the town itself was little more than one street. Not a street, really. It was more like what somebody once called "a wide place in the road." A whistle-stop. It was a lazy place. Easy to feel relaxed there. In Money, there were no obvious signs of trouble. None of the things Emmett had been warned about. No "White" or "Colored" drinking fountains, no segregated sections on buses, nobody stepping off sidewalks to let white folks pass. But that was because there were no drinking fountains, there were no buses, there were no sidewalks. Money wasn't like other places in the Jim Crow South. It was worse. It was much worse. The dangers were hidden, and a lot more treacherous. It was a place with racial attitudes as rigid as an oak tree in the dead of winter. People who lived in the area knew where the lines were, knew not to cross them. They didn't need signs to direct them. They didn't need help abiding by the rules, just like they didn't need help breathing. It was in them. A basic life function. For outsiders, things weren't that obvious.

The kids had driven uptown to buy a few treats at Bryant's Grocery and Meat Market. Roy Bryant, the owner, was out of town. His twenty-one-year-old wife, Carolyn, was working the counter alone that evening. On the porch, there was a checker game going on, as usual, with about four or five people involved. And there were other black kids hanging around. One at a time, the boys bought things in the store. Wheeler was inside when Emmett walked in. Wheeler left and then Simeon came to stand in the door to look out for Emmett, who paid two cents for some bubble gum and left. For Emmett, this little transaction was not all that different from any other one he might have had at Miss Haynes's store back in Argo.

A few versions of what happened next would emerge and even more variations on the story would develop over time. The kids were standing around on the porch outside the store when they saw Carolyn Bryant come out and head for a car. They kept laughing and talking as Emmett told everyone what he had bought. That's when the whistle was heard. Maurice would later tell reporters that Emmett made a whistling sound when he got stuck on a word. "Bubble gum" would have given him as much trouble in Money as "Moon Pie" once had given him in Argo. Roosevelt said he thought Emmett was whistling at a bold checker move on the porch. The others felt he was doing it as a joke, intentionally, to be playful. Whatever it was, it stopped all the laughter. Right away, someone said that Carolyn Bryant was going to the car for her gun. Everyone scrambled. The kids jumped into the Ford. But Maurice didn't get it moving quickly enough. Maybe it was that nasty gear problem again. And that made everyone nervous. They yelled at him to get going. Finally, he did, and they started on their way back home down Darfield Road. About two miles out of Money, a mile away from home, the kids saw something that upset them all over again. There were headlights in the rearview mirror. It had gotten darker by now and the headlights behind them were getting brighter, moving closer. Everybody knew right away what that meant. Somebody was coming after them. Maurice had a choice to make. But he knew he couldn't outrun another car in that forty-six Ford on that dusty road on that night. Without really thinking about it, he pulled over and jumped out of the car. Everybody jumped out after him. Everybody except Simeon. He just slid down on the seat to hide. The others ran through the cotton field hoping they could disappear into the darkness. Hoping whoever was following them wouldn't find Simmy in the car. As the kids ran, the bolls—the ones that hadn't opened yet—kept hitting against their legs.

Cotton may be soft, but those bolls were kind of hard when they hadn't opened yet. They hurt and they made Wheeler and Bo trip and fall to the ground. The boys looked back over their shoulders and watched. They saw the car continue moving down the road, right on past the Ford, where Simmy finally felt it was safe enough to sit up again.

Everyone agreed not to tell Papa Mose about the incident. Everyone agreed that would be the best thing. Nothing had happened. They didn't get in trouble, and Bo didn't want to make trouble for himself by making Papa Mose angry with him. By the end of the week, the kids weren't really thinking about that incident anymore. They even drove into Money again and nothing more was said about any of it. Then there was the night they drove to Greenwood and got back home very late. Saturday night.

That's when it happened. Somewhere around two in the morning, there was a violent beating on the front door of the Wright home, and a call from the front porch.

"Preacher. This is Mr. Bryant."

Papa Mose opened the door, stepped out onto the screened-in porch. He saw two white men standing there, Roy Bryant and his half-brother, J. W. "Big" Milam, towering over Papa Mose at six-foot-two and 235 pounds, balding. Papa Mose thought he could make out one other man standing outside, a black man, it seemed, who held his head down, probably so he couldn't be recognized. It was hard to get a good look at any of them, really. There was that flashlight beam that kept jumping in his face. Papa Mose had no trouble at all making out what else the big man was holding in his other hand. A Colt .45 automatic. Papa Mose knew what it meant when white men came banging on the door at two in the morning carrying guns. This was a terrorist assault, a surprise attack, and these men were moving quickly to take control of the Wright house. Bryant and Milam moved inside. It almost seemed darker inside than it was outside. The lights had gone out. So Milam flashed his light in Papa Mose's face. He asked Papa Mose if he had a couple of boys from Chicago there. Papa Mose said he did. The men told him that was why they were there. They had come for the boy from Chicago, the one who had done the talking.

Wheeler awakened. He was in the first bedroom with Maurice. He could hear the loud, angry voices coming from the front of the house. He heard "boys from Chicago." He was horrified. The two men were yelling and cursing by this time, and they were demanding to see Emmett. Aunt Lizzy came out and pleaded with the men to do no harm to the boy.

"Get back in bed," Milam told her. "I want to hear them springs squeak."

Papa Mose still didn't understand what they wanted from Emmett. But even though the boys had kept their promise not to tell, he had heard some mumblings about some talk a few days before in Money that didn't seem to amount to much. If Emmett had done something wrong, Papa Mose could take care of it, even whip him, if need be. Milam kept waving the gun around, the threat heavy in his hand. He demanded that Papa Mose take them to Emmett right then. All the yelling and cursing kept things off balance. Papa Mose had a shotgun in the house, but he didn't know how far this was going to go, who that was outside, how many more there might be, what they might be prepared to do. He thought he might still be able to reason with these men. And he would keep trying.

Bryant and Milam moved through that house like animals stalking their prey. There was nothing, it seemed, that could stop them. Wheeler knew from the tone of the voices that this was about as bad as it could get. He looked toward Maurice, who was still asleep. He said a prayer. He asked to be delivered from that place, from that night of terror. Then they came in. Milam flashed the light at Wheeler, and held it for a moment. They moved on, the only light in the house that night coming from the flashlight that jumped and jerked from one spot to the next. The second room was the one Robert was sharing with Curtis. The men kept going, finally down to the room where Emmett and Simeon were. Simmy looked up at them and they told him to go back to sleep. He lay back, but didn't close his eyes. They woke Emmett, lying next to Simmy, and told him to put on his clothes and his shoes. He was still half-asleep. Every time he tried to speak, he forgot the rule. He forgot to say "sir." Milam became violent, yelling and cursing and threatening Emmett about it.

Emmett wanted to put on his socks. They told him he didn't need socks. But he stopped. He said he didn't wear shoes without socks. To everyone, he seemed so calm about it all, standing there at the center of all the tension. He couldn't possibly have known what it meant for white men to come for you late in the night in Mississippi. Maybe it was the sleep in his eyes. Maybe he thought something would be done about this. Someone would call the police, the sheriff. Somebody. That's what I had told him to do. Call somebody when there's trouble. Don't try to handle it yourself. Maybe he thought he'd be able to talk his way out of it, as he had done with so many other problems he had encountered. Maybe it was his faith that, somehow, he would be okay. Whatever it was, he didn't seem nervous. And everyone remembered that. Aunt Lizzy, though, was frantic. She even offered to pay Bryant and Milam if they would leave Emmett. But they hadn't come for money. They continued to march Emmett out. Uncle Moses asked where they were taking him. Nowhere, they said, if he was not the right one.

Outside, they brought Emmett over to the truck, a green Chevy pickup with a white top. Uncle Moses could hear a voice from inside that truck. It was a light voice, a female voice.

"Yeah," came the voice from the shadows of that cab. "That's the one."

Emmett was put in the back of the truck, where it looked like that third man was holding him down. Then Milam turned back to Uncle Moses and warned him not to tell anyone. "Preacher," he added, "do you know any of us?"

"No, sir," he said. He had never seen these men before.

Milam had a second question. "How old are you?"

"Sixty-four."

"Well, if you know any of us tomorrow, you won't live to be sixty-five."

The men got in, drove down the path to the road out front, with the truck lights off.

Papa Mose stood there, frozen in place, watching the road. Aunt Lizzy ran right away to the home of some white neighbors nearby. The woman of the house was concerned about Aunt Lizzy. But the man of the house was slow to respond. That seemed to explain everything. Papa Mose and Aunt Lizzy figured the man must have known something about what had happened, even before it ever happened. There was panic. The whole family could be threatened and people nearby could be a part of that threat. Finally, Aunt Lizzy couldn't take it anymore. She insisted that Papa Mose drive her to her brother, Uncle Crosby, and he did. Back at their home, there was no more sleep for Simeon or Wheeler. Simeon waited up, watching every car that drove past their house, believing his cousin Emmett would be brought back. Wheeler waited up, too. He got dressed just in case the men did come back. Looking for him. He would be ready, if need be, to run out the back and into the woods.

"There is going to be hell to pay in Mississippi." Dr. T.R.M. Howard had stopped to talk to reporters, including the *Chicago Defender,* at Chicago's Midway Airport before he went back to his Mississippi home in Mound Bayou, not far from Money. It was Wednesday, August 31, and Dr. Howard, a wealthy and influential black leader in Mississippi, had been in Chicago as part of his organizing work. He stopped long enough to talk to reporters about Emmett's disappearance and about other things, horrible things. It was these other things that caused so much concern about what might be happening to Emmett. Two murders had been committed not long before Emmett's disappearance, and not far from Money. There were things going on in Mississippi I had never known about. In Belzoni, the Reverend George Lee had been organizing blacks to register to vote before he was shot to death that May. In August, only two weeks before Emmett left for Mississippi, Lamar Smith was shot to death on the courthouse lawn in Brookhaven—in broad daylight—for his political organizing work. Dr. Howard spoke about threats that had been received by his organization, threats that "blood would pave the streets of Mississippi before Negroes would be permitted to vote." Blood for something so basic, something we had come to take for granted in Chicago. This was the environment Emmett had walked into when he stepped off that train. It wasn't clear why Dr. Howard was tying Emmett's disappearance to these murders, but it was chilling to hear it.

Just the day before, Tuesday, August 30, I had to leave Mama's place to take money out of the bank to send to Uncle Crosby. I also had to talk to Attorney Huff, who gave me an update on his progress and showed me the telegrams he had sent to Illinois Governor Stratton and to Mississippi Governor Hugh White. Things were moving, people were on top of this, two men were in jail, and we were being heard. At least that.

When I got back to Mama's, there was something strange in the air. It was—I don't know, a sense of relief. It struck me as so odd. Then Mama told me that Bo was coming home. He was on his way home. That was incredible to me. How could that be? My heart wanted to believe, but my head wouldn't accept it. I had just met with Attorney Huff. He had shown me the telegrams. Surely he would have known if something, if anything, had developed. Especially this. I called the police and got referred to the criminal investigations branch and to people handling missing persons investigations. No one knew anything about it. It was a hoax. We had to accept that. And that was going to be only the first phase in discovering the full measure of human cruelty. It was like torture to us.

I talked with Uncle Crosby again and he advised me to wait another day before trying to make a trip to Mississippi. He was working with the sheriff. I started making plans to catch the *City of New Orleans,* the same train I had rushed Emmett to catch only eleven days earlier. Now it was Wednesday and there was a warning of "blood in the streets" and so much uncertainty. I don't remember sleeping at all between Sunday and Wednesday. There was no way I could rest until I knew where my baby was, until I knew what was happening to him, until I knew what had happened to him.

Then the reporter called.

I answered, but he didn't want to talk to me. He wanted the telephone number of someone else he could talk to. He really didn't have to say any more than that, but I gave him Ollie's number. And when I saw her later standing in the door, I had confirmation. Her being there said most of it.

Her look said the rest. It felt like an arrow had been shot through my heart as she approached me and Mama and pulled us aside, took our hands, told us what she really didn't have to tell us anymore. Emmett was dead. They had pulled his body from the Tallahatchie River, about twelve miles from Money. A fisherman, a white teenager, had found him there. His body was weighted down by a heavy gin fan tied around his neck with barbed wire. Mama broke down. I started taking notes. I had to get everything down. I had to get everything right. All the details. I was the one who was going to have to explain to people. Oh, God, how would I be able to do that? Please, tell me how? What was I supposed to do now? A moment from now? All I could do right then was write it down. It was like making up my bed all over again. Trying not to let it take me. Writing, keeping busy, would keep it from me. Over the weeks and months to come, I would try to keep busy, to keep it from me. But there really was no way to keep it from me. It kept hitting and hitting in waves. The reality was overwhelming. I began to cry. Oh, my poor sweet baby. Gone. What had they done to him? How was I going to live without my baby? I looked at Mama, and she was in even worse condition than I was. I moved over to try to comfort her. Other people started doing the same thing. And then I began to feel something, like a transfer of strength. It was coming from her to me. I was afraid at that moment of what might be happening, that I might draw too much from her. Oh, God, I couldn't lose Mama. I moved back and I told everybody else to move back, to give her room, to give her air. People cried and prayed.

Slowly, I began to pull myself together. I saw that Mama was in no condition to talk to anyone. It was going to fall on me. I could see it all around me: Everyone in the place was falling apart emotionally. The whole house was crying. I had to do what Mama had always been there to do for me. I had to take charge.

In a way, life had been too easy for me. Always someone there to look out for me, to take care of the hard things. Even Bo. I could see that things were about to get very hard, more difficult than they had ever been. Impossible, really. And the only one I could count on would be myself.

It seemed to take forever to get to a day that seemed to come much too quickly. Friday, September 2. I had to face it and I wondered if I would have the strength to get through it. I prayed for the strength, and I prayed for the courage. I prayed hard. I was staying with my mother. There were so many people around during those days while we waited for word on Bo. It must have been the sheer energy from all of them that sustained me in that time. I seemed to be drawing on it, as I had begun to draw on my mother's strength when we got the news about Bo. I can't recall whether I was eating much, although I must have been eating something. I really can't recall whether I was up early on this particular day or whether I had even slept at all the night before, but I do remember selecting the dress I would wear to Central Station at Twelfth Street. It was one of only a couple I had there at Mama's. It was a black sleeveless dress with beige figures, little geometric animals, one I had bought for myself. Mama was still making some of my dresses, even then. Black seemed like the appropriate thing to wear. I liked that dress, but I'm not sure whether Bo liked it. He never really told me whether he liked the clothes I wore. He wasn't big on compliments, but he certainly made it clear when he disapproved.

"Don't you want to go back and put something else on," he might say when I made the wrong choice. So, I thought about that—about making the right choice—and how I didn't want to disappoint Bo, how much I wanted to look nice for him. But then I stopped, and took a long, hard look at myself in the bathroom mirror, as if things were becoming clear to me for the first time. Not quite a week before, I had told my girlfriends how much I wanted to bring Emmett home from Mississippi. But not like this. He would arrive on this day on the *City of New Orleans,* the same train that two weeks before had carried him away from me down to Mississippi for the adventure of a lifetime, one he had so looked forward to having. But I wasn't greeting Emmett at the station; I wasn't welcoming him home from his Mississippi vacation. I was going to claim his body.

Emmett's murderers had tied a gin fan around his neck to weigh him down, figuring he never would be found. But they figured wrong. They had failed to weigh his feet down. Papa Mose was summoned to the scene by Tallahatchie County Sheriff H. C. Strider, a gruff, overweight, sweaty redneck. Leflore County Deputy Sheriff John Ed Cothran also was there. Several Delta counties would be involved before it was all said and done. Strider told Mose to look over the body sprawled out in the little boat there at the riverbank and tell him if that was the boy from Chicago. The body was facedown, and had to be turned over so Papa Mose could get a good look. From what I understand, Papa Mose saw nothing he could recognize until he came upon the one thing he thought he could. It was the ring, Louis Till's ring, the one I had given Emmett just before he left for Mississippi. Papa Mose thought he recognized it because Emmett was so proud of it, he had been showing it off to everyone. And he had let Simeon wear it, so they would need Simmy's help in making sure that was the ring, and that would tell them for sure that the body was Emmett's.

Papa Mose gazed down at the body. He never flinched in the face of this painful duty. Papa Mose knew the code. He and every other black person in the Delta knew it and lived by it. Never show emotions. You couldn't show joy. That would be suppressed. You couldn't show anger. That would mean defiance. You couldn't show sorrow. That would mean weakness. I guess as far as Southern whites were concerned, blacks had no feelings.

So Mose, looking down at Emmett, said very simply that he believed this, indeed, was his grandnephew, the one he had promised to look after and get home to Chicago safely. And Papa Mose dammed up his feelings, as he was so used to doing, holding back until later, until he couldn't hold back any longer.

Once the identity was confirmed, a black undertaker would be called in to handle things. Strider turned to walk back to his car with one last order, one last indignity: Get that body in the ground immediately.

Papa Mose was bound to oblige. The body was picked up by a local undertaker in Greenwood and preparations were being made to carry out

Sheriff Strider's command. Now, Curtis Jones, Emmett's cousin from Chicago, was down there since Saturday and saw how things were unfolding. He knew something about the way things worked in Mississippi, and he knew a lot about me. He knew how I would feel and how I would express my feelings, no matter who was around. He knew above all that I would not want Emmett buried in Mississippi. But they were racing against time. Preparations were under way. The grave was being dug. Papa Mose was considering the eulogy. What followed was a frantic relay of calls, from Curtis to Willie Mae, to my apartment, where my aunt Mamie got the message and told us.

"They're getting ready to bury Bo's body."

"No," I insisted. "I want the body here. I'll bury Bo."

We contacted Uncle Crosby and he promised to take care of everything, vowing to get Emmett's body back to Chicago if he had to pack it in ice and drive it back in his truck. He would work out the arrangements on that end, to put everything on hold. That gave me time to put things together in Chicago. Aunt Mamie suggested that we call A. A. Rayner, one of the biggest and most highly respected black funeral directors in Chicago. Mr. Rayner agreed to handle everything and told me he would call me back as soon as he figured it all out. He did call me back, to let me know that getting the body back was going to cost thirty-three hundred dollars. Oh, God. That was devastating. I wasn't even making four thousand a year. But I didn't have to think about it more than a second, really.

"Mr. Rayner," I said, "if I live, I will pay you. And if I don't live, somebody else will pay you."

Mr. Rayner accepted my assurances and then contacted people in Mississippi to have the body transferred from the Greenwood undertaker to one in Tutwiler, who made the arrangements for the shipment. Uncle Crosby made sure the body was placed on the train Thursday night with him for the long, sorrowful ride back to Chicago.

They were not going to bury my boy in Mississippi. He would be coming home. Finally, Bo would be coming home.

By the time we reached the train station at Twelfth Street early that Friday morning, there already was a huge crowd. The local papers had been carrying the story. So had the radio and television stations. *I Love Lucy* was interrupted with a news bulletin when they found Emmett's body. I wound up getting hate mail for that. It seemed to me that there were about a thousand people there in the train yard when we arrived. This was the first place so many black people saw when they stepped off the *City of New Or-*

leans from the South. This was their first glimpse of a new life, a new beginning. I only wish it had been such a joyful arrival for Emmett. There were so many people in such a small place, there was hardly room to move. I'm not sure what people expected. I didn't know what to expect myself.

I had to be brought up in a wheelchair. I was too weak and just couldn't stand up at the moment the train pulled in. But I was quite alert. I was aware of everything, *everything* that was going on. Even with that large crowd of people milling about, if a tiny mouse had peeked his head up, I would have noticed that, too. My father was there with me, and Gene Mobley, Rayfield Mooty, a few cousins. Bishop Louis Henry Ford and Bishop Isaiah Roberts were also there. And, of course, Uncle Crosby. Mama didn't come. She couldn't, but I had to.

Somewhere, Mr. Rayner was handling the details to accept the body and have it taken to his funeral home. Somehow, I was able to get the message out. To make sure he knew that I was going to be there, too. He knew why. We'd talked about it.

It had been something of a misunderstanding. Or, better said, Mr. Rayner had understood something I could not be made to understand. They were not planning to open the box to examine Emmett's body. The box would have to be buried intact, as it was being shipped. Oh, that could not be. I *wanted* that box opened. I insisted.

"Oh, Mrs. Bradley," Mr. Rayner had said, "we can't open that box."

Can't open it? "What do you mean?" I had asked.

He was very patient with me. He set it all out for me. It was being sent locked up with the seal of the State of Mississippi, which couldn't be broken. Promises had been made just to get the body out of Mississippi. "Mrs. Bradley," he explained, "I had to sign papers, the undertaker had to sign papers, your relatives had to sign papers."

I was not bending. That box had to come open. I mean, I didn't even know what we would find inside. There could have been bricks, mud, someone else's body. I would spend the rest of my life not knowing. Besides, I had heard so many things over the past couple of days, I had to see for myself what they had done to my son.

"Oh yes," I said, "I'm going to look at the body."

"But the box cannot be opened," he kept insisting.

Well, I couldn't take it anymore because I was really spent. Finally, I told him that if I had to take a hammer and open that box myself, it was going to be opened.

"You see, I didn't sign any papers," I said, "and I *dare* them to sue *me*. Let them come to Chicago and sue me." I just couldn't imagine a judge anywhere finding me guilty of viewing the body of my baby.

Finally, they unloaded the box that my son was in and placed it on a flatbed truck, a simple train-yard wagon that seemed so much like a caisson. I just lost it.

I looked up, saw that box, and I just screamed, "Oh, God. Oh, God. My only boy."

And I kept screaming, as the cameras kept flashing, in one long explosive moment that would be captured for the morning editions. It was as if everything was pouring out all at once. All the tension that had built up since Emmett left for Mississippi, all the fear that had grown in me since we had gotten word of his abduction, all the sorrow of a thousand people in that train yard, began bursting out of me. The box was huge. It seemed to me to be nearly half the size of the train car itself. Such a big box for such an itty-bitty boy. I couldn't imagine how they ever thought they could have buried that huge box intact. It would have taken up nearly three grave sites. That's the way it looked to me. At that moment, there was nothing in the world but that giant crate. Death to me was so much larger than life. It was overpowering. It was terrifying. It seemed that, if I could scream loudly enough, I could get that feeling out of me.

I reached out, as if to embrace the box moving toward us. I stood and I nearly fainted. Gene was right there, standing over me, helping me. So many other people rushed to my aid. People were trying to comfort me and keep the large crowd back to give me air. I wanted to pray.

The ministers helped me to my knees. "Lord, take my soul," I began, "show me what you want me to do, and make me able to do it."

Everything, everyone, the entire yard, fell silent.

It was the most terrible odor. We began to smell it about two blocks from the funeral home as we drove toward it. At first, I thought about the stockyards, where they slaughtered hogs and cattle. There was always a lingering odor from the stockyards that you could pick up even fifteen blocks away. This was much worse. This was overpowering. And the closer we got, the worse it got. It was the smell of death and it was everywhere. It seemed to cut a pathway right to the top of my skull. I will never forget that smell. It was Emmett.

At Rayner's funeral parlor, they were shooting off bombs so people wouldn't become ill from the smell.

As it turns out, the reason the box was so big was that there was a lot of packing inside. Locked and sealed. Somebody in the state of Mississippi wanted to make sure we didn't see what was inside that box. I had defied the people of Mississippi. I had insisted on taking one last look at the body of my son. What could they charge me with, anyway? Breaking and entering? I didn't care. The Mississippi officials were the ones with something to hide. What on earth was it? What was I about to witness? The rumors had grown and grown as they had made their way to me. Unspeakable, indescribable horrors. And now I was about to find out for myself.

Mr. Rayner directed me to the waiting room to give them more time to make the final preparations. I didn't think I could bear to wait any longer. I had already built up the strength and the determination to see this through. The longer I waited, the more difficult this was going to be for me. This emotional roller coaster was making my head ache and my stomach turn. But Mr. Rayner was doing his very best to help me. He was concerned about me and I knew that. He really didn't think I should look at Emmett like this. But I had kept insisting.

He just looked at me and he kind of shook his head. "You know, if you're *that* determined, I will get the body ready and let you view it."

They went back into a special room where they prepare bodies. I had no idea what kind of preparation was still needed. I certainly wasn't expecting to see a body dressed for funeral visitation. But then, I really wasn't sure what to expect. I took out the pictures I had brought with me. The ones we had taken at Christmas. I brought them to help me, as if I needed help to identify my son. When I was finally escorted to the other room, I found out why they had needed time. I found out why he had cautioned me so. I paused at the door. This was the moment I had insisted on and now I had to brace myself for the impact of it. There were two parts of me at war at that moment. One part that kept wanting to fight, one part that wanted to surrender. I dreaded the horror of recognizing my son, but I had to identify his body. While I wanted so much for my son to be alive, I desperately needed to make it all certain, to make it all final. I had to face the terrible reality: Emmett was dead, and the body was right there, just a few steps away, waiting for me.

To steady me, Gennie held one of my arms and my father held the other. I could see across the room on the table that the body had been hosed off. We moved in, closer to the table, and I couldn't take my eyes off it. I could see that there were these little white beady things all around. Of course, I had to ask about those things first. I wanted to know everything, every detail. Mr. Rayner explained that it was what the body had been packed in. Lime, I think he said, to make the body deteriorate faster, to make it even harder to identify. I guess those officials down in Mississippi felt a need to do that just in case the seal and lock didn't scare me off. Well, I was glad Mr. Rayner had gotten that white stuff off him. This was going to be hard enough as it was. When we reached the table, I told Gennie and Daddy to release me. I needed to stand alone. They didn't have to worry. I wasn't going to faint. I wouldn't let myself. I had a job to do.

At a glance, the body didn't even appear human. I remember thinking it looked like something from outer space, something you might see at one of those Saturday matinees. Or maybe that's only what I wanted to think so that I wouldn't have to admit that this was my son. Suddenly, as I stood there gazing down at the body, something came over me. It was like an electric shock. In fact, it was terror. I felt it through every bone in my body. I stiffened. The horror of this moment was as overwhelming as the smell had been before all this, and the sight of the box before that. And it was not because this body looked like something out of a horror movie. It was because I was getting closer to discovering, to confirming, that this body had once been my son. And I couldn't let anyone in the room know what I was feeling right then. I didn't want them to think even for a moment that I was not up to this. They might try to take this moment away from me. I couldn't let them stop me from going through with it. If I was stopped one more time, I don't know what I would have done. I'm not sure that I could have worked myself back up to it again. I had to steel myself like a forensic doctor. I had a job to do.

Quickly, I diverted my eyes down to his feet. That's how I needed to handle it. I decided that I would examine him from his feet to his head. I knew I could do it that way. I needed to do it that way. I just could not bear to examine his face. Not yet. I would have to get my courage back, let it build up again slowly as I moved back up his body to his head. So, I looked at the feet first and they were so familiar, and then the ankles. I knew those ankles because I had been so glad to see that they weren't like mine. I'd always thought of my ankles as rather fat in the back. Bo's were always shaped so nicely, so slender, so well tapered. I had always admired the shape of his little ankles, and I had always wished mine were like his. I examined them very carefully, the way a mother might check a newborn. Just to be sure. I *felt* them, so cold, so hard now. In the back where the tendon runs to the heel, I could put my finger in there and feel the indentation. Not like mine, round without that dip. Then I came on up the leg. How strong his legs had become. I recalled how worried I had been when he was stricken with polio. There weren't many people who had come back from polio the way Bo had, but he had been such a strong little boy, so full of life, so determined. And his knees. I paused at the knees. They weren't knobby knees, they were nice, fat, round knees and rather flat.

And they were *my* knees. I would know them anywhere. How the doctors had frightened me so, when Bo was born, and his knee had gotten tangled in the umbilical cord and had become so swollen. We showed them how wrong they had been. We proved that Bo didn't have to be institutionalized. Oh, how we showed them. He wasn't crippled for life, not crippled at all, the way they said he would be. I moved on up a little farther and stopped at his private area. Just long enough, really, to see that everything was still there. That had been one of the terrible rumors that had spread—that Emmett had been castrated. I was relieved for a moment before I caught myself. Oh, my God. Emmett would have a *fit* if he knew I was looking at him like this. He was *so* independent, especially after the polio. He always wanted to show me he could take care of himself. He even told me that he could bathe himself. At six. So young. He didn't need me to do that for him anymore. How hard that was for me, to suffer in silence, to give him his space and pray to God that he was getting everything clean. As I continued moving on up, I wondered how I had become so intimately aware of all the details of Emmett's body. It was as if I had just always known them, the way only a mother can know her child—by heart. In a way, it was better that I had let go earlier, let so much emotion pour out of me at the train yard, because I couldn't allow myself to get emotional, to lose control now. I had to get through this. There would be no second chance to get through this. I noticed that none of Emmett's body was scarred. It was bloated, the skin was loose, but there were no scars, no signs of violence anywhere. Until I got to his chin.

When I got to his chin, I saw his tongue resting there. It was huge. I never imagined that a human tongue could be that big. Maybe it was the effect of the water, since he had been in the river for several days, or maybe the heat. But as I gazed at the tongue, I couldn't help but think that it had been choked out of his mouth. I forced myself to move on, to keep going one small section at a time, as if taking this gruesome task in small doses could somehow make it less excruciating. I had started out doing this item analysis with the kind of detachment a forensic doctor might have, but I wasn't a forensic doctor. I was Emmett's mother and I was overwhelmed by a mother's anguish as I continued tracking Emmett through his night of torture. Step by step, as methodically as his killers had mutilated my baby, I was putting him back together again, but only to identify the body.

From the chin I moved up to his right cheek. There was an eyeball hanging down, resting on that cheek. It looked like it was still attached by the optic nerve, but it was just suspended there. I don't know how I could keep it together enough to do this, but I do recall looking closely enough to see the color of the eye. It was that light hazel brown everyone always thought was so pretty. Right away, I looked to the other eye. But it wasn't there. It seemed like someone had taken a nut picker and plucked that one out. Then I glanced down at the mouth, quickly now, because I needed to keep moving. Emmett always had the most beautiful teeth. Even as a little baby, his teeth were *very* unusual. And I recall how much I had hoped that his permanent set would be as perfect as his baby teeth were. Oh, and they were. Just beautiful. So I looked at his teeth, because I knew I could recognize them. Dear God, there were only two now, but they were definitely his. I looked at the bridge of his nose, at the point right between his eyebrows. It had been chopped, maybe with a meat cleaver. It looked as if someone had tenderized his nose.

From there, I went to one of his ears. Even though I could recognize the color of the only eye he had left, and even though those two teeth looked like his teeth, and his ankles and his knees were all so familiar, I felt that I still needed something, something more to let me know this was my child. With everything I had seen and touched, I still could not identify this body as Emmett. Or maybe I was just not ready to admit that this was my baby. So, I looked for his ear. I believe it was his right ear. The little curled-up part at the tip of the lobe. And that's when I found out that the right ear had been cut almost in half. The part I was looking for wasn't even there anymore. And I don't know what had happened to that part of his ear, but it wasn't on the back part of his skull. I did check. And when I did, I saw that someone—Milam or Bryant—had taken a hatchet and had cut through the top of his head, from ear to ear. The back of his head was loose from the front part of his face. As I moved around, I saw a bullet hole slightly back from the temple area. And I could see light shining through the hole on the other side, where the bullet left the skull. That's when I had to stop. My momentum was broken. With all the grisly things I had just witnessed in silence, it was that one bullet hole that finally caused me to speak.

"Did they have to *shoot* him?" I mean, he had to be dead by then.

It was Emmett. I knew it the way a mother knows every part of herself. Especially her child. I had examined every part of him I had ever loved, every part of him I had nurtured and helped to mend. I looked deeply at that entire body for something, anything that would help me find my son. Finally, I found him. And lost him.

I looked at Gene. He nodded. "That's Bobo," he said. "I know that haircut."

Everyone, it seemed, would recognize the parts of him they knew best. That's when it occurred to me that I had never used the photos I had

Smith family portrait, 1932. Young Mamie Elizabeth Carthan, age ten, is in the first row, far left; Mother Alma is in the second row, second from left, next to family patriarch George Smith and second wife, Clara.

Mamie Carthan Till with
baby Emmett Louis Till
in 1941.

Louis Till (seated), Emmett's
father, in Italy during World War II,
wearing the ring that would later
be given to Emmett.

"Mama and I would always make sure Emmett looked good." Emmett at two years old, in 1943.

Bo (Emmett) at three years old, in 1944.

Emmett at five years old, Easter Sunday 1946. "My mother gave Emmett this suit, and he put it on and told his grandmother he looked better than he ever looked in his life. Even then, he had a sense of what was important and how to make the important people around him happy."

Bo at thirteen, Christmas 1954. "There was something very special about this Christmas and I went all out."

Dear Mom.

How is everybody? I hope you and jean is fine. I hope you'll had a nice trip. I am having a fine time will be home next week. please have my motor bike fixed for me (pay you back). If I get any mail put it up for me. I am going to see uncle crosby Saturday. everybody here is fine and having a good time tell aunt alma hello. (out of money) your son Bobo

"Emmett wrote me from Mississippi, and I received the letter on August 27, 1955. I was so delighted to read it."

September 2, 1955, Emmett's body arrives from Mississippi. Mamie is overcome with emotion. Holding her up are, from left, Bishop Isaiah Roberts, Gene
Mobley, and Bishop Lewis Ford. (© Bettmann/Corbis)

Mamie at Emmett's funeral, wearing his watch. Taped to the casket are photos
from their last Christmas together. (*Chicago Sun-Times* Archives)

The Saturday morning service for Emmett was held at the Roberts Temple Church of God in Christ. The church was packed with at least two thousand people, with another five thousand waiting to get in. (*Chicago Sun-Times* Archives)

What tens of thousands of people filing past Emmett saw made men sob and women cry out. (*Chicago Tribune* Archive Photo)

As many as one hundred thousand people passed Emmett's glass-enclosed casket over the course of four days. (© *Chicago Defender*)

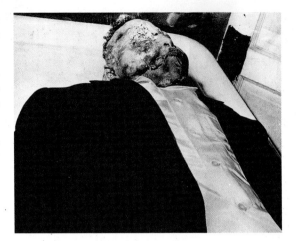

"People had to face my son and realize just how twisted, how distorted, how terrifying race hatred could be. People had to consider all of that as they viewed Emmett's body. The whole nation had to bear witness to this."
(© *Chicago Defender*)

Emmett was buried on September 6, 1955, at Burr Oak Cemetery. That same day, the Tallahatchie grand jury indicted Roy Bryant and J. W. Milam for his murder. (© *Chicago Defender* Digital Images)

Emmett's death certificate, signed by Sheriff H. C. Strider on September 1, 1955, and certified September 16, 1955, before the trial.

Mamie with her father and mother before leaving for the trial in Mississippi. (© *Chicago Defender* Digital Images)

On Wednesday, August 20, 1955, the kids went uptown to buy a few treats at Bryant's Grocery and Meat Market in Money. Emmett paid two cents for some bubble gum and left. For Emmett, the transaction was not at all different from any other he might have had at Miss Haynes's store back in Argo. (© *Chicago Defender* Digital Images)

Moses Wright's house, where Emmett was abducted early on Sunday morning, August 28, 1955. (© *Chicago Defender* Digital Images)

Roy Bryant and J. W. Milam in court with J. W. Kellum, one of their five attorneys. There were only five lawyers practicing in Sumner, Mississippi, at the time, and all of them volunteered to serve on the defense team. (© *Chicago Defender* Digital Images)

Mamie, left, sitting at the black press table at the trial. Counterclockwise, next to Mamie: Simeon Booker, *Jet* magazine; Alex Wilson, *Tri-State Defender;* Jimmy Hicks, *Baltimore Afro-American;* unidentified man; Clotye Murdock, *Ebony;* Congressman Charles Diggs of Detroit; and Ruby Hurley, NAACP Southeastern regional secretary. (© Ernest Withers/courtesy Panopticon Gallery, Waltham, MA, U.S.)

Ring marked as evidence identified at the murder trial as that taken from the body of Emmett Till. (AP/Wide World Photos)

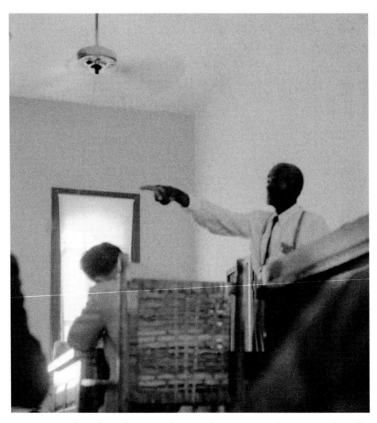

Moses Wright identifying Milam and Bryant as the men who abducted Emmett from his home. Through his testimony, Papa Mose crossed a line that no one could remember a black man ever crossing in Mississippi. (© Bettmann/Corbis)

"Surprise witness" Willie Reed escorted into court by Ruby Hurley and Dr. T.R.M. Howard. (© Ernest Withers/courtesy Panopticon Gallery, Waltham, MA, U.S.)

Courtroom drawing for *Life* magazine showing the first witness called by the defense, Carolyn Bryant, as she demonstrates for defense counsel C. Sidney Carlton how Emmett allegedly grabbed her in the store. (© Franklin McMahon)

Mother Mobley delivering a speech at the dedication of the Civil Rights Memorial, November 1989. In the background, from left: Chris McNair (father of Denise McNair, Birmingham church bombing victim); Dr. Carolyn Goodman (mother of Andrew Goodman, killed, with James Chaney and Michael Schwerner, by the Ku Klux Klan); and Ethel Kennedy. (Courtesy Southern Poverty Law Center)

"I ran my fingers over the letters of Emmett's name and felt the cool water. I began to weep. As I stood there shaking, I missed Emmett even more." (Courtesy Southern Poverty Law Center)

The Emmett Till Road dedication in Chicago, July 25, 1991. Front row, from left: Rosa Parks, Mayor Richard M. Daley, Mamie Till-Mobley, Gene Mobley. Young Ariel Mitchell, in the foreground, was also a member of the Emmett Till Players. (*Chicago Tribune*/Photo by John Irvine)

Mamie speaks at a rally in Kokomo, Mississippi, on July 8, 2000, about the pain of losing a son, after a young man, Raynard Johnson, seventeen years old, had died the previous month in a hanging ruled a suicide. At left is Raynard's mother, Maria Johnson. (AP/Wide World Photos)

Mother Mobley at the grave of her son, Emmett Louis Till, Memorial Day weekend, 2002. (Robert A. Davis, *Chicago Sun-Times* Digital Images)

"I never wanted Emmett to be a martyr. I only wanted him to be a good son." (Robert A. Davis, *Chicago Sun-Times*)

brought with me. In the end, we didn't need that kind of aid. In the end, we already had committed Emmett to memory.

I couldn't help but think of the first time I laid eyes on my son. I remembered my reaction to his distorted little face and how I made him cry. I would have given anything to take that back. That face seemed so adorable now. My first look and my last look at Emmett would forever be fused in my mind.

I kept looking at him on the table and I thought about what it must have been like for him that night. I studied every detail of what those monsters had done to destroy his beautiful young life. I thought about how afraid he must have been, how at some point that early Sunday morning, he must have known he was going to die. I thought about how all alone he must have felt, and I found myself hoping only that he died quickly. I can never forget what I saw on that table and how I felt. And I can never forget the complete devastation I experienced when I realized for the first time something that would haunt me for such a long time to come. At some point during his ordeal, in the last moments of his precious little life, Emmett must have cried out. Two names. "God" and "Mama." And no one answered the call.

CHAPTER 15

They say there's something to be gained from all of life's experiences. Even the bad ones. Especially those, really. But if the bad experience is a great loss, then what do we gain? Could it possibly be enough to make up for what is sacrificed? If it is, if things somehow balance out between what we lose and what we gain, if we only break even, then are we truly better off?

There were so many questions during that time, so few answers. The coming months would be such an intense period of hard questions, and answers that never seemed to come easily. I had prayed for answers and when they didn't come right away, I became angry. I became angry with God. Why had this happened to Emmett? Why had this happened to me? What could I have possibly done to deserve this? What would become of me as a result of this?

So much was running through my head at the moment I stood there, at the funeral home, with A. A. Rayner and Daddy and Gene and Rayfield all standing by as I gazed at the mutilated body that once had been my son. At that moment I didn't see what I possibly could gain from the worst experience anyone could ever have. All I felt was the vast emptiness left by what had been lost.

Into that void, I kept pouring so much pain and, oh, yes, so much anger. Emmett hadn't done anything to deserve what was done to him. What was done to him by those men was savage, it was barbaric, and I wasn't about to let them get away with it. Roy Bryant and J. W. Milam had been arrested on Monday and charged with kidnapping. On Thursday, the day Uncle Crosby boarded the train in Mississippi to bring Emmett's body home to Chicago, on that day the charges against Bryant and Milam were upgraded to murder. Even so, before they'd stand trial, they'd have to be indicted by a grand jury in Tallahatchie County. The place where Emmett's body was found. Just miles from the place where I was born.

I told Mr. Rayner I wanted an open-casket funeral. He looked at Emmett, that horribly distorted face, then he looked back at me. He asked me if I was sure. I was never more certain of anything. He asked me if I wanted him to retouch Emmett. If I wanted him to work on my son. If I wanted to make him more presentable.

I shook my head. "No," I said. That was the way I wanted him presented. "Let the world see what I've seen."

I didn't really know what was motivating me, what was making me do what I was doing during this period. It was something I can't explain, something working through me, something that would cause me to say things that would only become clear to me the instant I'd speak them. But the feeling was strong in me and I understood clearly what had to be done. It would be important for people to look at what had happened on a late Mississippi night when nobody was looking, to consider what might happen again if we didn't look out. This would not be like so many other lynching cases, the hundreds, the thousands of cases where families would be forced to walk away and quietly bury their dead and their grief and their humiliation. I was not going quietly. Oh, no, I was not about to do that. I knew that I could talk for the rest of my life about what had happened to my baby, I could explain it in great detail, I could describe what I saw laid out there on that slab at A. A. Rayner's, one piece, one inch, one body part, at a time. I could do all of that and people still would not get the full impact. They would not be able to visualize what had happened, unless they were allowed to see the results of what had happened. They had to see what I had seen. The whole nation had to bear witness to this.

So I wanted to make it as real and as visible to people as I could possibly make it. I knew that if they walked by that casket, if people opened the pages of *Jet* magazine and the *Chicago Defender,* if other people could see it with their *own* eyes, then together we might find a way to express what we had seen. It was important to do that, I thought, to help people recognize the horrible problems we were facing in the South.

We gave Mr. Rayner the clothes to be used to dress Emmett. The black suit I had bought him for Christmas. The last Christmas. The best ever. I also gave him three photographs from that holiday. The shot of Emmett in his fine clothes, the shirt and the tie and the hat we had given him. The picture of Emmett leaning on his television set. And, of course, the one of Emmett and me together. Our mother-and-son portrait. I wanted the photographs displayed inside the open casket. People needed to see those, too. People needed to see what was taken away from me, what was taken from us all.

Aunt Lizzy wasted no time getting out of Mississippi. She had come to Chicago and would be there at Bo's funeral. The boys would join her. But Simeon would stay behind for a while with Uncle Moses. They were waiting behind, the two of them, to serve as witnesses against Bryant and Milam. It was a very dangerous thing to do. Aunt Lizzy would write to Uncle Moses every day, begging him to leave. But he wanted to stay, to see it through. He didn't always stay at his house, though, and Simmy stayed with other relatives. That was a good thing. One night after Bo's abduction, cars and trucks had pulled into Papa Mose's lane. White men had come knocking on his door, looking for him. He had slept in his car, parked next to the cemetery behind his church, where nobody could see him. There were other restless nights. Nights when he slept in the house with his shotgun under the bed. Times when he might stay in the wooded area outside his home. One morning he came back to the house and found his screen door cut and the house ransacked, beds turned. He knew then that his days in Mississippi were numbered.

It was late on Friday when I viewed the body. Mr. Rayner did some work to prepare Emmett for the public viewing, despite our talk. Looking back on it now, I think he probably felt he had to do something. Emmett was in such bad shape when we got him back. Monstrous condition. But Mr. Rayner did what he could. That tongue had been removed, I guess, and put somewhere. The mouth was closed now. And you could see on the side of Emmett's head that some coarse thread had been used to sew the pieces back together. I guess it was like that on the right side, too, but I couldn't see that. The eye that had been dangling, that was removed, too, and the eyelid closed, like on the other side, where no eye was left. I told Mr. Rayner he had done a beautiful job. You would have to have seen Emmett when I first saw him to really appreciate what Mr. Rayner had done before my son's body was viewed by the public and photographed for public view. What I had seen was so much worse than what other people would ever see. And what tens of thousands of people filing past Emmett would see would make men cry and women cry out.

It was reported that about five thousand people viewed Emmett's body that night, and they would go on until the chapel closed at two in the morning. As I left close to midnight, it seemed that there were hundreds still waiting to get in. I stopped to speak to them. I felt that I had to. As I had looked upon my son, something was shaken in me. Things had changed for me in an instant. They would never be the same again. I understood now that this was about more than Emmett. There was nothing more we could do for my baby, but we could honor him by recognizing that we all had a responsibility to work together for a common good. I could not accept that my son had died in vain. *We* could not accept that. So I told the crowd that the first step we had to take was to make sure the people who lynched my son were convicted, to make sure the world would be safe for so many other young boys. I was so caught up in my own passion and the energy of the crowd at that moment that I never paused to consider just how difficult that first step was going to be.

The service was scheduled to start at eleven. We were all pleased that Uncle Crosby's son, Crosby Junior, was able to fly in. "Sonny" had been training as a paratrooper at Ft. Campbell down in Kentucky and was only one jump away from qualifying when he got the news about Bo. His commander got the Red Cross involved and arrangements were made right away to fly him in for the funeral. He would ride over in the family car with Gene, Mama, Papa Spearman, and me. As I had done every morning since Emmett had left for Mississippi, I wound his watch and put it on my wrist. I could practically feel it ticking. My pulse timed to Emmett's. Two hearts in sync. For all time.

The Saturday-morning service would be held at Roberts Temple Church of God in Christ. That was Mama's first church in Chicago. It was the mother of all the Churches of God in Christ in Illinois. It had been the place Mama had been sent when she first moved to Argo from Mississippi. So I thought Bishop Roberts, pastor of that church, would preach the funeral. But Mama said he would serve as the host pastor and her new minister, Bishop Ford, of the St. Paul Church of God in Christ, would preach the funeral.

When we arrived at the church, it was packed, at least a couple of thousand people inside, a capacity crowd, with at least another five thousand outside, unable to get in. They were lined up around the block, four deep at some points, just to be able to walk through the church for the viewing. Loudspeakers were set up so that people outside could hear. We decided to postpone the burial until Tuesday, just to let everyone have a chance to see Emmett. So many people wanted to do that. At least they felt they could do that.

One report showed that more than twenty-five thousand people would view Emmett's body that afternoon and evening. As many as one hundred thousand people would file past Emmett's glass-enclosed casket during the four days he lay there. Emmett's Argo friends were there. His Chicago friends, too. They would serve as pallbearers. There were so many people there. So many people who had known Emmett, so many more people who would come to know him only like this. I was told that every fifth person or so had to be assisted. Nurses were on hand to help. People were falling out, fainting. Extra chairs had been set up outside to assist the people who didn't have the strength to go on. I could only imagine the reaction if they had seen what I had seen. On the one hand, as a mother, I couldn't bear the thought of people being horrified by the sight of my son. He had always been such a fine young boy and I was so very proud of him. But, on the other hand, I felt that the alternative was even worse. After all, we had averted our eyes far too long, turning away from the ugly reality facing us as a nation. I know, because I was guilty of the same thing. But to let that continue, to think that even one more mother, one more mother's son, would have to suffer, well, that was too much for me to bear. People had to face my son and realize just how twisted, how distorted, how terrifying, race hatred could be. How it had menaced my son during his last, tortured hours on earth. How it continued to stalk us all. Which is why people also had to face themselves. They would have to see their own responsibility in pushing for an end to this evil.

People had to consider all of that as they viewed Emmett's body. The impact was like being hit by a sledgehammer. I knew how it had hit me that first time and how it kept slamming into me each time I would see that image of my son, and I would see that image forever. How else could I have made people understand something like that? Even after the viewing, so many people were left speechless. That's not surprising. We're taught to describe things by comparison. Something we've seen, something we've done. But what did we have to compare to Emmett? Nothing in our experience. Nothing in our expression. The English language is so rich with contributions from so many other languages around the world, yet it was inadequate for us when we needed it the most. We just did not have the vocabulary to describe the horror we saw, or the dread we felt in seeing it. Emmett's murderers had devised a form of brutality that not only was beyond measure, it was beyond words.

Bennie Goodwin, Jr., was among the many people who came. He was the son of my pastor, Elder Goodwin, at Argo Temple Church of God in Christ, where I was still a member and where Emmett attended the service on the last Sunday before leaving for Mississippi. Like so many others, Bennie was shocked by what he saw. But he also was comforted in a way no one else might have recognized at that moment. As he gazed down at the casket, he could only wonder what had become of Emmett's body, but he knew what had become of his soul. He remembered his encounter with Emmett on that streetcar from Argo one Sunday night, when they prayed together, when Emmett accepted Jesus Christ, when my son had the most incredible aura. Emmett was so calm, at peace, as he was when those men took him away. That experience on a streetcar from Argo would be the way Bennie would recall Emmett for years to come, and for that memory, for that awareness, he felt truly blessed.

When I stood at the casket, as I looked at Emmett, I felt a deep loneliness, like I was in a vacuum. There were no tears at first. I was reminded of what I had thought when news had reached me that Emmett's body had been found, just after that initial shock, when I realized that I would have to take charge. I had a vision of my heart encased in glass—for protection, for preservation—so that nothing more could harm it. I gazed down at the casket, and there, encased in glass, I saw Emmett, my son, my child, my heart. At that moment, though, I began to feel my own resolve cracking. So much of my energy had been consumed by handling all the little things that had to be handled. All the details, keeping track, taking notes, making arrangements. I had lost myself in all those details. That had been part of my own defense. But, as I stood there, I had no activity to hide behind, no little detail to handle. I was defenseless. Something started coming over me. I couldn't take it. I was overwhelmed. I couldn't get it through my head that this was a human being, let alone my child. I became hysterical, weak, and had to be carried back to my seat. I had no idea how I could make it through. But I knew that I had to do it. And I knew that it wasn't going to get any easier as we prepared for what was ahead.

During the better part of the next two hours, a number of ministers and politicians made that point, and they told people about their responsibility in the struggle we were about to face. The funeral service became sort of a forum. At least in part. How could it not be? Illinois State Senator Marshall Korshak was there to represent Governor Stratton. He called Emmett "a young martyr in a fight for democracy and freedom, in a fight against evil men." One minister, the Reverend Cornelius Adams, urged people to contribute "fighting dollars" to help with the legal efforts, the political organizing. Money would be collected throughout the viewing of Emmett's body, and on into the weeks and months ahead. Bishop Ford questioned how this country could be a world leader if it couldn't lead at home, if it couldn't protect its own citizens and guarantee full equality. He recommended that President Eisenhower and Vice President Richard Nixon work on this Southern problem. Archibald Carey, a former alderman and a former alternate delegate to the United Nations, urged people to allow the legal system a chance to work. He cautioned everyone against trying to seek revenge. "A mob in Chicago," he said, "is no better than a mob in Mississippi."

There came a point, in the middle of everything, as I was listening to the speakers, when I had a sensation. It was something I could just barely make out. Something fluttering somewhere. It seemed like it was in the corner of my eye, at the edge of my awareness. As my eye darted to get a better look and as my head turned to follow, the image seemed to move, just ahead of my glance, always just a flutter ahead like that, always on the borderline between conscious and subconscious. It would happen like that over and over again. And it looked to me like a dove. I wanted to see it fully, but never could. It would always move away just when I'd turn my full attention to it. I came to realize that it was a sign. The dove. A sign of peace. A sign from God.

Finally, with that, I was able to take a deep breath and draw in some measure of peace, place everything in the hands of God. Bishop Ford would reflect that feeling in his sermon, based on Matthew 18:6: "But whoso shall offend one of these little ones which believe in me, it were better for him that a millstone were hanged about his neck and *that* he were drowned in the depth of the sea."

Bishop Ford did a masterful job. I will always be grateful for that.

Things had begun to heat up right away. Even while thousands of people were turning out in Chicago to view Emmett's body, the press coverage of his death was spreading the word and the pictures around the nation, and people everywhere were outraged. The pressure had started coming down on the state of Mississippi even before the funeral service.

I had said that Emmett's death was part of an oppressive pattern in Mississippi, "an everyday occurrence."

My words echoed across the country in waves of headlines. The papers also carried the words of other people who condemned the killing and called on Mississippi for swift justice. Mayor Richard J. Daley had said it was a "brutal, terrible crime" and had sent a telegram to President Eisenhower calling for a federal investigation. Governor Stratton urged Mississippi authorities to investigate thoroughly. And the NAACP, through Executive Secretary Roy Wilkins, issued a blistering attack: "Mississippi has decided to maintain white supremacy by murdering children." The NAACP statement said Emmett's murderers "felt free to lynch him" because of the racist climate that state leaders there had accepted.

These voices were heard in Mississippi, where officials started digging in. What began to take shape was just unbelievable. Even Mississippi officials had to admit that the murder of my son was a horrendous crime. Who couldn't see that? But, when the pressure began to build from outside the state, the people in the state began to build up their defenses. Mississippi's governor—with the ironic name Hugh White—shot back a telegram to the NAACP to argue that Emmett's killing was not a lynching, but a "straight out murder." What a strange debate this was turning out to be. Lynching or murder. As if defining it one way or the other would make a difference. This was the vicious torture/killing of a defenseless boy, by men who had seemed to turn it into a good time. Blood sport. And the only reason Emmett was killed was because he was black. That sure sounded like a lynching to me, and to every other reasonable person who would come to see my son's killing as part of a pattern. But what difference did it make what it was called, anyway? That was my first reaction to what seemed like a silly little diversion. I have learned, though, that it could make a big difference. And, although they would not be called to testify about the matter, Roy Bryant and J. W. Milam ultimately would answer that question for the entire nation.

Meanwhile, some members of the Southern press tried to turn these heartless murderers into heartwarming human-interest stories. They were veterans, we would learn. J. W. Milam was thirty-six and had served in Europe in World War II. Roy Bryant was twenty-four and had served more recently as a paratrooper. Milam had been a lieutenant, given a field commission. He was known as the man who could be counted on to deal with German prisoners, a harsh but efficient interrogator who would not hesitate to use his Colt .45 automatic. He had taken shrapnel and had won a Purple Heart. He was a celebrated killer. The papers also gave a full presentation on the wives and the kids. Each of these men had two sons. And there was a story on the mother of Bryant and Milam, creating public sympathy for her plight. She was proud of her boys, and so troubled by the murder trial.

Meanwhile, one Mississippi newspaper writer called Emmett's funeral a "Congo circus" and Roy Wilkins a "witch doctor." Oh, it was getting ugly, and that was not to be the worst of it in what some began to call a new war between the North and the South, a new Civil War, a war of words that was anything but civil. In a statement that showed just how twisted the logic of racism can be, a spokesman for the segregationist White Citizens Councils took the opportunity to point to the murder of my son as yet another justification for keeping the races apart. Emmett wouldn't have been killed if he hadn't been allowed to have contact with whites.

The war of words, though, was beginning to have consequences. It was beginning to look like it would have an effect on the course of events. Even while we were sitting in the Saturday funeral service, Tallahatchie County Sheriff H. C. Strider, the man who was supposed to enforce the law, the man who was supposed to investigate the murder, the man who was supposed to assist the prosecution, that man was sending a signal, an indication just where this trial was headed. He really wasn't sure, he said, that the body pulled from the river was, in fact, the body of Emmett Till. The body might have been in the water too long to have been Emmett's. Strider said he didn't even know whether the corpse was black or white, because of the deterioration. Never mind what Strider had done, what he *would* do. What he *had* done was to release the body to a black undertaker, which he never would have done if he thought the victim might not be black. What he was *about* to do was to permit the death certificate to be formally certified by the county with information that contradicted everything he said. The death certificate showed Emmett's full name, his race, his age, the names of his parents, the date of death, the cause of death. Sheriff Strider signed the certificate affirming all these things on September 1, two days before he gave his outrageous statement to the press. But I didn't know that at the time. The death certificate wouldn't be delivered to me for some time to come.

Strider didn't stop there. "I'm chasing down some evidence now that looks like the killing might have been planned and plotted by the NAACP," he said. So, instead of doing his duty, chasing down evidence against my son's killers, he was going way beyond the call of duty to make it impossible to convict these murderers in his county. It was reported that he was concerned about the safety of Bryant and Milam sitting in a Charleston jail. He had seen hate mail with Chicago postmarks. He said there were people planning to drive down to Tallahatchie County and take the law into their own hands. A black lynch mob, I guess. He felt there was a need to call out the National Guard to prevent that kind of mob action. Mississippi newspapers picked up on that one, too, and published stories on why local citizens didn't need to panic, stories that only drew more attention to the rumors about bands of angry black men riding down from Chicago to seek revenge. Imagine that. My son was the one who was brutalized and murdered, and I was the one getting hate mail in Chicago, all those threatening letters about my call for justice. But here in the inside-out world of Mississippi, it was the white murderers who felt they were being victimized. It was the white people who needed protection from the angry hordes. Of black folks. Incredible. They were going to turn the murder of my son into a case of self-defense—defense of the Mississippi way of life. The state of Mississippi had become the mirror image of the rest of the world. Normal at a glance, until you realized it was all completely backward.

Even Mississippi's native son William Faulkner had to speak out on how ridiculous things were becoming. He wrote a commentary from Rome that was featured in publications all over the United States, including *The Crisis,* the NAACP's magazine. If people cared at all about holding on to our unique way of life in America, if they valued our special form of democracy, he wrote, they were going to have to think about how this country fit, how it would advance, how it would be judged by the rest of the world, a world where whites were in the minority. "Because if we in America have reached that point in our desperate culture when we must murder children, no matter for what reason or what color, we don't deserve to survive, and probably won't." Faulkner's was a lonely voice warning other white Mississippians about the rumble that was on the way. Nobody in the Delta, it seems, was listening.

So Sheriff Strider was showing his true colors, much of the Southern press seemed to be putting its stamp of approval on it, and we refused to let them get away with it. When we got news of Strider's remarks, Rayfield Mooty shot back right away that his comments smacked of a cover-up. It looked to us like Strider was trying to influence the grand jury, which still hadn't convened to consider the murder indictment. Rayfield Mooty was good at this sort of thing. He was a union man, an organizer. He was a hard-hitting fighter who understood what it took to win. He was a shrewd negotiator who understood the timing of every aspect of bargaining with other tough people. He knew when to talk, when to walk. He knew when no was the best way to yes. He also knew all the people he needed to call on, in doing what he did so well. Not just the labor people, the civil rights people, and the politicians, but also the reporters, who were so important in getting the message out. Rayfield was just the person we needed to manage all the things we were taking on. I was glad when he worked out a leave of absence from his job. I was impressed when he was able to keep the leave open-ended so that he could be available to help us get through the difficult days ahead.

On Tuesday, September 6, the day we buried Emmett at Burr Oak Cemetery, the Tallahatchie grand jury sitting in Sumner, Mississippi, indicted Roy Bryant and J. W. Milam for Emmett's murder. There had been a lot of back-and-forth discussion for a while. There was a question whether the trial should be held in Leflore County or Tallahatchie. Emmett was abducted from Papa Mose's house in Money, which was in Leflore County, but his body was found in Tallahatchie County. That left the question of where the murder had been committed. At some point, it was decided that Tallahatchie would have jurisdiction over the murder, and Leflore would have jurisdiction over the kidnapping. Since Bryant and Milam had already admitted to the kidnapping, that seemed like it would be an open-and-shut case. The murder trial was another matter altogether.

M ama didn't want to hear it. She wouldn't have it. But I had to do it. I had to go to Mississippi for the trial. I told reporters that I was ready to give my life to make sure that what had happened to Emmett would never happen to anyone else. I meant those words.

It was the possibility behind those words, wrapped up in that meaning, that upset Mama so. She saw the very real risk in all this, and she was terrified. She couldn't bear the thought of it. The threats had been coming in and she knew about them. Even Mayor Daley had received threats because of his support for us. He placed a police guard at my home. But Henry Huff, the NAACP attorney, had encouraged us. A little. He told us he had gotten threats all the time and it never stopped him from going to Mississippi to do the important things he had to do. He would travel with us to Mississippi to advise us. Attorney Huff also had gone public with a statement that he was looking at the possibility of filing a civil action against Bryant and Milam. He wasn't afraid. Still, Mama didn't want me to take the chance. She didn't want to lose her only daughter after all she was going through, all her suffering in the loss of her only grandson.

"I've lost one," she said. "If I lose you, it would be the death of me."

I had to stop and consider my mother's feelings about the whole thing. I didn't want her to be hurt. I didn't even want to cause her discomfort. But this was something I simply had to do. Something deep inside was telling me that I had business in Mississippi. I felt that I had no choice but to go. And this is what I finally explained to my mother, what I finally got her to accept.

I could see the way things were going down in Mississippi and believed I could make a difference. Sheriff Strider already had shown his hand.

Emmett's identity was going to be an issue. I knew my son. Who could have known him better? I was ready to testify that I knew my son, that I had recognized him, identified him. Maybe, even in Mississippi, there would be twelve people who would consider the testimony of a grieving mother on the stand.

Despite my determination, there was an indication that we were going to have a very difficult time trying to reason with anybody down there. There was a gloating editorial in a Jackson, Mississippi, paper after the murder indictment was handed down. Basically, the paper claimed that the state of Mississippi had gotten back at the NAACP by deciding to put Bryant and Milam on trial for murder. The point the paper was making was that the NAACP didn't really want a trial at all. According to this paper, the organization was making Emmett's death into a political issue. The worse the state of Mississippi looked, the better the NAACP would look. There were others—newspaper writers and politicians—who warned that "outside agitators" were threatening the outcome of the case. In other words, by talking about it, by condemning a system of racism that was supported by elected officials, by criticizing a law enforcement officer who was practically standing in the courthouse door blocking all fairness and integrity, by insisting that justice be done, we actually were risking that justice would be undone. How ridiculous. How telling.

First of all, the so-called outside agitators, like me, were only pushing for the conviction of two murderers, Bryant and Milam. If Mississippi citizens really were fair-minded, as the editorial writers argued, then they would have supported a just outcome in this case. They would have done that no matter how much outside agitation there might have been. There would be no way for a fair-minded jury to consider anything else, under any circumstances. After all, a fair-minded person is not going to be petty and make a decision just out of spite, just to make a point to outside agitators. If that was even a possibility, as some people in Mississippi were suggesting, then the people who would be sitting in judgment wouldn't be fair-minded to begin with. And, if that was the case, then we had very good reason to be concerned, we had the right to speak out, and we had the duty to agitate. That was, after all, the American way.

Instead of serving the ends of justice, it was beginning to seem like the trial was serving the ends of ego. It wasn't the state of Mississippi versus Bryant and Milam. It was the state of Mississippi against just about everybody, to prove a point: that all the state's critics were wrong. It made me think that there was some other purpose here. The murder case had two defendants, and a whole state on the defensive. So, it was beginning to seem like a decision had been made that there would be a fair, impartial trial. And then Bryant and Milam would be acquitted. I was getting the sickening feeling that I just might see these murderers go free.

As it turns out, Henry Huff would not make the trip to Mississippi after all. He developed a problem with his foot and couldn't travel. Daddy and Rayfield would travel with me. I would have to rely on the Mississippi state prosecutors for any legal advice I might need while there. The money we got from the donations at the funeral, all the public events, and from the unions would cover our expenses. Rayfield worked out all the arrangements. We were ready to go. I don't know that we were ready for what we would encounter. But I was as firm, as decisive as I had ever been. I was channeling my anger now in the direction where it should have been going. I wanted to rip the sheets off the state of Mississippi, shine the light on the night riders, who seemed to be in charge. They had brought the worst of Mississippi racism right to our Chicago doorstep and I was going to take a little Chicago right back down to them. "Someone is going to pay for this," I declared. "The entire state of Mississippi is going to pay."

Once we made the decision to go to Mississippi for the trial, there was still another very important thing we had to figure out. Where would we stay? Even under normal circumstances, we really would have had to think about something like that. We would have had to think about it long and hard. There was no hotel or rooming house that we knew about that would accommodate blacks in Sumner, where the trial would take place. If we stayed with other black families in town, well, that could put those families in danger. It was that bad down there, and we surely didn't want to cause problems for anybody. Of course, we also had to think about our own safety, and that was no small thing, either. Somewhere in all the discussions, somebody was able to work things out with Dr. T.R.M. Howard, a contact of the NAACP, and also William Dawson, the powerful congressman from Chicago. Dr. Howard was the man who had made the statement to the press at Midway Airport in Chicago on the day they found Emmett's body that "There will be hell to pay in Mississippi."

Dr. Howard was a very successful surgeon, and he was a major force in the push for civil rights in Mississippi. He had a huge estate in Mound Bayou, an all-black town that had been founded by an ex-slave. It was roughly an hour's drive from Sumner. Dr. Howard would keep us safe there at his place. As it turns out, all black folks attending the trial from outside Mississippi would stay in Mound Bayou, a number of them at Dr. Howard's place. Now, to work out how to make it into Mound Bayou. Getting us there was almost like traveling the underground railroad in reverse, with "conductors" and safe houses along the way. There was a whole lot of anxiety about black folks traveling the roads of Mississippi about that time. There was some talk about how state troopers would target black folks who were involved in civil rights organizing. The word was that some officials would pass along license plate numbers to Ku Klux Klan members, who would lay in wait on dark, lonely roads. In Mississippi in the fifties, "driving while black" could be a capital offense.

Our plan involved several steps and, of course, quite a few people to make sure there were no missteps. We knew we could expect a hostile reception by Mississippi white folks. I mean, that whole state was on edge. So everything had to work smoothly. Rayfield, Daddy, and I flew into Memphis on Friday, September 16. When we got off the plane, there was a delegation to receive us, and all I know is that they took us to the home of a prominent black dentist. I say home, but it really looked more like a mansion to me, and there was a huge feast prepared in our honor. I was so amazed that black people were living like this in the South. All the places I'd ever seen were, well, they were a lot more modest. In fact, some had been pretty basic. Shotgun houses where you could look through the cracks in the floorboards and see the chickens underneath, scratching and whatnot.

The next morning, Saturday, September 17, we were driven to Clarksdale, Mississippi. The Clarksdale connection had been set up by Bishop Ford. We were taken to the home of his brother. It was Bishop Ford's brother who saw us safely to Dr. Howard's house in Mound Bayou. Dr. Howard would look after us from that point until the trial was over.

We learned very quickly that Dr. Howard was as friendly and generous as he was well off. And he was very well off. His huge home rested comfortably on nearly two hundred acres, sort of a farm, sort of a ranch. He also had set up a zoo in Mound Bayou. He felt that black children ought to at least know what it was like to see exotic animals. And where else were they going to be able to do that? He kept monkeys and alligators and peacocks and all sorts of exotic fish. There was a public swimming pool he had built for local residents. And he believed in creating greater opportunities for people who worked for him. He had come to Mound Bayou as chief surgeon at the Taborian Hospital. Later he formed his own Friendship Clinic. He would provide training and tutoring for nurse's aides, take them up to Memphis, have them tested and certified to become nurses so they could take advantage of the greater job opportunities they might find in the big city. It was fascinating to learn about Dr. Howard, a man who could have rested comfortably with his fortune and never worried about a thing. But he didn't seem comfortable at all resting with his own while there was so much deprivation around him. He didn't seem like a man who could just sit back and refuse to get involved. He was committed to making things better.

Dr. Howard's civil rights work had been covered in the *Tri-State Defender*, which had called him "a modern Moses." And, years later, his impressive life's work and contributions would be documented by scholars David T. Beito and Linda Royster Beito. As they would tell it, Dr. Howard was an important man. As a black organizer in Mississippi, he had formed the Mississippi Regional Council for Negro Leadership, which sponsored huge rallies in Mound Bayou each year that would attract up to ten thousand people. There would be parades and entertainment and, most important of all, there would be leadership development with speeches by national political figures like Congressman William Dawson of Chicago, Congressman Charles Diggs of Detroit, and NAACP Counsel Thurgood Marshall. His organization rivaled the NAACP in Mississippi. So, according to the Beitos, in 1954, when the Supreme Court announced in *Brown v. Board of Education* that school segregation was unconstitutional, Dr. Howard was summoned by Mississippi Governor Hugh White to discuss a way that Mississippi could keep its schools segregated, but give equal funding to black schools.

Dr. Howard said no thanks. Or words to that effect. "We are demanding a chance to help shape our own destiny," he declared to shocked white politicians.

For his efforts, his hard work for black equality in Mississippi, Dr. Howard was put on a hit list, along with a number of other black activists.

In the days we would stay with Dr. Howard, there was so much activity at his home, which became sort of a black command center during the trial. There were strategy sessions each night. And there were so many impressive people there during those days. Medgar Evers was the NAACP field secretary for Mississippi, based in Jackson. He had once worked for Dr. Howard, selling burial insurance to blacks. He was so impressive. He had been in the army, and he was a very strong and decisive young man, who seemed so comfortable taking charge. He had a great passion for what he was doing and a deep understanding of just how all the pieces came together. How the grassroots work being done there in Mississippi fit into the larger picture, the national struggle for civil rights. Medgar Evers could have been content to make a living for his young family instead of driving every day between Jackson and the Delta, risking his life. I was grateful for his commitment and his compassion. He had been really moved by Emmett's murder. He was the one who had done the initial investigation to brief the NAACP head office. Investigating racist crimes was just one of the many things he did back then. But you could see in his eyes that this one was personal to him.

Ruby Hurley was there, too. She was the NAACP's Southeastern regional secretary. She was intense, she was intelligent, and she was never intimidated, as tough and as forceful a woman as I had ever met. Besides Mama, of course. She seemed fearless to me, never hesitating to move forward in any situation where she might be needed. And, oh, that woman could hold her own in a room full of men, all the while never forgetting that she was a woman. I liked her and I was proud to know her. And I was impressed by the courageous work of all the other NAACP people who were around in those days as well, people like Amzie Moore, head of the NAACP office in Cleveland, Mississippi, and Aaron Henry. These people were heroic, but never seemed to have time to stop and think about how special they were. They just did what they did, it seemed, because they couldn't help doing it. I would come to understand and appreciate them and their bravery as I learned just what was being put on the line down there in Mississippi, and how it all related to Emmett and to me.

They had tried to set out a case for the federal government. Before we even made it down to Mississippi, the U.S. Justice Department decided that it did not have jurisdiction to enter the murder case against Bryant and Milam. A delegation from the NAACP had met with Warren Olney, the head of the Justice Department's criminal division. This was a high-powered delegation that included Roy Wilkins, the executive secretary; Thurgood Marshall, the NAACP chief counsel; Clarence Mitchell, head of the NAACP's Washington office; Ruby Hurley; and Medgar Evers.

It was through the regular discussions and strategy sessions in Mound Bayou that I was able to learn why it was important for the NAACP elite to make that plea in Washington. This case was so important in a larger way, as part of the overall struggle for black rights. I learned about things I had never bothered to consider before. Things we had come to take for granted in the North. Things we often failed to respect and utilize. By the time we arrived there in Mississippi in late September, things were hot in the Delta. Emotionally hot. The whole place was on a slow boil, and building. Everyone felt tense and threatened. Blacks were threatened by whites who felt threatened by blacks. There was a vicious cycle of fear and violence. In so many ways, Mississippi was the worst of the Southern states for black folks—more lynchings than anywhere else—and the Delta region was the worst part of Mississippi. Things were intensifying throughout the South in the summer of 1955. There was so much anxiety about the Supreme Court and the way it was ruling against the rule of the

South. In May 1954, the Court had decided that "separate but equal" was not equal at all. And then in May 1955, the Court had ruled that states had to start putting desegregation plans in motion "with all deliberate speed."

The reaction in Mississippi was immediate and widely reported. Senator James O. Eastland had been heading up the white opposition. That man lent so much support to the White Citizens Councils, which had been such a critical part of the Mississippi civil rights backlash. The Citizens Councils worked to ruin black folks who fought for their basic rights, and they made sure other whites toed the line.

Just days before Emmett arrived in Money, Senator Eastland had made a speech before the Citizens Councils condemning the Supreme Court's *Brown* decision. "You are not required to obey any court which passes out such a ruling," he declared. "In fact, you are obligated to defy it." He had warned Mississippi whites about the possible "death of southern culture and our aspirations as Anglo-Saxon people." To make matters worse, all this public debate was going on during a state election in Mississippi. All five candidates running for governor of Mississippi during the August primary campaigned against desegregation. It wasn't just a platform, it seemed like the whole structure of their campaigns. It was the order of the day in Mississippi.

As *The Crisis* reported, this was a costly struggle for black Mississippians. It was costing them their livelihoods, and their lives. White Citizens Councils would take voter registration lists and petitions for desegregation and turn them into "black" lists, and hand them over to landlords and bankers. Black people were fired from their jobs just for trying to register to vote or seeking to enforce the Supreme Court decision. Their home mortgages and their farm loans were called in. People were threatened with eviction, foreclosure, and bankruptcy.

As a result, the NAACP had worked with the Tri-State Bank of Memphis to set up a loan plan to help black people in Southern states who were victims of this kind of awful economic reprisal. According to *The Crisis,* black organizations shifted about three hundred thousand dollars to the Memphis bank, which was made available to save black folks from financial ruin. But there was little the NAACP or Dr. Howard's forces could do to save blacks from another threat: murder. The tension was rising in the Delta, as widely reported, and summarized by the Southern Poverty Law Center in its publication *Free at Last.*

Reverend George Lee had been a minister in nearby Belzoni. There were twice as many blacks as whites in Belzoni, but not one single black person was permitted to vote. Reverend Lee organized an NAACP chapter in Belzoni and began registering people to vote. He refused to give up, refused to back down when whites came to talk. Then in May, somebody fired a shotgun at Reverend Lee while he was driving his car. The sheriff ruled the cause of Reverend Lee's death an auto accident. The sheriff ignored all the lead pellets that were found in Reverend Lee's face. He said they were probably only dental fillings.

Lamar Smith was a farmer and World War II veteran, who had been pretty successful in the local community in Brookhaven, another Delta town. He urged blacks to register to vote, and even passed out campaign literature against a white candidate he didn't think was good for black people. In August, just two weeks before Emmett's visit, Lamar Smith was passing out leaflets on the courthouse lawn in Brookhaven. Several white men approached him. Lamar Smith was gunned down in broad daylight in front of so many witnesses who didn't see a thing.

Dr. Howard said these men were friends of his. He was outraged by their murders and the lack of justice. He knew he also was on a hit list. But you'd never know it to look at how he conducted himself. He had a ready smile and an oversized appetite for life. But, then, there were the bodyguards. On the day we arrived, as soon as we had turned onto his property, we were stopped by an armed guard. There were others around the grounds, I understood. And the guards were only part of it. *Ebony* writer Clotye Murdock had a little trouble bringing her suitcase through the front door. The door wouldn't open wide enough. She realized just why, when she looked behind the door and saw a small arsenal at the ready. I guess all the guards and all that firepower should have made us feel more secure. In fact, it was just a reminder to me of how much danger there was all around us.

Dr. Howard left nothing to chance. Like his decision once to place flowers in the back of the car that would shuttle people back and forth between Mound Bayou and Sumner during the trial. That was so no one could see who was in the car. He was known to take the long way around through Louisiana on his own car trips from one Mississippi spot to another, so as to spend less time on the roads of his own state, less time exposed to an increasing threat. Then there was the time he had to be driven home from Natchez by Audley Mackel, Jr., son of the head of the NAACP in that town. There were threats in the air. So, on that trip, Dr. Howard was driven back to Mound Bayou in the back of a hearse.

Everyone might have felt a little more at ease staying in Mound Bayou, staying among our own, but not all of the local people felt comfortable having us there. On the one hand, they felt a great deal of pride in Dr. Howard. But there also was a great deal of anxiety. They knew white folks weren't playing. They knew what the murder trial in Sumner was going to mean for them once it was all over. They might have their own mayor, their own police chief, but there were still ways that white folks could mess with them. Officials reportedly had thrown out Mound Bayou ballots in the last election. There was concern that things could get a whole lot worse than that. There were a number of black folks throughout the Delta who probably wished we had never come down there. As bad as things were, there were some people who had adjusted. They knew how to make out and figured they were better off that way. They figured there would be much worse in store for them once we all left, left them on their own, with nobody watching. They figured they'd be left to pay the price. So, there were some black folks down there who wanted to stay as far away from this whole thing as possible, figuring they'd be better off throwing their lot in with white folks.

This was the vacation spot Emmett had reached when he stepped off that train, the outsider from Chicago. He might not have been a civil rights organizer or involved in any of the activities that had gotten white folks so worked up. But his killing was part of a pattern. One thing connected to the next thing and the thing just before it. White folks were desperate. They felt they had to send a signal. White power would be protected at all costs, and the value of black life was cheap. Emmett's murder was the latest example of how brazen it had gotten. They called it "a reign of terror."

Monday, September 19 was the first day set for the trial, and I was feeling opening-day stress. There had been so much pretrial publicity, so much tension created by the publicity. There had been that war of words that had ended in a stalemate. Even though Sumner was not far from where I had been born and even though Uncle Crosby lived there, this place did not seem anything like home to me. At home, there was love. In Sumner, in the late summer, there was nothing but white-hot hatred.

There had never been anything like this in Sumner, a town that was supposed to be "A Good Place to Raise a Boy," as the motto boasted. The total population was fewer than six hundred people. As we got close to the trial, there were reports that there would be more than a thousand observers in town during that week. Somewhere between seventy and a hundred of those people would be from the press. It seemed like there were reporters and photographers and camera people and sound people everywhere you looked. It was reported that this trial drew more coverage than the sensational Bruno Hauptmann trial with journalists coming from as far away as London. Many future media stars were covering the trial. Television's John Chancellor was there. Murray Kempton of the *New York Post* would write impassioned columns. John Popham of *The New York Times* also was there, and so was David Halberstam. I've read what he has written about the trial, which he would later refer to as "the first great media event of the civil rights movement." A black writer and scholar, Clenora Hudson-Weems, would make a very interesting point about that many years later. She talked with me, she talked with Rayfield, she talked with other family members, as she put together a report on Emmett's murder and the trial for her dissertation and book. She commented on the irony she saw in one of those Christmas photos of Emmett, the one of him leaning on the television set. It was his television set and he leaned on it like he owned it. That photo would come to define him for everyone. It would become so important in telling his story, starting at his funeral, where it had been on display in his casket. How ironic, she noted, that the photo seemed to foreshadow something with such profound historical significance: the role that the media—especially television—would play in covering the civil rights struggle, a struggle that would intensify with the coverage of the murder trial. Something was starting right there in Talla-hatchie County, and the world would be watching. Intently.

With all the media glare that focused on tiny Sumner during the five days of the trial, no one would cover this event with the same energy, the same passion as the twelve or so black reporters and photographers who came into town like troops landing behind enemy lines. *Ebony, Jet,* and the *Defender* sent teams to cover the trial. Writers like Simeon Booker of *Jet,* Clotye Murdock of *Ebony,* L. Alex Wilson and Moses Newson of the *Tri-State Defender,* the Chicago paper's Southern arm. They would all go way out on a limb in pursuit of the absolute truth. And then there was James Hicks of the *Baltimore Afro-American,* who always seemed to be working three or four stories at once. That man was relentless in probing, pushing, prodding, to the point of putting his own life on the line. There were black photographers like David Jackson of *Ebony* and *Jet,* who would come face-to-face with a gun-toting white band. And there was Ernest Withers, who shot for the *Defender,* and who would risk a judge's contempt to cap-ture the single most significant photograph of the entire trial. Everywhere I turned in the close-knit group that surrounded us during our stay, I saw heroes and I was inspired by them. I also was strengthened and encour-aged by them.

Much of what I learned about what was really going on down there in Sumner—not just what I could observe for myself in court or on the way to court, but the behind-the-scenes maneuvering—much of that I learned from so many reports and stories that were written. And I made a point of reading everything I could get my hands on: the news reports, the jour-nals, the books. There would be comprehensive works on Emmett's mur-der and the trial produced by people like Clenora Hudson-Weems, Stephen J. Whitfield, and Christopher Metress over the years. I read them all. But the black reporters who covered that trial would provide a unique source of information about what went on. They were an amazing and courageous group of people who took great risks to uncover the facts about what had happened to my son in Mississippi. And not just for the sake of getting their stories, either. It was as if they wanted to find the truth for the sake of truth itself, for the sake of justice. The black reporters, in their conversations, in comparing notes, in the strategy sessions so many people would participate in each night, would show that they were not only fine journalists, but, along with Dr. Howard, and Medgar Evers, and Ruby Hurley, they also were advocates. In a very important way, these journalists would help to alter the course of events as the trial progressed.

As it turns out, I was not always permitted to be in the courtroom, although even when I was outside, I was always somewhere nearby. Since I was there as a witness, there were some parts of the proceedings I could not be allowed to hear. But I would always be informed one way or the other; Rayfield and Daddy were constantly soaking up everything to tell me. The first day, I was kept in seclusion. That day wound up being consumed by jury selection. There were 120 white men selected for the jury pool and, my God, it seemed like the prosecutors and the defense attorneys were going to have to go through all of them just to find twelve who could sit and render a verdict without getting confused by other things. There were quite a few other things that could confuse a white man sitting in judgment of two other white men accused of killing a black boy in Mississippi. One of those things was whether these prospective jurors had contributed to the defense fund for Bryant and Milam. Local stores had put up jars to collect money. My goodness, it looked like they had pulled in more for their defense than we had collected in Chicago to get my son back, to bury him, to arrange for our trip, to seek justice. There was a report that as much as $10,000 was collected for the defense fund in the couple of weeks leading up to the trial. A number of potential jurors were excluded when they revealed that they had dropped a dollar or so in one of those jars. Others were eliminated when they said they had strong feelings about race. Still others were blocked from the jury when they admitted they had already made their minds up about the case. A few were connected in some way to the lawyers and they had to go.

It seemed like it would have been very hard down there not to have a connection to somebody connected to this case. In the tight white world of Tallahatchie County, social inbreeding was a way of life. There were only five lawyers practicing in Sumner at the time. All five had volunteered to serve on the defense team for Bryant and Milam. Two of the lawyers were partners, and were politically connected: J. J. Breland, who later would make no attempt at all to try to hide his hostility toward black people, and John Whitten, a cousin of Jamie Whitten, the segregationist congressman from the area. There were three lawyers for the prosecution. Gerald Chatham was the district attorney for a four-county area. He was close to retirement, and this was going to be a taxing trial for that man, but he would hang in there. Robert Smith was more energetic. He was an ex-marine and FBI agent, who had been appointed by the governor as a special prosecutor. Finally, there was Hamilton Caldwell, the county prosecutor.

Even with this team of lawyers, we didn't get a lot of preparation. The prosecutors didn't seem to have much time for that kind of thing since they were so busy rolling up their sleeves and digging into the investigation. Sheriff Strider was no help at all. At least not to the prosecution. As a result, I don't recall being asked too many questions about my background or Emmett's character. I wasn't coached on what to expect from the defense team or how to handle it. I knew why I was there. I was Emmett's mother. No one could know a son like his mother. The identity of the body pulled from the Tallahatchie River was going to be crucial in this case. And I had to be firm, I had to be certain, I had to be convincing in my testimony that the body was that of my son. So that was pretty much it. And, of course, one other thing: I was cautioned always to put a handle on those responses from the witness stand. "Yes, *sir.*" "No, *sir.*" Oh, that was so important down there.

A quiet debate was still going on about just where this trial should be held. The question hadn't been completely answered about exactly where Emmett's murder took place. He was kidnapped in Leflore County and his body was found in Tallahatchie County, so the assumption was that he was killed in Tallahatchie. But there was a lot of talk—more like whispering, really—among black folks that Emmett could have been murdered in Sunflower County. From there, he could have been carried to the spot where he was found in the Tallahatchie River. If that could be established, then the whole trial would have to move, which would suit a lot of people just fine. Black people who knew these things knew that this case would have a much better chance of reaching a just result in front of a jury in Sunflower or even Leflore County than in Tallahatchie. The defense lawyers seemed to be aware of that, too, based on reports about their strategy. Leflore County was holding on to the kidnapping part of the case and would decide whether to indict after the murder trial. The defense lawyers wanted everything tried together in one big bundle. Apparently, the defense lawyers wanted it all handled right there in Tallahatchie County for the same reason many black folks wanted it anywhere but there. Tallahatchie had a reputation for being a mean place, very hostile toward blacks. And when I say "mean," well, we're talking mean by Delta standards, which was as bad as it gets.

Nowhere was the hostility more clear than with Sheriff H. C. Strider.

Oh, God, if that man had been an actor, he would have played the part of a racist Southern sheriff. He looked the part. He *lived* the part. Every day of his life, he lived it. He was malicious, he was hostile, he was in charge. Of everything, it seemed. Even the courthouse. That's how it was in those Southern counties back then. And county sheriffs got to be well off because of their power. Strider owned a large plantation, which was the key to finding him if you bothered to look in the telephone book. Under *P*. David Halberstam learned that's where you'd have to look for Strider. Under *P* for "plantation." So he ran everything and he was determined to run a tight ship during this trial.

Monday, the first day, started off with a meeting run by Sheriff Strider. He was laying down the law. He told the press that there would be reserved seating for twenty-two white reporters up front, near the judge's bench. He also had arranged for seating for the black press. Four seats, off to the side, behind the railing, next to a window. It didn't matter to him whether or not the black reporters could hear anything that far away. It didn't matter to him whether the black reporters even had access to his courtroom, when you got right down to it. One thing did matter to him, though. There hadn't been any race mixing in his county up to that point and there wasn't going to be any during that trial. To make matters worse, there was no "Colored" washroom, no "Colored" drinking fountain in the courthouse building. Black folks would have to go down the street to a black diner, where the black reporters would set up shop during the day. Bryant and Milam would use the washroom in the judge's chambers. Strider made it clear he didn't want the white and black reporters getting cozy, consulting, comparing notes. The *Ebony-Jet* team had brought along two photographers, David Jackson, who was black, and Mike Shea, who was white. It was a shrewd decision by publisher John H. Johnson to have someone who might get into places the black team members might not be able to go. Strider did at least allow the black reporters to take the back stairs to the courtroom along with the white reporters and jurors, according to Jimmy Hicks, the reporter from the *Baltimore Afro-American*. That way they could avoid the crush of spectators coming into the court on the main stairs up front. Strider handed out press passes. That would be a help. One of the things black reporters wanted to make sure they'd avoid was having any incidents while they were there. Even accidental contact with white folks: bumping into somebody on crowded stairs could have been a disaster. But accidentally bumping into each other was what some of the black reporters and the white reporters wound up working out, just so they could talk things through, sort them out every now and then. The white reporters out of the North already were starting to challenge the rigid Southern way of life. But quietly.

The court was packed on that first day. There were reports that there were up to four hundred people in a courtroom with seats for less than half that many. Blacks could take a few seats in the rear, or stand in the rear or along the sides toward the rear. That crowd was unbelievable. It was intolerable. The heat was in the upper nineties, but someone said the temperature in that courtroom was at least 118 degrees. Judge Curtis Swango, who sipped Coca-Cola, told the men they could shed their jackets. That was some relief. Vendors squeezed by the people in the aisles to sell soda pop. To everybody, except black folks. People brought box lunches. Anybody who was not known to the deputies at the door had to be searched. Strider made a big deal out of the death threats he said he had received. Even so, there was a rumor that many whites carried weapons all the time, even into court.

Up front, Roy Bryant and J. W. Milam sat with their wives and their sons. Two sons each, running around, playing constantly up front where the attorneys were questioning and challenging the potential jurors until they had run out of time for the day. The lawyers had only selected ten and would wait until the next morning to pick the last two. Court was adjourned. But, for Dr. Howard, Ruby Hurley, Medgar Evers, the black reporters, and the rest, the work was just about to get started.

Tuesday, September 20, was to be my first official appearance in the courtroom. Before nine in the morning, Rayfield, Daddy, and I made our way to the courthouse. Even in the morning, the weather was pretty much like the town itself: oppressive and unforgiving. The temperature was bad enough. But the humidity and the heat together made it so much worse. It felt like we had walked into hell.

There was no protection arranged for us. I kept looking around expecting to have somebody, federal marshals, the FBI, anybody. But we were on our own. The only thing that made me feel somewhat protected was the fact that there were so many reporters all over the place. I figured nothing could happen with all the reporters there to see it. People had so little experience with the media that they actually thought television cameras and radio microphones were broadcasting live. In fact, the media were flying their film back to New York every day to be processed.

As we made our way past all the people and the reporters to the courthouse, I couldn't help but look up at the statue of a Confederate soldier that stood in the blazing heat outside the courthouse building. Straight up, he stood, like the point on a sundial. Marking time, keeping watch. As we approached the building, gazing at the soldier, I heard the pop of an explosion. It startled me, made me jump. I looked up to see some white boys hanging out of the courthouse window with their fathers, laughing. One of the boys had aimed a cap pistol at me and fired. They all thought that was very funny. They *would* think that. These were the same people who would joke about how only a black boy would steal a gin fan and then try to carry it across a river. And then say straight-faced that they didn't know what all the fuss was about. After all, that Tallahatchie River was full of niggers. That's what they would say. There would be so many more heartless things they would say as they stood around out there or hung out of windows. The attitude of that place was simmering. Somewhere, not far from the court, it was reported, somebody had burned a cross. In the crazy carnival setting of Sumner, with children taking target practice out of a courthouse window, and soft drink vendors turning that Mississippi heat into profit, and cruel jokes passing around in the slow-marching shadow of a Confederate memorial, and news organizations rushing film each day to New York, somehow in the midst of all that, nobody even seemed to be distracted much at all by a burning cross.

Rod Serling, like so many other writers, would later draw inspiration from this event, this trial of the human experience, by crafting several television dramas. That seemed so fitting to me, because, looking back on it, that place *was* "the Twilight Zone." I mean, I felt like I had been transported to some distant time and place, a very strange world. Planet Mississippi. Everything there seemed so different from the place I had left behind. There, everything was hostile and insecure and threatening.

There was all that and the absolute pressure of the moment for me.

Inside the courtroom, I was mobbed by the reporters, who wanted to record Mamie Bradley's first appearance at the trial. The questions were routine and I was able to keep my answers brief. There had been a slight delay of the proceedings on this morning. Someone must have decided that four seats would not be enough for the black press and all the black witnesses and other special observers who would attend the trial. So there was a short recess to dig up a table for us. When I say "dig up," that's about what they seemed to do. I mean, that table was rough and unfinished and the splinters tore into my dress and scratched my arms. We also would wind up playing a strange game of musical chairs. Whenever we'd recess, some of the white folks would take some of our chairs and the black reporters would just take it in stride. They'd have to stand up nearby. But who was going to complain?

There was a bit of commotion shortly after I came in. It was Charles

Diggs, the congressman from Detroit. Congressman Diggs had written to Judge Swango asking if he could sit in on the trial as an observer. The judge had given his permission, but somebody forgot to tell Sheriff Strider and his crew. When Diggs and a couple of associates couldn't get in the door, the reporter Jimmy Hicks got involved and offered to take the congressman's card to the judge.

Hicks recalled a deputy taking the card and remarking to one of his cronies, "This nigger says that other nigger is a congressman."

"A nigger congressman?" the second deputy exclaimed. "It ain't possible. It ain't even legal."

Somehow, everything got worked out and the U.S. congressman, the highest-ranking public official to attend the murder trial of Roy Bryant and J. W. Milam, finally was given a seat. At the Jim Crow table.

It was so uncomfortable in that courtroom. The temperature was bad enough. But the heat from those people—not their body heat, but their emotional heat, their hatred—made it all so much worse. I could stand the heat, but the hatred was intolerable. I had brought a little silk fan with me, but it didn't do much good. At one point, I raised my hand to order a soda pop from one of the white vendors. What was I thinking? All he served up was disgust.

Somebody must have said something to Sheriff Strider about trying to be more polite to the black visitors, the press, the observers, the rest of us. So he began greeting us all, "Mornin', niggahs."

As we sat there and as I fanned away the indignities and tried to listen to the jury questions, I glanced in the direction of Bryant and Milam. I could only see the backs of their heads from where we were sitting. And, really, that's about all I cared to see. I didn't want to look at them. But I was kind of drawn in that direction. Even from behind, they seemed so calm, like they didn't have a care in the world. There was no stress. They smoked cigarettes, at times they read the newspaper. Their wives were constantly at their sides; sometimes even their mother was there. Mostly, though, I found myself watching their children. The way they played with their daddies. I watched those four little boys. I could see those babies playing on their daddies' laps, pulling on their noses and their ears and doing all kinds of things that they might well have been doing at home. I thought about how Emmett used to play like that. On my lap, or Mama's. I thought about how I had looked forward to his children one day doing the same thing. I considered that, how I would never have the chance to play with my grandchildren on my lap. And then I thought about those little boys across the way from me, the Bryant boys and the Milam boys, and how I could take each of those boys and raise them as my own, and love them in the process. I caught myself. That thought even shocked me. But, then, maybe it shouldn't have. Maybe I just wanted to save them from their fathers, save them from themselves. The way any mother might want to do. Or maybe it was to save other mothers and other mothers' sons from the legacy of hatred that just might be handed down to them by their fathers. That is, after all, how it works. We don't come here with hatred in our hearts. We have to be taught to feel that way. We have to want to be that way, to please the people who teach us to want to be like them. Strange, to think that people might learn to hate as a way of getting some approval, some acceptance, some love. I thought about all that before I realized that I couldn't let myself think about it any longer.

There was tension in the air. It wasn't just the hostility of the white folks, the antagonism they felt just seeing all the media attention that had been given to me and to Congressman Diggs. There was something else, too. It was just beneath the surface, or maybe floating just above it, at the table with the black press. The proceedings were dull as the lawyers worked their way through the jury prospects. Someone mentioned that you could tell by the questions that the prosecutors didn't plan to seek the death penalty. You have to ask jurors how they feel about that if you expect them to decide on it. The prosecutors didn't ask about that and it meant they might not have felt they had a strong enough case. That wasn't reassuring. It wasn't that I wanted the death penalty for those men. But I wanted to know that the prosecutors felt they had a solid case to get a conviction.

I looked across our table and Ruby Hurley was taking notes. She would take notes like that during the entire trial, just like the reporters. She wrote the field reports for *The Crisis,* but she always seemed to be noting things, analyzing things, keeping records.

Finally, the lawyers came up with two more people to sit on the panel. It took all morning to do that, but it meant they were being very careful in making the choices. There were ten farmers, an insurance man, and a carpenter. And that tension lingered. It was like everybody at the black press table knew something was about to happen and nobody was saying anything. We had had a discussion earlier. I can't recall who came up with the plan, but somebody thought we needed one. There had been a story about a trial somewhere in the Delta where a black defendant had been shot and killed by one of the white spectators right there in the courtroom. If something happened in this trial, we would not be in a good spot, since we'd have to run through a huge mob of angry white folks just to get to the doorway in the back. So somebody had suggested a plan to head for the window right there next to the table. If a problem should arise, somebody would help the ladies out first and then it would be every man for himself. I didn't know how serious this plan was. It was quite a drop down to the ground, but that had been the nature of the anxiety there at the table. Even so, that wasn't it. This tension was more like anticipation. Something was about to happen. Everybody knew it, but nobody was saying anything about it.

With the selection of the last juror, the judge dismissed the rest of the prospects. Nobody left their seats. Everybody wanted to stay for the trial, for the show. But it would be a short day for this audience. The district attorney, Gerald Chatham, stood to ask for a recess. He had been given information about surprise witnesses and needed time to locate them. J. J. Breland, the lead defense lawyer, rose to object. The judge ruled that the request was a reasonable one. He adjourned until nine the next morning. So, for the second time, there would be a recess: the first to serve the interests of Jim Crow, the second to serve the interests of justice. And there was an odd sort of balance to that. The judge also told the crowd that he was going to have to limit picture taking while court was in session. No exceptions. There also would be no one standing in the aisles the next day. If you didn't get there early enough to get a seat, you couldn't stay if you weren't taking part in the trial.

The black reporters at our table didn't say anything. There would be plenty of time to talk later about the things that were yet to unfold. Plenty of time to write about them. Jimmy Hicks would report the whole thing in a four-part series that would run in the *Baltimore Afro-American,* the *Cleveland Call and Post,* and the *Atlanta Daily World,* compiled years later by Christopher Metress. Simeon Booker would call it "an incredible interracial manhunt" in his version of the story written for the *Nieman Reports,* published by the Nieman Foundation for Journalism at Harvard University, which would come out within a month or so after the trial. But at the black press table at that moment, on Tuesday, as the judge ordered a recess until Wednesday, the reporters said nothing about it. Reporters can be like that. They are used to protecting their sources. In this case, though, they were protecting lives. And to hear their chilling accounts of this story is to learn why they felt they had to do it that way.

All of the twelve black reporters and photographers covering the trial were based in Mound Bayou. Dr. Howard's place was big, all right, but not quite big enough to accommodate everyone, so some out-of-town people stayed at a motel owned by a woman named Mrs. Anderson. But it seems no one could stay put. Almost as soon as they landed in town that Sunday,

Simeon Booker, Clotye Murdock, and photographer David Jackson traveled to Money to talk to Papa Mose. Jimmy Hicks went a different way; he always seemed to be going his own way. But they would all have fascinating stories to swap sometime later. The *Ebony-Jet* team ran into a truckload of white men carrying guns. It was not hunting season. But, as Papa Mose would remark, that depends on "what you're hunting." The journalists took this as a warning not to stray too far. When Strider would set down the rule the next morning that there would be no mixing of black and white reporters, it would become clear that all the local forces were working together to draw a sharp line for blacks covering the murder trial. It means something to a reporter when you start drawing lines. It means you have something hidden somewhere. Something hidden is exactly what a reporter wants to find. Digging for something hidden is exactly what a reporter lives to do.

Jimmy Hicks knew how to dig. He was a seasoned investigative reporter and, as he would recall in his series, his nose took him to the black juke joints of the area. There were stories in those juke joints. Stories that had been carried on hot summer breezes out of the cotton fields. Stories that had been served up by the shot at the bars. Pickers in overalls and barefoot gals in cotton dresses like to tell stories straight up, or over the rocks, and over the blaring music in the juke joints of the Delta. There were stories about people who saw things, people who heard things. Jimmy Hicks listened and over time he heard names and facts and situations. What he learned most of all was that there was more on the line in the Delta than just a story.

Dr. Howard had been hearing stories, too. Stories about people who had seen things, people who had heard things. He didn't have to go to the juke joints. People came to him. They came to him with names. Dr. Howard had found out about a witness who had seen two black men on the back of a truck with Emmett in Sunflower County. Milam and Bryant and maybe one or two other white men had been on the scene. Jimmy Hicks had heard a couple of names, the names of two black men connected to J. W. Milam. Two men who had disappeared after Emmett's murder: Henry Lee Loggins and Levy "Too Tight" Collins, sometimes called "Leroy."

Meanwhile, a couple of white reporters violated Sheriff Strider's rule about talking to blacks, and comparing notes. These reporters slipped out to Mound Bayou on Monday night and told Simeon Booker and other black reporters they thought the trial was doomed. The only eyewitnesses for the prosecution were going to be Papa Mose and little Simmy. They could only testify about the abduction. The investigation into the rest of it had been limited because the prosecutors hadn't gotten any help. There hadn't been any resources to speak of. And Sheriff Strider, the chief investigator, was working for the other side, raising questions about the identity of Emmett's body. There was some talk that the defense might not even put on one single witness. The fear now was that there was only going to be a show trial for the media.

No one was going to let that happen. Jimmy Hicks had information, Dr. Howard had information, and Ruby Hurley felt that might be enough information to have everything moved to Sunflower County, where it was beginning to look like the murder actually had occurred, and where everybody thought there might be a better chance of getting a conviction. They knew they would have to reach out to the witnesses, Hicks and Booker reported. The NAACP folks had been out looking. They knew that people were scared about giving up information. They knew they were going to need more time. The only way to get more time would be to reveal the information to the authorities. But the white authorities couldn't be trusted and probably wouldn't take the word of NAACP people and the black reporters, anyway.

Despite it all, the decision was made to bring in some white reporters who could reach out to the authorities, maybe get them to do the right thing. The decision was made that Simeon Booker would talk to Clark Porteus of the *Memphis Press-Scimitar*. Like Booker, he was a former Nieman fellow. A couple of other white reporters were brought in and, after a little arguing and a lot of negotiating, an agreement was struck to share information, according to the reports. But they would hold off on reporting any stories until the witnesses could be secured. The white reporters would appeal to the authorities for help in protecting the witnesses and delaying the trial.

Now, ordinarily, there are two things reporters will never do. The first is to share information with one another. They're much too competitive to do that. The second is to get involved with law enforcement, revealing information to help the police track down criminals or witnesses to a crime. That crosses the line. The reporters are supposed to stay outside the stories they cover. If they are out there helping, then they're part of the stories. But these reporters quickly worked it all out. This trial was the biggest story many of them had covered. It was not going to be a complete story without these witnesses, and they needed one another to get the information together. As for the second part, well, somebody figured out that they would have been obstructing justice if they didn't help out, Booker wrote. Now for the final part, the safety of the witnesses. How could they trust the law enforcement people? Strider already was showing his true colors. These reporters might be jeopardizing people who came forward. Dr. Howard agreed to pay for the relocation of any witnesses who agreed to testify, and hopefully that would take care of everything.

The call for new witnesses may have been a surprise to the court, but it was a shock to the defense team. No one had ever imagined that witnesses might come forward to testify against white men accused of killing a black person.

As both Hicks and Booker reported later, teams were formed of sheriff's deputies, reporters, and NAACP people. The black journalists included Hicks, Booker, Clotye Murdock, L. Alex Wilson, Moses Newson, David Jackson, and Ernest Withers. NAACP representatives included Medgar Evers, Amzie Moore, Aaron Henry, and, of course, Ruby Hurley, who put on a red bandanna and work clothes to help her fit in when she walked out into the fields, trying to convince people to trust her. That was the only way it was going to work. Black witnesses might trust other black folks, if they would trust anyone at all. But they were not going to trust anybody they thought was an outsider.

There were other risks, too. On Monday, Moses Newson had made the rounds with Medgar Evers, Ruby Hurley, and Amzie Moore, all dressed in work clothes. As they searched the plantations for witnesses, they talked about how careful they would have to be. Newson would recall later that they didn't want to scare anybody away. But they also didn't know who to trust. After all, there was talk that at least a couple of black men had been loyal to J. W. Milam. There had even been talk that it was a black man, not Carolyn Bryant, who first told Roy Bryant about "the boy from Chicago." So, there was no telling who might turn you in, once you got to talking out there in those fields. Besides all that, Newson remembers, those sheriff's deputies had a strange way of just popping up out of nowhere. Right in the middle of a cotton field, where there was no place to hide.

With all that in mind, the teams started out making the rounds to plantations on Tuesday and found several cases where potential witnesses had disappeared. The word was that they had been visited by whites.

Many people began to believe Collins and Loggins had been killed to keep them quiet. Jimmy Hicks believed something else. He had developed some amazing sources in such a short time, impressive when you realize just how wary those Delta black folks could be. But Hicks had good information that Too Tight was in jail in Charleston. Maybe Loggins, too. The prosecutors asked about it. Sheriff Strider denied it. And that seemed to be good enough for all the white folks. But the names Levy "Too Tight" Collins and Henry Lee Loggins would continue to haunt the proceedings. For Jimmy Hicks, though, these men would become an obsession.

Even though the whereabouts of Collins and Loggins would remain a mystery, the teams were able to reach several witnesses and convince them to come forward. Still, there was one critical person everyone wanted to find. And the teams were racing the clock. Everything had to be in place by the following morning. Leflore County Sheriff George Smith was heading up one of the search parties. He had been the man contacted by Papa Mose and Uncle Crosby when Emmett was taken. This team finally got a break, a lead they couldn't afford to pass up. Smith would lead the way, followed by Booker and Porteus in one car and Hicks in another. As it turns out, the sheriff's team was traveling so fast, Booker and Hicks lost him and, the reporters wrote, they were left to wonder how things would turn out.

Willie Reed stopped what he was doing as he watched across the field. He didn't know the names of the people, black people and white people, walking in his direction, and he wouldn't remember their names after it was all over. He did know why they were there. He knew that even before they started talking to him. He had heard all about it on the radio, he had seen it in the paper, when he wasn't picking. He had heard something else even before anybody heard anything on the radio. His own relatives had advised him to stay out of it. Not to tell what he had heard. He thought about all that and about what these strangers were talking about. But he didn't think long. What they talked about would put his life in danger. His relatives had told him that much. That thought made him nervous. Very nervous. He was only eighteen. He had to live in this place for a long time and he didn't want to live with the constant fear of dying. If he was going to keep living at all. But he agreed to cooperate. He recalled the horror of what some men had done early on a Sunday morning in a plantation shed, when they thought nobody was around. He had been unable to do anything to stop it from happening. Maybe now he could do something to keep it from ever happening again. Maybe.

The story was front-page news Wednesday morning. That's the way everybody had agreed it would go. The three white reporters were able to go forward with their insider accounts. They wrote about how the surprise witnesses were found and brought in to testify. That had been their reward, but it also had been part of the strategy of Medgar Evers, Dr. Howard, and Ruby Hurley, working with the black reporters. The Clark Porteus story in the *Memphis Press-Scimitar* made news across the country through the Scripps-Howard news service. Porteus wrote about how Dr. Howard had identified five witnesses who might be able to show that Emmett's murder had taken place at the Sheridan Plantation in Sunflower County. Like Leflore, Sunflower was right next to Tallahatchie County. The Sheridan Plantation was managed by Leslie Milam, J. W. Milam's brother, and Roy Bryant's half-brother. The Porteus story gave a detailed account of Dr. Howard's discussions with a witness about the possible scene of the crime. As many as four white men and two black men were seen with Emmett at the Sheridan Plantation in a green Chevy truck, like the one that drove off from Papa Mose's place with Emmett in the back. Porteus had been the person who delivered Dr. Howard's report to the prosecutors. Everyone saw right away that this new evidence might mean the whole trial would have to move to Sunflower County. They brought in Leflore County Sheriff George Smith, along with his deputy, John Ed Cothran; the Sunflower County district attorney; the Sunflower County prosecutor; and a forensic specialist sent down by Governor White. After Judge Swango granted the recess on Tuesday, Porteus wrote, the white officials went to the Sheridan Plantation to examine a shed. There was some information that the shed might have been the place where Emmett had been beaten, and where someone had been trying to clean up bloodstains. The officials didn't find any traces of blood, and they probably scared off quite a few potential black witnesses in the process.

Even though Porteus didn't mention Jimmy Hicks, he did report that two more potential witnesses, Levy "Too Tight" Collins and Henry Lee Loggins, were still being sought. And that only fueled the growing feeling that these two men were long gone.

Papa Mose was sworn in at nine-fifteen Wednesday morning. He had been waiting there in court over the last two days just for this moment. On Tuesday, he had stood around because there were no vacant seats. He'd just stood, waiting to be called. Then court was recessed so that the surprise witnesses could be found, and he'd had to wait overnight. But he had been waiting for this moment even longer than that. He had been waiting nearly a month to have the chance to bear witness, to tell everybody what had happened at his home the night Emmett was taken away.

Papa Mose wasn't a tall man, but people had always looked up to him. He was respected by the people who knew him. When he spoke, they listened. In court, they listened intently, not so much because the white folks there cared about what he was saying, but because they cared more about what he was speaking against. Yes, he was testifying against Bryant and Milam. But, more than that, his very presence there spoke out against a custom that said you don't do what he was about to do. You see, through his testimony, Papa Mose would cross a line that no one could remember a black man ever crossing in Mississippi. He wasn't afraid of Bryant and Milam, sitting there in court, staring him down. "They oughtta be scared of me," he had said before he got his moment, before he was sworn in, before he settled into the cane chair on the witness stand. This was Papa Mose's chance. He had been waiting for this chance, for this moment. He was not going to let Bryant and Milam off. They had violated his home. They had terrorized his family. Beyond all else, they had tortured and killed Emmett.

The District Attorney Gerald Chatham started off. He addressed the witness as "Uncle Mose," and the witness addressed him as "sir." On questioning, Papa Mose once again told the story about how he was awakened at two in the morning by the banging on the front door and the voice calling out to him, the one identifying himself as "Mr. Bryant." He told how he came out to the screened-in porch to see that there were two men, one with a flashlight and a gun, who asked for the boy from Chicago, the one who had done the talking. There was a third man, who stayed behind on the porch outside when the other two came in.

Papa Mose testified how the two men woke Emmett and threatened him and took him out to the truck. He told how he heard Milam ask someone in the truck whether Emmett was the right boy. There was that voice from inside the truck: "Yes." A fourth person, a person with a voice that was lighter than a man's voice. They put Emmett in the back of the truck. And they drove away.

Chatham looked straight across at Papa Mose. "Did you ever see your nephew alive again?"

Papa Mose swallowed. Then he spoke in a low voice. "No, sir."

Chatham asked Papa Mose if he could identify the two men. This was the moment. A black man was actually being asked to take a stand in a Mississippi courtroom and accuse a white man of kidnapping a black boy.

"Yes, sir," Papa Mose said. He could identify them, all right.

Chatham asked him to rise.

Papa Mose did right away. He stood up, straight, erect. He did not waver, he did not shake. It was very dramatic, and everything was suspended in the heat of that moment, the very moment Papa Mose had been waiting for. Chatham asked Papa Mose to indicate the men who came to his house that Sunday morning. Without hesitating, as if he had seen himself doing this in a thousand moments before this one, Papa Mose raised his arm.

At the black press table, off to the left, behind the rail, and near the window, Ernest Withers, the photographer shooting for the *Defender,* was also waiting for that moment. Ernest Withers knew what that moment meant, and what it would mean. It was a defiant moment that had to be preserved, even if the judge had restricted picture taking. So Ernest Withers pointed his camera very carefully, aimed it between the people in front of him, straight through the opening, right at Papa Mose. That's where everybody else's attention was drawn, too. Nobody, it seemed, was watching the black press table at that moment. At least you might hope that would be the case. So, with hope, with patience, and with a steady hand, Ernest Withers waited for the moment.

As Papa Mose pointed, he felt the rush of anger in that room. The heat of the moment. As he would put it later, he could feel the blood of all those white people boiling. But there was scarcely a peep from the crowd. In fact, it was so quiet in that courtroom, you could hear the gentle whirring sound of the ceiling fans stirring the hot air. That, and a single click of a camera shutter over at the black press table. Papa Mose stood straight and firm against the weight of that room. "There he is," he said, as he pointed directly at J. W. Milam. "And there is Mr. Bryant."

That done, the moment past, Papa Mose took his seat once again.

As he did, from a spot near the jury, artist Franklin McMahon was preparing for *Life* magazine a drawing of the same dramatic event photographed by Withers. While he finished his work, McMahon heard a juror mutter a reference to Papa Mose: "Sambo, Sambo."

When the defense attorney, C. Sidney Carlton, started his cross-examination, it became clear that he wanted to make this *his* moment. He tried to pin Papa Mose down on how he could recognize anybody in the dark with the flashlight pointed mostly at him. Carlton tried to get Papa Mose to admit that the only reason he even thought he recognized Milam was because Milam was big and bald and white. And couldn't that description fit a lot of people? He wondered how Papa Mose could even identify Bryant, ignoring what Papa Mose had said under oath. Bryant had identified himself when he came banging on his door. Oh, that man was getting on Papa Mose's nerves. In fact, at one point, he became so annoyed that he just stopped saying "sir" when he answered.

"So there were four persons there that night?" Carlton asked.

Papa Mose sat back in the chair. "That's right."

Finally, Carlton asked about the third man who had come that night, the one who had stayed out on the porch. "Was he a white man?"

"I don't think so," Papa Mose said.

"He might have been a Negro?"

"He sure acted like a Negro," Papa Mose said. "He stayed outside."

People laughed at this answer and the judge slammed the gavel and shut everything down right away. He was determined to keep control of his courtroom. After about an hour, Papa Mose finally was released. The moment had come and it had passed. An hour that seemed like only a heartbeat, and an entire lifetime.

Leflore County Sheriff George Smith was called next. The judge excused the jury while he listened to what the sheriff had to say. What Smith had to say was how he went to Roy Bryant's store later that Sunday, after Emmett was taken. Bryant was asleep in back of the store at two in the afternoon. Bryant admitted that he took Emmett out of the house and back up to the store. But he told Smith that he turned Emmett loose, when he found out from his wife that he wasn't the one. The defense lawyers made a big deal out of the fact that Sheriff Smith and Bryant were friends. They tried to say that the conversation between them was confidential. But the judge wouldn't allow the objection. The whole thing just seemed too cozy. The sheriff who was investigating the kidnapping was a friend of one of the kidnappers. It looked like the sheriff wanted to do the right thing, but in that crazy place, you could never be sure how things might turn out.

The recess for lunch was going to be two and a half hours long. The defense team wanted to have time to question the surprise witnesses being called by the prosecutors.

As people began filing out for the extended break, somebody approached Ernest Withers, stopped him in his tracks. Somebody had seen him take that picture, capture the moment: Papa Mose standing to accuse Bryant and Milam. As it turned out, the man was from one of the wire services. He bought the film right out of Ernest Withers's camera.

It must have been unsettling for Willie Reed. Awful, really. It sure had been that way for me. Walking into that court for the first time, not knowing what was in store, what to expect. Oh, for me, it was the worst. But, for him, it was worse still. He had never been inside a courthouse in his entire life, and what he was about to do there would change his life from that point on. His first stop on this first trip on Wednesday was the judge's chambers. There, seated with their feet up on Judge Swango's desk, were Roy Bryant and J. W. Milam. Their lawyers were there, too. That was not a good sign to Willie. He might not have ever been in a courthouse before, but he didn't have to have experience in a courthouse to know what it meant for a black man to be in a room like that with people like those. He had lived in the Delta long enough to know this much: Even when you're brought into the room, you're still an outsider.

Willie didn't take a seat. He didn't even think about that. He just stood there and answered the questions about the testimony he would give. The same way the other surprise witnesses would be doing. Willie was under a great deal of pressure, but he believed he could get through it. He had gotten so much support during his stay at Dr. Howard's place the night before. People knew he would need that. Willie had been very hard to find at first because his grandfather had moved him about three miles away from his house when things had started heating up, when word started spreading about the people who might have information about Emmett's death, especially Willie. His grandfather needed to protect Willie. Even so, even several miles away from his grandfather's place, he hadn't felt completely safe. Somebody still could have gotten to him. As it turns out, the people who finally did get to Willie wound up bringing him to safety in Mound Bayou. He thought about that. That, and all the encouragement everybody had given him the night before. He had been impressed to meet a U.S. congressman, a black congressman. He told Charles Diggs as much. He told me he wanted to help and I told him how much I appreciated his help, how grateful I was. He felt relieved being in an all-black town, on Dr. Howard's grounds, with bodyguards. Oh, that made him feel very good, and very safe. To him, it was like being at the White House. Trying to get to Dr. Howard, he said, would have been like trying to get to the president.

That was Tuesday night. Being in that court on Wednesday morning, though, being invited into the judge's chambers and still being an outsider in the presence of all those insiders—well, that was another thing altogether. But he was prepared to do what he had promised he was going to do. So he answered the questions about his testimony, about what he had seen, what he had heard very early in the morning on the fourth Sunday in August, about the two white men sitting there with their feet on Judge Swango's desk. He was prepared to do what he had promised he was going to do, and he was approved as a witness to do just that.

That afternoon, the state called Chester Miller, the black undertaker from Greenwood; Robert Hodges, who discovered the body; and Sheriff Smith's deputy, John Ed Cothran. Robert Hodges told about how he contacted Sheriff Strider after seeing Emmett's foot rising above the surface of the river, and how the body was towed to shore. Chester Miller described the condition of the body he came to pick up in his ambulance. He also saw a hole above the right ear, probably the bullet hole. Part of Emmett's head had been crushed and a piece of the skull had fallen off into the boat. He remembered that. Who could forget seeing something like that? He also described the gin fan and the several feet of barbed wire tied around Emmett's neck. The fan had been brought into court, all seventy-five or eighty or ninety pounds of it, and it sat there, like a silent witness or an accomplice to the murder. Deputy Cothran had arrested J. W. Milam. He testified that Milam admitted taking Emmett and, just like Bryant, said he had let him go when they found he was not the right one. That was their story. That they had just released Emmett, let him walk back the three miles from the store in Money to Papa Mose's home. That Emmett had simply disappeared into the early morning darkness.

Chick Nelson, the first witness on Thursday morning, seemed to blend into all the rest. He was the undertaker from Tutwiler, the white man who ultimately was the one who took the body from Chester Miller and turned it over to Uncle Crosby to bring back to Chicago. In fact, everything after Papa Mose's testimony on Wednesday morning seemed to blend together. In that horrible compression chamber of heat and hate, it all seemed like one big transition from Papa Mose to me, the second witness called on Thursday.

The prosecutors hadn't done very much to prepare me for the experience, but there probably wasn't very much anyone could have done to prepare me. As I walked forward to be sworn in and take my place in that old cane witness chair, I was overwhelmed by the mood. You could feel it, thick as the humidity.

You really can feel things like that. It's in the air in most places. In church you can feel it. Even when nobody is around, you can feel what was brought there when everybody was around. People who want to connect with God bring a special kind of spiritual power to a place, and it stays there long after they have left. It's the power of faith, the power of love. You can breathe it in. God is there. It is so uplifting. That was not the feeling I got as I walked to the front of the court. That place was not church. That crowd did not come to sing His praises. In fact, those white folks looked to me like a lynch mob.

For the first time, it seemed, I took a good look at the witness stand. That's what it was, really. A stand, not a box. There was a chair, but no wall separating you from the lawyers, from the crowd. You would just have to sit there, facing out, up against that wall of hostility, all alone, exposed. So vulnerable.

Special Prosecutor Robert Smith called me "Mamie." And I called him "sir." We had already been through why we'd have to go through all that. In court, we worked our way through all the "how-do-you-do" kind of questions, the preliminary things I guess lawyers have to put on the record when they know a record is being made of what they say. That kind of stuff. And then he got right into it. The reason I was there. How did I know the body that was sent to me was my son?

I went through the scene at A. A. Rayner's, how I had examined Emmett's entire body, the legs, the torso, the face, mouth, teeth, eye, ear. Everything. And, as I explained it all, I turned from the prosecutor to the jurors. I wanted to talk to them, to reach them directly. I had to. If there was any chance at all that they might even consider a murder conviction, let alone hand one down, then they were going to have to get beyond some things. They had to see past the color of a witness's skin, and feel the anguish of a mother's loss.

The prosecutor asked if I could recognize the body.

This was *my* moment. And I knew how closely everyone would be listening to my words, my voice, my delivery. They were going to measure it all, evaluate it, analyze it, pick it apart a thousand different ways. The strength, the certainty. I had to demonstrate these things just by the way I spoke.

"I positively identified it," I said firmly. "It definitely was my boy. Beyond a shadow of a doubt."

The prosecutor showed me the police photo of Emmett, the one taken right after he was pulled from the river. My God. He looked even worse there than he did when I saw him, which was worse than he did when the rest of the world finally saw him. Oh, everything just washed over me again. The force of it rocked me in that old cane chair, back and forth. I bowed my head. I had to do that to collect myself. I mean, the tears were welling up and I wanted so much to hold them back. I wanted to hide them. No one should see them. I had to be strong up there. I couldn't be weak. I had to be strong for Emmett.

I breathed deeply, worked through it, and, one more time, I made the identification. I nodded. "That was my son," I said.

He turned to walk back to the table for more evidence. As he did, I took off my glasses, wiped my eyes. There was a job to do. Emmett. *We can do it.*

The prosecutor brought over another picture. This was one of the Christmas pictures and I said that, too, was Emmett. Next was the ring. I told him it was the ring I had given to Emmett before he left Chicago. I recognized it because of the inscription: LT MAY 25, 1943. I explained that the ring had been left by Emmett's father, Louis Till. Louis had died July 2, 1945, in the service in Europe. He didn't ask any more about that. I don't know what else I would have been able to say, since that was about all I had ever known.

Next, J. J. Breland took his turn on me for Bryant and Milam. He was the oldest defense attorney. But that attack dog hadn't lost his bite. In another setting, he might have been considered the dean. I saw him there as the ringleader. The first words he spoke were to the judge. He asked permission to keep his seat while he questioned me. He never asked my permission to call me "Mamie." And that was just the beginning. But there was no way to turn back. I had come to testify, to cooperate, to help find some measure of justice. Whatever it took. I always knew I would be in the spotlight, on the stand. I always knew there would be pressure. But, still, even though I knew all these things and thought I had braced myself, I had no idea that a trial could be such an ordeal.

Breland wanted to know whether I had insurance on Emmett. It was so nasty. I knew the defense had already set the stage for what they were trying to do. They wanted to create the impression that I could have had something to do with the death of my own son. Maybe I had my son killed for the insurance money. Yes, I had insurance. Yes, it provided for double indemnity in the case of accidental death. Or murder. Breeland wanted to know if I had collected. Well, how could I? Sheriff Strider hadn't released the death certificate yet. Okay then, so maybe I had worked with the NAACP, digging up a body in the cemetery, putting the ring on a finger, weighting it, and throwing it in the Tallahatchie River. Or, better yet, wasn't Emmett, at that very moment, walking around the streets of Detroit with my father? Well, my father was sitting just across the room. So how could that be? Breland was doing everything he could to play on the doubts and the suspicions he knew the white people of that community had. After all, he was one of them. Much better off, but no better, really.

Oh, it was like I had been tied up to a target and he was throwing darts at me. Even so, I kept my composure. I responded to every question, and always remembered to say "sir." Well, almost always. I slipped once and just said "no," and I hurried up and added "sir." I mean, there was a gap between those words, but I tried to hook them up before anybody could notice. You didn't want people to notice something like that. It felt like that place could erupt at any minute. I knew I had no protection. They could drag me off that stand and tar and feather me. Or worse.

Then Breeland shifted gears. "Do you read the *Chicago Defender*?"

Well, everybody knew where he was about to go with that. The *Defender* was about as bad as the NAACP to those people. He wanted to try to prejudice the jurors against me. As if they needed any more help with that. But Judge Swango ordered the jury out to see how far he would let this go.

I told him that I bought the paper and read it, even though I didn't subscribe to it.

Now, to pursue this line, he finally had to stand, after all, and come to me. He handed me a copy of the paper, asked if I had seen it. When I told him that I had, in fact, seen the paper, he directed me to a picture and asked if I recognized it as a picture of Emmett's body. I told him that I did, and it was Emmett's body. The judge said there would be no further references to the newspaper or the photo during the trial. There obviously was no point to any of it, except to get people all excited.

Then Breeland shifted again. He asked first if I was from the South. I told him I was born in Webb, not that far from Sumner. He wanted to know what I had told Emmett to prepare him for his trip to the South. How to act around white folks. I said that I had done just that. He wanted to know what I had said.

I repeated a summary of what I had told Emmett, to be very careful how he spoke and to say "yes, sir" and "no, ma'am" and not to hesitate to humble himself, "if you have to get down on your knees." That's what I told him.

All the while I was on the stand, I never looked at Bryant and Milam. Never even glanced in their direction. A part of me wanted to do it. Wanted to look into the eyes of my baby's killers. But I didn't. It wasn't so much that I was afraid to do it. Oh, I was very anxious just being there, on the spot, in the spotlight. But, as for Bryant and Milam—well, there was nothing more they could have done to me. Nothing at all. They already had done as much as anyone possibly could have done. Still, I knew that I had to keep it all together, maintain a delicate balance in that courtroom. If I had any chance at all to appeal to that jury, to reach out to them, then I could not let them see me challenge those two monsters. And that's how it would have been interpreted if I had been seen looking at them. So I looked only at the lawyers who interrogated me and the jurors who evaluated me. And I answered all questions as directly as I could, until my hour was up, and I was dismissed.

As I stepped off the stand, though, I felt, I don't know, like I really hadn't connected at all. Like I didn't matter at all. Like they had blocked out everything I had said. I felt that my words didn't mean any more to those people than a piece of paper, like trash, blowing down the street. On top of that, I had to walk past all those angry white folks on my way out. There were daggers in their eyes. So I had to stop making eye contact to avoid the cutting looks. I had to start looking ahead to the door, where I was happy to see Daddy waiting to escort me out. It was so good that I had somebody in the courtroom just to be with me at that moment. But then I realized I wouldn't have been alone in any event. I had faced the cruel stares and the hostile questions with the strength of someone who knew that she was not alone. I had prayed for that strength.

That place was not church. Far from it. But, in the end, God was there for me.

CHAPTER 19

He was the first of the surprise witnesses called by the state that Thursday. And Willie Reed looked so nervous about it. He should have been. There was a lot at stake for him. There was a lot at stake for the trial. A whole lot. Of all the witnesses who would testify that day, he was the one who held the link that would connect all the other stories. And, with all the threats and intimidation that had surrounded this whole event, it was going to take a special kind of courage for Willie to take the stand. To tell the story. He looked nervous, but somewhere deep down inside him, Willie Reed had that courage.

Seeing Congressman Diggs there helped. The black congressman represented so much to Willie. Something he had never imagined before. In Diggs, Willie saw power, the power of possibility. He drew on that power source. It was the encouragement he needed to get through. He saw me and was reminded of why this had been something that he felt he had to do. He was just eighteen. Emmett had only been fourteen. As far as Willie was concerned, it could have been him. And he would have wanted somebody to come forward for him, even at such a great risk.

He spoke softly, so softly the judge had to ask him to speak up several times. But Willie Reed would be heard on this day, loud and clear.

About six in the morning on Sunday, August 28, Willie was sent to the store by his grandfather to buy some meat for Sunday dinner. He took a shortcut walking across the Sheridan Plantation near Drew in Sunflower County, where he lived. He hit the road just about the time a pickup truck passed. He noticed the truck because it was so early in the morning. It was a green fifty-five Chevy with a white top. There were four white men riding in the front. In the back of the truck, there were three blacks, two men and a young man, a teenager. The two black men were sitting up on the sides of the truck in back. The teenager was sitting on the bottom. On his way back from the store, Willie cut across the plantation again and saw the truck parked outside a tractor shed attached to a red barn. No one was inside the truck at this time, but there was something unusual about the whole scene. Something caught Willie's attention and just would not let it go. So, he walked near the shed, and as he did, he heard sounds.

"Licks, a lot of licks." He also heard screams. Painful screams.

Then things got quiet. Willie kept going, but he saw a white man come out of the shed and walk over to a water pump to take a drink. It was J. W. Milam. He knew that because he had seen Milam around the plantation before. Milam's brother, Leslie, was the Sheridan Plantation manager. Milam had a holster strapped around the waist of his khaki trousers. There was a pistol in the holster.

Willie felt helpless to do anything about what was going on, so he did the only thing he could. He stopped at Amanda Bradley's place, just across the way from the shed. He asked her what was going on, who was getting beat to death out in the shed. Then he went out to get a bucket of water from that pump near the shed. The same one Milam had used. The sounds had died down. From the window back at Mandy Bradley's place, he could see a tractor being pulled out of the shed and the truck backed up. Something wrapped in a tarpaulin was placed in the back of the truck before it was driven off.

Willie seemed less nervous as he continued his testimony. Like the rest of us, he felt better knowing the press was there to observe everything that was going on. He was betting no one would try anything as long as the reporters were around to see it. It was the watchful eye of the press that seemed to keep things in line. It was the press that had helped me get so much attention when Emmett was taken, when his body was found. In fact, that's how Willie had connected it all up. He had seen Emmett's picture in the paper and remembered what he had seen days before that, early in the morning, before he went to Sunday school.

Willie looked at the Christmas picture of Emmett, the one that had been marked for evidence after my testimony earlier. He said the person in the picture looked like the person he saw in the back of that truck. Prosecutor Smith asked Willie to identify the man he saw at the Sheridan Plantation that Sunday morning, the white man with the holster and the pistol. As Willie pointed out Milam, he noticed a slight smile on his face. Milam was just looking at Willie. And Willie looked back at him. Milam's little smile seemed to tell Willie that his testimony would not mean a thing. To Milam, or to the jury.

Defense counsel J. W. Kellum wanted to make sure Willie's testimony didn't count. He moved to have it stricken. It was irrelevant, he said. The judge ruled against him. Well, then, Kellum argued, the testimony shouldn't apply to Bryant since Willie had identified only Milam. The judge said the defendants had decided to be tried together so the evidence applied to both of them. Kellum also tried to shake Willie's testimony, asking him questions about distance, testing him to see if he really could have seen what he said he had seen. How far was he from the pump when he first saw Milam? How far was the truck when he saw it? But Willie stuck it out. He had been encouraged to do that and he made it through.

The other surprise witnesses called by the state that day were Add Reed, Willie's sixty-five-year-old grandfather, and Amanda Bradley, who was fifty. They basically confirmed parts of Willie's story. Add Reed testified that he saw Leslie Milam near the shed around eight o'clock Sunday morning. He also saw the pickup truck parked near the shed. Mandy Bradley testified that she looked out the window and saw the green and white Chevy truck. She also said she saw four white men going in and out of the barn. J. W. Milam was one of them.

The prosecution rested. It was around two that afternoon and like clockwork, right away, the defense made its move. The lawyers said the judge should order the jury to acquit Bryant and Milam right then and there. A directed verdict of acquittal, that's what they called it. These defense lawyers argued that the state had not even set out a case for murder, so there was nothing for them to defend. Judge Swango denied their motion. He argued that there was something for the jury to consider in all this. Enough evidence had been presented to move forward.

The way things were going, there was new reason to have hope. The prosecutors had put their case together with some thought and care, even with no help in the investigation and no time to do it all. Papa Mose had sworn that Bryant and Milam took Emmett from his house. Sheriff George Smith and his deputy John Ed Cothran had testified that Bryant and Milam admitted taking Emmett, even though they said they let him go. Now there were witnesses who said they saw Milam and three other white men early Sunday morning, just hours after Emmett was taken. And Willie Reed actually saw Emmett in the truck with the white men and two black men, before he heard beating and screaming in that shed. And, of course, I swore to the identity of my son. One of the men who had come to Sumner with Congressman Diggs, a lawyer, thought it looked like the state had done a pretty good job of setting things out. And it was a good sign that the judge thought there were enough issues to be considered by the jury. Well, that sounded encouraging to me. But this game was still in play and we couldn't trust that the defense team would play fair.

The first witness called by the defense was Carolyn Bryant. It was clear right away that Defense Attorney Carlton wanted to put Emmett on trial. His line of questioning focused on that Wednesday night when Emmett and the other kids had come into Money and walked into Bryant's store. As soon as the lawyer began, the judge ordered the jury out of the room. He wanted to see where this was all going before he allowed the jury to be inflamed by it. And it was enough to set anyone's passion on fire. To me, it was pure drama. And the audience was ready for the show. It seemed like the entire courtroom tilted in that woman's direction; all the white people moved forward, sitting on the edge of their seats, as if they wanted to embrace every word of their star attraction, the woman billed in the Southern press as the "pretty twenty-one-year-old mother of two."

Carolyn Bryant told the story of how she worked alone in the store on the night of August 24. What she meant by this was that her husband was out of town and her sister-in-law, Juanita Milam, was in the living quarters in the back of the store. So, while Carolyn Bryant was out front, behind the counter, this black "man" with "a northern brogue" had come into the store and had gone over to the candy counter. He was buying bubble gum.

When she held her hand out for the money, she claimed that he grabbed her arm and spoke to her. "How about a date, baby?"

She said she broke free and that he came around and grabbed her by the waist and spoke again. "What's the matter, baby, can't you take it? I've been with white women before."

Carlton got her to stand and acted out the scene with her, touching her waist the way she claimed the black man had done. She said he used foul language. So foul, in fact, she just hung her head as she thought about it in court and said she could not repeat it there. She *would* not. At a certain point, she claimed, a Southern Negro came in and grabbed the man and took him out. She said she ran out to get a pistol from the car and saw the man standing there on the porch with the other Negroes. As she made her way to the car, she says, she heard the whistle.

Carlton decided to demonstrate for everybody in the court. He blew a whistle. A wolf whistle. Two notes that slashed the air of that packed courtroom like a knife. She swore that was the sound.

Oh, that woman's testimony was outrageous. It just seemed obvious to me that she had added so much to this brief encounter to try to justify what her husband and brother-in-law had done to my son. Emmett might not have known everything about the way things worked down South, but this white woman certainly did. She would have never held out her hand to take Emmett's money. Black folks always dropped their money on the counter. That was the best way to avoid even looking like they had physical contact. Even if Emmett had held out the coins in his hand, she would have let him drop them. That was the Money way. Second, by all accounts, Emmett wasn't in the store long enough to have had that much conversation with the woman. Much of that time, Simeon was standing in the door waiting for him, looking at everything. He surely didn't have time to chase her around the store. Third, if she had been insulted and had been afraid, as she swore she had been, her sister-in-law was right in the back of the store and there was a gas station only steps away from the store. She went to the car. She could have called for help when she was there, or run across the way for protection if she felt somebody was assaulting her, as she swore some black "man" had done. And, if things had happened the way she claimed, then why did it take so long for everything to heat up? I doubt that those boys would have even made it three miles back to the house that night, let alone come back to Money a couple of days later, when it seemed that the whole thing had blown over.

The defense wanted the judge to allow Carolyn Bryant's testimony to be heard by the jury. Special Prosecutor Robert Smith argued that whatever happened that Wednesday night in the store should not be connected up to what happened early Sunday morning. It was irrelevant, he said. In any event, it certainly was no justification for murder.

The judge saw it his way. He refused to allow the jury to hear her testimony. But the damage was done already: You could be sure the jury would hear it. After all, the judge had allowed that fantastic story to be told in open court in front of all those other white people. Even though the jurors were kept at the Delta Inn Hotel each night of the trial, and even though they were told not to speak to anybody about the case, there was going to be so much buzzing about that testimony that there would be no way the jurors could keep from hearing the story. And they would wind up hearing the story in all the twisted and distorted ways people could possibly tell it. That is, if they hadn't heard it already, long before the trial even got under way.

For the time left, the defense lawyers called a bunch of character witnesses, including Milam's wife, Juanita, and other people they paraded in front of the jury as "experts." Since the defense opened the door to character, the prosecutors tried to raise questions about whether people knew Milam had been arrested for bootlegging. But the judge didn't permit them to go there. He did allow people like Sheriff Strider to come in to twist things up even more.

Strider testified that the body he saw looked like it had been in the water for somewhere between ten and fifteen days. Emmett had only been missing for three days. He said he couldn't tell whether it was black or white. He just knew it was human. And, in a comment that I know was directed at me, he said he wouldn't have been able to recognize that body if it had been one of his own sons. The special prosecutor asked him if he had signed a death certificate that identified the body as Emmett Till. Strider swore that he had not done that. It would be some time before I would finally receive Emmett's death certificate that showed Strider had done exactly that on September 1. Twenty-one days earlier. But, of course, we had no way to know that at the time.

Dr. L. B. Otken, a physician, said the body could have been in the river for up to two weeks and was so bloated that a mother couldn't have even identified him. He was able to give this "expert" opinion even though he never moved any closer to Emmett than the riverbank, because of the odor. Finally, H. D. Malone, the embalmer, said it looked like the body had been in the water for up to twenty-five days and was "bloated beyond recognition." Each one of the defense team's so-called experts seemed to be taking it up a notch. I mean, if this had gone on much longer, they might have tried to say Emmett's body had been in that river since the end of the Civil War. None of these witnesses was a pathologist and they all had to admit when they were asked by the prosecution that a badly beaten body would deteriorate much faster and look like it had been in the river much longer.

Clotye Murdock, the *Ebony* writer, was so upset about Strider's testimony that she approached the judge as court was recessing. She asked a question that the judge thought was a pretty good one. If Strider couldn't tell whether the body pulled from the river was black or white, how come he turned it over to a black undertaker? It was a bold thing to do right there on Strider's turf, and she realized it. Only after the fact. As it turns out, word never reached Strider. At least he never said anything or did anything about it.

There was plenty of reason to be concerned about harassment. Jimmy Hicks found that out. On his way into court one day, he was pulled aside by a deputy and taken before some kind of justice of the peace in another building. He was accused of passing a stopped school bus on the road. After a nervous moment, the whole thing wound up being thrown out. But Jimmy Hicks and everybody else got the message: People were watching and they wanted us to know they could come after us when we least expected it.

Things were shifting again. After the defense began playing its cards, it was beginning to seem like none of our evidence, none of our testimony was going to matter. In a criminal case, all the jury needs to let somebody off is a reasonable doubt. What might have seemed irrational and distorted to the rest of the world came off as very reasonable in the upside-down world of Sumner, where it seemed people were looking for any reason, any excuse to set two murderers free. Once again, I was beginning to fear that things were not going to turn out well.

I really wasn't sure I wanted to return on Friday. Not after listening to all those lies on Thursday afternoon. I mean, I just had this awful feeling, knowing now that it was possible for these people to take lies for truth and truth for lies. They had been living such dishonest lives for so many years that they probably didn't even know the difference anymore. Oh, God, it seemed like all the blood drained out of my body. I just had to pray, and brave it. And so I did.

Friday, September 23, was the first day of fall. Summer had ended. But the heat was still on. In court, the morning was taken up by more character witnesses before the defense rested, and closing arguments were set to begin.

Well, I thought I had heard it all during the testimony, but those defense lawyers were saving the worst for last. They really wanted to end on a low note. They had built their whole case around creating doubt that the body pulled from the river was Emmett's. They could have left it at that. But they didn't. John Whitten practically accused Papa Mose and the NAACP of grave robbing to find a "rotting, stinking body" that could be thrown into the river with Emmett's ring. He told the jury that he had confidence "that every last Anglo-Saxon one of you has the courage to free these men. . . ."

Special Prosecutor Robert Smith said that was about "the most far-fetched thing I ever heard in court." But the defense team was hammering the point home that this was about more than the murder of my son. It was about showing who was in charge. J. W. Kellum made that point crystal clear when he told the white men on the jury "your forefathers will turn over in their graves" if the defendants were convicted.

The District Attorney Gerald Chatham gave a moving summation, filled with emotion and delivered with great passion. Emmett's murder was ". . . morally and legally wrong," he said. Chatham told the jurors they should not pay attention to the testimony of the so-called experts who wouldn't have known Emmett under any circumstances. But they should take the word of his mother, ". . . someone who loved him and cared for him," he said, "God's given witness to identify him."

They say you can tell a lot about the outcome of a trial when you watch the expressions of the jurors. That might be. I couldn't tell much by looking at that jury because I had always had such a bad feeling about them anyway. But I could tell a lot by watching the faces of some of the black spectators in the back of the court. Some stayed in their places, but some were getting out of there, and those are the ones I studied.

So, as the jury retired, I measured the looks of the folks in the rear and I turned to Congressman Diggs and the others. "The jury has retired and it's time for us to retire."

"What?" Congressman Diggs said. "And miss the verdict?"

I told him I thought that was one verdict he might want to miss. If that jury came back with an acquittal, then white folks were going to know for sure that they could get away with murder. It was going to be open season on black folks and we were going to be the prime targets. I was not about to wait around for that.

The jurors deliberated one hour and seven minutes. They took a soda pop break, it was said, to stretch it out a little, make it look better. They reached their verdict. Not guilty. We were on the road, about fifteen minutes out of Mound Bayou when it was announced on the radio. There was such jubilation. The radio reporter sounded like he was doing the countdown for a new year. You could hear the celebration in the background. It was like the Fourth of July. The defendants kissed their wives for the cameras, and lit their cigars. I felt despair. I was speechless. I didn't know what to say. I didn't know what to think. But I knew one thing for sure: I was not going to be vacationing in Mississippi anytime soon. In fact, I was going to get out as quickly as I possibly could.

In the end, the jury said, they did not think the state had proved that the body was Emmett's. I had done what I was supposed to do, all that I could have done. It wasn't enough for them. I had sworn that I recognized my son and had simply been dismissed. I had pleaded for justice and had the courtroom door slammed in my face.

I wonder how different things might have been if the laws and practices of Tallahatchie County had been different. What if blacks could vote there and had qualified to be on that jury? Would there have been enough black folks with the courage of Papa Mose or Willie Reed to convict two white men of murdering a black boy? Could that have happened? What if the law had allowed women to serve then? What if only one woman had been allowed on that jury? Even a white woman in Sumner, in Mississippi, in 1955 would have had to feel something for another woman who had felt what I did. Wouldn't she? A mother, someone who understood, as only a mother could, what it felt like to become a mother, what it must feel like to lose a child, a part of yourself. I wonder if a woman could have had much influence over the way things turned out. Then again, a woman did have influence over the whole thing, didn't she? In this case, a woman was at the very heart of it all, the accusation, the abduction, the acquittal. And, of course, the cause for celebration.

Dr. Howard arranged a driver for Daddy, Rayfield, and me to get to Memphis, where we would catch our plane. Somewhere along the way, someone asked the driver, a black man, if he knew who he had in his car.

"Three very nice people, seems to me," the man said.

When he found out that I was Emmett Till's mother, my God, that man went into such a cursing panic. He knew, as anyone from that area would know, that it could mean a death sentence for him just to be seen with us. He actually turned off the headlights for a while as it was getting dark, and he seemed to be taking all kinds of back roads. But what would I know? They all looked like back roads to me. Especially in the dark. His reaction scared me. It reminded me of just how much we had to fear down there. How much of a threat existed down there. Oh, I was terrified and could only imagine the horrors that lay around every turn. And then an even more terrifying thought rushed over me: Was this what Emmett saw, was this what he thought on his last ride in Mississippi in the pitch black of night?

Finally, at the airport in Memphis, the driver could not seem to get us out of his car fast enough. He did not even want to stick around long enough to collect his money, which we kind of tossed onto the backseat as he tore off into the night. I have no idea whatever became of that poor man. But I will never forget the great fear he had. Later, back in Chicago, I would remember his face and the terror he and so many others had to endure in Mississippi, USA. I prayed for his well-being and for all those we left behind.

CHAPTER 20

It was the shock heard around the world. The newspaper headlines only echoed the public outcry over that Sumner jury's verdict. They told of one hundred thousand people who turned out across the country to protest, to demonstrate their outrage. New York Congressman Adam Clayton Powell called for an economic boycott of everything from the state of Mississippi. There were demands for antilynching legislation, the end to racial segregation, black voting rights. Some even suggested sending federal troops down to Mississippi. In Chicago, NAACP attorney William Henry Huff announced that he would file a civil suit against Roy Bryant, J. W. Milam, Carolyn Bryant, and Leslie Milam, seeking $400,000 in damages.

There were demonstrations as far away as France, where Josephine Baker led a protest rally. In Germany, an editorial writer commented that a black life in Mississippi wasn't "worth a whistle." Ten thousand people turned out at a rally in Chicago to hear journalist Simeon Booker and others. As many as sixty-five thousand people rallied in Detroit, where Congressman Charles Diggs and Medgar Evers talked about the trial. In Baltimore, nearly three thousand came to hear Dr. T.R.M. Howard. I was brought fresh from Mississippi to New York, where about fifteen thousand people came to a rally headed up by Roy Wilkins and A. Philip Randolph, head of the Brotherhood of Sleeping Car Porters.

People were energized, they were angry. They were moved to action in ways they hadn't been before. It had been a little more complicated sorting Supreme Court decisions, as people began to realize that "all deliberate speed" meant just the opposite of what it sounded like it meant. That took a little more thought.

The message of the Emmett Till story was a lot simpler. And it only took feeling. In New York and in so many other cities where I would appear, I spoke from the heart about what it meant to send a boy away on vacation and bring him home in a box. I spoke of what it meant to have to examine every inch of a body to even recognize it as a human being, let alone your own flesh and blood. I spoke about the pain a mother feels when she learns about the suffering of her baby. And I spoke about a murder trial that was really a farce. I spoke about Mississippi justice, where the laws seemed to be turned inside out. Where innocent people were punished and guilty people went free. I spoke about just how close Mississippi really was to Chicago and to New York. How I once had believed that the problems of the people of Mississippi and the rest of the South were not my problems. I knew better as a result of my great loss. As a people, we had to see that what happened to any of us, affected all of us. Which is why I urged people not to give up on our fight for justice, equal justice and equal rights. I had come to see that Emmett had died for a reason. That's what I had learned from my own reflection, and from listening to all those dedicated black people back in Mississippi. I had come to realize that we had to work together to turn the sacrifice of Emmett's life into some positive gain. As I had heard the NAACP leaders in Mississippi say, we, as a nation, had to work as hard at breaking through the "Cotton Curtain" of the Deep South as we were working at breaking through the Iron Curtain of Eastern Europe. I would not harbor any hatred toward whites. But I could no longer accept their hatred of me or black people. I had learned what their hatred had cost us. As important as anything else, of course, I urged people to contribute money to help finance the fight that we could see ahead of us.

Oh, and those contributions just rolled in. Thousands and thousands of dollars, I was told. It had started at Emmett's funeral, when huge tubs of money were collected, as one minister had said, to help the NAACP. Rayfield Mooty had arranged other public appearances for me before the trial through his labor contacts and organizations. There was always a collection. At the rallies following the trial, tens of thousands of dollars were collected. NAACP membership also increased dramatically, I was told. As I understand, the organization had been strapped following the costly school desegregation fight. But following Emmett's death and the trial, contributions would hit new highs.

Apart from the fund-raising, the New York stop had been important to me for another reason. That meeting with Roy Wilkins led to discussions about my public speaking. From the very beginning, it had been so hard for us to manage all the requests that came in. Rayfield Mooty had done a pretty good job with many of the early arrangements. But we would get so many more requests following the trial. And there were quite a few groups that would announce my appearance even when they had no confirmation, sometimes misrepresenting that I would appear when they had never contacted us.

Rayfield also was concerned about being able to screen the groups that were asking for appearances. There was so much concern back then about communism. I heard that J. Edgar Hoover said that I was a little "pink." I didn't even know what that meant when I first heard it. But it was chilling when I finally realized how even little things like that "Cotton Curtain" remark I would make in my speeches might be misconstrued in ways that could be used against me. And to think, if Mr. J. Edgar Hoover had spent more time trying to build a federal case against Roy Bryant and J. W. Milam, and less time trying to make Communists out of law-abiding citizens, then maybe there would have been at least two more cold-blooded killers taken off the streets. Anyway, with public appearances, we weren't always sure when we'd get requests whether there was some connection that might have been embarrassing. We had to be careful. There was too much at stake.

Beyond all this, we had questions about what was going on behind the scenes of some of the events at which I was being asked to speak. We had been noticing that so much money was being collected through contributions at my early appearances; it was hard not to, with all the buckets and pails and tubs being passed around. But we weren't sure exactly what was happening to all that money. We were blessed to have received enough to handle the funeral expenses for Emmett, and there were contributions to help with travel to Mississippi. But some people told us that so many thousands more had been collected to help the NAACP, and it wasn't clear whether all that money was making its way to the organization. I remember one appearance I made at a large church in Detroit where people were just packed in like sardines in a can. They were even standing around outside, listening on loudspeakers. Great sums of money were collected there. I mean, when it came time for collection at this service, they didn't pass the plate. They didn't pass the bucket. They passed around big wastebaskets. I mean, *garbage cans.* And the people were filling them up. It was just amazing. After I finished my remarks, I asked to see the pastor, a prominent, respected man. I hadn't seen him since I started speaking. I was told that he was indisposed, or something like that. But I kept insisting and finally barged into his office, just broke past the people out front, opened the door, and went in to find him standing there, putting on his suit coat. Well, on the desk between us there was a satchel, just sitting there wide open, filled to the brim with greenbacks. I mean, that bag was *stuffed*. My first thought was to wonder how on earth he would even get it closed. But it definitely looked like he was on his way out, and he was not leaving without that money. That church gave me $175 for my efforts that day. But I'll never forget that satchel and I always wondered what happened after I left.

Now, that was only one situation I happened to see. People were telling me all the time about other cases much like that one. Money was being raised, money was being diverted. There were so many good people who wanted to help us back then, and organizations did all they could to make sure people's intentions were fulfilled. But, obviously, there also were good reasons for us to raise questions about whether Emmett's name was being used by some people for their own gain. During the murder trial, Ruby Hurley had issued a statement for the NAACP confirming that it had not participated in any fund-raising activities tied to Emmett's death and that it had not received any funds that were collected. Well, you can just imagine how alarming that would be. So, there were many reasons for us to try to get some help in managing these public appearances. To make sure there was no overbooking, to make sure we were not being used by the wrong groups, and to make sure that the money would wind up at the NAACP, where it would do the most good.

Rayfield worked something out with A. Philip Randolph, who arranged a meeting with Roy Wilkins in New York. We met to discuss it all. Roy Wilkins seemed like a very serious and determined man, but different from the other NAACP people I had spent time with in Mississippi. He seemed cooler than people like Medgar Evers and Ruby Hurley, who were always so passionate about the work they were doing on the front lines. But, of course, they would be different. The frontline officers deal with people. The generals deal with battle plans. He had come up from the front lines, though. In fact, I had heard about the stirring address he had given at the funeral service for Reverend George Lee in Belzoni. But, unlike the people out in the field, Roy Wilkins had to think about an entire organization as well as all the people in it. He had to think about an agenda. He made that clear in our meeting. And it was with that in mind that he told me at first that he had reservations about working with us to manage a public speaking tour. He had been executive secretary for less than six months, but he had been in important positions at the NAACP for quite a few years before that. He said he felt that some people in the past had used the organization, only to abandon it once they had gotten what they wanted. We talked it through and told him that would never be the case with me. And, besides, we thought there would be benefits for the

NAACP. There would be a chance to raise money and increase the NAACP's membership at a time when the organization needed both. Finally, he agreed and we worked out the terms. I would receive a fee for speaking, and the NAACP would manage a tour that also would bring in contributions and memberships.

It seemed like a very good arrangement and I could move forward with peace of mind, not worrying about whether I was being used. There would be so many appearances over the coming weeks. It was important to me to be able to share my message with the huge crowds.

It had been awkward at first, being in the spotlight. My family had always had such a quiet, normal existence, and I had been so happy to lead an ordinary life. I didn't ask for everything that was happening to me. Lord knows, I didn't ask for any of it. But I acted on what I was given. There were decisions I had made without really thinking much about them at all. It had been as if something was working through me, guiding me through a mission I never would have recognized before. I had made a choice to share my loss with the public, to share my pain in a way that would energize and motivate people to take action.

This activity came with a price. Behind every public exposure, there was a flurry of telephone calls, letters. Thousands of letters. Some were very unkind, some even worse. It just brought on a whole lot of trauma, really. I kept going, because it was important. I felt that. But there was something else, something very personal about this public experience. I needed it. In so many ways I could never have explained back then, I needed to continue talking. I needed it so very much. I don't know what I would have done if I had been all alone during this period or if I had tried right away to go back to the normal life I had always thought I would live. I doubt that I could have survived it all. There was just too much sorrow for one person to endure, too much pain for one person to absorb, too much anger for one person to express. So the crowds helped me get through it. They listened as I talked about Emmett and his trip and the brutal murder and the horrible injustice that I had suffered, that black people were suffering every day in so many ways. We connected. I talked, they listened. But, in a way, it was a dialogue. Just by being there, they were saying something to me. Something very important. They were saying that people cared about what had happened. That's what I needed to know, especially after spending a week at the Sumner trial, where it didn't seem that people cared at all. I am so thankful for the crowds that turned out to listen to me, and to communicate with me in the process. Indeed, they helped me find a reason to keep going. Talking helped me sort through the horror. The more I talked about it, the more relief I felt, relief from the agony. Something deep inside me was just boiling up, and if I hadn't been able to talk about it, I would have exploded. I was getting it out. I was grieving by talking. In the process, I was finding my voice and finding some meaning. It was cathartic.

Papa Mose had lived in Mississippi all of his life and had never really wanted to live anywhere else. There had been a good crop that year. He had expected to pick about thirty bales of cotton. But now, with the help of Dr. Howard and Medgar Evers, he would leave. Aunt Lizzy had been begging him to do it, to join her in Chicago. The time had come, and he wouldn't wait, couldn't wait, until the end of the year to settle up. That's how families had always done it before they left Mississippi for a better life up North. Wait until the end of the year, settle up, move in December or January. But Papa Mose was leaving even that behind, settling as best he could right then and there. He had survived the most difficult experience of his life, sold all his farm animals, given away his dog, Dallas, told his brother to pick up that forty-six Ford, the one with the stripped first gear, just pick it up at the train station, sell it. He would come back only one more time, in November, for the grand jury in Greenwood, the one that would consider indicting Roy Bryant and J. W. Milam for kidnapping.

Amanda Bradley had to flee to her mother's house. Even there, she was not safe. A white mob came looking for her and she saved herself by hiding under her mother's bed. The mob left, but not before warning Mandy's mother that if they found her, she would never testify at another trial. She made sure they weren't going to find her. She made her way to Mound Bayou and to Dr. Howard, who arranged to get her on a train to Chicago. She would have liked to have been able to settle up with Leslie Milam before she had to leave, before Milam evicted her husband, who stayed behind for a while. They had been sharecropping on the Sheridan Plantation for three years and had never done better than break even, she told the *Chicago Defender*. In fact, the year before, they wound up owing eleven dollars to Leslie Milam after it was all said and done. At least, according to his calculations. It was going to be hard in Chicago, but at least there was some hope. At least she was alive and could try to do better than just breaking even.

Willie Reed made a run for it. With only the clothes he was wearing, an extra pair of pants, and a coat, he traveled by foot about six miles to the special meeting place that had been set up. He was picked up and driven to Mound Bayou, where Dr. Howard arranged for his safe transit, too. Medgar Evers drove Willie and Congressman Diggs to Memphis, where they boarded a plane to Chicago. Willie would join his mother and other relatives. His grandfather Add Reed planned to stay in Mississippi, Willie told the *Defender*. His grandfather, like Uncle Crosby, was not afraid. There was only a small amount of relief for Willie when he arrived and was greeted by an uncle who would take him to his new home. His whole world had been set on edge and it was hard for him to feel at ease. He was still distracted by what he had left behind.

Willie and his uncle probably should have noticed the two men. After all, the men kind of stood out in that neighborhood. But they didn't notice, not until they were noticed.

As Willie and his uncle made their way up the steps, they heard the voice. "Willie? Willie Reed?"

It was a moment of terror for Willie and his uncle. The people back in Mississippi had promised to get him out of danger. They had flown him all the way to Chicago to guarantee that he would not be harmed. They had promised he would be protected. When Willie and his uncle turned to see who was speaking, they were greeted by two plainclothes Chicago officers. The police would be assigned to protect Willie for the next couple of months.

For Willie, the relief would not last long, though. Soon, he was rushed to Michael Reese Hospital. He had suffered a nervous breakdown.

I also collapsed. The pressure had been incredible. I felt like I had been carrying the weight of the world on my shoulders and it was pure adrenaline that had helped me carry that weight. But it simply got to be too much for me. I was exhausted and had to be put under a doctor's care.

So many lives were changed by what happened there in Tallahatchie County. In fact, the whole county went through changes. Nearly a quarter of the entire population had left by the end of the 1950s. But there was something else that was transforming.

I'm no historian. But you don't have to be a historian to tell about the history you have lived. You just need a long memory. There are things that happened to me a long time ago that I will never forget. There are things that happened *because* of the things that happened to me that I will always consider.

There was no justice for me in Mississippi. Nothing about that trial was even remotely related to justice. I had a door slammed in my face. To add insult to injury, there were Southern papers and Southern politicians who had the nerve to suggest that things would have been different if we had kept our mouths shut. If only I hadn't let the world see Emmett the way they had sent him home to me. If only the NAACP hadn't demanded justice in a little country courthouse down there in Mississippi. If it hadn't been for us, there could have been a different outcome in the murder trial of Roy Bryant and J. W. Milam. So, it was our fault, the "outside agitators." But what did they base that opinion on? You didn't have to look that far to find other cases where whites had gotten clean away with murder. In fact, the same week the Sumner jury acquitted Bryant and Milam, a grand jury in Brookhaven failed to indict any of the three white men accused of murdering Lamar Smith in broad daylight. No witnesses would come forward.

I never felt that I had done the wrong thing by exposing what was going on down there. And I never will. It was the outside agitators who revealed to the world, not only the injustice I had suffered, but also the unfairness blacks were suffering every single day of the year. Even so, it would take time for me to realize everything that had happened down there in Sumner, Mississippi. Those lawyers, J. J. Breland and John Whitten and the rest, hadn't really defended Roy Bryant and J. W. Milam so much as they had defended a way of life. Tallahatchie County was like so many other places in the Delta. The places they had always been. Tallahatchie County had a population of eleven thousand whites and nineteen thousand blacks. Almost twice as many blacks as whites, but not a single black person in that entire county was registered to vote. It was only through intimidation that white folks were able to hold on to their power and all that their power brought them. That must have been clear to somebody like Sheriff H. C. Strider. I can't imagine that he ever would have come into office if the black majority down there had just been allowed to vote. So, the last thing people like Breland and Whitten wanted was to have the spotlight shine on their dirty little secret, to have anyone coming in from the outside telling them they couldn't do the only thing they were used to doing: stay in power.

That's not to say that racism wasn't a factor. The murder of my son, after all, was a hate crime. And the acquittal of Bryant and Milam had as much to do with racism as anything. That point would be made crystal clear in an unpublished master's thesis produced in 1963 by Hugh Stephen Whitaker at Florida State University in Tallahassee. Whitaker was sixteen years old at the time of the murder trial. As a white Tallahatchie County resident, he was able to talk to a lot of the key people involved in the trial, including jurors, defense attorneys, and Special Prosecutor Robert Smith. What Whitaker found might shock some people, but it wouldn't surprise those of us—the black reporters and civil rights workers and witnesses—who sat in that courtroom and felt the heat.

Whitaker would write that the defense team felt they had won the case once the jury was selected. They had relied on Strider and the newly elected sheriff, Harry Dogan, who would replace Strider. These men helped the defense lawyers screen prospective jurors, since these men knew just about everybody in the county. As a result, the defense team knew more about the jury than the prosecutors did. The jurors weren't really affected at all by the pretrial publicity, according to Whitaker. And, even though the jurors had been instructed by the judge not to talk about the case with anyone, there were wide rumors around Sumner that they were contacted by members of the White Citizens Councils to vote "the right way." Still, even this did not have an effect on them. In fact, the evidence didn't move the jurors one way or the other. According to Whitaker's interviews, they were unaffected by the evidence, by their peers, by the pressure of the press and the "outside agitators." It was like they lived in a cocoon, insulated by their own racism. They had heard Carolyn Bryant's fantastic account long before she gave it in court, long before that testimony made it around town on the rumor mill. Whitaker would write that the jurors didn't doubt that Bryant and Milam had killed Emmett. They didn't doubt that at all. The jurors heard one thing that was important to them, and that was a white woman's claim that a black boy had insulted her. That was all they needed to hear. It was all they needed to know. In the end, according to Whitaker, it was all they would consider in making up their minds.

So it looks like the jury would have voted the same way even if the NAACP and I hadn't made all that noise in the days and weeks leading up to the trial. The outcome would have been no different even if I had chosen to stay quiet, as thousands of other black people had done when their loved ones were lynched. But there would have been one very important difference if I had not done anything, or said anything about Emmett's murder: No one else would have known about it, and no one else would have been moved to action because of it.

I had to consider all of that, as I went through the lineup of speaking appearances arranged by the NAACP that October. I was on the cusp of my thirty-fourth birthday, on the brink of being reborn. I had been so naive for so much of my life. I had lost my darling son and my own innocence all at the same time. But I hadn't been alone. The entire country had been forced to open its eyes, too.

Emmett represented so many things to so many people. To Bryant and Milam, he had represented everything they had refused to recognize in black people. He was confident and self-assured, and he carried himself with a certain dignity they felt they had to beat down, beat back, beat to a bloody pulp. To little black children who gazed upon the images of my son in the pages of *Jet* magazine, Emmett was the face of a harsh reality that left no place to hide. To all black people, he was a reminder of the common problem we faced in this country, whether we lived in the North or the South. He was a unifying symbol. And his name would be spoken at so many rallies and fund-raisers and even in congressional hearings.

We were in the television age now, and the media had seen the light. Many of the reporters who covered that travesty in Mississippi had been awakened to the great social and legal injustices confronting us. These were hard things to forget. And injustice would be a recurring theme playing out in the months and years to come. Those people down there in Mississippi thought that they could stage-manage a trial, and force people to accept their warped version of reality. They thought wrong. Those lawyers down in Mississippi figured they had stopped the NAACP in its tracks. They miscalculated. They might have won a battle, but they were about to lose the war.

Things would never be the same again. No one could plead ignorance. Everyone had to take responsibility for what our society had become. Anybody who did anything to make it happen. Anybody who did nothing to stop it from happening. There could no longer be any innocent bystanders. For an entire nation, the murder of Emmett Till marked the death of innocence.

CHAPTER 21

The story broke around the middle of October. We were in Washington. And that kind of made sense, the timing and all. This was all about politics, every last part of it: the trial, the intimidation, and now the revelation.

The Washington trip had been arranged as part of a national drive to push for an end to racial intolerance. It was called the "Spiritual Mobilization," and we would travel to a number of cities to appeal to people to get involved and, of course, to contribute to the cause. It was a very busy and stressful time. I was making two or even three speeches in a single day. Rayfield, Aunt Lizzy, and Bishop Isaiah Roberts traveled with me to Washington, so that helped me a lot. Now, everyone had always known that getting the federal government involved would be a very important part of the drive. We had asked for a meeting with Maxwell Raab. He was the secretary to President Eisenhower's cabinet and the White House aide on minority affairs. We were told that Raab had a very heavy schedule and that he would not be able to meet with us. But, at least there had been a response. President Eisenhower never even answered the telegram I had sent asking for his help with a federal investigation of Emmett's murder.

We also had wanted to schedule a hearing before the Senate Subcommittee on Civil Rights while we were in Washington. But we were sent regrets by Senator Thomas Hennings, the chairman of that subcommittee. Unfortunately, we were told, there would be no session during our visit. There was no word on any future hearings. That really shouldn't have surprised us. The chairman of the full committee, the one that basically controlled Senator Hennings's subcommittee, was Mississippi's own Senator James O. Eastland, who had fought tooth and nail to resist any desegregation in his state. I would find out that Senator Eastland had another card up his sleeve in this dirty little political game, and he would use his government connections to play it.

Despite the fact that the federal government was leaving us out in the cold, the main event of our trip would go very well. About six thousand people would attend the mass meeting that had been scheduled. A second meeting would be arranged for the overflow crowd of more than four thousand.

The headline for the day, though, would not be the story about mass meetings or racial intolerance or calls for government action. The headline would be a story that was leaked to the Southern press. It was the story of Louis Till. It finally would clear up for me what the army had meant when it had classified his cause of death as "willful misconduct." But it would do a whole lot more than that. Private Louis Till was court-martialed and, on February 17, 1944, he was found guilty of murdering an Italian woman and raping two others. He was hanged on July 2, 1945, and buried in a military cemetery in Naples. The execution order was signed by General Dwight David Eisenhower.

The uproar was deafening. That story was used in Mississippi just the way it was intended by the people who leaked it. For people who didn't know any better, it would provide the justification for everything that happened to Emmett. The suggestion was clear: "Like father, like son." That story fed the most horrible stereotypes and played on the greatest fear white Southerners had about desegregation. It was an irrational notion that more contact between blacks and whites would mean greater risk for white women. Oh, it was terrible.

It was so unfair, too. Especially since these same records that had been given so easily to reporters were never released to me. I had tried. And that was on the record. Among the other documents that were released with this revelation was a 1948 letter. It had been written by the lawyer Joseph Tobias on my behalf and it sought an explanation of why benefits were cut off. The records that were coming out now showed why I could never get an explanation from the army, from Louis Till's commanding officer, or from the chaplain. Even many years later, when I filed a Freedom of Information Act request, the documents I received were so censored that it wound up being a waste of my money. The army, it seems, only released this kind of information to the next of kin. Louis and I had been separated, so he had listed an uncle as his next of kin. The only reason I ever got any information at all was that I was listed on the allotment Louis had worked out. But that was it. After our efforts failed in 1948, I had settled into the uncertainty of it all, feeling that I would never find out what had happened. I never imagined I would find out like this.

Ethel Payne, a writer at the *Chicago Defender,* dug into the matter. She reported that the judge advocate general would never release such information to the press, and hadn't done it in this case. The army had rigid rules about the release of records like those. The reporters who broke the story wound up giving credit where it was due: Senator Eastland had helped.

This was an outrage and, while I was caught off guard in Washington trying to answer reporters' questions while preparing for the speech later that day, Attorney William Henry Huff was in Chicago blaming Mississippi's two senators, Eastland and John Stennis, for the controversy. The whole business was insulting, unfair, and misleading. And, it seems, it was starting to cause a breach in my relationship with the NAACP. Roy Wilkins reportedly told someone he was glad he hadn't gotten caught in that "Louis Till trap." Apparently, he had intended to include a reference to Louis and his service to the country in some remarks he had been planning to make. I was demoralized by something that was not even my fault, and certainly wasn't Emmett's. In a strange way, he was being held to account for a father he never knew. Even worse, there was some talk that Louis himself could have been misjudged.

The most terrible stories were told to me. Nightmare stories about how a number of black soldiers were treated during World War II. With the revelation about Louis, I began to hear from his army friends. The unit he served in was an all-black unit made up mostly of fellows from the Chicago area, so it was not hard for them to locate me. Louis's friends told me they thought he had gotten set up. First, they didn't believe Louis was capable of doing what he was accused of doing. Second, there was a larger problem the black soldiers were dealing with. It was a problem that had followed them overseas from the United States. Gene's brother, Wealthy, talked about it, too. He had served in Europe and recalled how black soldiers would get roused at three in the morning. Military police would look over the black soldiers in formation. The MPs would bring in local women who would point out someone in the line. One night, Wealthy recalled, a woman was walking the line and stopped when she got to his section of the formation. He knew what that meant and he was terrified. He began to sweat, knowing that black soldiers who got pointed out at three in the morning were always taken away. They were not brought back. He knew he hadn't done anything wrong, but that didn't seem to matter. As it turned out, the woman pointed to the man standing next to Wealthy, not that he found a whole lot of relief in that. That man was taken away and he was never seen again. Wealthy was distressed about it. The man slept in the bunk next to his, and Wealthy knew the man had been in his bunk every night.

It seemed that the army really didn't need much more proof than a late-night identification to take black soldiers out. But based on what Louis's friends told me, it seemed the real offense wasn't always against white women. Often, it really was against white men. A number of women in those late-night lineups, it seems, were only identifying the men who slept with them, not men they were accusing of rape. There were rules about soldiers fraternizing with local women—white women. But for many of the white officers and soldiers from the South, there also was a custom about that sort of thing. They wouldn't tolerate seeing a black soldier with even a *picture* of a white woman, let alone a relationship. There were friends of Louis's in the service who wondered whether he really was guilty. Like Wealthy had wondered about that fellow in the bunk next to his. But they could only wonder.

Louis died before he could see what would happen to his son. Bo died before he could learn about what had happened to his father. Yet they were connected in ways that ran as deep as their heritage, as long as their bloodline. I was left behind to think about all the ways they were connected. J. W. Milam had served in World War II. He had become a lieutenant. He was just the kind of tough guy the army would honor, reward with a field commission. I couldn't help thinking about so many Milams and Bryants in the armed services, good ole boys. I couldn't help thinking about how much power these men would have had over the lives of black soldiers, just as they would one day have again back home on their farms and their plantations. I couldn't help thinking about all of that, and how maybe, just maybe, Louis Till had been set up, as his friends believed. So, in the end, Eastland and his supporters just might have been right after all. Maybe Emmett did wind up like his father, an echo of what had happened ten years earlier. Maybe they both were lynched.

The timing of the revelation could not have been better for people with the worst of intentions. On November 8, 1955, the grand jury of Leflore County, Mississippi, sat to consider whether to indict Roy Bryant and J. W. Milam in Emmett's kidnapping. Under Mississippi law at the time, Bryant and Milam could have faced ten years in prison, or even death, if convicted. Bryant had admitted to the kidnapping when he was questioned by Leflore County Sheriff George Smith. Milam admitted to it when he was questioned by Smith's deputy, John Ed Cothran. The sheriff and the deputy were both called to testify at the grand jury hearing in Greenwood. Papa Mose and Willie Reed also were called and they both traveled back to Mississippi from Chicago to testify. Papa Mose spent about twenty-four minutes with the grand jury, and Willie spent about nineteen. In the end, it seemed like a waste of time. Nothing seemed to matter to whites in the Delta. Despite the testimony, despite the admission by Bryant and Milam, the grand jury refused to indict. This was outrageous even to people who might have quibbled over whether there had been a strong enough case for conviction in the murder trial. This had been an open-and-shut case. But, of course, the grand jury sat within a couple of weeks of the Louis Till story, which had been widely circulated in the area. And that might have been all the "evidence" that was needed for people who wanted to rush to judgment. I was physically ill. The *Chicago Sun-Times* published an editorial on the Greenwood grand jury that pretty much said it all: "There was no lack of evidence that would have justified an indictment by any grand jury. . . . Somewhere along the line something went wrong—and it was a shameful, evil wrong."

The NAACP had arranged to send me on a speaking tour of the West Coast. Ruby Hurley would also be featured on the November tour. The plan was for me to deliver speeches over a two-week period. As my public appearance schedule began to pick up, my father had agreed to go on the road with me. He took a leave from his job just to accompany me. He had been there for me in Mississippi during the trial. I had needed his help so desperately then. I promised that his expenses would be covered and that I would pay him for lost work. It was a great comfort to me that my father would be there during the trip and at all the speaking engagements. I was still getting threatening letters and I felt better knowing there would be somebody there to look out for me. Besides, I was so confused during that time that if somebody had asked where I was, where I had been, or where I was going next, well, I would have needed some prompting. The doctor had released me to travel, but I was still in such a state. My sense of time and place had gotten scrambled. But my daddy, oh, he could tell me everything. I mean, he was not an educated man, but he had a computer in his head and it really was something. He could keep details in order. He knew where I'd been, where I was, where I was going, everything. And, as important as anything else, he protected me from the crowd. He had to be there for me. I was happy he'd agreed.

There were a number of discussions about the details of the trip, the expenses and the amount I would receive. I had been offered fifteen hundred dollars for the two-week tour. Now, there were a lot of people around me during this period. Rayfield certainly was always there. He was so good at handling details, keeping track of things, contacting people to make sure we got pictures, and advising me. He was a shrewd and tough negotiator. He had worked out the initial arrangement with the NAACP about handling the speaking appearances, and he seemed to always be thinking about plans for me. But there were others, as well. Many people were there to talk to me and to offer advice. A woman was taking care of my administrative affairs and handled most of the discussions with the NAACP about the West Coast trip. She also handled record keeping and, as important as anything else, tracking those expenses. There were quite a few new expenses to track. It was almost like running a little business. I had come to rely on the advice of others back then. I needed to be able to rely on them, since it was all I could do most of the time just to show up where I was told I should be. Show up and speak. At one point, my assistant looked over everything and told me that I couldn't afford to make the Western trip for only fifteen hundred dollars. I guess I was trying to do too much—covering my father's expenses and my own, her compensation, and all the rest. I heard from others at different points, too. There was so much that I was urged to think about. Would I return to work anytime soon? Could I even consider it? If not, then how would I live? What about the large debt that had piled up? Shouldn't I be thinking about that, and about trying to prepare now for an uncertain future? And what about all those people who had made money off my name, off Emmett's?

I had confidence in the NAACP and felt comfortable with our new arrangement, and that the money that was supposed to go to the organization was reaching it. There was nothing I would ever be able to do about the people who had taken advantage of me and the circumstances in the past. They would take care of themselves. But other considerations—ongoing living expenses and, now, operating costs—caused me to think. My goodness, the telephone bill alone had gone up to a couple of hundred dollars a month. I needed to know that I could make the trip out West and still take care of everything back home, as well as all the people. When my assistant told me that I'd wind up having to reach into my own pocket to make ends meet, well, I knew that wasn't going to work.

There was a minister out West who was coordinating on that end. When he was informed about the circumstances, he said he would consider the situation and the possibilities. When he called back, he had good news. Wonderful news, really. They had increased the payment to three thousand dollars. Oh, my God, that would be great.

Then he called again. He said they might be able to go up to six thousand dollars, and somehow, I was told, they finally settled on five thousand.

I was so relieved when I got that information, because I would not have to be distracted by financial worries. My needs would be taken care of.

Then another call came in. This one came late, about eleven o'clock one night, directly to me. It was from New York, not California. It was Roy Wilkins. He was mad. I mean, he was *very* angry. And he bawled me out. He told me I was like all the rest, the other people, the ones he had told me about, the ones who had turned on the organization the minute they got a little attention, a little fame. They wanted everything for themselves. They weren't loyal to the NAACP.

"But I'm not going to do that," I said. I never would have done anything like that. I thought about all the crowds I had addressed and how I had urged everyone to support the NAACP. I remembered the work and the commitment of people like Medgar Evers, Ruby Hurley, Amzie Moore, Aaron Henry. The people who had done so much for us down in Mississippi. I had been impressed by everything they were willing to put on the line. I had learned about the supreme sacrifices of people like the Reverend George Lee and Lamar Smith. And I was moved by it all. I felt that I had become part of it all. I had come to understand things I had never understood before, about how important it was for everyone to do something, anything, whatever we could, to help in the progress we deserved to make. I thought about all that and how I had pledged my complete support to the NAACP. That's what I had told the crowds, that I would do anything I was asked to do, and that they should do the same. And I thought about the advice I had gotten—advice that was spinning in my head as I listened to him speak, advice about how to handle these business matters and how to make sure things were taken care of and how to negotiate.

So I tried to explain to Roy Wilkins that I was not turning away from the NAACP and that I was just trying to take care of the important needs I had at that time. I even tried to explain to him what they were.

That's when he spoke the words I can never forget. "You're trying to capitalize on the death of your son."

I was stunned. There was nothing to do but hang up.

Things were in such a state of turmoil over the next few days. I was deeply hurt, but I still tried to reach out, to repair what had been damaged. I even wrote a letter to Roy Wilkins. "The objective of the NAACP is of much greater concern to me than my pocketbook," I wrote. "I set out to trade the blood of my child for the betterment of my race; and I do not wish now to deviate from that course. . . . Please let me go forward for the NAACP. It is a duty. I would not want it said that I did anything to shirk it."

It was too late, though. I was told that I wouldn't be going to California, or anywhere else. That message was confirmed in the newspapers that would report on the split, and the miscommunication, the advice I had been getting, and how some people had not been representing me well and, oh, I was just devastated.

Roy Wilkins had a job to do, and I recognized that and supported that. A war was being waged on injustice and inequality and he was the general in that war. All generals have to keep their eye on their objectives, on winning the war. They must accept that there will be casualties along the way. I just never imagined that I would wind up as one of the casualties.

The NAACP announced that it would not pursue a civil action against Roy Bryant and J. W. Milam, as Attorney Huff had been considering. Such a case would have to be filed in Mississippi. The feeling now was that it would be futile after the jury acquittal in Sumner and the grand jury decision in Greenwood. The federal government had decided some time ago that it was not going to step in. So, it seemed that all the possibilities had been exhausted.

Papa Mose agreed to fill in on the West Coast speaking tour, so at least the rallies were able to continue. But it all would continue now without me.

During this period, Rayfield Mooty arranged a meeting. We were going to see an attorney somewhere up on Forty-seventh Street. He wanted me to keep it confidential and not tell anybody—not even my mother—where I was going. I agreed, even though I wondered why I wasn't supposed to tell anybody. I was a little concerned when I arrived and saw a run-down building and had to climb those rickety steps. But I was greeted very warmly by Rayfield and an attorney. They laid out a program for me that would have allowed me to continue my speaking appearances, but under Rayfield's management. He told me all the things he would be able to do to make it happen and to make it successful. It all sounded good and I wanted so much to be able to reach out to people again. Then he set the terms. Rayfield would be paid 40 percent of my gross earnings. The attorney would get 10 percent. I would get 50 percent, but I would have to pay all expenses out of my 50 percent. And that would be the arrangement for the next twenty years. A twenty-year contract. Now, I'm no lawyer, but I really didn't need to be a lawyer to know that this deal didn't sound quite right. I wasn't sure I could even sign a twenty-year agreement to stay married to the same man. Not with the kind of experience I had been having.

I had learned quite a bit from Rayfield Mooty in those weeks we had spent together. I saw him in action and he was something to watch. I learned what it took to be a tough negotiator. When to talk, when to walk.

I learned when no was the best way to yes. But I also learned when no was just the best way, period. I appreciated the time Rayfield had spent with me, the time he had spent thinking through his plan for me. But I was going to have to let this one go. With everything that had happened, well, I just felt that it was best for me to take some time to reflect on it all. I felt that it was best for me to do that alone.

Gus Courts was a black grocer in Belzoni, Mississippi. He had been a close friend of the Reverend George Lee, and had picked up the baton after Reverend Lee was murdered. Even though he faced a great deal of risk and intimidation, he took over the NAACP recruitment and voter registration work that Reverend Lee had been doing. In the eight months that followed Reverend Lee's murder, Courts was made to suffer for his bold decision. The White Citizens Councils blocked deliveries to his store to try to drive him out of business. When this didn't seem to work, men came looking for him. He was shot in his store. As God would have it, he survived. But he decided he had to leave the South. Over in Mound Bayou, Dr. Howard had a similar revelation. He was on the same hit list as Courts and Medgar Evers and so many others. Dr. Howard sold his property at a great loss and moved his family to Chicago, where he set up a new medical practice. It might have seemed like the racists of Mississippi had won. But this would only be the beginning. Dr. Howard would stay active and would even get involved in politics. As a Republican. He had had his fill of Democrats down in Mississippi.

For a moment, I had been part of something, the beginning of something that now seemed to be leaving me behind. That was something I had to accept and, even though there was so much despair for me, I was comforted by the thought that Emmett would not be forgotten. By December, in Montgomery, Alabama, something was happening. The spark of Emmett had caught fire. Another mother figure would warm our hearts, nurture our spirits, inspire our work. I had been there at the center of the media storm and I understood what she was experiencing. I knew the tests she would have to endure. I knew these things and I reached out to her. I did it quietly. I did it privately. I did it through prayer.

P eople were determined to keep Emmett Till alive. The tragedy had moved them to tears. The injustice had made them angry enough to fight back. And the unanswered questions, well, they kept nagging for some kind of resolution.

Jimmy Hicks, the reporter for the *Baltimore Afro-American,* couldn't let it go. In the weeks following the murder trial in Sumner, he published his series revealing all the things that had gone on behind the scenes, all the efforts by the reporters and the authorities in that frantic search for the surprise witnesses. The series was published in several black newspapers. But Jimmy Hicks still couldn't let it go. He went back down there to Mississippi and covered the kidnapping grand jury in Greenwood. He did that even though he admitted that, like so many of the rest of us during the murder trial, he also had been afraid of those white folks. This was a man who was bold enough to want to be among the first reporters to fly up in a rocket ship, whenever we got to that point, and he, too, had been afraid of those folks in Mississippi. That was how bad things had been. And that was how courageous all the people were to stick with it down there, in the face of all that intimidation.

Jimmy Hicks kept pushing the questions about Levy "Too Tight" Collins and Henry Lee Loggins, the two black men people believed to have been in the back of the truck with Emmett. Hicks had been told that these black men had been kept in the Charleston jail by Sheriff Strider to keep them from testifying. But the prosecutors didn't follow up on this. The prosecutors accepted Strider's assurance that it was not true. And the black reporters were not allowed to visit the jail. So all they had were the rumors and the source stories. The rumors were persistent and just kept swirling around and growing until they became the stories that other people would report. Others would come forward after the trial to say they, too, had seen the truck that morning, the one with whites up front and blacks in the back. They would say, off the record, that they later saw two black men washing blood from the back of that truck, blood these men said was from deer hunting. It was not deer hunting season. During the murder trial, many people had begun to feel that Collins and Loggins had been killed to keep them quiet. But Jimmy Hicks couldn't let it go. He was a reporter every day of his life and he knew when he was onto something. He was convinced of it. But he had run up against that wall of indifference and racist hostility down in Tallahatchie County, and, in the end, he just could not break through it. He urged the federal government to investigate possible obstruction of justice. And he wrote about it.

L. Alex Wilson couldn't let it go, either. He had covered the murder trial for the *Tri-State Defender* from his Memphis base. His publisher, John H. Sengstacke, had offered a reward for information on Emmett's killers. But that wasn't all that was done. Alex Wilson spent four days after the trial working with informants in the Delta tracking down Too Tight. He wrote a front-page story for the *Chicago Defender* about the "four harrowing, danger-filled days" it took for him to find Too Tight, to lure him into a gambling game that never happened, and finally to convince him to drive to Chicago with Wilson. As it turns out, Henry Lee Loggins had already gone to St. Louis. At the Chicago offices of the *Defender*, Too Tight was interviewed by the paper's general counsel, with the publisher and Wilson. The entire interview was published in the paper and included in Christopher Metress's book. But, after all the speculation, all the effort to find him and to get him to talk, Levy "Too Tight" Collins didn't help resolve a thing. He said he was working in Clarksdale, another Mississippi Delta town, with Henry Lee Loggins the entire time of the trial. They were driving a gravel truck for J. W. Milam's brother-in-law, Melvin Campbell. He said he had never been to Papa Mose's house in Money and he didn't feel Milam had anything to do with Emmett's death. "No, I believe he was too nice a man to do it," he said.

As it turns out, though, Jimmy Hicks might have had some pretty good sources after all. Eight years later, when Hugh Whitaker would work on his master's thesis at Florida State University, he would talk to people who never would have given up any information to black reporters. He was white and he came from Tallahatchie County. There was no wall for him, just open doors. People told him things. He interviewed defense attorney J. J. Breland and others, who told him that Collins and Loggins had been held in the county jail at Charleston. Whitaker was told that Sheriff Strider had issued the order and that these two men were held under assumed names, probably so that they could be hidden in the jail records, as well as in their cells.

We can only wonder now why somebody might have wanted to keep these two men away from everybody during the trial, to keep them from talking. If Collins and Loggins knew anything at all about what had happened to Emmett, then we can only wonder why they were still around to have the chance to talk about it at all.

After the first of the year, there would be yet another shock, at least for those who ever believed Roy Bryant and J. W. Milam were not guilty of murder. In the January 24, 1956, issue of *Look* magazine, William Bradford Huie, a white Alabama writer, reportedly paid nearly four thousand dollars to interview Bryant and Milam to get their account of how they murdered my son.

The tale that unfolded in *Look* was horrible. In fact, it was unbearable. And that was not just because of the description the killers gave of that night of terror, but also because of the distorted picture of Emmett that was presented.

In the *Look* version of events, Carolyn Bryant was not in the truck when Roy Bryant and J. W. Milam took Emmett from the house; this story never mentioned that anyone else had come to the house with them, ignoring Papa Mose's version of events. Carolyn Bryant was never involved in any way in identifying Emmett, according to this account, even though Bryant and Milam had both told Sheriff George Smith and his deputy that she had been involved. They had said they let Emmett go after bringing him before her to identify.

Since there was no third man there to hold Emmett down in the back of the truck, Emmett just sat there and went along for the ride, according to this story. He was taken to J. W. Milam's place, where he was pistol-whipped with the guns Bryant and Milam had been issued in the army. Milam was using the one he had used to beat answers out of German prisoners. They claimed Emmett kept talking back to them the whole time. They claimed he had a picture of a white girl in his wallet and that he bragged about having white girlfriends. So, they kept beating him with the pistols they had taken as mementos of their service to the country. And, they said, after all this beating, he got in the back of the truck to ride around some more. With only the two of them in the front, Emmett still just sat there passively in the back of the truck all by himself while they drove around searching for a gin fan. It was getting light out by this time and Milam said he was starting to get concerned that somebody might stop them. For stealing the gin fan. They said Emmett was still defiant as he stood on the riverbank and was told to strip and as the gun was pointed at his head.

Reporters ask questions. They ask questions and they examine records. They probe. That's how they find out things. That's how they get at the truth.

William Bradford Huie negotiated for this story. His interview with Bryant and Milam had been cleared by their lawyers, and they were very careful not to bring anyone else into the picture. Bryant and Milam had already been acquitted of murder. They could never be tried again for murdering my son. Other people didn't have that kind of protection. Lawyers would understand that sort of thing and advise their clients accordingly.

So, the Bryant and Milam version of events, the one that looked like it had been cleared by the lawyers, did not include the Sheridan Plantation in Sunflower County, where Leslie Milam was in charge. That's where Willie Reed and Amanda Bradley had both testified that they saw J. W. Milam and his truck and three other white men the Sunday morning Emmett was killed. Willie even saw Emmett in the back of that truck with the two black men. Willie's grandfather Add Reed testified that he saw Leslie Milam there about the same time the other men and the truck were there. But the *Look* article ignored all this witness testimony and accepted J. W. Milam's version of the story that they went to his place way over in Tallahatchie County. That would take Leslie Milam out of the picture altogether. It also left everybody else out.

This article seemed to go out of its way to exclude Carolyn Bryant from anything besides being insulted and telling her husband about it. And here Huie seemed to rely on that exaggerated story Carolyn Bryant told in court, the one that presented Emmett as brash and boastful. And worse. It was a picture of Emmett that easily fit a stereotype one white Southerner might easily have presented back then, and another white Southerner might easily have accepted. And published. Oh, God, if Huie had only looked at the photograph of Emmett's body, he would have known that Emmett was in no condition to stand at the riverbank and talk back. Milam claimed he did. Huie accepted that claim, it seems, without question. After that savage beating Emmett took, I doubt that he could have stood at all.

The portrayal of Emmett in this story was just awful and seemed to rely not only on what Carolyn Bryant had said in court but also on what people had been spreading around Money a couple of months after the fact. But stories in the Delta pop up as fast as the cotton in late summer, another cash crop. And they grow even faster in the hands of each picker passing them on. There was one that Jimmy Hicks had picked up in one of the juke joints where Too Tight Collins used to hang out. It was said there that the hole in Emmett's head was not a bullet hole at all. It had been made by a drill. All sorts of horrible stories sprouted up after the trial, like the one about the picture of the white girl. It seemed as if stories about Emmett and what went on in that store that Wednesday night were going to continue to grow and be cultivated.

The money must have been a great temptation for Bryant and Milam. But they also seemed to have a strategy in mind. They must have known after their acquittal that there was some support among other white racists in the Delta for what they had done and some lingering questions in the minds of others. In painting the picture of Emmett as an arrogant and defiant black boy from Chicago, they finally were doing something that they could have never done in court: They were telling a version of events that could not be challenged under oath, and appeared to go unchallenged by the journalist taking it all down. They obviously wanted to show that they had justification for doing what they boasted about doing to Emmett. The way they saw it, he had provoked them by talking back to them. In the minds of so many whites in the Delta, it would have taken far less than what they described in that story to provide a justification for his murder. And, in the process of telling this story, Bryant and Milam also accomplished something else: They had protected other people.

I wasn't there in Money at the store. But people who were there have said things did not happen the way Carolyn Bryant told the story in court, or the way they were embellished for the *Look* article. They never saw Emmett showing off a picture of a white girl. The only picture I could imagine Bryant and Milam finding in Emmett's wallet was the one that came with the wallet. The one of Hedy Lamarr. I can't imagine these killers could have mistaken a picture of Emmett's favorite actress for his girlfriend. But, then, for a black person even to carry around a picture of a white Hollywood star would have been enough to offend the likes of these two. Sadly, the people who talked to me about what went on down in Money didn't have their stories published in *Look*. That is the thing that is so troubling about this article. It seems to be built on an assumption that, where there is a conflict between two different versions of the same story—one black, one white—the white version is the one to be accepted. When you consider that the white version tends to play on black stereotypes, it was inevitable, over the years, that this story came to be the one that was relied on as the actual, factual account of what went on in that store in Money.

How sad. After all the relentless reporting that had been done by black writers like Jimmy Hicks, L. Alex Wilson, and Simeon Booker; all the courageous undercover work that had been done by NAACP people like Medgar Evers, Ruby Hurley, Amzie Moore, Aaron Henry, and others; after the persistent efforts of Dr. Howard in coaxing testimony out of eyewitnesses, paying for their relocation to Chicago; after all that work to uncover the truth of what happened to my son, the story people would often cite over the years was the one *Look* published.

William Bradford Huie negotiated for that story. Usually, when you negotiate, you agree on a price, you agree on terms. We can only wonder what terms were set for Huie's interviews, for what could be included, what would be excluded. In the end, Bryant and Milam were able to tell the story they seemed so eager to tell. And, for that, they collected close to four thousand dollars. For killing my son and boasting about it, they collected their reward, their bounty.

One thing about the Bryant and Milam version that is striking: Milam boasts about killing Emmett to teach him a lesson, and also to send a message to others. Whatever happened in that store in Money, whatever was said to have happened, whatever grew out of the imagination of people who told the story over and over again—the fact remains that Milam saw it as his duty as a white man to send that message. And sending a message to black folks is one of the key factors that distinguishes a lynching from a murder.

When it comes to a lynching, it is not just the actual killers who are guilty. It is the dominant culture, the entire society that permits such a thing, that encourages it. Bryant and Milam were not the only guilty parties in the lynching of my son. Witnesses have pointed to at least six or seven people. But, in a way, there were so many thousands more. People who were responsible, powerful, influential. People who could have chosen to lead, and chose instead to incite. People who could have condemned hate crimes and chose instead to condone them. People who could have come clean, and chose instead to live the rest of their lives with blood on their hands.

Many people were outraged when they read the admission of guilt. There was a call for a new kidnapping grand jury. Since Bryant and Milam hadn't been tried on that charge, double jeopardy wouldn't apply. But there would be no new grand jury. There even was a report that the new governor of Mississippi, James P. Coleman, said Bryant and Milam should have been executed. But he later claimed he never said that. The whole thing was just unbearable to me. On top of everything I had been through, this was just too much. Eventually, I filed a one-million-dollar lawsuit against *Look* and Huie. Attorney Joseph Tobias represented me with that claim. The story had defamed Emmett. He was not the person who was portrayed in the article. I had not raised a person like that. What had been written about Emmett was simply not true. And it hurt so badly. Eventually, that suit was dismissed. Libel is a personal claim, I was told. In the end, as God would have it, the only person who could have filed that lawsuit was Emmett.

I had been asleep in my room up front one day and finally pulled myself up. I was groggy and tried to blink away what I thought I saw. It was a lump under my rug. Finally, after looking at it for a moment, I tried to smooth it out with my foot, but there was something there, underneath. I lifted the rug and saw what it was. Dirt. *Emmett.* That boy had been sweeping dirt under my rug. I laughed out loud, thinking about how we both had laughed so many months before that. It was after we had seen that cartoon, the one about the kids sweeping dirt under the rug. I had warned Emmett about doing such a thing. And he got me anyway. He was still making me laugh. But, in a way, he would have the last laugh on this one. I started to cry. There I sat, unable to decide whether I should clean up this dust under my rug. After all, this was Emmett's last practical joke. Even this seemed like a keepsake, somehow. His memory, the spirit of his humor, written in that dust. Oh, God, he must have been so disappointed that he didn't get a chance to see the look on my face when I found out about his little prank. He would have given anything to be there. I would have given a million times that much.

People have expectations. They don't mean any harm by them at all. But they do have expectations. They might not tell you directly. In fact, they will probably be much too polite to ever say it directly. But you know or you feel that, even with the most horrible things that can happen to you, people sort of expect that you somehow will get on with your life. Trouble is, I didn't think I had much of a life left to get on with. I wasn't sure about returning to my job. It was hard to consider going back to anything familiar, although I should have been able to take at least some comfort from the familiar. My whole world had changed. And the new world that had only recently opened up, well, that world seemed to have spun away from me. Things had moved so quickly after Emmett's death that I never really had a chance to grieve, to release the pain. Now, it seemed, I had nothing but time, and the pain was unbearable to me. I needed to talk, I needed to sort, but I was beginning to feel a little self-conscious about doing that. At least the public appearances, the speaking and all, that really helped me, because I was able to talk about it. That was like sharing all that grief with thousands of others.

One day I was sitting at home all alone in the dining room, feeling so sorry for myself. Mama had gone home. Gene was working. When he'd get off from work at Ford, he would go home first, take his shower, and go to the barbershop. I might not see him until ten o'clock in the evening, when he'd come by to check on me, see if I'd had anything to eat. But he usually couldn't stay long, because he had to go to work the next morning. So I was just sitting in the dining room feeling sorry for myself.

"What am I going to do?"

Almost as soon as I asked that question, the answer came. "End it all."

Oh, I don't know what possessed me. I really don't have any idea at all. But I got up and walked over to a window. Well, that window was painted shut, so I went to another window. That one led out to a gangway, a stairwell, where I figured no one would find me until my body started to smell. No, that wouldn't do. I looked at the front windows. One was a picture window that didn't open, but then I couldn't jump from those windows on the sides, either. Children played out front and that would be so traumatic for them. Besides, after I thought about it a little more, I realized something else that was very important: I wasn't wearing pants. I didn't wear pants back then. I was wearing a dress that Mama had made for me. Oh, I remember that dress. It was sleeveless, real tight in the waist with a long flared skirt. It was a white dress, white with a floral pattern, some kind of design in it, and that design was pink. That was one of my favorite dresses. I couldn't stand the thought of jumping in that dress. More important, I couldn't stand the thought that my skirt might fly up.

Just then, as I was thinking about all that, the phone rang. It was a reporter. He was thinking about doing a follow-up story on me and he wanted to know what I was planning to do. Well, I couldn't tell him I was planning to jump out the window. So I said I wanted to go back to school and become a teacher. I turned around as if to ask, "Who said that?" Now, I don't know to this day where it came from, but he said he would take me to register for classes. I mean, he was just going to carry me down to the college and walk me through it. That was fine with me, because I didn't even know where to go. I hadn't exactly given this a whole lot of thought.

As it turns out, the place to go was Chicago Teachers College. He took me there and, unfortunately, we were told that registration for classes had just closed. Before I even got a chance to start thinking about those windows back home again, he somehow convinced them to admit just one more student, and that's how it all started. That's how I was able to start over. I was going to go to college. I was going to become a teacher. I would be able to work with children, to teach them, to help shape them, to introduce them to a whole world of possibilities. In the process, a whole world of possibilities was opening up to me.

Throughout my life I have heard a great many stories about how people received the call to their life's mission. I have to smile when I recall how I received mine. For me, the call came by phone, from a reporter.

It had been a whole year, and only a moment, since my entire life changed. September was so much like the beginning of the year to me. Everything seemed to be running on that cycle. For the folks who stayed behind in Mississippi, there was a new cotton crop. For me up in Chicago, there was a new school term. Fall is a transitional season, and I sensed myself moving between the extremes of my life.

As lonesome as I felt at the time, I was not alone. Mama was always coming by to see about me, sorting my mail, checking my bills, making sure there was enough food in the place. And she had pulled Gene aside to urge him to do the same thing, to look after me, to stick around, to make sure I was going to be all right. She trusted that he would do all that. She knew how he felt about me, how we felt about each other. After his early-morning shift at Ford, Gene was still doing afternoons at Polk's Barbershop, the place around the corner, the place where we met. He didn't live as far away as Mama, so it all made sense, really, that he would come around. Besides, he wanted to be there. He wanted to be there with me. I wanted that too.

During a quiet moment some time later, he would tell me about that conversation with my mother, when she had asked him to do what she had. "You know," he said, giving me one of those looks, "Mama didn't have to tell me to do that. As long as I have breath, you'll be protected."

I believed that, I felt that. I felt it all the way through. Gene impressed me so much with the way he could take care of things, and the way he did take care. He would be a big help emotionally, just showing such care. But it was also good to know that he could handle any other problems that might arise. Besides, I mean, you just never know what might happen. So it was good to know he could handle things. Gene was at least six feet tall and, my goodness, that man had the longest arms. Thirty-five sleeve length. A collar size around seventeen and a half, or eighteen. Oh, he was a good-sized man, all right. Such stature, he had. And just to look at him made me feel safe, secure.

So, while I might have felt lonesome at the time, I wasn't alone. Not by a long shot. There were loving people around to tend to me. But there was something else going on. Quite a bit, in fact. The whole world was shifting, even as I was shifting. It felt like we were changing together in a way, the world and I, caught up in that transitional season, moving between the extremes. In Montgomery, Rosa Parks, a strong and determined black woman, had drawn a new line on a public bus, and had set things in motion. She took a stand by keeping her seat. The black folks of Montgomery stood with her, walked with her, and with a young minister, a powerful new voice rising above so many other voices. Dr. Martin Luther King, Jr., would guide this transition and, by December 1956, a little more than one year after it began, the Montgomery bus boycott would end in triumph. It wasn't just that accommodations were made in Montgomery, as important as that might have been. People throughout the nation were moved to push for change.

The *Pittsburgh Courier* would look at so many events of that year following the murder trial and echo the words I had spoken during the days when Emmett lay in state. I had promised that Emmett's death would not be in vain. The paper presented the evidence of a single year to show that my words had become prophecy. "Negro America had been aroused as it had never been," the paper declared. NAACP membership and contributions were soaring, and the people of Montgomery were moved to the point where they could hold the bus boycott together and make it succeed.

The following year, in 1957, Congress would pass a civil rights act. Among other things, it would establish the new position of assistant attorney general for civil rights at the Department of Justice, and the Civil Rights Commission, with the power to investigate complaints. This was the first civil rights act passed by Congress since Reconstruction. But as significant as anything else was Emmett's impact on the whole thing. According to scholars Hugh Whitaker and Stephen Whitfield, a number of witnesses came before Congress during the hearings for the new law and testified about Emmett, about the murder trial in Tallahatchie County, about the need for federal involvement to protect us from that kind of brutal injustice. This was to be the first step in a long march forward. It would be a difficult and painful and costly road to freedom. There would be so many sacrifices along the way. And so many people would look back at Emmett as the first. Indeed, they would point to my son, Emmett Louis Till, as the sacrificial lamb of the civil rights movement.

So, if I felt lonesome in September 1956, it wasn't because I was alone. It was because I felt that I was sitting apart from something I felt so much a part of. How much I would have wanted the impossible. For Emmett to see what had been born of his death. How much I would have wanted even to represent him there in the thick of it. How much I still wanted just to be there in the center of it.

It was a season of transition. Back in Tallahatchie County, Gerald Chatham, the district attorney, died. Heart failure. I recalled his closing argument back in Sumner, how much heart he had put into that. The news of his death mentioned that he had tried the murder case against Bryant and Milam. It probably would have been enough to have said, quite simply, he tried.

There were many things on my mind, so many things to ponder, as I made adjustments to the transition all around. It had been so long since I had been a student. Now, I had always done very well in school, the best, actually. So I had no reason to think that I wouldn't do the same in college. I don't know why I thought college would be as easy as grammar school and high school. Had no idea at all that instructors had so much freedom to do what they wanted to do, to talk about everything except the lesson, to give you too much to read with no explanation. I definitely had to make adjustments. It was quite a challenge at the beginning of my college career. For one thing, I was about fourteen or fifteen years older than my classmates. Many of them were fresh out of high school. I had been out of school sixteen years. So my skills were not quite as sharp as theirs, and they were not as rusty as I was, but I was ready to work hard at it. I wanted to learn as much as I could. I wanted to understand all the things that were happening in the world around me. I especially wanted to be well trained to work with children and teach them the important lessons of a lifetime.

As much as anything else during that period, I wanted to stay busy. I still needed to do that. College, in a way, was like making my bed in the middle of a crisis, or taking notes to keep up a buffer, some protection from the pain. And, believe me, there would be enough notes to take, and still a great deal of need for just that kind of avoidance. I was going to dive into those books and keep my mind on my studies. As long as I was doing that, I figured, there would be no room for other things. I wouldn't be able to think about other things—so many other things. Study for me would be like therapy. I would become absorbed in it.

It was odd at first, being there in college around all those other people, yet not really around them at all. It seemed that people knew who I was—I mean, the way they were looking at me and all. But it was always at a distance early on, like they didn't know how to approach me, like I was an untouchable. No one seemed to know what to make of me. It didn't faze me, though. I was there to do what I had to do, and I focused on doing just that: trying to learn everything I could.

Looked like I was going to need that kind of focus, too. Starting with the basics. On our first day in psychology, the instructor asked us what we thought psychology was. Trick question.

I didn't have a clue when he got to me. I shrugged. "The ability to read people's minds?"

Without a doubt, I had a lot to learn. A whole lot. But I was ready to do it, to work hard at it. So hard, in fact, that I would go from that low point at the beginning of psychology to getting an A in that course.

That would help in a couple of ways. I wound up working for the psychology department earning thirty dollars a week. That was great, because I could buy my books and I could feed myself. I could buy gasoline to get to school and back home again. I didn't have to pay rent. Mama and I had worked it all out. On top of that, Congressman Dawson had promised me fifty dollars a month, as long as I maintained a B average. I was determined to get that stipend.

After an awkward beginning, it was good to start developing relationships, to interact with the kids. The students, I mean. There were so many people with such different backgrounds and experience, and that made it very exciting to me. I had quite a bit to learn inside and outside the classroom. I joined a study group. Actually, I put it together.

There was a group of girls in my gym class, and they were very sweet to me. They only greeted me and smiled at first, but soon they just started gathering around me. There were seven. I was number eight. And we came together because we were all frustrated with the gym teacher, who was making that class so difficult. Impossible, really. We were taking square dancing, of all things. I don't know what I was thinking about even enrolling in a class like that. I never had been able to dance. Emmett had told me that much when he laughed at me trying to do the Bunny Hop. Anyway, when I found out that we would have to learn all of those lyrics and calls to all those songs and the dance patterns, too, well, it just made sense that we work together. So, I gathered the girls one day and suggested that we form a square-dancing group. We could meet at my house every Saturday and go through the routines. I would type out the lyrics and duplicate them and everybody could have a copy to make it easier to follow everything. They agreed. And we wound up doing very well. So well, in fact, that we began studying other subjects together, too. We were in a number of classes together.

Even outside of square-dancing class, those younger students really kept me on my toes. They helped me fill in what I couldn't comprehend right away on my own, and they challenged me to get better at doing it on my own. I was learning from them how to learn from the teachers. I was absorbing it all like a sponge, adjusting, making up for all the time I had been away from school. I was so focused on what we were doing that I often would forget the basic things I needed to do just to take care of myself. Poor Gennie. I know he felt neglected back then, and he saw how I was neglecting myself. I was immersed in my books. Didn't have time to eat, let alone talk. There were times when Gene would come over and I'd be there studying with the youngsters from Chicago Teachers College and, bless his heart, he would sit down right there beside me and put food in my mouth as we studied. Sometimes I would get irritated with him because his arm was coming between me and the written page. That's how determined I was to try to learn what I had to learn. But he understood that. He never gave up on me. Never.

It didn't take me long to adjust to the process. I was getting good grades. So good, in fact, that when I got my report card, I marched into my math instructor's office and demanded to know why I'd only gotten a B. I mean, that was low for me. I'd been getting perfect scores in his class.

"Well, Miss Bradley," he explained, "you improved less than anybody. You only missed five at the beginning of the semester, and so you only made an improvement of five problems."

What? Okay, so now I knew. Performance was important, but improvement was the key. Learning, after all, was what I was there to do. Learning would be my strategy as well as my goal. I made sure that I would always show more than five problems' worth of improvement.

Still, even though I was doing exceptionally well, it was taking so much effort for me. I was not remembering things as well as I thought I should have been. Throughout grade school and high school, I had always marveled at the gift I felt I had for learning. Anything I read would be right there for me, entire chapters. I could close my eyes and the words would run before me like credits on a screen, whether someone else had written the words or whether I had written them. It wasn't exactly a photographic memory. It was more like intense concentration. When I focused on something, I mean, when I really zeroed in on it, there was nothing else in the world at that moment. Once I knew I could do that, I would write everything down, all my notes, review them, concentrate, then close my eyes and read every one of those notes. In my mind. Or every word in a section of a book. Throughout school, I always had a funny feeling that I was cheating somehow, being dishonest. In fact, I was being diligent. I was working hard for everything I achieved. In college, though, the work was a lot harder and things at first seemed to slip away.

One day, I talked with an English professor about it all. He heard me out, reflected on it a moment, picked up a raggedy piece of chalk, then drew a circle on the blackboard.

"Now, this is your brain," he said, before putting little dots in the circle. "And these are all the bits of accumulated knowledge you have."

After filling up the circle with those little dots, he explained that I had filled my brain up with everything I had accumulated and I was just going to have to make room for the new stuff. Well, that kind of made sense until I thought about something we'd learned in another course. We don't use up all of our brain, so there was no way to fill it all up.

That professor had a point, though. It wasn't that I was filling up my brain physically. But I was filling it up, using so much space in another way. It was Emmett. As much as I might have tried to avoid being consumed by the memories, I had to realize that there are some things in life that cannot be pushed aside while you make your bed or take notes. No matter how much you might try to concentrate, they will be there, tapping on your shoulder, whispering in your ear, taking even the smallest bit of your attention. So I came to accept that and decided to work with it, to let Emmett and the whole experience of his loss guide me in my learning and eventually in my teaching. Somehow, I would find a way to make it all work together, even while I was adding more dots to the circle.

In my second year of college, I would get my first chance, and I would learn so much more than the instructor ever could have taught me. It was a speech course, and that instructor was giving me such a hard time. Now, his speech was—well, his speech was letter perfect. It was as if he were holding a basket in one hand and picking out words with the other. He would regard each word he held there, sizing it up, giving it full measure. Every syllable. Every sound. Every single letter would get his complete attention and respect. And I would hang on to those words. And he would hang me on mine.

Between Mama and Aunt Rose Taliafero, and all their attention, I had always spoken very distinctly. Mama would compliment me on my diction. But I guess I had gotten a little more relaxed in my years away from school. Well, this instructor made me feel anything but relaxed in his classroom. He pointed out every mistake, the smallest ones, when I spoke. He even criticized my Southern accent. I saw nothing wrong with that. After all, my whole family came from the South. Oh, I was determined to prove something to that man. We had to deliver a number of speeches in class for our grade. We came to one assignment that had special meaning to me. It was a eulogy.

I talked about Emmett to the point where I think I took up most of that class period. I connected so much in his life from those first steps as a little boy to the time he climbed the steps onto that train platform. I talked about how he never let anything stand in his way, how nothing could stop him from moving forward. There was meaning in his life and I tried to draw it all together for the class. I brought props, pictures, playthings. By the time I finished, the class was completely silent. Some people were tearing up. Finally, someone asked the instructor what grade I was going to get. He had to admit that it was not possible to grade my speech. To grade it would be to diminish it.

Gene was spending more and more time at my place, mostly looking out for me, but often just looking at television. Relaxing. I had bought Emmett a red lounging chair. It was a model that had just come out. I bought one with a separate ottoman and placed it in front of the television where Emmett liked to sit. That wound up being the place where Gene liked to sit, after coming from the barbershop, before going home for the night. I remember one evening he came over and he was sitting in Bobo's red chair. Just stretched out right there, feet up, snoozing like, well, like he lived there. He was in another world, perfectly relaxed.

Finally, I had to say something. "Gene, I think you're kind of hanging around here a little too much. I mean, you really don't have a legal right to hang around here like this. What will the neighbors think?" He was half-asleep and he looked so surprised, but I kept going. "I think it's time for us to go downtown and get you a license to be here."

Well, he straightened up in that chair and just started smiling. The following Monday when he got off from work, he went home to take his bath, as usual, but he didn't make his usual run to the barbershop. He picked me up and we went downtown to apply for a marriage license. That following Sunday, June 24, 1957, we went with my mother to the home of Bishop Isaiah Roberts, the host pastor for Emmett's funeral, and Gene and I were married.

At one point, Gene looked at me, remembering how he and Emmett used to play with each other about this event. "Do you think Bo would think we're ready yet?"

I closed my eyes. A blink, really, but just enough to consider it all in a flash. How my son had looked at me before he left for Mississippi. "Don't you and GeGe run off and get married before I get back," he had said. I looked up at Gene again, a tear in my eye, but so much joy in my heart. "I think he's given us his blessing," I said. And Gene agreed.

As Bishop Roberts led us in prayer, we were asked to pull together in faith. We did, and I bowed my head believing that my life with Gene would be as blessed as that moment.

By September, another cotton crop, another school term. There was a crisis in Little Rock, Arkansas. Nine children would integrate Central High School, but not before President Eisenhower reluctantly federalized the National Guard and sent in paratroopers from Ft. Campbell, Kentucky, where my cousin, Crosby Smith, Jr., had been stationed and where he had made his one last qualifying jump right after Emmett's funeral. L. Alex Wilson was there in Little Rock, and so was Jimmy Hicks. They were in a group of black reporters who were chased by an angry white mob. Alex Wilson was hit in the head with a brick.

Those poor children were threatened and harassed, too, just for doing what the law and what the courts finally said they could do, attend school with white children. Such anguish, such pain. Oh, who can forget the sight of little Elizabeth Eckford, who got separated from the other eight black kids that first day? How she was made to suffer so much emotional torture. How she kept her dignity. How she never let them see her cry.

I have learned the importance of theme in writing and in public speaking. Taking an image that you can use to create a feeling, a reaction, to get across a message. Threading that imagery through all the words. The same thing applies to great social events in a way. I was a grieving mother. That was a universal theme the media could present, and the public could understand during the trial of my son's murderers. Motherhood, children, would come to symbolize so many aspects of the movement that was growing out of our suffering. Children and the mothers of children would be there. They would be there on the line, marching. They would be there at the lunch counters, sitting-in. So many people have told me over the years how they were affected by the news of Emmett's death or the sight of his body. But it seemed to affect children the most. Children who were Emmett's age when he was murdered, and at a legal age when it came time to for them to act.

A new generation of leaders ultimately would point our way. But it was their mothers who would nurture the movement. Mothers also would guide and they would lead. Too often, though, they would lead us in mourning.

amily has always been important. It was important to Mama. She believed in keeping her family close to her, and she had done a great deal over the years to help so many of our folks get out of Mississippi to start a new life in the North. Family was important to Gene and me, too. He was always close to his four brothers. But the closest in every respect was his older brother Wealthy, who also worked at Ford. Wealthy and Gene were right next to each other in age, but they had a closeness that went beyond just the family head count. They were like twins, really, that kind of close. There would come a time when both Gene and Wealthy would have to be hospitalized at the same time for the same surgery. Wealthy was to be released first, while Gene would have to stay in for a second procedure. Wealthy insisted on staying in as well. If his brother was going to be in the hospital, then Wealthy would be there with him. That's how close they were. Wealthy had also been part of Emmett's life. He went along with Gene and Bo to a lot of those ball games they all loved so much. And it was always such a joy to have Wealthy come by to visit us after we got married.

One day in particular was kind of, well, sweet. I was taking a break from my studies and baking a cake. Now, with all the things Gene was doing for me, there were two things I always tried to do whenever I could. One was the laundry. Now, Gene was *too* clean. I thought Emmett was meticulous about his looks, but Gene always wanted to have his clothes just right. So I tried to give him a break from doing the laundry. I mean, I didn't want dirty clothes in my house, either. I kept all the whites bleached and sparkling. I would tie his socks together at the top because he was color blind; as fussy as he was, I couldn't have him put on a black sock and a blue sock or a brown sock. He was very, very pleased with the way I kept him dressed, kept him clean.

The second thing I tried to do was bake. Gene was cooking all the time; it was the least I could do. So, one day, there I was in the kitchen, cake in the oven, and in walked Wealthy, who let the door slam. I just stood there for a moment. I really didn't have to open the oven door to know what I would find.

"Oh, look at that," I said, as I gazed down at the fallen chocolate cake. "I can't give this to my husband."

Wealthy looked at the cake, too. He wanted to know what I planned to do with it.

"Throw it away," I said. I mean, what else?

He convinced me to give it to him and, don't you know, he took that flat cake home, sliced it up, and carried it up to the Ford plant to share with all the boys. They must have had a good time, too, because he came back and told me they wanted him to slam the door every time he walked in our place. They just might get lucky again. We had a lot of fun together. Wealthy was so much like the brother I never had. That's why he understood why I was going to start all over again to make a brand-new cake for Gene that day. Maybe the boys at the plant were right. Maybe even the bad ones I made were good. But good was not quite good enough. I wanted to give Gene the very best, because he always gave me the best. Of everything. I called him "Daddy." He called me "Baby." And that pretty much says it all.

There was another special part of Gene's family I accepted as my own. For some time, I enjoyed a very good rapport with Gene's daughters, Lillian Gene and Yvonne, and was so happy to have had the chance to attend Lillian's graduation from grade school the year Gene and I were married. In 1959, Gene's ex-wife, Dorothy, came to see me. She wanted to ask a favor. It was very important to her. She was moving away from Chicago, farther south in Illinois. But she wanted her daughters to be able to complete the school year in Chicago, where they had started. Of course, they could, and they did. That was the start of what became a very close relationship for so many years to come. It added something quite special to my life at that time. When Lillian Gene and Yvonne came to stay with their daddy and me, just like that, we had a family household. At least for a while.

It hadn't taken me long to adjust to the routine of college and I was doing quite well. I had close to an A average and had been told by Congressman Dawson's office early in my second year that I no longer had to bring my grade reports in to qualify for my stipend. They assumed I was a good student and I kept getting that money, which really came in handy.

Even though I was doing well, I never let up on my intensity. In fact, I worked so hard that I wound up graduating cum laude in January 1960. I had done it in only three and a half years.

In no time at all, I had a placement at Carter Elementary. I felt that I was ready. I knew when I started teaching that it was time to step up to the plate or sit on the bench. I had been out of work for nearly four years, and had left a pretty nice paying job before that. I couldn't *afford* to sit on the bench. Besides, I was eager for this new experience.

The first thing I had to do was to take charge of the classroom. I made it clear to those kids that they were there to learn and I was there to make sure they did what they were there to do. If they didn't do as they should, then the wind would begin to blow. I did not tolerate back talk or any kind of rude behavior. I was determined that, by the time those kids left my classroom, they would be better people as well as better students. So, first I had to show who was in charge. The affection would come later.

I developed a technique for getting the kids involved in their own learning, so they wouldn't just sit there passively while I threw everything at them. I would identify the students who had the greatest skills and have them work with others who might need to strengthen theirs. One of the most important lessons a black child can learn is how to work together with others as a community. We were like a family in my classroom. Everyone knew where they stood, everyone knew what was expected. At the beginning of each day, I would put the objectives up. Before those kids were dismissed in the afternoon, we would review. And they were so excited every day to see exactly what they had learned. They were active participants in the process. We set goals, we met goals, and my kids walked away every day with a sense of accomplishment. I actually had students asking me for homework. That's how driven they would become under my care. This was about more than lesson plans and grades and passing and failing tests. This was about developing an approach to life. That was important to me. So many of the students I would meet over the years had never been given that kind of guidance. It was my duty to provide it, to show them that they should let nothing stand in the way of their success. I knew how important this would be for them. I knew how important it had been for me.

I will never forget what I found the day I returned to school after being out ill so long. It was when I had the heart condition at twelve, after my father had moved away. I loved school so much and missed the experience while I was out, so I was overjoyed when I returned. Until I saw what I saw in my classroom. What I saw was another pupil in my seat. The first chair. That was the place of honor for the very best student in the class.

From the time I had been in first grade, no one even thought about taking that first chair on the first day of school each year. That seat practically had my name on it. I was always the top student in the class and everyone knew that. But now things were different. The first chair and the second were taken by two students who had just transferred in. And they were very smart. I had to go to the end of the line. And I cried. After school, I asked my teacher how this could happen, and how I could regain my position. She explained that I would have to work my way back up. When she said that, I got an idea. I knew I would work very hard and get top grades. But the other two students were working hard, too. I had to do more to set myself apart. I had to do something special, something to earn extra points.

We had a sand table in our classroom, but nobody ever used it. It was just there for displays. I got the idea to work up a Thanksgiving display on that table, and asked permission to stay after school and come in thirty minutes early every day. I began crafting a scene depicting the first Thanksgiving. I started with a piece of broken mirror I got from my mother. I put that in the sand and banked the sand up around it to make it look like a lake. Then I made some little cutout ducks and geese and put them on the water. I made my benches out of little sticks, and my Pilgrims out of clothespins. I used thimbles for hats and put little black paper around their bodies and added white paper collars. The Indians were made out of clothespins, too, and had the most colorful feather headdresses. All of them had big headgear. Even Pocahontas. Then I made turkeys. White walnuts for the bodies, toothpicks for the legs. I had opened the shells just enough to force the toothpicks in, so the turkeys could stand. I used cardboard and colored paper to make the trees and placed the turkeys among the trees, where they were hiding out. I worked on that display for weeks, taking care to cover it up every day so no one could see it before I was ready for them to see it.

When my display finally was unveiled, the teacher made the announcement to the class, "Well, Mamie Carthan has taken back the first seat, first row."

For me, there was a compelling lesson in my experience, and what it said about the drive I always had to succeed at everything. It was a lesson that would become so important to share over the years. We should never rest on a single success. Good was not good enough. Better was just another step along the way. I taught my kids to want to be the best, the best they could possibly be. Each child has to figure out what that means on a personal level. I was there to provide the guidance. But the key was to keep working, keep striving, keep pushing on. After all, how will you ever be sure you have achieved your very best if you stop trying? Never be satisfied. Never settle. If you believe that the horizon is the finish line, then you will keep moving forward. Success is perpetual motion. It was a lesson I had learned at home. It was a lesson that echoed in those days in Mississippi during the trial. We can never stop.

As a teacher, I knew my kids would have to have a sense of determination, the will to succeed. Many had natural ability. That was obvious. But some needed a little help. Some needed a little more. My mother had always been there to help me. She pushed me. She pushed so hard, in fact, that she got me to do the pushing myself. That's what I wanted for my kids. They had good parents to do all the things parents are supposed to do. But some still were in need. That's how I saw my job, my mission: to serve that need. I would become a parent as well as a teacher. I taught as a mother might. I nurtured, I disciplined, I cared. My class, in effect, was my extended family.

And I would learn so much about helping myself through the help I would provide to others.

Over the years, there would be so many difficult questions I would confront concerning the loss of my son, my only child. Of course, there were the questions about the murder and the social and legal issues that were raised. But there were deep personal things that also would take a long time for me to resolve. One was the sense that so much was cut off with Emmett's tragic death. After all, it is through our children that we achieve a certain immortality. Through our children and our children's children, we leave something of ourselves that lives on forever. So I've had to adjust to a life without promise of future generations. It has been a terribly difficult thing to consider, and I would get reminders all the time. But in getting the reminders, I have been blessed to have had the chance to consider just how my promise really has been fulfilled. And that answer has come from something much greater than me. I prayed so long for guidance, and my prayers were answered. God told me, "I have taken one from you, but I will give you thousands." The words just came to me, quietly. Words of great comfort to me. A revelation can be like that. Not always like the thunder we hear in movie versions of the Bible. But more quietly, like a whisper. It's just there in your awareness, as if it had been there all along, waiting for just the right circumstances for you to notice.

So, I came to know what was revealed to me, to experience it, to live it, for so many years to come. I have left something of myself in all the children I have touched.

In a way, it was hard at times even to think about having a normal life. In a way, it was important to try.

In 1960, the same year I started teaching, Mama and Papa Spearman were planning to move into a new home. Mama had been involved from the ground up. First she had picked out the lot. There were three choices together on a South Wabash Avenue block, and they were building pretty fast, so Mama had to make the selection without delay. I went with her, of course. One lot was next to a lady who didn't want to have any children nearby. Well, Mama always had children nearby. There was a long line of kids coming through Mama's place, so that wasn't going to work. Another lot was next to a lady who came right out to greet us. "Hi, neighbor," she said. She had heard that Mama was going to buy in that block. As it turns out, she was a member of Mama's church and was so friendly that she basically made the choice for my mother. That lot would need some work, though. Mama insisted that the builder remove the seven cottonwood trees from the backyard. She wanted a garden and needed that space. After a whole lot of to-and-fro, they worked it all out. By the time the house was built, though, something had happened. There was an urgent call. Mama was in tears asking me if I could help her out with some money. Papa Spearman had changed his mind. After talking it over with his nephew, Rayfield, he decided that the new house would not be a wise move, so now Mama had to figure out how to keep from losing her down payment. That's when we stepped in. Whenever Gene found out Mama needed something, he would always be there for her. He had no reservations whatsoever. So we wound up taking over everything. We worked with Mama to sell our two-flat apartment building to Elder George Liggins from her church, and we bought the house that Mama built. The one that would have such a nice neighbor, such a nice garden. The one she had wanted so much for her own.

Not long after that, Gene decided he was going to open up his own barbershop. Now, I was a little concerned, because I had only started teaching, we had a new house note to pay, and we also were buying a new car. But Gene wanted that barbershop. He wanted it very much. So I got behind him. I promised I would help. Besides, I figured, at least he still had his job at the Ford plant. Of course, I didn't figure on Gene taking a leave of absence from that job. I thought he could have managed the shop after three in the afternoon, just like he had worked it out at Polk's for years.

But he saw it differently and, like I said, I got behind him. I only hoped *we* would not get behind in the process.

Gene found the perfect spot just around the corner from our new home. We called on quite a few relatives to come in and help with the remodeling, to customize the place. And Gene wanted a top-rate customized shop. Somebody came in to lay the tile. We went to the place that sells barber supplies and I started heading over to the section with the reconditioned chairs and things and I turned around and saw Gene talking to somebody in the brand-new, brand-name, up-to-the-minute, top-of-the-line section. He picked the very best of everything for his new shop. Chairs that were second to none. They were called "the Cadillac of barber chairs." That was all Gene needed to hear. He didn't drive a Cadillac, but I could kind of see the wheels turning on that one, too. He paid fifteen hundred dollars for a back bar and bought the best face bowls—one for each station he planned to set up. Oh, my God, the man was killing me. Our first note on the house was coming due in April. That was $142.10. The rent on the shop would come due at the same time. That was one hundred and fifteen dollars. I didn't know what the new car note was going to be yet, and Gene had taken a leave of absence. An unpaid leave. I just swallowed hard and kept smiling. I was behind him all the way.

By the time Gene finished, that shop was sparkling. I mean, it was beautiful. Word spread very quickly that Gene Mobley had opened a new shop. Well, when he got home at the end of that first night, he laid out a stack of money that was almost too big to count. But I managed.

There came a day when Gene had to go in to Ford to talk about his leave. I told him before he left for the meeting to hold on to that job no matter what. But we didn't get a chance to go into all the details. Later he told me that he had left Ford. I couldn't believe it. I knew things were going well at the barbershop, but Ford had such great benefits. With just another couple of years, we would have been able to retire with a wonderful health plan that would carry us for the rest of our lives.

I just looked at him. "Gene," I said, "next time you want to do something like that, think 'Mamie.' What would *I* want? Just think 'Mamie.' "

He explained that he couldn't extend his leave and he couldn't go back. He was happy at the shop and wanted to devote all his time to that. I accepted it. I could have never stood between Gene and his dream. That would have been the worst thing I could do. And I wanted only the best for him. I took a long, hard look at my husband, and I saw something I really admired. I saw what Emmett might have been, if only he had been given the chance. Gene was strong, he was resourceful and industrious.

He would have made a good father for Emmett. I saw so much of Emmett in Gene. But, then, I was seeing Emmett everywhere. I was looking everywhere for him.

Gene and I settled into our life together. Family was so important. In fact, it was vital. Gene's brother Wealthy and his new wife, Euthenia, or Lou, as we called her, became such wonderful companions. And, even though we would spend time at the homes of all of Gene's brothers and would go to the family events hosted by his ex-wife, Dorothy, we felt a special kinship with Wealthy and Lou. Just as Wealthy had become a brother to me, Lou would be like a sister after they married in 1962. She never hesitated to help me with everything, including all that schoolwork I seemed to be doing all the time back then. Evenings, weekends, all the time. She seemed to actually enjoy helping me get through it, partly because we just got along so well, partly because I know she was in a hurry to get to those Uno games. I do believe Lou is the only person who ever beat me at anything.

One night, we were all sitting around talking. Wealthy always was a good conversationalist. I turned to him at one point and said I thought he should become a preacher. He just kind of looked at me at first. And I kept going. Wealthy could become a minister, Gene could become the deacon, Lou could be the usher, and I could become the secretary. Everybody had a good laugh over that one. But I guess that was the way I thought about our close-knit little group. For me, family time was a spiritual experience.

Nothing was more enjoyable to us all than fishing. Now, Emmett had been an avid fisherman and loved going out with Mama and with Wheeler Parker. But the first time I did it was in 1963. I must have spent a hundred dollars on equipment so that I would have everything I needed. Lou taught me how to bait the hook and cast my line. And that was it. I was ready. Caught my first fish and I was so excited. Over the years, Gene, Wealthy, Lou, and I would spend days up on rivers and lakes in Illinois and Wisconsin, talking, cooking out, and catching so much fish: bluegill, bigmouth bass, silver bass, catfish, walleye. *Oh,* we could catch some fish. So much, in fact, that sometimes we'd bring back enough to give to the church. It was always a great time. It gave me a chance to collect myself. And talk. Lou had not lived through our loss and she always seemed as ready to listen as I was to talk. There was no end to my talking about Emmett and all that had happened. Sometimes, Lou would convince me to let it go for a moment, to get into the peace of the environment all around us. And I would.

Fishing for me would become a great need, one that I don't think I fully understood right away. There is something so refreshing—spiritually refreshing—about the experience. Being with family. Being so close to nature. I would cast my line and feel connected. A ripple that would go on forever. You could feel the rhythm of the riverbank, the pulse of the ages. It was natural, it was easy. Oh, it was perfection in slow motion. It was at times like those when you could feel your place in the scheme of things, and know that there is so much in the world beside you, and ultimately, that it all is the way it is supposed to be. God doesn't make mistakes. You come to realize all that when you cast your line and make the connection. Of course, it's also nice to catch a fish or two.

Every now and then, Gene would kind of give me that look and sigh. We agreed that Bo would have really enjoyed the experience, fishing with us.

We know Mama enjoyed it. Eventually, she would join us on some of those fishing trips. And she was serious about her fishing. So serious, in fact, that it was hard to tear her away from it. Once, we were fishing on the Rock River in Wisconsin and Mama was bringing in a nice catch. As she grabbed at the fish, got it off the line, the hook somehow swung back and caught her arm, tore into a vein. She looked up at Wealthy and asked him to take it out. He didn't want to mess with it. Much too dangerous. Mama just calmly wrapped a towel around her arm, we asked directions to the nearest hospital, and we got moving, not because Mama was concerned about her bleeding arm, but because she said she wanted to hurry up and get back to catch some more fish. And we did. What amazed everybody that day was that Mama and I were so calm about the whole thing. We never got excited during that crisis. Others have noticed that sort of thing over the years. People have said that Mama and I had ice water in our veins. I think really it was that we had God in our hearts. It is what we have learned, what we have held deep inside us: "Be still, and know that I am God."

There have been times when I thought that Mama hadn't prepared me for some of the challenges I would face in life. And there were some things that it would have been helpful for me to know sooner than I wound up learning them. But I know now that, somehow, she taught me one of the most important things I could ever know. It would be there for me when we got the news of Emmett's death. When I felt something transferring from Mama to me. In a way, what I was feeling was an awareness that I would have to stay composed under the most difficult circumstances I would ever experience. What I felt was God moving through Mama and me. There was a great calm. And, as I would learn, such a strong connection to fishing. The still peace of that riverbank would always be there, and so would God. So Mama had helped me realize so much in the way she lived her life and showed me how to stay calm with the deep understanding, the knowledge that all things are possible with God. And all the rest? Just details.

It seemed like the whole world was there that day, August 28, 1963. Eight years to the day since Emmett was murdered. The Lincoln Memorial, the park area around the reflecting pool, the National Mall stretching back to the Washington Monument, were jammed with people, speakers and spectators. They had come to Washington, D.C., a quarter of a million strong to demonstrate, to show their support for civil rights legislation. It was summer and it was hot and people were shoulder to shoulder across that west end of the Mall. Roy Wilkins was there. So were many other civil rights leaders and religious leaders and labor leaders and politicians. It was a most impressive lineup of dignitaries. But it was Dr. Martin Luther King, Jr., who stirred everyone that day.

He shared a vision and a mission and, of course, a dream: "I have a dream that one day the state of Mississippi, a state sweltering with the heat of injustice, sweltering with the heat of oppression, will be transformed into an oasis of freedom and justice."

He spoke about it in ways that would move a nation to share in the dream. That march on Washington would be followed by historic civil rights laws over the next couple of years, and great progress in tearing down the walls of inequality. Everything was coming together.

It seemed like the whole world was there in Washington on the anniversary of Emmett's murder. That's the way it looked as I watched it all, the way so many others watched: from a distance. On television. Yet I still felt so close to it all. I would watch a great deal on television over the years, and I would read the newspapers, tracking the progress. But it was progress, as we would all see, that came at great cost.

Just a little more than two weeks after the march on Washington, white racists bombed the Sixteenth Street Baptist Church in Birmingham. Four little black girls, Addie Mae Collins, Denise McNair, Cynthia Wesley, and Carole Robertson, were killed. And their families were left to sift through the rubble of their shattered lives, and their broken hearts. Oh, God, the children. Why were they being made to suffer, again and again?

In June that year, Medgar Evers was gunned down in the driveway of his home, the same night President John F. Kennedy told the nation "that the rights of every man are diminished when the rights of one man are threatened." Medgar Evers was given a soldier's burial at Arlington National Cemetery, and I wondered how many people realized, as I did, just how much of a hero he had been. My heart went out to his wife, Myrlie, and their children. I knew, as only a few could possibly know, the depths of their despair.

Everything seemed to be turned upside down. People were being brutalized. The Freedom Riders were dragged off buses and beaten. Peaceful marchers crossing the Edmund Pettus Bridge in Selma, Alabama, were attacked by a merciless mob. White state troopers. Peace officers. People would call it Bloody Sunday. And blood was being shed everywhere. No one seemed to be safe from the violence. Not even a man who dreamed of peace. When Dr. Martin Luther King, Jr., was assassinated on April 4, 1968, I shared the pain of his loss with everyone. As I watched the sorrowful funeral, I wanted to be there for Coretta Scott King and for her children, as I had wanted to be there for Myrlie Evers and her children. I never met Dr. King. But Mama did. It was when he brought his campaign for equality to Chicago in 1966. Mama happened to be driving by the place where he was staying, saw him, and stopped to talk. Just like that. She told me they talked about Emmett. The black people of Montgomery were outraged and determined following Emmett's murder when Dr. King led the bus boycott there. They were moved by it.

As unbearable as it was to consider our loss and a family's grief, it also was hurtful to watch the violence that exploded in the wake of Dr. King's death. He was a man who had stood for turning hate into love, and here just the opposite seemed to be happening. I had gotten the message. I had lived that message. I was determined to share it with everyone I could.

Once, for a moment, I had been part of something, something important. Although I was, in a way, left behind by events, I made a point of keeping up, keeping informed. I knew at this point of great national crisis what I had learned at the point of my greatest personal crisis: What happened to any of us affected all of us. And each of us had a role to play in the struggle for justice and equality. There were people who were prepared to make the ultimate sacrifice for what they believed in. There were too many families and loved ones left in the unbearable wake of so much sacrifice. At the very least, everyone had a duty to understand the meaning of all that. I felt a special personal need to understand, to know everything I could know about everything that was happening. If ever the call came for me to be there again, I would be ready.

CHAPTER 25

M
ama moved in with Gene and me. It was not long after Papa
Spearman died, in 1967. I don't recall that we talked much about
it at all. Mama was alone, we had the space, and that really was
about all there was to it. Gene had always felt close to Mama, partly because he had lost his own mother when he was so young. We wanted my
mother to be with us and, eventually, we put an extension on the house to
make it more comfortable for everybody. So, Mama finally was able to live
in the house that she built, with the good neighbors and the garden she
had wanted so much to tend.

As it had always been with my mother when I was coming up, there
seemed to be a constant flow of relatives staying with us at various times
over the years. Mostly the younger ones. Oh my, we loved that. There
were young cousins Bertha Thomas and Abriel Thomas and all their
brothers and sisters. Their mother, Juanita, was Uncle Crosby's daughter
and Mama's favorite niece. There were so many others who would stay
with us from time to time: Shafter Gordon, and my cousins and god-
daughters Ollie Gordon and, later, Ollie's daughter, Airicka. And you
could be sure that every child who walked through our door would get the
family lessons from Mama. Whether they were coming for dinner, the
weekend, or whatever, she would sit them down and tell them about Emmett. The whole story. Family was always so important to Mama, and she
felt it was her duty to teach the family history. It was their duty to know it.

Daddy even stayed with us for a short while, about a year or so after
Mama had moved in. Gene and I wanted to go to California during my
summer vacation. Daddy wanted to come down from Detroit to go with
us. He had made all the arrangements and bought all his provisions for the

road trip we would make. Daddy kept insisting on bringing a washbasin and cooler. We could sleep in the car, wash up in the morning along the side of the road, and eat meals from the cooler. That was Daddy's plan. But Gene and I had other ideas and tried to convince Daddy that we would all be more comfortable staying in motels along the way. While we were going around and around on all this, Daddy took ill. He had been diagnosed with diabetes, had already lost a toe, and now was having some complications with his heart. The doctor said he should stay in, stay quiet, stay cool. I had installed central air-conditioning in the house years before when I found out Gene was spending so much time at that barbershop because it was more comfortable there in the summer. So Daddy would stay at our place where the air was conditioned and the environment was quiet, just as the doctor had ordered, until he recovered. Daddy and Mama insisted that Gene and I should still make our trip. Mama arranged with her good friend Annie M. Goodman to stay there, too, to help with Daddy.

Now, this arrangement seemed a little unusual to us, but Daddy's wife, A.D., back in Detroit, was relieved that he would be cared for, and that's all she cared about, so we made our trip. When we got back, we found Daddy and Mama had been sitting around talking, patching up their differences. Daddy had accepted Christ. You couldn't spend two weeks around Mama without doing that. Daddy played my piano, played his heart out, the way he must have done all those weekends when he would disappear from our place back in Argo so many years ago, working that juke joint for shots. There in my home, he tickled the keys and made us all smile. Mama and Mother Goodman sang along, happy songs. And everything was in tune.

We all went up to Detroit for Thanksgiving. Mama wanted to take the turkey with us—the turkey, the roast pan, and everything she needed to work with. She went into that kitchen at Daddy's place and prepared the whole Thanksgiving dinner, including the yeast rolls. A.D. just sat there and watched in amazement as it all came together. Daddy returned to Chicago early in 1969 to visit. We had dinner at our place and he was getting ready to carry a couple of cousins home before he returned to Argo, where he was staying with his brother, Uncle Emmett, and Aunt Babe. He didn't look well and I wanted him to lie down and let me drive our cousins. He insisted that he was all right. Mama and I both stood outside watching as the car disappeared into the night.

Inside the car, he was chatting away with our cousins, glancing up at the rearview mirror with a smile. "See how much they care about me," he said. "They're just standing out there. Watching me."

Back in Argo that night, Daddy could barely get up the steps to Uncle

Emmett's house. He sat on those steps for a while. He had eaten at our place, so he refused all the comfort food Aunt Babe offered him inside. Around three that next morning, Aunt Babe thought she heard labored breathing coming from Daddy's room. When she and Uncle Emmett checked on him later that morning, Daddy was cold.

It was Mama who called Daddy's wife in Detroit to break the news about Daddy's passing. She wanted to know what should be done. A.D. asked Mama to take care of everything. Mama was there and, well, Mama always took care of everything. As God would have it, Daddy's brothers already had bought plots for all of them at Lincoln Cemetery in Chicago. So Mama took care of it all, as A.D. had requested. She contacted the mortician, selected the things for Daddy to be put away in, the casket, everything. After it was all over, Daddy's wife put her arms around my mother's neck and spoke to her softly. "I couldn't have done a better job myself. I appreciate everything you've done."

In the end, Daddy had been there for me, as a father should be. He had helped Emmett and me in Detroit, he had traveled with me to protect me in Mississippi and in so many cities we visited after the trial. Mama had made her peace with Daddy; she had forgiven him. Even though I never actually spoke the words of forgiveness, they were there, between everything else the other words we spoke, and the hugs we shared, and the lyrics to so many songs we sang around that piano in my living room.

Although we know that death is a part of life, knowing it never makes it any easier to accept. In 1970, Aunt Lizzy died, and Uncle Moses would follow her seven years later. They had adjusted to their life in Argo, but were forever saddled with the horrible memory of the thing that had carried them out of Mississippi. A lot of people were left damaged by that nightmare. A lot of people who tried to make sense of it. Papa Mose talked about it for years with his grandson William Parker, one of Wheeler's brothers. He shared all the details, searching in vain for ways that it might have turned out differently. You can adjust to a new life but, try as you might, you never quite let go of the life you've left. You never get comfortable with the pain of what has been lost. It just sits there on top of everything else you ever feel or next to everything else or between it all, elbowing everything aside when you least expect to have to face it. I know what Papa Mose felt, and Aunt Lizzy. I felt their pain and Emmett's and my own.

There is no way I ever could have endured as much as I have had to bear without my faith. It is a deep knowing, even at the moment of greatest despair, that things will be okay. Emmett had to stand at the darkest point he had ever reached at Papa Mose's place in order to be able to look up and see a billion stars in the nighttime sky. So I had to reach the darkest point in my life to see the light. And I made it through because I believed I would. Something pulled me back from the abyss. It was faith. In my deepest despair, when I thought there was no reason for me to go on, God reached out to me. He had a plan for me. I followed the plan. I followed it because I believed. When there are questions, I know how to find the answers. It is through dealing with the deep sorrow of death that I have found my own words to live by: Life is fragile, handle with prayer.

Someone asked me once whether I tithed and I said I couldn't afford to do it. Well, that was the wrong answer. She explained to me that I could afford to do a lot more than I thought, but that I had to believe that I could do it and never doubt that. In fact, she told me that I should not only tithe, but that I should also make regular deposits into my savings account. Well, I didn't know how she expected me to do all that. With all our expenses at the time, we were just breaking even. But I decided I would try it, and when I made that decision, I believed I would do what I set out to do. So I started contributing 10 percent of my biweekly paycheck to the church. After I deducted that forty-five dollars, then I set aside another five dollars to put into my savings account for the pay period. Well, before I knew it, my little five dollars had grown to five hundred dollars. And I got a raise.

On top of all that, Gene wound up bringing in even more money. He was selling Cadillacs. It started some time after he bought a used one for us in 1968. People kept admiring that car. Oh, and it was something, too. He finally started carrying folks down to Hanley Dawson, the dealership, to help them pick out cars for themselves. He knew what to ask for, how to negotiate a good deal. Well, he was carrying so many people down there that they started giving him a finder's fee and eventually a job. He became the top salesman with wonderful commissions and incentives. We were sent on trips to the Caribbean and, oh, just everywhere.

So, of course, I increased my tithe, bumped my savings up, and I never looked back.

Tithing was only part of my contribution to the church. Periodically I would get invitations from local churches to speak about Emmett and his connection to the events that followed. These were small affairs and that suited Mama just fine. She saw no need for me to travel or to take part in the big events that were unfolding throughout the country. She felt I had enough to keep me busy right there in Chicago. But I knew there were other reasons she felt that way. She wanted to keep me close. She wanted to keep me safe.

Mama had taken a leave of absence from Roberts Temple Church of

God in Christ to help start another church, Corinthian Temple Church of God in Christ. I had gone with her, helped her with all the fund-raising, listened to all the planning. That woman was something to behold. She helped to found five churches since coming North, starting with the Argo Temple Church of God in Christ. But not long after this latest church was set up, she was ready to return home to Roberts Temple. There would be no more church founding for her. I asked her what I should do, since I had followed her to the new church. I should have known that Mama had another plan for me. She told me she wanted me to follow Elder George Liggins, who was called to establish another church. I felt I had worked enough with Mama founding churches, but she insisted and I finally sat in on a meeting about it. I was so happy I did. I became captivated by the whole idea of this new little church and I had to be a part of it. I worked with Mother Goodman, Mama's buddy, and Elder Liggins, who had bought our two-flat building on St. Lawrence when we moved to the new place. We were so committed. After I left work, I wouldn't head home, I'd head off to work on our little church, helping to make sure it got off to a great start. I became one of the seven founding members of the Evangelistic Crusader Church of God in Christ, which was established on May 13, 1973. By the time the church would celebrate its thirtieth anniversary, it would have five hundred members, and it has been said that thousands more have been part of the congregation before getting the call to go on to found other churches. Many have grown from what we started. I would serve as the first church secretary and, of course, as a Sunday school teacher. I looked for every opportunity to work with children, wherever I found myself. It filled so much of my life and seemed to keep me young. So young, in fact, that when I asked Gene how old you have to be, how long you have to wait to become a church mother, that special rank of responsibility and leadership, his response was quite simple: "When you start acting like a church mother."

Well, I did just that. And I was rewarded for all my efforts. I was elevated during this glorious experience and would come to be known as Mother Mobley, and a member of the Mothers' Board, under the guidance of Mother Goodwin.

That same year, my principal at Carter Elementary School had come to me with an urgent request. He wanted me to put the Black History School Assembly together. The whole thing. Organized, produced, and directed. It was a huge undertaking and I wasn't sure at first what I would do. My mission was to teach, so anything I was involved in had to involve some kind of learning. I saw how much children really wanted to learn, wanted it as much as they needed it. So, for me, the real challenge always was to find the lesson to be learned. In developing a concept for the school assembly, I was able to find that lesson. I found it through my own experience, all the parts of my life coming together. I conceived a program built around speeches by Dr. Martin Luther King, Jr., linked by a narrative that showed the kids the significance of it all.

Many students thought they would never be able to remember their speeches and then get up before an audience. It would be like that for many years. Kids can get so caught up in telling you what they can't do. I'm sorry, but I just can't accept "can't." I handed out multiple copies of their speeches. So they *could*. I told them to put a copy of the speech on the mirror of their dresser. Put one on the bedroom door. Another one on the bathroom door. The refrigerator door. I wanted them to have speeches everywhere. Even under the pillow. If they were going to have a dream, it would be a speech by Dr. King. Every spare minute was to be put on that speech. No time to giggle, no time to dawdle; they had a job to do. I told them that if I were to call and wake them up at three o'clock in the morning, they should be able to say that speech before they said "Hello."

Something was triggered in their minds. I thought about how I would concentrate as a child, close my eyes, and remember things as if I were reading them all over again. It took discipline and a refusal to acknowledge that something could not be done. The kids would be concerned about standing up there in front of people, reciting. But I taught them to move beyond that. To focus on the words and the message, to become one with the message. As my children would learn, something is impossible only until you decide that it is not.

Well, I think they got the message, and, oh, I was so proud of them. People were moved by their presentation. Their knees didn't knock and they didn't stutter. Once they took that mic in their hands, they were transformed. They internalized. They became the message they were delivering. They became the Emmett Till Players.

Hundreds of children have learned so much about their history and about themselves, their ability, through participating in my programs, starting as annual assemblies at school, and becoming regular events sponsored by my church. I wanted the kids to know these things. More than just the words they would memorize, I wanted them to know the meaning of the words, the message behind them. More still, I wanted them to have the attributes they would need to excel in anything they chose to do: confidence, discipline, industry. They have developed those attributes that carry them on to success in so many fields. And they have learned their history, that so many sacrifices were made for the opportunities they enjoyed. That's why I named the group in honor of my son. But I have learned something, too. I struggled for so long with my responsibility, questioning the role I would play sitting on the sidelines as great social changes unfolded. But I have come to realize that there was a message for me in the speeches of Dr. King. One of my favorites urges people to be the best they can be at whatever it is they have chosen to be, even if it is a street sweeper. I learned that our progress as a people would come in two steps. The first was to make sure our rights were secured, that opportunities were created. The second part was my part, and the part so many of us can play. To make sure young black kids were ready to take advantage of the opportunities that were created. One step would be no good without the other. So there was purpose in my life, as there is in every life. The blessing is discovering our purpose. The commitment is living it. I thank God that I have had both experiences.

Teaching never ended with me. It was my passion. Not even my family could escape. Of course, all the kids in our family would learn about Emmett, and develop a deep understanding of their own history as a result.

History wasn't the only thing I shared with all the kids. I just couldn't help myself. When my cousin Ollie Gordon let her baby Airicka stay with us while she worked during the week, I began working too—working on the baby. As soon as she started talking, she started asking questions, trying to define her little world.

"She's ready to start learning," I said to Mama. And I was ready to teach.

I used pop bottles to make bowling pins. I would papier-mâché the bottle just to mold it to the right shape, then cut the paper off, tape the two sides together, and paint on numbers. She used a beach ball to knock down the little papier-mâché pins. The first lesson was to count how many pins were knocked over. The second lesson was to learn how to read the numbers on each pin. The final lesson was to add the numbers on each pin knocked over. After we progressed through that game, we set up a little grocery store with a box and empty soup cans. I would put my own labels on with names and prices and we would do our shopping right there in the kitchen. Airicka became quite a little helper when we really did go to the store, too. She could call off items from the shelf and pick out the ones that were low enough. Oh, my, when that child finally went off to school, she already knew her ABC's and her 1-2-3's. Later she would become one of my Emmett Till Players, and add so much to our ensemble with her beautiful singing voice.

It is so important to make every experience a learning experience for children and to help them find the lesson in each experience they have.

There are life lessons in everyday life. Kids who don't get started until they attend school get off to a slow start. I know. I've seen the result. I have seen children with all the potential in the world who wind up getting written off, just because nobody worked with them early enough. There was one little boy just like that who came to my class. People told me he was learning disabled. A fourth grader who walked around with his fingers in his mouth all the time. He was not very expressive and, whenever his mother was around, he clung to her leg. Where so many others had seen hopelessness, I saw hope. I started teaching that little boy speeches. He began to excel. Even in class, when he stood to give his speech, all the other students stood with him, to get a good look at him, to flow with his rhythm. He was so happy to get the attention, to realize that he could do something no one ever expected him to do, and he began to move with so much confidence as a result. At one presentation, a Chicago alderman was so impressed, he presented the little fellow with a hundred dollars. I was overjoyed to learn years later that this little boy, the one who was headed for failure only because everyone expected that of him, this same little boy whose body wiggled with excitement as he recited his speeches and heard the sweet sound of approval—this little boy I believed in was awarded a full four-year scholarship to a state university.

Over the years, I developed such a reputation that I would be given the most difficult students to try to turn around, particularly at the Scanlon School, where I taught for a number of years. Some only needed to find a reason to apply themselves. Odel Sterling was always a very bright student, but he was a cutup in class. He also had a stuttering problem. I reached out to him and gave him Dr. King's "Mountaintop" speech to learn, figuring he might get inspiration from that. But Odel heard the "I Have a Dream" speech and wanted to do that one. He wanted to do it so badly that he struck a bargain with me on a Monday morning. I told him I'd let him have the "Dream" speech, if he learned both speeches by that Friday's rehearsal time. Every day that week, every time Odel would see me, in the hall or anywhere in the school, he would recite a line of the "Dream" speech just to show me his progress. Oh, he was so proud of himself.

"We'll see," I would always say. "Just know 'every village and every hamlet' by Friday."

At Friday's rehearsal, I announced to all the students that we would have a special treat. Odel would do two speeches. I asked him to do "Mountaintop" first. He did it perfectly. Now, for the real test. The "Dream" speech. And that one was just as good as the first.

I saw his anxious glance at me when he finished, and I finally spoke. "Did you hear that?"

"Hear what?"

"Do it again," I said.

He was puzzled. It showed. But he did it again.

"Did you hear that?" I asked him again.

He shrugged.

"Do it again," I said.

Well, this time, he put so much power into what already had been two fine performances that everyone in the rehearsal was moved. But that wasn't my point. He had delivered a flawless performance the very first time. And that was the point.

"Did you hear that?"

He was so frustrated with me. "Hear what?"

"You didn't stutter," I told him, touched by the moment, a moment that reminded me so much of one I'd had so many years before. Another moment, another boy, another stutter. A once-upon-a-time moment with Emmett.

As I look back on those years after Emmett's death, I realize that I was filling the empty places in my life with work. And I couldn't seem to get enough of it. Even in the middle of all the work as a teacher, leading the Emmett Till Players, and helping to get our new little church started, I was working on another degree. My dear friend Ann Brickel, Mother Goodman's daughter, had convinced me to register for the graduate program at Loyola University in Chicago. She wanted to have a companion as she went through the program. We both earned master's degrees, and I earned additional hours toward a doctorate, while Dr. Brickel went all the way. But, even with all that, and with all the children in my family, who were so much like children of my own, there still was something missing: I couldn't help but think at times what my grandchildren would have been like.

At Scanlon, there was an attractive young kindergarten teacher I had seen for years. One day she approached me, and said something very special.

"You know," she began, "I could have been your daughter-in-law."

She had been in school with Emmett and it seems he'd had a crush on her. It never developed into anything, probably because he really was too young to know how to express those feelings to a little girl. But she knew, the way a girl would know such things. And I knew what she meant, the way a girl knows how a girl would know such things. I looked at her as she was telling me this story and I saw what I missed so much. I saw children.

Beautiful children who might have called me "Nana" or "Mimi." Or maybe just "Grandma."

There was something in our blood. I always knew family was important. More than knowing it, though, I felt it. It was clear to me in the way Mama always embraced our whole family. Oh, we have so many cousins that we just stopped counting years ago. Family for us has never been paint-by-numbers. So it doesn't matter whether it's a first, second, third, fourth, or fifth cousin. To us, it's just "Cuddin' So-and-So." There was a powerful reason why relationship was always so important—something we felt. It was in the blood. We were getting ready for a huge family re-union in 1975, and Mama wanted to do a family tree. Now, Mama being Mama, she put in all the branches, all the stems and the fruit of that tree. But that still wasn't enough. She dug all the way down to the roots.

There had been stories handed down for generations. Stories about five sisters who were taken from Africa, brought to America. Five sisters who somehow were able to hold tight, stay close, pleading with the flesh merchants and the slave owners to keep them together. For these five sisters, family wasn't just important, it was life itself. Our lifeline to Africa, as well as the life forced upon us here. Betty Alexander, my great-great-grandmother, held on to her family and some of her family ways she remembered from Africa. But there was a price. She was married to the master's son, Hilliard Tolliver, another slave, but her firstborn was by the master himself. My great-grandmother Laura. Mama knew the story of Betty Alexander Tolliver, and shared it with everyone. It must have been the reason she always felt it was so important to protect her own family. To keep us close. She had done her best and now I was all she had left, the last of her line. It would be some time before I would learn how much she had done to keep me close, to keep me safe.

From the beginning when we formed the Emmett Till Players in 1973, I would work with students from my school and with members of my church. We would travel across the country over the coming years, per-forming before family members of Dr. Martin Luther King, Jr., in Atlanta, and even folks in Mississippi. One trip would have such special meaning to me.

For years I had hoped that there would be a memorial to Emmett, something to reflect his memory and his connection to everything that followed. By the mid-seventies, I received notice that such a memorial was being planned. And what a fitting one. In Denver, a statue was to be dedicated in honor of Dr. King and Emmett. I was overwhelmed by the tribute. This was the first official recognition that Emmett had not died in vain, that something had been gained by my tragic loss, that there was a link between Emmett's death and the push for change.

So many family members and church members and, of course, Emmett Till Players went with us to share in this joyous event in 1976. And then there was the unveiling itself in Denver's City Park. The statue of Dr. King looking out, with his hand on the shoulder of the statue of Emmett. I was speechless. I mean, I was unable to say anything. But everyone was waiting for me to say something. Say something was what I was there to do. Oh, but the weight of that statue just came down on me, knocked me out of the box. Mama was there for me. She always was there, like the statue, looking over my shoulder. I was listed as the first speaker and she was to follow. But she didn't hesitate for a moment. That woman saved the day. She just walked forward and took the podium, allowing me to catch my breath, regain my composure, and take the baton back from her. My mother. That lady was simply awesome. And her influence ran deep and wide.

The year after the Denver dedication, Wheeler Parker, Jr., became a minister. He had prayed for deliverance in the darkness of Papa Mose's home when those men came to take Emmett. Wheeler had made a promise for that deliverance. And in 1977, Reverend Wheeler Parker, Jr., kept his promise. By 1993, he would become pastor of the Argo Temple Church of God in Christ. My mother would have been so proud to see Reverend Parker as pastor of the first church she had helped to establish, the one that had been founded in our home.

By April 1981, Mama had to be hospitalized. It was her heart. Although she was released, this was a very anxious time for me. As it turns out, there was reason for me to be concerned. Mama had to return to the hospital that August. Gene and I were there every night of the week, often together, sometimes in shifts. No matter how tired we might have been after work, we were there, all the time she was hospitalized, from August to November.

We did our best to make her feel comfortable, but that was not always easy to do. They had these tubes going down her throat. She was in and out of consciousness.

There were times when she was alert and I would step out to talk to the doctor or the nurse, leaving Gene to talk to Mama, keep her company. But when I'd walk back into the room, she would stop talking. Strange. I didn't understand that. So one night, after we left, I asked Gene what that was all about. He looked at me long and hard and finally revealed what Mama had been telling him, what she had been urging him, what she had been hoping and praying he would do. She wanted him to take care of "Baby." That was me. Hearing that was the end of me.

"You're all she's got now," Mama had told Gene. She wanted him to look after me. And to be good to me. Oh, God. I couldn't bear it. I started crying so much Gene needed a mop and pail to clean up after me.

The next time we were there together with Mama at Michael Reese Hospital, she looked at me and must have known that Gene had told me. A look is all it would have taken for a mother to read a daughter, a daughter who was her best friend in the whole world. Finally, she turned to Gene.

"Son," she said.

"Yes, Mama."

"I want to go home."

Gene turned to me, and then back to her. "Well, Mama, we can't take care of you at home like they're doing here." He knew there were so many things Mama needed that we could never provide at our place.

She shook her head. "That's not what I mean. I want to go home."

That's when I broke down. That's when I broke in: "No, Mama! You're not going anywhere. We need you. I need you." She had taught me to be a fighter and I was ready to fight even her if that's what it took to keep her.

Mother didn't try to talk to me any more after that. Everything she had left to say, she would say to Gene.

On November 11, 1981, I was there in the room by myself with Mama. Everything was quiet at first. Then she began to have seizures. Violent seizures. It terrified me to see her whole body jerk up into a full sitting position then fall back again. I called the doctor. He had to do something. I couldn't take it, seeing her like that.

The doctor called a nurse, told her to give Mama an injection. Just as the nurse came back in ready to follow the doctor's order, my mother fell back to the pillow. She never moved again. In the end, I was thankful that they didn't give her that injection. I would be left forever to wonder if it was the needle that killed her. God simply answered her prayer. He took her home.

Oh, my God. I had lost Mama. What was I going to do? I felt life would be impossible without her. I cried so hard I was in pain. I stood there, alone, after the doctor and nurse left. Someone came in later and said I was just standing there gazing down at Mama in the bed, my arms outstretched, my fingers spread wide. They said it looked like I had released her. Finally.

I couldn't remember a time when my mother wasn't there for me. Now she would be there no more. She was seventy-nine years old and had so much wisdom. What is it worth to gain so much knowledge if you can't stay around for others to benefit? Then again, maybe that was the selfish reaction. Mama had been able to influence a great many people in the years she had been given. Without question, she had left a mark, an impression on the people she met. She was a strong, determined woman other women wanted to emulate. Yvonne, Gene's youngest daughter, named her oldest daughter Alma.

We are only given a certain amount of time to do what we were sent here to do. You don't have to be around a long time to share the wisdom of a lifetime. You just have to use your time wisely, efficiently. There is no time to waste.

At Mama's gravesite at Burr Oak Cemetery, where we had buried Emmett, I watched as they began to lower the coffin, as the pallbearers threw the gloves in, as they dropped the first shovelful of dirt, and prayed. Ashes to ashes, dust to dust. And suddenly, there it was, just as I had seen it before. At Emmett's funeral. That fluttering, right there at the corner of my eye. I looked only to see it escape me. As if it was flying away. Off into the sky. It was the dove. I saw it again, just for a moment. And then I let it go.

A t Scanlon School, I had developed a reputation as a tough teacher. Tough, but understanding. I was known as "the little lady in the Cadillac you don't mess with." Yes, I was still driving Cadillacs in the early eighties. Things had been working out so well for Gene at Hanley Dawson that he was selling Cadillacs full-time. Word spread so far about how good he was that everybody was going down to see Gene about buying a car. In addition to the money, we also were still getting all those wonderful incentive trips and we had new Cadillacs all the time. Gene thought they were his, I thought they were mine, but as long as Mama was around, she would always trump both of us. Oh, she did enjoy driving those cars.

So, anyway, I was tough. But I felt that I had to be. I could see what some of the kids couldn't see for themselves. It was my job to see these things. How important their education would be, how many sacrifices had been made for the opportunities they had, how tragic it would be to waste any part of their lives. I looked at my kids and I saw what they were going to be. And I never let up. I found myself once backing a boy into a wall, grabbing his collar, and laying it all out for him. Now, I'm barely five feet tall on my tiptoes, and this kid was nearly a foot taller than I was, so the first reaction everybody had was utter shock. But I was not giving up on him, and I was not about to let him give up on himself. Oh, no, that was not going to happen. I told him I was his last chance and that he was going to do well if it killed him. I never let up. He was going to be a better student, a better person if it killed *me*. It was a challenge. His father was not around, his mother had a drinking problem, nobody had ever done more than just move him along. He had no respect for women. But I knew from my own experience that when a man, or even a man-child, has no respect for women, it's because he has no respect for himself. No one had ever shown him they cared about him, or that he should care about himself, for that matter. I showed him. I proved it. He settled down, he applied himself, he adjusted to being a good student. I was tough. But it was tough love. A parent's love. I used the strong arm of a father and the tender touch of a mother to get through to my kids. They knew I loved them when I didn't have to, and that made an impression. The ones who turned out the best were the ones who could work their way through the tough part and feel the love. Everybody has had that one teacher who turned a life around, made something click, made a difference. For so many children, I was that teacher and nothing would give me more satisfaction than to hear that from former students over the years. I moved them to want to become the best they could possibly become, and they knew that *becoming* was an ongoing process. They learned to keep their eyes on the horizon, and to never, *never* let up.

One day in 1982 I got a call. I was at home that day and not in school because the Chicago teachers were out on a job action for better working conditions. It seemed that the people who appreciated us the most were the kids we were helping. But we needed help in order to provide help. The call was from a former student of mine. It was Odel Sterling, the boy who had worked through his stutter by learning Dr. King's speeches. He wanted to come over to my house and bring a few of his friends. I told him they could all come. And, oh, my, there were about eight of these boys who showed up at my place. I had to wonder what this was all about. Well, they told me. They wanted to be in school. I was shocked. But that's what they said. They wanted the teachers to go back so that *they* could go back. I explained what the action was all about, that there was more than money involved, and they seemed to understand that.

Then something happened. I noticed that they were kind of hanging their heads, and I never wanted kids to do that. I would tell them about that sort of thing all the time. "We're not in Mississippi anymore. We have rights. Hold your heads up."

One of the boys lifted his head. "I'm sorry."

"Sorry," I said. "Sorry for what? I said it was okay for you to come by."

Odel explained. "We're gang members."

My goodness. Eight members of the Black Gangster Disciples sitting right there in my living room. And they were telling me they wanted to get off the streets and go back to school. They were reaching out to me because somehow I had reached them. Some had been students of mine, others only knew about me. But they were looking for help. The teachers' action would sort itself out, but the most important thing to me was making a point with these boys, a point I always made with my Emmett Till Players. Life is all about choices. Every choice you make comes at the expense of so many other choices you *could* have made. We must be careful to consider all our choices, and what they will cost us. I could only hope that they were thinking about what I was saying as much as I was thinking about it myself. The choices I had made. The costs I had paid.

Later, Odel would take part in one last school assembly I would produce before my retirement. He did the "I Have a Dream" speech. And he did it with such power and passion that the entire assembly was silent for a moment after he finished. Just a moment. People had been so moved by him that they couldn't move themselves. Finally, there was an outpouring of appreciation. Teachers were in tears. They recalled the day Dr. King delivered the speech and what it had meant to all of us. And the students would learn all that.

Odel walked over to me after the assembly. "I'm through," he said. "I'm getting out of the gang."

I looked at him and I knew he knew how proud I felt. "Well," I said, "the only one who can get out is you."

I had always been firm with my students. But I also gave them some room to figure things out, to solve problems without having the solutions dictated to them. I knew that success as a teacher was not seeing a child meet your expectations. True success was in seeing a child exceed your expectations. Children can only excel when they are given a chance to go beyond merely solving the immediate problem, when they reach the point of learning an important lesson in problem solving, working it through themselves.

That is the lesson Emmett taught me when he would not allow me to walk him through his school assignments. And, oh, how I wanted to help him, especially with his writing and his spelling. But he only wanted me to answer a question here, a question there, and then he'd stop me: "Okay, okay. I got it."

What he had gotten was just enough to go and work it through himself. The confidence he gained from doing that made him believe he could do anything, solve any problems he confronted. I remembered how disappointed I had been when Emmett hadn't allowed me to see him through the process. That was because I didn't fully understand the process back then. Now I could quietly thank my son: "Okay, Bo. Okay. I got it."

So, I guess I had given Odel just enough to figure the rest out on his own. There was no future in gangbanging. That was a choice that would cost way too much. At least five of the other boys who had come to see me with Odel that day also would quit the gang. Two others who stayed in were killed. Odel and I would enjoy a special relationship long after I moved on from teaching. He would make good choices, profitable ones. His mother, a minister, would be so pleased to see her son graduate from Southwest Baptist University and become an investigator with the Chicago Board of Election Commissioners, and provide service as a motivational speaker and church deacon. Through it all, Odel would always remember the speech he had learned, in part, to impress me. "I Have a Dream." The speech that helped him lose his stutter. The speech that helped him find his direction.

Following my retirement from teaching in 1983, I was able to step up my work with my church and with the Emmett Till Players. Gene would tell people that I was working harder in retirement than I had all the years I held jobs. Occasionally, I would still get requests from local, Chicago-area churches and community groups to speak. But retirement also would give me more time with family, and I was so happy about that. Gene and I were able to spend more time fishing and traveling with Lou and Reverend Mobley. Yes, Wealthy might have dismissed me when I first suggested that he become a preacher, but my voice kept playing back in his head over the next ten years that followed our little chat. He would get more and more involved with his church until he was called to the ministry in 1974. By 1988, he would establish his own church, the Gospel Truth Missionary Baptist Church in Chicago, and Gene and I would be right there to help in every way we could. Pretty much the way I had envisioned it. In the meantime, there was so much joy in the moments we all had together, especially during our travels. We even drove down to Mississippi once to visit Uncle Crosby and see the new home he was building. But I'll never forget the monthlong trip we made out to California when Lou and I sat in the back of their new 1985 Crown Victoria and played Uno. We spent three days touring the Grand Canyon, and Reverend Mobley was acknowledged by the congregation of a Los Angeles church we visited. He was invited to preach the sermon.

In addition to the family bonding, 1985 was a very important year for me for another reason. It was the thirtieth anniversary of Emmett's murder and the Sumner trial. Every fifth year since 1955, I had been contacted by media. I would relive the tragedy in newspapers and on television, most of it local. But the thirtieth anniversary was different. There was a spark. There seemed to be even greater interest in the Emmett Till story than at other times, interest that came from way beyond Chicago. Maybe the country had just needed time to process everything. It had been a generation since we had seen the great victories of the civil rights movement, the social, legal, and political changes. The country had been so caught up in the sheer energy, the drive of the movement, and the afterglow that it had taken a while for people to sit down and reflect on the causes of the effects.

There were so many calls and interviews that year. A wonderful documentary was produced by the NBC television station in Chicago. The reporter Rich Samuels and his production team actually tracked down Roy Bryant in Mississippi, but Bryant wouldn't talk. That documentary wound up winning an Emmy Award. But, more important, the attention to the story created even more interest and the calls kept coming. Then in 1987, a major documentary series was shown on Public Broadcasting Service stations all across the country. *Eyes on the Prize* was an acclaimed documentary on the significant developments in the civil rights movement. The first segment showed the spark for the movement that came from the events surrounding the murder of Emmett Till.

I was delighted to have the chance to meet Henry Hampton, the documentary producer, when I was in Boston that year to receive an award. My cousin Thelma Wright Edwards was living there at the time and we talked to him about his work and Emmett and Thelma's father, Uncle Moses. Of course, we couldn't help pointing out a few details that only family members would have known.

By this time, the requests for public appearances really began to pick up. We had been through nearly two full terms of the Reagan administration and there was a lot of concern, a lot of anxiety about civil rights. Something had shifted. New leaders were bringing a new message on social issues and government policy. People were raising questions about things that had been beyond question for so many years, questions about the fairness of so many things that had been done to achieve fairness. Conservatives wanted to turn back the clock on social progress. So people were interested in talking about civil rights. Not just current policies, but the history of it all. It was important for everybody to understand what I had been teaching my students and my Emmett Till Players, that great sacrifices had been made for the progress we had seen. I was becoming part of this dialogue. It was what I had wanted for such a long time. After all, the story of the civil rights movement would be incomplete without a discussion of Emmett Till. And who could discuss Emmett Till better than his mother? Thank God I had prepared myself. I had read everything I could get my hands on. And I had been getting practice at public speaking with the local churches and other groups that had invited me over the years after that college speech class, where I had eulogized Emmett. Be-

yond all that, though, I had studied the master, as I considered the important meaning and style of all those speeches by Dr. Martin Luther King,
Jr., the ones I had been sharing with my kids.

In 1988, I was honored to be invited by Mrs. Coretta Scott King to
make a presentation at a very special event sponsored by the Dr. Martin
Luther King, Jr. Center for Nonviolent Social Change in Atlanta. The
event was called "Women in the Civil Rights Movement: Trailblazers and
Torchbearers." It was to be a four-day conference held that October and
would include an impressive lineup of women. I turned to Gene, who
told me he would be delighted to go with me, as he was for so many out-
of-town appearances yet to come. But this one was to be the first big one
for me, and I wanted to do a good job. I felt that I owed that to the people
who were coming, looking for answers. I was told to prepare for fifteen
minutes, but I brought plenty of material to go longer, just in case.

My presentation during the conference was held in a room that filled
up very quickly. Someone wound up moving a back wall and that gave us
the other half of the room. As that second section began to fill up, they
started opening the two side panels of the room. It seemed like everybody
at the conference had come to this session. Every chair was taken. People
were standing. They were sitting on the floor. I wound up going for much
longer than fifteen minutes and I was so pleased that I had prepared myself for a longer period.

At one point, as I was speaking and looking out at the huge crowd, my
attention was drawn to an entrance where I saw two more people walking
in. It was Mrs. Coretta Scott King and Mrs. Rosa Parks. Oh, I was just ec-
static to have them come to hear *me*. And, as I continued my talk, I suddenly felt so connected. There was a bond between me and them, even
across the room. I wanted to talk to them, but things were hectic as we
broke up, and I didn't get the chance.

Later, as Gene and I walked into the reception that evening, the first
person I saw was Mrs. King, who came over to greet me. "Well, *finally* we
meet," she said.

I wasn't sure at first what she meant by that, but I certainly was thrilled
to meet her. She was so warm, so gracious. As it turns out, what she meant
was that I had never responded to other invitations that had been sent to
me over the years. Invitations to attend the 1963 March on Washington
and the funeral of Dr. King in 1968. I didn't know anything about those
invitations. I had never received them and didn't really have time to consider it much right then because things were moving so quickly. There
was so much excitement with so many important people at the reception.
Dr. Dorothy Height, president of the National Council of Negro Women,

hugged me and kissed me and made me feel so welcome. There would be many hugs and kisses that evening, many greetings, but there would be one embrace that would be especially dear to me. The last one. The one that came rushing over to me. The one that held on so tightly. One I would hold on to for so many years to come. It was the one from Mrs. Rosa Parks.

It was almost as if she was apologizing for something, trying to make up for something. I shared that feeling. It just seemed like we should have met so many years before we did. But we would waste no time making up for lost time. I would bring my kids up to Detroit, where she was living, to perform their program. Some of my kids also would participate in her "Pathways to Freedom," a bus tour that familiarizes children with the significance of the Underground Railroad. She and I would also be there for each other during the special times, like when she would receive the Congressional Medal of Honor. Gene and I would become very close friends with Rosa Parks and Elaine Eason Steele, the cofounder and director of the Rosa & Raymond Parks Institute for Self Development. Over the years, we would share so much appreciation and so much love. We would share something else, too. Something that had connected us for so many years. Something that should have brought us together so many years before. It was that something that had made us hug each other so tightly when we met. Rosa Parks would tell me how she felt about Emmett, how she had thought about him on that fateful day when she took that historic stand by keeping her seat.

At the King Center event, I would be puzzled for some time about what Mrs. King had said to me, about those invitations that had never reached me. It was so nice, so satisfying to learn finally that I had not been left behind after all. That people had tried to include me in the events that unfolded after Emmett's death. That's when I realized what had happened. Mama. Oh, Mama. I thought about how she had never wanted me to consider being in the thick of it all during the 1960s, how concerned she had been for my own well-being, how she had wanted to keep me close, keep me safe, and told me I had plenty of other things to do. I thought about how she had been there so often to help sort my mail. And open it. Mama had intercepted those invitations. She did it to protect me. I thought about it and I understood it. As only a mother could.

In 1989, there was another special invitation. The Civil Rights Memorial was being dedicated at the headquarters of the Southern Poverty Law Center in Montgomery. Morris Dees, the head of the organization, is a passionate and committed lawyer, who dedicated his career to fighting injustice, and who engineered a major blow to the Ku Klux Klan when he won a seven-million-dollar judgment against the Klan on behalf of Beulah Mae Donald in the lynching death of her son, Michael Donald. That judgment left the KKK bankrupt. Morris Dees raised money to commission a monument by Maya Lin to commemorate the sacrifices made by so many during the civil rights movement. Along with major events, the names of forty people were etched in black granite. Emmett's was included.

It was a tremendous honor and I quickly gathered up my family to travel to Montgomery for the dedication. Gene's two daughters, Lillian and Yvonne, went along. Yvonne's husband, Ron, drove us all in their van. Ollie Gordon went, along with my cousin Deborah Watts from Minneapolis, and Ollie's friend Bobby Bradley. And Thelma Wright Edwards flew in to join us.

It was bright and hot in Montgomery during that first weekend in November. Still, there was something chilling in the air. The police were all around for protection. They were on rooftops and on the street surrounding the grounds of the center. It was the kind of scene I had expected and never saw during the Sumner trial. There was a reason for all the protection. There had been threats by white supremacists who apparently didn't want to see this tribute to civil rights so close to the Alabama State Capitol, or anywhere, for that matter. The tension had been building for a while. The former headquarters of the Southern Poverty Law Center already had been firebombed.

It also was chilling to see the monument for the first time. It is a beautiful work of art. It takes your breath away. There is a curved wall of black granite with water flowing over the etched words from Dr. King's "I Have a Dream" speech, the words of the prophet Amos: ". . . Until justice rolls down like water, and righteousness like a mighty stream." A round black granite table sits in the middle of the plaza, like a timepiece that connects important events and the names of martyrs of the movement, a movement that goes around and around and seems to never end. A continuous flow of water rises up from the center and washes ever so gently over it all.

On the day before the main dedication ceremony, we viewed the monument. I couldn't hold back. I approached, I searched, following the dates, and I found what I was looking for.

28 • AUG • 1955   Emmett Louis Till • Youth Murdered For
                          Speaking To White Woman • Money, MS

Emmett's was the third name in the time line following the Reverend George Lee and Lamar Smith, a little before reaching Rosa Parks and the

Montgomery bus boycott. I ran my fingers over the letters of Emmett's name and felt the cool water. I began to weep. As I stood there, shaking, I missed Emmett even more. And I realized that my heart was still wrestling with something so enormous that even this great honor could not resolve it for me. It was quite a moment and it would take me a while to get over it. It was like touching my son. Like reliving his funeral. But, as I told people there, it also filled me with such joy to see Emmett honored, to see him included among the martyrs of the movement. A list that included everyday people who did amazing things. A list that included Dr. King and Medgar Evers. Myrlie Evers was there, too, at the dedication. It was so good to see her and to hear her wonderful banquet speech. I looked around as I stood there at the monument. I saw others walking up, running their hands over the letters, the words, the names. So many families. So much loss. So much gain.

I would speak about that at the dedication ceremony the next day, there on the platform with Rosa Parks and Julian Bond, Martin Luther King III and Ethel Kennedy, among others. Looking out at thousands who had turned out for the event. Looking down at the monument and the names etched in stone and the water that flowed liked so many tears.

"We cannot afford the luxury of self-pity," I said in my speech. We had responsibilities, all of us, the families of the victims of the movement. We had been chosen to bear the burdens we bore and I recognized that we had held on to our hope. I had found such peace in working with children, helping them "reach beyond the ordinary and strive for the extraordinary."

We all rose on the platform to sing "We Shall Overcome," the other speakers and I. Others who had suffered the great pain of lost loved ones, including: Chris McNair, father of eleven-year-old Denise McNair, the youngest of four girls killed in the 1963 bombing of Birmingham's Six-teenth Street Baptist Church; Dr. Carolyn Goodman, mother of Andrew Goodman; and Rita Schwerner Bender, widow of Michael Schwerner. In 1964, civil rights workers James Chaney, Goodman, and Schwerner were murdered by the Ku Klux Klan in Philadelphia, Mississippi. On the plat-form, as we sang, our hands and our hearts, like so many events in time, were linked.

I thought about the meaning of the words of the song. I thought about the meaning of the words I had spoken. How "Emmett's death was not a personal experience for me to hug to myself and weep, but it was a world-wide awakening that would change the course of history." In looking at his name on that beautiful monument, I realized that Emmett had achieved the significant impact in death that he had been denied in life. Even so, I had never wanted Emmett to be a martyr. I only wanted him to be a good son. Although I realized all the great things that had been accomplished largely because of the sacrifices made by so many people, I found myself wishing that somehow we could have done it another way.

Despite all the recognition Emmett was getting around the country, I had always hoped that there would be some monument, some honor bestowed on him in Chicago, his hometown. Since I had dedicated my life to teaching, I often told people that a school would be a wonderful tribute. Eventually, an honor would come. Not a school, but a street. A sign of Emmett that people would have to look up to for a seven-mile stretch of Chicago's South Side. We were thrilled when the city of Chicago agreed to give a section of Seventy-first Street the honorary name "Emmett Till Road."

The dedication was held on July 25, 1991. It was Emmett's fiftieth birthday. And it was a beautiful day for a party. There were so many people there. My family, of course, as well as Mayor Richard M. Daley, whose father had been moved to help us with appeals to the state of Mississippi and the federal government when Emmett was taken. Rosa Parks came down from Detroit to be there with me, and tell reporters what Emmett's death had meant to her and to black people in Montgomery during the bus boycott. Privately, she would tell me how she felt that history should remember Emmett as a hero. I thought about it all in the motorcade as we made our way down Emmett Till Road from the dedication ceremony to another press function at the South Shore Country Club, where I would call for a reopening of the investigation into Emmett's murder.

What an appropriate choice Seventy-first Street had been, as the street renamed for Emmett. It connected so many communities, both black and white. It also was a street that ran as a sort of time line, linking so much history. A. A. Rayner's funeral home was located there. It was the street where Dr. Martin Luther King, Jr., was heckled and stoned by angry whites when he marched in Chicago. It also was the street that bordered the cemetery where Harold Washington, Chicago's first black mayor, had been buried. There was so much to think about as we sped along. I thought about the connections. Those, and a motorcade of dignitaries honoring my son, and a motorcycle cop who could have been my son. If Emmett had lived to become the motorcycle cop he had wanted to be.

There would be continuing interest in Emmett Till in the coming years, partly because our story would connect to so many other recent events that showed how far we still had to go in getting beyond hatred. I would be invited to participate in events along with so many activists, like the Reverend Al Sharpton and, of course, the Reverend Jesse Jackson, Sr., who had become a good family friend. Regrettably, there were still too many incidents of racial hatred that would remind people so much of Emmett's death. I was always willing to lend my support, and try in some way to help people understand through my personal experiences.

In October 1992, I shared that experience with a national audience on the *Oprah Winfrey Show*. It was a show devoted to hate crimes, and Myrlie Evers also was a guest. The producers sent me down to the Delta for part of my segment. It was like being transported back in time. So many things were brought back to me, yet so many new things came down on me. I looked out at the Tallahatchie River from the spot where Emmett's body was brought to shore. I was sickened by the memory of the police picture that was taken of his body. The one that had been shown to me in that blazing-hot Sumner courtroom. I gazed upon the dilapidated store in Money and could hear the echoes of the black kids who had gathered in front there that Wednesday evening, August 24, 1955. I could see the porch where they had watched a checkers game and talked about the treats they had bought inside the store. Emmett had bought two cents' worth of bubble gum. I thought about his stutter and how I had taught him to whistle when he got stuck on a word like "bubble gum." I thought about a possibility, a horrible possibility that would plague any mother. The possibility that something I had suggested as a way to help my son could have hurt him so badly.

There would be so many calls following my appearance on the *Oprah Winfrey Show*, and even more requests for other interviews. One caller would stand out. A radio talk show host contacted me to discuss the case. Like so many people, he had been moved by Emmett's death. He had spent a great deal of time looking into it himself and had actually located Roy Bryant, who was living in Ruleville, Mississippi. Somewhere in our conversation, this man asked me if I wanted to listen in while he interviewed Bryant. The very thought stopped me for a distressing moment. Then, in the next moment, I heard myself agreeing to do it. So, he set up a three-way call and Roy Bryant never knew that I was listening in.

Bryant didn't want to talk at first. But the man on the other end kept at it. Bryant had been getting a lot of calls about Emmett Till. He said that Emmett Till had ruined his life. *His* life? He began using a lot of vulgarity, and saying so many hateful things. "Emmett Till is dead," he said. "I don't know why he can't just stay dead." Oh, it was all I could do to keep my breathing steady and not make a sound. But that man was very belligerent. Oh, my God, his language was so filthy, you could almost *feel* the dirt. When he was asked if he had any remorse, he said he didn't. If he had it to do all over again, he would. When the phone call ended, well, I was just shaking. That man had lived his whole life filled with so much hatred. How could he have enjoyed anything?

I knew his story. I had kept up with him and J. W. Milam in the articles I had read over the years. They were abandoned by all their supporters after the trial. I guess the white folks of the Delta didn't appreciate having all that attention that Bryant and Milam had attracted down there. Bryant and Milam had trouble getting credit, blacks boycotted the stores their families had run, and eventually they had to pack up and leave. Things never really worked out for them after that. Their wives left them. Bryant lost a lot of his vision when his eyes were damaged while training as a welder. Milam died of cancer in 1983, and Bryant would die in 1994. Legally blind.

Not long after that phone call, I had a dream. It wasn't the first time I had it, but this time the dream would have new meaning to me. I was on a high bridge, sort of like the Golden Gate. And there were thick clouds all around me, a fog. I was walking, but couldn't even see where my feet were stepping. All of a sudden, the clouds parted and I could see that the water was black. Not muddy, just black, and roiling. I heard a voice in this dream. "I have suspended you high above the troubled waters. Keep moving forward. You are headed in the right direction."

When I awakened from the dream, I had such a sense of peace. I knew that the troubled waters had been hatred and God had guided me over it and away from it. I would not take that plunge, and I was so thankful. Hatred is a self-inflicted wound. And it is so destructive. I never felt any hatred for Bryant and Milam. And I didn't want them to be executed. I wanted justice. I wanted them to be sorry. I wanted the state of Mississippi to be sorry. I want it still.

My great disappointment in listening to Bryant was not in what I heard him say, the insults, the obscenities. No, the disappointment was with what I didn't hear him say. He spoke no words of remorse. Bryant and Milam left a lot of people damaged. But as horrible a crime as they committed against my little boy, against me, against society, their true crime was against God. They were given enough time to redeem themselves, to show remorse, to beg forgiveness. And it seems that they refused to do it. As I taught my kids, life is all about choices. Bryant and Milam made a terrible choice, the most expensive one of their lives. It cost them their eternal souls. I feel so very sorry for them. In this world, they only had Mamie to deal with.

In February 1993, Uncle Crosby died. I had always felt a special closeness to him. For one thing, he was my mother's favorite brother, and she always looked out for him, for his kids and his grandchildren. Not long after he moved to Argo—right next door to us—Mama even handled his money for a while. When I was younger, I never really understood why Uncle Crosby moved back to Mississippi, since everyone else seemed to be coming the other way. But there are some things you don't understand until it's time for you to understand. That time would come. Uncle Crosby was there in Mississippi when we needed him the most. He brought Emmett home. There was no amount of intimidation that could have stopped him from doing that, or from returning to Mississippi to live out his life. I have been blessed to have known quite a few heroes in my life. Ordinary people who are moved by nothing more than a sense of moral obligation. They don't get headlines or parades or medals. Like Uncle Crosby, they don't expect any of those things. Like Uncle Crosby, they just do what they can't help doing. They rise to the occasion.

S o many people drew so much inspiration from Emmett Till over the years. Of course, there were those who were moved to action. People took stands they had never taken before, spoke out in ways they had never imagined before, got involved in ways they might never have considered before. But Emmett inspired art as well as activism. Gwendolyn Brooks and Langston Hughes wrote poems, Bob Dylan, a song. Rod Serling wove themes of Emmett's story into several teleplays. In fact, I was invited once to serve on a panel to discuss these themes in his work. I was struck by words that hit so close to home, words Serling wrote at the conclusion of a 1958 *Twilight Zone* episode, defying network censors and national sensibilities to tell us that "prejudices can kill, and suspicion can destroy. And the thoughtless frightened search for a scapegoat has a fallout all of its own for the children and the children yet unborn. . . ."

There was more to come. Bebe Moore Campbell's novel *Your Blues Ain't Like My Blues* explores, in part, how people live with the memory of such horrors as the murder of a child. And there were several plays, including one written by Toni Morrison and, of course, James Baldwin's *Blues for Mister Charlie,* which he dedicated to Medgar Evers, to Myrlie, and to their children, as well as the children who were murdered in Birmingham. The attention to children certainly has very special meaning. James Baldwin wrote in his "Notes for *Blues*" that we all have a special responsibility to try to save the most wretched man among us, and if we can't do that, at least we should "begin working toward the liberation of his children."

Even as I had sat there listening to Bryant spewing all that hatred on the three-way telephone hookup, I thought again about his children. His and

Milam's. I thought about them with love. Their wives had left Bryant and Milam, and I wondered whether the children had been saved from the terribly ironic burden of earning their fathers' love by adopting their fathers' hatred.

Saving children, serving children is what my life has been about. That is why I wanted for so many years to join all those who had written about Emmett. I wanted to tell the story myself. I had come close. But only close. I had cooperated with scholar Clenora Hudson-Weems, and was pleased to share my recollections for the research for her dissertation on Emmett, which was later published. Still, I wanted to do my own book, my own story. There were other writers who wanted to do a slick Hollywood version with an Emmett Till his own mother wouldn't recognize. And there were book authors, collaborators, who would fail to deliver. Oh, I was so very disappointed by the false starts and the people who would remove documents from my files on the promise that my story would be written. It was heartbreaking for me to have so many promises broken, and so many documents never returned.

So I was more than a little wary when I was approached by a writer in 1997 who said he wanted to tell my story. He wanted to tell it in a play. Well, I had never really considered that before. But this young man was quite insistent. He had grown up in Hampton, Virginia, and like so many young people I have met over the years, he told me he had been shocked by the pictures and story of Emmett his grandfather had shared with him as a little boy. It had all been burned into his consciousness. I was impressed by his sincerity. But I also took a little time to read the reviews of his work. It took a couple of months for us to discuss how things would work. He thought it should be my story, my recollection and his dramatic presentation. It would be a collaboration. The speech I delivered at the dedication of the Civil Rights Memorial would drive the drama. Finally, everything was presented to my lawyer, former student and Emmett Till Player Lester Barclay. Lester worked it all out, and David Barr and I began to write my story in a way I had never imagined before, as a play.

This would be a difficult time for me and for Gene. Our health was failing. Our health plan was failing even more. We both were having such difficulty getting around. Thank God for the relatives who were there for us, like my cousins Abriel Thomas and Shafter Gordon. Abe and Shep were always willing to help us with the driving. My problems were serious enough. I had diabetes. I was taking insulin. I was swelling from water gain, and slowed by the constant pain. But Gene's problems were worse. He had suffered a stroke in 1987 and had slowed down quite a bit with a limp that would forever mark that distinctive walk that had always impressed me so. Gene would go to prayer meeting every Wednesday night. One Wednesday night, Gene's daughter Lillian was visiting. She had started spending a lot more time with us after her husband died in 1989. She and I were sitting around talking and waiting for Gene to come home from prayer meeting, but it was getting so late and we hadn't heard anything.

Lillian had been concerned for a while. "Daddy, do you have to go to prayer meeting every Wednesday night?" she had asked.

Gene laughed, the way he always would. "Oh yes," he'd said. "Especially now."

So we waited this one Wednesday night, waited and worried about where he could be. And it grew later and later, until finally, he walked in and we were relieved.

Until he told us what had happened. He had fallen on the way from the garage to the house. He was out there, on the ground, helpless, not fifty feet from the back door as we sat on the other side of that door, in the kitchen, totally unaware that he couldn't reach us.

"Well," he said with a laugh, "I guess I've learned how to fall now."

This was no laughing matter.

In 1999, we traveled to the Mayo Clinic, more than once. Lillian went with us. We would pay for the treatment ourselves, out of our own pockets. We had no patience for haggling with an HMO. All the fluid gain was difficult for me. I mean, my legs were as tight as a drum. It would hurt me to reach for a phone or shake hands with people, and I was doing a lot of both. But the treatments at the clinic would help. At least for a while.

With my health causing such difficulty, I was beginning to feel a certain urgency in getting my story told. That is why I was so pleased that, by the summer of 1999, a draft of the play was completed and edited. *The State of Mississippi v. Emmett Till* would open the fall season for Pegasus Players, a Chicago theater company. Lester and I met with officials of the company to sign the agreement. Before the first word had even been written, Arlene Crewdson, the artistic director, had said she wanted the play for Pegasus, knowing the significance of the story and the impact it would have as a dramatic presentation. Everything was coming together and I was so excited about sharing my story with live audiences. David told me that opening night would be my night.

"Well, well," I said, after signing the contract. "Looks like we have a show." And I was so happy that we did.

On the second night of rehearsals, Gene and I were invited to come to talk to the cast members about my story. We were only supposed to be there for an hour but, my goodness, it was so wonderful to talk with all those actors who would become the people who would bring the story to life. I mean, we just talked and talked for four and a half hours. I guess they had to make up for that rehearsal time.

There was so much press attention leading up to the opening. Television, newspapers—every major media outlet in Chicago did stories. Some did more than one. For me, this was a good chance to help people understand the important message I wanted to come out of all the effort.

Opening night, September 7, 1999. Everything was in place. There were 265 seats in the theater. Producers had to set up extra chairs so that everyone who wanted to see the play that night could do so. I believe my whole family must have been there in that theater. Gene and I came in after everyone was seated. Since I was in a wheelchair, we had a special place in the rear of the theater. Only David and a few production people knew we were back there.

I had never watched the actors perform during rehearsals. I had wanted to see the play unfold the way everyone else would. It was so moving. The part where the "Mamie" character describes what she saw as she examined Bo's body—oh, God, every sentence was punctuated by gasps and moans from the audience. There were no pictures. But the words had such power. One lady had to leave. David stood nearby and would check on me from time to time. I was fine. I had lived the story.

By the time the play ended, the audience members were on their feet. There was a special encore. The cast began singing one of my favorites, "I Woke Up This Morning with My Mind Set on Freedom." I wanted to hear the song, but someone escorted Gene and me around to the back, where we waited in the wings. As they finished the song, the house lights went up and the entire cast turned to me and blew a kiss. Well, I'm sure no one in the audience knew what that was all about, because I was out of sight in the wings. But they soon found out. Gene wheeled me out onto the stage. I rose, slowly, from my wheelchair and stepped up to a podium that had been set up there. And, oh, the people just showed me so much love. I cried, and had to gather myself before I could speak.

I told the audience how much I appreciated their response. How blessed I felt to still be around to appreciate so many people who had appreciated Emmett and my lifelong efforts to share his story. But the work was not over, I said. There was so much still to be done to prevent that kind of horror from ever happening to even one more child.

I acknowledged Gene, my life partner, who for forty-two years had been with me every step of the way. If not for him, I said, I didn't know where I would have been. I thanked him for being so strong and so brave even at times when I couldn't be. Then, I looked for David Barr. I said that it felt a little alone up there, without my writing partner. I finally saw him standing way in the back of the theater.

We stayed in that theater lobby until midnight, nearly two hours. So many people wanted to talk and share their experiences, how the story of Emmett Till had affected them. Even theater critics stuck around. I was told that was very unusual, since critics have deadlines they must rush to meet.

As we were about to leave, I realized that I still had not spoken with David. I asked for him. He had stayed behind in the theater, away from the crowds. But we found him.

"I told you this was going to be your night," he said to me.

I took his hand, squeezed it. "Oh, and what a night. What a night."

After that, I must have seen that play on at least twenty other nights. It was extended an extra month. And the news spread with all the press attention we got. The city of Aurora, Illinois, negotiated to have the play staged there that following January.

For the cast, every night's performance would be a religious experience. Without question, my story involves a tragic loss. The worst experience a mother could ever have. But there also is the celebration of life, the lessons of a lifetime. For black people, every generation has had its cautionary tale. Emmett Till became that story for an entire generation coming of age in the fifties and the sixties. But that's not what I wanted for my son. I didn't want Emmett to become a cautionary tale. I wanted people to know his story and to learn from it. What I wanted them to learn was what I always thought my son should represent. I have wanted Emmett's name to stand for healing, reconciliation, forgiveness, and hope. It seemed that people were getting that message. The ovations said it all. The audiences were expressing their love. It was love for my son. And what more could any mother want?

March 5, 2000, would mark the thirty-fifth anniversary of Bloody Sunday. As on past anniversaries, there would be a ceremonial march across the Edmund Pettus Bridge in Selma, Alabama. But this year would be different. This year would be special. This year, the president of the United States would lead that march along with the Reverend Jesse Jackson, Sr., and so many other dignitaries. This year would be different for yet another reason. I had sat on the sidelines during the civil rights movement, and watched in horror with the rest of the nation as Alabama troopers brutally beat voting rights demonstrators back in 1965. But I would be there this time. I would cross that bridge. Gene would be there with me. And so would my daughter-in-law Lillian.

As we came closer to the event, we became more concerned about Gene. I had noticed that he was having trouble eating. He would hold his fork in one hand and use the other hand to lift that hand to his mouth. I asked him about it and he just said that his hand was heavy. He also was falling more often. Even in our hotel room, down in Alabama, he fell, and he laughed about it. Lillian was there to help him. She was there to help us both, and she really had her hands full. Our biggest fear was that Gene might fall on that bridge. That would not be so easy to laugh off. Not with all those people out there.

There were thousands who turned out for the march across the Edmund Pettus Bridge, named for a Confederate general. Many of the people were veterans of the civil rights movement. John Lewis was there. He had been there in 1965, an organizer for the Student Nonviolent Coordinating Committee. When police charged the demonstrators in 1965 with cattle prods and bullwhips and clubs, John Lewis got his skull cracked. Now he was a U.S. congressman from the state of Georgia, and there were black police officers along the way who saluted him and the congressional delegation that accompanied him and the president, who led them all.

Bill Clinton was at the head of the procession along with Reverend Jackson, Coretta Scott King, and Congressman Lewis. I was not far behind. We had asked for two wheelchairs. Gene and I both needed one, but only one was provided. Gene looked so weak, but he told me to take it and he would walk across the bridge. Lillian would help him. Someone was assigned to push me and they would be somewhere behind in the crowd. Oh, that crowd was packed in there, too. And the security kept things even tighter. I mean, it was so tight, the flies couldn't even get through.

We hadn't gotten very far at all when the crowd started closing in around me. There were about two people between me and that front row with Reverend Jackson and President Clinton, but the ends were going faster than the middle. We were getting crushed and my wheelchair kept banging into people, who didn't look too happy about it. Farther back, Lillian also was having trouble with Gene. In a way, the crowd kind of helped her hold him up. But Lillian wasn't taking any chances. She pulled somebody in to take Gene's other arm. Finally, the whole march stopped. Probably to get everything aligned again.

While all that was going on, I spoke up from the crush of the crowd. "Reverend, Mr. President. Would you rescue me? The Red Sea is falling in on me, and I need help."

When Jesse looked back and saw it was me, oh, my goodness, he just had such a reaction. He got the attention of the president, who parted that Red Sea once again.

"Move back," President Clinton said. "Let this mother through. Don't you know who this is?"

Jesse came up with a plan. "Why don't we send Mother Mobley on first," he said. "And she can watch the rest of us come across."

So I crossed over first. Gene and Lillian would follow with everyone else. Gene wanted to be there for me. He wanted to be there with me. Even with all the difficulty, he wanted us to share this moment. And we did. Even with the Alabama River between us, we did.

Oh, and what a moment it was. When I saw that wall of people coming across that bridge, it was just awesome. There was so much power in the peace and unity of the whole thing. I thought back to the images of the original march and the police riot that had broken out. How the marchers had met hate with love, violence with peace. How outraged an entire nation had been to see the bloody confrontation. How the Voting Rights Act had been signed later that year. It was signed in ink in Washington, but, as Bill Clinton would say, ". . . it was first signed in blood in Selma."

There were a number of us who spoke during the anniversary march and surrounding events. But I will always remember the remarks by President Clinton, who said that the people who had marched across the Edmund Pettus Bridge in 1965 had set him free, too. Discrimination had limited whites as well as blacks.

Within a couple of weeks after we got back to Chicago, Gene was scheduled for a medical appointment, a biopsy. I always wanted to go with him even for the routine exams, because I always knew the right questions to ask. Gene couldn't even tell me what his blood pressure was after he came back from the doctor. But he never wanted to wait for me to get ready. And, I have to admit, it was hard to have to wheel me into the hospital, get me situated, park the car, then come back. So I started writing notes for the doctor to send me the information.

The morning of Gene's appointment, I told him not to leave without waking me so I could talk to him before he left. I heard the bell, and knew it was Abe who had come to take Gene to the hospital. But I fell asleep again. Then I heard the door close and before I could get up to catch Gene, they had driven off.

Within a couple of hours, I got a call. It was my goddaughter Airicka. She had gotten a call from Abe at the hospital. The doctor wanted to see me. But she didn't tell me why. Not until we were halfway to the hospital.

Now, Airicka doesn't hold up any traffic. That girl knows how to move a car. But on this day she was not moving fast enough for me. Not after she told me Gene was having some trouble. I wanted her to slide over and let me take the wheel, as I had done when Gene was driving me to Mama's the morning I got the news about Emmett's disappearance. I felt that the clock was running and there were so many unanswered questions. Gene's biopsy was completed pretty quickly. As Abe went to the hospital garage to get the car, Gene wanted to use the washroom. When Gene didn't come out soon enough, Abe went back in to check on him and found him still in the washroom. He couldn't move. He had suffered another stroke. He was admitted immediately.

Airicka drove me up to the door and Abe met us there with a wheel-chair and he wheeled me to where Daddy was. Gennie looked good, not like anything was wrong at all. But he could not speak. Oh, God. That just sent chills down my spine. I called out to him. He would look at me but he wouldn't say anything.

I took a deep breath. "Do you know me? If you know me, just squeeze my hand." I took his right hand and felt no pressure at all. Nothing. I thought he couldn't hear me. I could see his eyes moving, but I don't read eye language very well.

Then it occurred to me to move over to the left side. "Daddy, if you know me, squeeze my hand."

Oh, my God, the squeeze he gave me nearly broke my hand. It was the most reassuring pain I had ever felt. I thought then that Gene was such a strong man, he would beat whatever this thing was. I felt that squeeze and I felt at ease.

So that's how we communicated for a while there in his hospital room. I would ask yes-or-no questions and he would give my hand one or two squeezes to answer. Is anything hurting? Are you hungry? Things like that.

I wanted him to eat something. He hadn't eaten since the night before because of the biopsy. He had to be hungry. Very hungry. But the nurse told me they couldn't feed him just yet. They didn't know what condition his throat was in, whether he could swallow. So they had to keep feeding him intravenously until tests could reveal what condition he was in. I had to accept that. It was close to one in the afternoon at this point and I stayed on until after midnight, asking questions, chatting away, feeling the connection while Gene squeezed my hand and rolled his eyes.

Abe drove us back that next morning, Friday, March 18. As Airicka wheeled me toward Gene's room, the nurse came out and rushed over to us. "Mrs. Mobley," she said, "Mr. Mobley hasn't closed his eyes all night long."

Oh, my heart just dropped. I had them rush me in. But, when I looked at Gene, he was looking so pretty. He was clean. It looked like he'd had a shave. I knew he hadn't but it looked like he had. He just looked good to me, better than I'd ever seen him look. I asked him how he felt and he gave my hand two squeezes. I guess that meant "okay." I had to remember to ask yes-or-no questions. I asked if he had eaten. He gave me one squeeze for no. That still bothered me, but I accepted what they were telling me.

I began to just talk. I told him how hard he had squeezed my hand when I asked him if he knew me. He sure knew me, all right. He kind of laughed at that. With his eyes. We went on like that for a while before he started getting restless. Like he wanted to get up. I got him to settle down, told him I'd have to leave if he didn't. He seemed to relax again. So I started talking again. I just went on about things we had done, things that had made us laugh in the past.

All of a sudden, Gene sat up in that bed. I thought at first that he was trying to get up again. I was wrong. He was having a seizure. I yelled and Airicka ran to the door to call for the nurse.

By the time the nurse rushed in, he had fallen back but he was still breathing. The nurse told us to clear the room. What was happening? What was wrong? I was his wife, shouldn't I be told something? The nurse just had somebody turn me around in the chair and take me out of the room. As we left, Abe heard them call the code.

Oh, my God. I was losing Gennie. What was I going to do? I had never prepared myself for that. In fact, I had been preparing *him* to lose *me*. We had talked about it. I had walked him through it. I knew he'd be strong enough to survive me, but how on earth could I live without Gennie?

It wasn't long before they came to the waiting room to get us. They asked us to go to the family room. Not back to Gene's room. I knew what that meant. They said they had done all they could do. They said they were sorry. I said nothing. I just screamed, and thought about all that I had lost when I lost Gene.

"As long as I have breath," he had once told me, "you'll be protected." Oh, God. Who would be there for me now? Who would protect me?

Only much later, as I thought about that painful moment, I realized that I had been saying a prayer. God answered. God was there to protect me. God was always there. And Gene? He was my angel.

CHAPTER 28

We were always fishing. Oh, how we loved to fish. We often thought about Emmett and how much he would have loved to be there with us. We talked about him. Sometimes Gene would give me a wink. "Do you think Bo would think we're ready yet?"

We were in Wisconsin. It was such a great spot. My goodness, there were so many fish there. I could see them in the water, all around, just waiting to be caught. And Reverend Mobley and Sister Lou, they were just catching those fish. But I couldn't get my pole in the water. The line kept getting tangled and Gene would have to help me out. Or he would be trying to get the bait on, or trying to get the hook on before that. There was always something that kept me from getting that line in the water.

We found another spot. Deeper in Wisconsin. Much deeper. We went all the way to the Mississippi River, the place where Wisconsin and Minnesota are separated by the river. Close to the beginning of it all. The source. It was beautiful, standing there on a very high bluff. We laid all our stuff out and were arranging our rods and reels. Gene and I were closer to the edge than Lou and Wealthy were. So, while they were getting everything together, I decided to look over the edge. We had been in such a hurry, nobody had even taken time to check. My goodness, that was a long drop.

I turned around. "Oh, Gennie, we might not have enough line to get our hooks into the water."

Gene came over to look. That's when he lost his footing and fell over the cliff. I screamed and, as I did, I saw that Gene had fallen into a net. It was a big net, a fishing net we had. It broke his fall, scooped him up, and brought him back up to the bluff, where he very gently tumbled out onto the ground.

Gene just laughed as he picked himself up. The way he had done so many times before. "Well, I guess I've learned how to fall now."

Then, I would awaken. Every night it would be the same thing. Always about fishing. There were variations. But it always was about fishing. The Lord had me dreaming about Gene, trying to tell me something.

When Gennie died, I reached such a low point in my life where, once again, death seemed more attractive to me than life. It was something I began to look forward to. I could see no purpose in going on. I had never stopped to think how much I had come to need Gene. When he was here, he'd never given me a chance to think about that. He just took care of everything. Things were done. And that's all there was to it. But, more than that, there was the emotional connection. We were two people who had lived as one. And Gene had been my last direct link to Emmett. The best father figure Bo had ever known. When I lost Gene, it was like I was losing two people, like I was losing Bo all over again. I felt so alone. I just wanted to go where everybody else had gone. I was assuming, of course, that they all were in heaven.

I would talk about things like this with Lillian. She had lost her husband in 1989 and now she had lost her father. She could understand what I was feeling, just as I understood her feelings. So we could talk. Most of all, we could listen.

It was while I was in this frame of mind that I turned to the Lord and I cried, "Lord, why did you take Gennie? You know how much I loved him, how much I depended on him." I prayed and I prayed. And soon the answer came: "I want you to depend on Me."

It was a horrible discovery. Another mother's son had been found dead in Mississippi. He was found on June 16, 2000, with a belt around his neck, a noose tied to the pecan tree in his front yard in Kokomo. Raynard Johnson was only seventeen years old. He had been friends with a white girl at school and it was believed that there were people who were very upset about that. The death was ruled a suicide. The belt around Raynard's neck was not his belt. He was six feet tall and his legs were touching the ground. The branch on the tree was low enough and his legs were long enough to have stopped any strangulation. That would have been his natural impulse. Unless he was dead already when he was strapped up there.

The Reverend Jesse Jackson, Sr., was going down to Mississippi in July. He called on me. He wanted me to go with him. He told me there was a job to do. There was a great public uproar over the case. There was a great deal of tension. A mother was in need of comfort. And there were many people who needed to hear things that only could be spoken by someone who had traveled this road. A very long road, stretching back for many miles and many years. Although I had been to Mississippi on personal trips a few times since the Sumner trial, this would be the first time I would return for this kind of event. I agreed to go. Lillian would go with me. Reverend Jackson arranged for a Learjet to carry us all down there. As comfortable as it all was, it became a very uneasy flight for me. I had forgotten my insulin and there were urgent calls ahead to Mississippi from the plane.

Down on the ground in Jackson, Stephanie Parker-Weaver had everything in place. She's the executive secretary for the Southern Christian Leadership Conference in Mississippi and the go-to person when civil rights leaders come in for important events. So she had everything in place, but she got the call about the one thing nobody could have anticipated. The one thing I needed—insulin. And it was an emergency.

When I stepped off that plane onto the tarmac in Jackson, Mrs. Maria Johnson emerged from the delegation there to greet us. She and I hugged so strongly. Motherly hugs. Of course, we had never met before. Oh, but we knew each other. We knew each other in the way that two people know they share a bond. It was a connection only we could feel. We spoke a silent language only we could understand. For us, it needed no translation. So we hugged, and we communed. And then I made my way to the paramedics, who were waiting nearby. With that detail out of the way, we soon were on our way.

A busy schedule had been planned. A rally was set for the next day. There would be a march to Mrs. Johnson's home in Kokomo and there would be speeches. On this day, there would be a meeting with the governor, Ronnie Musgrove, and a meeting at the John the Baptist Church.

At the meeting that had been arranged with the governor, Reverend Jackson was going to discuss the investigation of Raynard Johnson's death and all the concerns about the findings and the suspicion that they were incomplete. And then there was me. I had to hold back. I was filled with so much emotion, anticipation. Oh, my God, I had waited forty-five years for such a moment. This would be the highest-ranking Mississippi official I had ever met. It would be the first time such an official would have the chance to talk to the mother of Emmett Till, to offer any promise at all that the murder investigation would be reopened, to offer an apology for all that had been done. For all that had not been done. We waited for that meeting. And waited. Finally, the wait was over. We were told that the governor would be unable to meet with us after all. There was a conflict.

So we left, and Reverend Jackson said something about sorting it all out in future elections. For the governor, there had been a conflict, but nothing, it seemed, like the ones that lay ahead, nothing like the one that lay in my heart. The expectation, the disappointment.

There was too much ahead of us to dwell on what we left behind there at the meeting that would never be. We had to get to Hattiesburg, where we would stay overnight before the next day's rally and march. Of course, we also had the church meeting, where I thought I still needed my wheelchair, until Reverend Jackson spoke up. "Oh, Mother, you don't need a wheelchair. Let the spirit move you." He took my arm and I realized that his call, the call to go with him down to Mississippi, that call had come at just the right time in my life. It was a call that pulled me out of my despair over losing Gene. Reverend Jackson had brought me back again, to Mississippi and to myself. He had given me a reason to move forward, and we did. We walked down the aisle of that church and I felt energized by all the love and support of the black people of Mississippi, by having the chance to meet them, to talk with them. The pain of loss, of children murdered, it just seemed to be felt by everyone. In a way, I suppose I represented the survival of such great loss. The hope that gets us through the things we might never imagine getting through.

My hope during that trip was that I might provide some comfort to Mrs. Johnson. I knew what she was feeling during this time, a time when even all the family love, all the public support couldn't fill that hollow loneliness. I felt that, too. So deeply. We talked about that feeling. About that and the need for her to find peace within herself and with God. She had to accept God's will even if she didn't fully understand it right away. That was the first thing to do. Once she could reach that peace, she would receive spiritual guidance to handle everything else that she would have to handle: finding the truth, finding forgiveness. She would have to be strong to endure what lay ahead: the outside pressure, the inner turmoil. Oh, I knew those parts so well. I could see how difficult it was going to be. I knew that, as much as things in Mississippi had changed, they seemed to have changed so little in ways that are close to the heart. I felt that based on what I had heard about the way the Raynard Johnson case had been handled. And how we had been handled by a conflicted Mississippi governor. She would have to be strong to keep fighting, as I had kept fighting, as I would continue to fight for the rest of my life. So I talked about all that, and urged her never to give up. But most important of all, I listened.

There was so much pressure on Mrs. Johnson. And there was so much heat in Mississippi in July. People from Mississippi said they had never felt such heat. Mrs. Johnson suffered from it. She had to be rushed to the hospital to be treated for heat exhaustion. But there were other concerns, concerns that were not shared with everybody at the time. Only a few people would know where Mrs. Johnson had been taken. There was tension in the air that was hotter than the temperature and thicker than the humidity. There was a death threat. It was against Reverend Jackson, and no one knew how far hostile people might go. We all would have to be protected, secured against any possibility. As God would have it, the march and rally went on without incident. Mrs. Johnson's doctor advised her to stay inside, to stay quiet. But she refused to follow the doctor's orders. She wanted to appear at the rally. She said she could do it. And she did it, because she said she could do it, because she believed what she said. That was the kind of determination I knew would carry her beyond that weekend.

Things began to pick up again. There had been calls about the play after the Chicago and Aurora performances, and the Pegasus Players theater company served as the broker for deals for the work to be performed by the Unity Players in Los Angeles in September 2000, then for another run in San Diego that November, and by the Paul Robeson Theater Company in Buffalo in February 2001. I traveled to the opening of each run and spoke to the press and the audiences in each city and, oh, the reaction was just amazing to me. I mean, there were traffic jams around those theaters on opening night and, if you didn't have tickets, you weren't going to get them. Travel activities can wear a lot of people out. But I was energized by it all, and by hearing so many wonderful things from the producers, the directors, the actors, and all the people who came out to see the performances.

With all the new media attention, I began to hear from others as well. Two documentaries were being planned. Keith Beauchamp, a young man from New York who had been inspired by the Emmett Till story, had begun working on a treatment of the story that became a documentary project. He has a background in criminal justice and began his own investigation of the case as he interviewed people in the South. One day, he decided to call me and was amazed that he got through and that I talked so freely. Stanley Nelson got inspired to produce an Emmett Till documentary after he saw an interview I had done. His company already had produced an acclaimed documentary on the black press and he would go on to win a MacArthur Foundation grant. Stanley's documentary would be included in the *American Experience* series on Public Broadcasting Service stations. Keith was in discussions with HBO and CourtTV. These would be the first documentaries for a national audience devoted entirely to Emmett Till. Of course, I was eager to tell my story, and to have it reach a national audience.

Despite the boost I was getting from all the activity, my health was in crisis. One night at home, I fell. This was not the first time. Once I had fallen and it took me hours to drag myself from my bedroom through my office and into my kitchen, where I finally was able to pull myself up by the banister at my basement stairs. But this time, I couldn't even do that. I was home alone and I fell on the floor, on the side of the bed in my own room, where I had to stay until my cousin Abe Thomas came in to check on me the following morning.

I was taken to Christ Hospital. It was my blood sugar, and there was excess fluid building up. The doctors told me they were going to release me after a few days. But I didn't feel comfortable going home alone. Not after that latest episode. So they sent me to a rehab center where I stayed for almost a week. There, I started having shortness of breath and had to be rushed back to Christ Hospital. I saw a different group of doctors from the ones who had treated me before. Immediately, they said I had to go on dialysis. There was way too much fluid for my own good. I went through a couple of sessions a day for a while and wound up losing eighty-five pounds from the excess fluid. It was a real miracle. Had they sent me home when they'd planned to do so, who knows what might have happened?

This had been a terrifying episode and we had a family meeting about it. The time had come for me to decide how I was going to go on living the way I had been living. Alone. Or whether I even could anymore. A few plans were put on the table. One possibility that was suggested was to have me check into an assisted living facility. As it turned out, that plan was not a workable one for me. My assets would have to be turned over to the facility, and I just couldn't have that.

We finally worked it out so that I could stay at home with virtually my whole family looking out for me. A longtime family friend and nurse, Earlene Greer, had been coming in to help me with personal needs. Now she'd be there every day during the week. Abe would drive me to dialysis three days a week, and he and Shep Gordon would help with shopping and general household repairs. Ollie and Airicka would also be part of the emergency check-in list. And either Abe's sister Bertha Thomas or Lillian would be my travel companions. Bertha also was a big help with business matters, especially the Emmett Till Foundation, which raises money for college scholarships and the Emmett Till Players. Bertha is a paralegal and very good at these things. I also would have an emergency notice system, a lifeline button I could push to call a neighbor right away in an emergency.

Although my health situation was still fragile, losing all that water weight was a tremendous help to me. And the arrangements we worked out gave me peace of mind and made it possible for me to continue to be active, to do all the work I still felt I needed to do.

So many issues would become important to me over the years as I increased my awareness of them through their close connection to the one issue that has always been central to my life. No matter what condition I've been in, I've been ready to lend my support to the causes I believe in. Capital punishment is one of those. As the mother of a murder victim, I feel that I have been victimized, too. But we have seen so many people on death row who also are victims. They have been wrongly accused. Too many times, they are black. I've spent too much of my life speaking out against injustice against black people to be able to live with that. Besides, it seems that even guilty people should be given a chance for redemption. I would hope that a life sentence would give people that chance. That was my hope even with Roy Bryant and J. W. Milam. That at some point before they closed their eyes for good, even if it had only been a whisper, or a flash of a thought, they would have been sorry for what they did. That was my hope, and one very important reason why I would call on Illinois Governor George Ryan to abolish the death penalty.

The call for reparations has caused a lot of controversy. And I don't think everybody sees all the aspects of it. It is not a simple matter. The more it is debated, the better chance we might have to reach an understanding about a very serious and unsettled part of our history. So, when I got the call from Chicago Alderman Dorothy Tillman to travel to Mississippi again for a conference on reparations in May 2002, I was very happy to take part. I arranged to have dialysis in Jackson, and I was ready to go.

The first day of the two-day conference was conducted as a hearing by the Jackson City Council at City Hall, a building that had been constructed with slave labor. There was a huge turnout. My goodness, I never imagined that there were so many people who were involved in so many different aspects of the fight for justice. And everyone had stories to tell about injustices they had suffered. There were people who talked about the need to make up for slavery itself. Some talked about the effects of slavery. Others, like me, talked about the brutality and the need to address the needs of the families of victims. But it really wasn't about money. The focus was on repairing the damage left by so many years of discrimination. Ways that go beyond money. After all, when it comes to victims of brutality, there is no way to provide enough money to make up for the loss of a loved one. But there is a need for counseling and other help for people who have lost family members to hate crimes.

I was moved by the stories people told, people like Mrs. Maria Johnson, whose son's death was not reinvestigated. Although the file was reviewed, the original finding was not reversed. The official cause of death was still listed as suicide. Mrs. Johnson is determined to keep pushing for an answer her heart can accept. There were so many people at the hearings who had to live with great anguish. People who never even got so much as an apology. That had always been so important to me, for some official of the state of Mississippi to do even that much. In a way, that is what the reparations debate represents. An apology, an admission. After all, things can't be set right until we face up to what's been done wrong.

There was a surprise in store for me on the first day of the hearings. Jackson City Councilman Kenneth Stokes issued an apology to me, speaking with the authority he had earned with the rights that had been gained as a result of so much sacrifice that had been made. It wasn't surprising to me that a black elected official in Mississippi had done what a white elected official could never bring himself to do. But it touched me so deeply to know that in 2002, quite unlike 1955, there was a black man in Mississippi who had the power to do it.

Willie Reed called me. Out of the blue, he just called and then came by to visit. We hadn't seen each other in years and it was so good to sit down and talk. Willie was working at Jackson Park Hospital in Chicago.

We ordered Chinese food and reminded each other of things some people might have wanted to forget. Things people can never forget no matter how much they might want to do so. Things about the trial and all that hostility, and how we both knew the way things would turn out, and how we kept moving forward anyway. And, oh, yes, how we couldn't wait to get out of Mississippi. I thanked Willie for his courage. He had put so much on the line in agreeing to testify. He would forever give up his life in Mississippi. Yet, he told me, he would do it all over again, if the situation presented itself. He thought about it, he said, practically every day. To get to work, he would drive down Emmett Till Road. And he would think about it all. How there came to be an Emmett Till Road. Willie felt a kinship with Emmett. For one thing, they were close in age. Willie was eighteen at the time and Emmett was fourteen. Willie was an only child and he knew Emmett was an only child. He said that if what happened to Emmett had happened to him, he would have wanted somebody to come forward for him.

It occurred to me after Willie left that I had never asked him what prompted him to call me. But, then, I guess there are some things you really don't have to ask.

For years, I have hoped to have the investigation of the murder of my son reopened. There still are so many unanswered questions. Even though Roy Bryant and J. W. Milam could never be convicted of murder once they were acquitted, there were other reasons to take a fresh look at this case. We knew what reporters like Jimmy Hicks and witnesses like Willie Reed had told us years ago. This crime was not committed by two people alone. Others were there. Others participated on one level or another. Until we know, this case is unresolved. I have said repeatedly that I was determined to work until my dying day to search for answers and to make sure that the story of Emmett Louis Till would never be buried. I have my own determination, but I also have been able to draw on inspiration from others. I have seen how Coretta Scott King would never let the dream die, how Myrlie Evers continued to pursue Medgar's assassin.

Mine is not just the passion of an aggrieved mother. This should be the sentiment of an entire nation. As long as the Emmett Till murder is unresolved, this case will sit there like a thorn in the side of our sense of justice and fair play. It will continue to poke at us, to prick our conscience and irritate. Without a resolution, we can never be at ease.

There have been many others who have shared this feeling. For years, Keith Beauchamp has wanted to find answers, too. His documentary was the first step. The first screening was scheduled for November 2002 in New York, co-sponsored by the Africana Studies Department at New York University in connection with the release of the University of Virginia Press book *The Lynching of Emmett Till* edited by Christopher Metress. The reaction was incredible. An extra screening had to be added and people lined up in the rain to get into both sessions. The press would take the story of renewed interest in Emmett Till all over the country. *The New York Times* (including an opinion piece by Brent Staples), *The Washington Post,* the *Atlanta Journal-Constitution,* ABC News—everyone, it seemed, wanted to talk about a quest for justice that would not die.

Later, Keith teamed up with Alvin Sykes and Donald Burger of the Justice Campaign of America to present information to the attorney general of Mississippi and to the U.S. Justice Department to try to reopen the investigation into Emmett's murder. Eyewitnesses are still around. Maybe even a few accomplices. It has been difficult sorting through the technicalities of the law to show that the state has cause, or that the federal government has jurisdiction. But the effort continues.

Although I have lived so much of my life without Emmett, I have lived my entire life *because* of him. Everything leading up to his birth, everything following his death was for a purpose. Unfortunately, so much of that time, I have suppressed the horrible feeling that only a mother can have when a child is lost. Was there something I could have done? Was Emmett's death something I could have prevented? Emmett was a good boy, a good son, and I know that I was a good mother. But you can't help but wonder about such things.

I think about that dreadful day at A. A. Rayner's when I had to examine Emmett's horribly disfigured body. How could I ever forget that? I remember how I thought about Emmett in that shed, how no one had answered his call. I know now that I was wrong about that. God answered the call when He embraced Emmett and showed the world what race hatred could do, how much better we should be than what we had become. So much good has come of that. And I have answered the call in all my life's work, nurturing young minds, providing much-needed guidance. And in that, there is redemption.

The work is not done. So many of our young people still need so much guidance. There is much they don't know and we must take responsibility for that. We can see it in the recent debate about the movie *Barbershop,* where a character jokingly questions whether Rosa Parks did anything worth honoring by refusing to give up her seat. Rosa Parks is a friend I have come to love very much. We have talked about that historic day when she would not be moved. She was tired. But not physically tired. She was tired of the indignities that we as a people were made to suffer. It was an act of courage. I know from experience just how much people put on the line during the civil rights movement. People risked their lives. People sacrificed their lives. And they did it so that our young people now can enjoy certain rights without having to think about it. But we *should* think about it. Young people must be taught to think about it. They should know, as they say, that freedom is never free. Lord knows, as much as I speak out, I am not in favor of censorship. But there are some things that are so precious, they become sacred. It just should never even occur to us to joke about sacred things.

There still is much that needs to be done to educate white people, too. The fact that we still have to debate whether more needs to be done to repair the damage left by so many years of racial discrimination shows that much. The fact that a U.S. senator could fantasize about the presidency of an arch-segregationist shows that much. White people need a lot of guidance in matters of race. Just as they did in the 1950s, they deserve leaders who will enlighten rather than incite. We all deserve that.

Oh, God, how blessed I have been to have taken part in something as significant as our national debate. I have come to realize that we are all here for a purpose and we have unique gifts to share with the rest of the world. I have enjoyed a full, rich, meaningful life because I was able to discover my reason for being and to perfect my gifts in fulfilling my purpose, touching so many lives in the process. Hopefully, I have left each one just a little better than I found it. Hopefully, I have made a difference. That is, after all, how our lives are measured. By how many other lives we touch and inspire. By how much of life we embrace, not by what we reject. By what we accept, not by what we judge. Still, even with this understanding of a lifetime, the tears do flow from time to time. But I see much more clearly now through my tears, and that is a good thing. Rainy days always help us appreciate the sunny ones so much more, don't they? Besides, it is in crying that we are able to let go. In letting go, I have experienced what it is like to bring hope from despair, joy from anguish, forgiveness from anger, love from hate. And if I can do it, I know anyone can. And if everyone does it, just imagine how much better we all can be.

With each day, I give thanks for the blessings of life—the blessings of another day and the chance to do something with it. Something good. Something significant. Something helpful. No matter how small it might seem. I want to keep making a difference. Although I am much more aware now of the limits of my own life, I am not afraid. My son has taught me so much about facing all aspects of life with courage. I have planned for the end of my life as carefully as I planned so much of the life I have lived recently. We have made arrangements with Mrs. Slivy Edmonds Cotton, president of Perpetua, Inc., the owners of Burr Oak Cemetery, for the establishment of a mausoleum and museum at the cemetery. Emmett, Gene, and I will be there together with pictures and other remembrances of our lives in a setting that will enable children to learn. Not just about our history, but also about the transition in store for every life. The cemetery is for the living, after all, not the dead. And I want children to be able to touch my life and Bo's life and Gene's in ways that I hope we have touched everyone else's.

I just want to make sure now that I tie up all the loose ends, finish the work God put me here to do, see Mama again in the still peace of the riverbank, and prepare to live in eternal bliss with Emmett and Gennie once again, finally as family.

And, Bo, I do think we're ready now.

Every now and then, you have the good fortune to meet someone who changes your life. When you consider the impact a life-altering experience can have, every now and then is plenty.

Mamie Till-Mobley became such a person for me. One day this past December, I sat in her kitchen and watched her in action. Now, getting to that kitchen had been a two-step process. The first time we met, we sat in the dining room. There had been a certain formality to that, proving my-self worthy of crossing a threshold in our relationship, moving into the kitchen. Much cozier, that kitchen, the nerve center of her home. As in the dining room, there was a table to bring us together. That was a big part of her life. A table, and all that it represented: business, as well as food, nurturing. The table was where she did her work, and where she said her blessings.

So one December day we sat at the kitchen table, in the middle of one of our many interview sessions for this book. She was involved in so many other things at the same time. To know Mother Mobley was to know that there always would be so many other things. There were constant phone calls, from schedulers for upcoming events, out-of-town events that would force her to change her three-day-a-week dialysis schedule, and there were media inquiries. At times she would just hand the phone to me. She knew *I* could say no. Wait for the book, I would say. It's only ten months away. She couldn't say those things, couldn't hold back. She had been waiting too long already. "I'm like a glass of champagne that keeps bubbling up," she'd say. Vintage Mamie, consumed by the moment. So, ten more months seemed like a lifetime to her.

There was all that, and then there was the food. The chicken and dumplings, the yeast rolls, the banana pudding, and so much more sustenance that Mother Mobley and her family friend and nurse, Earlene Greer, always were so eager to provide. On this one day, at the height of just that kind of activity—the calls, the conversation, the cooking—she did something that really amazed me. She walked. Just stood on her own and walked from the kitchen to her adjacent office and back again, without her walker, without her cane, without even an arm to lean on. I waited for her to take her seat again before calling all this to her attention. It just seemed like a good idea to wait.

She hadn't even noticed that she had done this thing that had amazed me, this thing I hadn't seen her do before. But then she gave me a wink of a glance. "Well," she said, "I have to be able to get around if I'm going to go out on the road and talk about my book."

Indeed. And I wanted that for her. I wanted that very much. For her to be strong and healthy, to be able to go out, tell the story she had waited so long to tell. When you care about somebody, you want them to have what they want. Everyone who knew Mother Mobley cared about her. People who only knew *about* her cared about her. She once jammed the aisles in a local grocery store when her cousin Abriel Thomas told only a couple of people that Emmett Till's mother was there shopping. Word spread. People knew her story, parts of it, anyway, and they wanted to tell her how it had changed their lives. It was like that wherever she went. But there was much more than the pieces of a story. There was Mother Mobley herself. She was Everymother. She had an aura, a smile like the sunrise, and a way of making you want to make her smile just to get warmed by it. There was a magnetism, a way she had of drawing you in like a loving embrace. It would make you just want to do things for her. It made me want to call ahead of time, every time I'd come over, to see if she needed anything, anything at all, from the store. Of course, she needed that, the attention, the care, the help. Just as other people, especially the family members who looked after her, needed her to be pleased. She was that special person who said the things we always want to hear: *I missed you. God bless you. I love you, too.*

She was the teacher we'd always remember. You know, the one who changed our lives. She might have retired from teaching twenty years ago, but for Mother Mobley that was a minor administrative detail. She continued to teach in her own way. She teaches us still. She teaches as a mother would, warming our hearts, nurturing our minds. She teaches about the importance of living a committed life, a purposeful life. Of squeezing every ounce of enrichment out of every moment we are given. To live on purpose. She taught me these things, as I sat there in her kitchen, as I listened to her, watched her on the move. She taught me the best way you can teach anybody anything: by example.

On January 6 of this year, Mother Mobley died. She suffered a heart attack. She had just started walking again, or trying to. She was on the move that day, on her way to another accelerated dialysis session so she could make an early-morning flight to Atlanta the next day. She was scheduled to speak at Ebenezer Baptist Church in connection with the exhibition "Without Sanctuary: Lynching Photography in America" at the Martin Luther King, Jr., National Historic Site. Abe and Earlene were with her on that last ride, one so much like others she had experienced, like the one the morning she got the news about Emmett's disappearance, and when she heard about Gene in the hospital, racing the speed limit, hoping against hope that the outcome would be different from the expectation.

Maybe it all makes sense, that she would die as she had lived: on the move. At eighty-one, she showed just how short life really is, how important it is to seize the moment, to push beyond our limitations. She did that, stayed active, kept moving forward, knowing the great risk to her personal health. She did it because she wanted so much to tell the story, the story she had lived.

Her story was very important to her. She recognized the power of her message was in its simplicity. A boy was brutally murdered, the confessed killers were set free, an aggrieved mother found no justice, and race hatred was at the very heart of it all. It is a story that clawed at our conscience like fingernails on a blackboard. It challenged a nation in the most fundamental way. We looked at the tortured face of Emmett Till and saw what a nightmare the American dream had become for so many of us. One newspaper headline got it exactly right when it noted quite simply that Mother Mobley had opened a casket and opened our eyes. She made us face what we all must experience at some point in a full and complete life: a move away from our own naïveté, our own ignorance; an increase in our awareness. For it is only in the sacrifice of our innocence that we can achieve absolute understanding.

Mother Mobley's message is political, it is spiritual. And people get it. Mother Mobley made sure of that. In fact, she *became* her own message. In the example of her life, we were able to see so much more than individual despair. She was a metaphor for the community she represented. Not just the abuse, the injustice we had suffered, but also the hope for a better day, the courage to fight for it, the faith that it eventually would come. She taught us that and she inspired us to put the lesson to work.

She also inspired us in the way she continued to live her life without bitterness. Her last public appearance came at the special request of Renny

Cushing, executive director of Murder Victims' Families for Reconciliation. On December 8, 2002, she participated in Victims' Voices, a Loyola University forum in Chicago, sponsored by Cushing's Cambridge-based group, which is opposed to the death penalty. Mother Mobley explained that she had never wanted to be consumed by hatred—the same destructive force that had driven Emmett's killers—as she used the platform of the event to call upon Illinois Governor George Ryan to abolish the death penalty.

"For her, speaking against the death penalty was life affirming," Cushing told me. "It was a way of keeping Emmett alive."

On January 11, 2003, the day Mother Mobley was buried, Governor Ryan commuted 164 Illinois death sentences to life in prison without parole. Among so many other things, among so many other names, Mamie Till-Mobley was on the governor's mind at the time, and in the speech he delivered when he cleared Death Row: "Mamie's strength and grace not only ignited the civil rights movement—including inspiring Rosa Parks to refuse to go to the back of the bus—but inspired murder victims' families until her dying day."

There seemed to be so much left for Mother Mobley to do, events to attend, business to attend to. *The State of Mississippi v. Emmett Till* was scheduled for a January reprise in Aurora, Illinois, where Mayor David Stover had been so moved by the first production and by meeting Mother Mobley that he had insisted on a return engagement. There would be a full run in the fall by the Pegasus Players in Chicago. Artistic Director Arlene Crewdson had chosen the play to lead off the twenty-fifth anniversary season of the best works the organization had ever mounted. There was the annual prayer breakfast in Chicago in honor of Dr. Martin Luther King, Jr., where Mayor Daley would honor Mother Mobley, telling the capacity crowd that she deserved the Nobel Peace Prize for her work in leading us to a better place. There was the Chicago screening of Stanley Nelson's Emmett Till documentary, to which I was to escort her. There was discussion about other joint appearances with Emmett Till documentarian Keith Beauchamp, including a screening and panel discussion at the United Nations. And, of course, there was the book.

So much left to do. Mother Mobley wanted to live. But she was ready to die, emboldened by her unwavering faith. She wanted to be able to do much more than she already had done, but she had done so much already. In the end, God decided that she had done enough. As Dr. King might have said in one of her favorite speeches, she had swept her job so well.

Part of that job was in making sure there would be others to carry on the work she had started. And she was a tough taskmaster, too, in making sure. She was as demanding of those around her as she was of herself. I had been warned that she evaluated people by an exacting standard, one that had been set by the last good person who had done the last good thing for her. Or, as David Barr so aptly put it after introducing us, "Mother Mobley grades on the curve." I can only hope that I made the grade.

I know I kept up. And keeping up with her was no easy thing, especially when she wasn't slowed by the walker or the cane. In every conversation we had, even between the formal interviews, there was at least one story, often more. But what I heard was so much more than stories. There was an urgency. It was the kind of thing you might expect to hear from a person who knows that ten months can be a lifetime. She wanted to make sure she said it all, shared it all, got it all down. She even made her own notes. Copious notes of every conversation, indexed and dated in her notebook. Everything had to be recorded, documented. She was her own archivist. She didn't want to miss a thing. And although we never really spoke about that feeling of urgency, there was always the sense that we were racing the clock. I only wish we could have turned the clock back. I wanted to hear more stories, I wanted to have more time together, I wanted more banana pudding.

Then again, Mother Mobley never really stopped talking to me. In the months after she passed, I would sit in my study and hear her voice. The echoes were everywhere, in the words of the transcripts and the many scattered notes, rising and falling on that gentle cadence of hers, that distinctive clip in her pronunciation, each word spoken so carefully, so thoughtfully, so perfectly. I could look up from my computer monitor and see the newspaper clippings and pictures taped to the walls, and the words "Think Mamie" I had posted there. But there was something else. From my apartment, I can see the train tracks that run south all the way off to the horizon. Many mornings at 8:35, or maybe it was 8:37, or 8:52 (we're talking Amtrak time here), as I was writing, I would hear the sound of a distant horn. It was the horn of a train, one that had crossed that horizon from the South, traveling all the way from Cairo, Illinois, and Memphis before that, and Mississippi before that; the train that would come barreling through my Hyde Park neighborhood on its way to the end of the line at Union Station in downtown Chicago. It was the *City of New Orleans,* the train that had brought Emmett's body home. So many mornings I thought about that, about a mother and son, about tracks that disappear over the horizon, about a life's journey, about homegoing, and about so many stories trumpeted by the horn of a train.

Early on Mother Mobley had described herself as an ordinary person who had faced an extraordinary situation. I wonder about that. Having come to know her, I believe she was truly an extraordinary woman who had only been waiting for circumstances to arouse her power. Learning that has helped me realize that the same is true of all of us, really. We all are capable of extraordinary things when we open ourselves up to the possibility of the extraordinary. An evangelist as well as a teacher, Mother Mobley spent the better part of her life inspiring that discovery in the people she reached, especially the children. She saw the possibility for greatness everywhere she turned. And she left her mark, arousing an awareness, sharpening the vision in others. That was her gift. Her legacy.

Franklin McMahon felt the touch. He is the artist who was assigned by *Life* magazine to produce courtroom drawings of the 1955 murder trial in Sumner. It was his first assignment, a transforming experience. As a result, he wound up spending much of the rest of his career covering the civil rights movement and political campaigns. Drawing on the human spirit. He often would take his children with him to the marches and demonstrations. White kids, who would grow up knowing the struggle for full racial equality was their cause, too.

Willie Reed felt the touch. He told me, as he had told Mother Mobley, that he was moved by her courage. He never forgot it. He never will forget it. On the morning of January 6, Willie Reed called in sick. He was not feeling up to going into work that day at Jackson Park Hospital. Later that afternoon, his wife called out to him. There was a report on the news that Mother Mobley had been pronounced dead at Jackson Park Hospital. It hit Willie, hit him hard. He thought about the last time he had seen Mother Mobley, at her home the summer before, how they had talked and laughed and eaten Chinese carryout, how he might have seen her one more time if he had not been ill that day and had been able to go into work. He thought about what he might have said to her if he had seen her that one last time.

"That she's a beautiful person, a kind person, and a lovely person," he told me. "I would say, you know, I would tell her, I just love her."

And she would say she loves you, too, Willie.

Motherhood is about love. Motherhood is about sacrifice. Mother Mobley knew about motherhood. She knew about motherhood cut short. She came to see Emmett as a sacrificial lamb. But the sacrifices for her did not end with his death. She sacrificed her own privacy in permitting the solemn experience of her mourning to become a public event, and in giving up the comfort of being the ordinary person she thought she was to become the public figure we came to know. In the end, you can't help but think there also was the sacrifice of her own life. She knew, she had to know, that she was pushing herself beyond her own physical capabilities.

But she couldn't say no. She had a job to do. She had been able to mine her grief for meaning and a mission, one she had vowed to serve until the day she died. There was no task too big, none too small. She once urged Abe to drive her up and down Seventy-first Street, Emmett Till Road. She wanted to count the street signs honoring her son, to make sure the city of Chicago had kept its promise to post those signs on the entire seven-mile stretch. As far as she was concerned, every single sign carried a message, and every city block presented an audience for that message.

In every way, she was true to her vow to devote a lifetime to service, as the Reverend Wheeler Parker noted during one of two funeral services for Mother Mobley. "She died with her boots on," he told the huge crowd at the homegoing service. "How do you plan to die?"

The same way—that's my answer. The same way she lived. On the move. That is her challenge to all of us. I made my commitment to her to meet the challenge. And my life will never be the same for the experience. It will be so much better, because of what I have learned. Lessons of a lifetime, lessons from my favorite teacher: Live a committed life, a purposeful life, and make each moment count. If there is something you have to say, say it now. If there is something to do, don't wait: not a month, or two, or ten, as I had urged interviewers calling on Mother Mobley. I see now what she saw back then, one day in December. Ten months can be a lifetime.

CHRISTOPHER BENSON
Chicago
May 1, 2003

MAMIE TILL-MOBLEY died on January 6, 2003, at the age of eighty-one. Following the death of her only child, Emmett Till, she entered Chicago Teachers College in September 1956, graduating cum laude and fifth in her class three and a half years later. In 1973, she earned a master's degree in administration and supervision at Loyola University. Till-Mobley was a frequent lecturer throughout the country, recalling the struggle for civil rights and urging her listeners to be the best they could be.

A Chicago-based writer and lawyer, CHRISTOPHER BENSON is features editor for *Ebony,* and a former Washington editor for *Ebony* and *Jet.* His articles also have appeared in *Chicago* and *Reader's Digest.* Benson is the author of the novel *Special Interest,* which will be published by One World/Ballantine in December 2003.

This book was set in Bembo, a typeface based on an old-style Roman face that was used for Cardinal Bembo's tract *De Aetna* in 1495. Bembo was cut by Francisco Griffo in the early sixteenth century. The Lanston Monotype Machine Company of Philadelphia brought the well-proportioned letter forms of Bembo to the United States in the 1930s.